PRAISE FOR

WALKABLE CITY

"If Jane Jacobs invented a new urbanism, *Walkable City* is its perfect complement, a commonsense twenty-first-century user's manual." —Kurt Andersen, author of *Evil Geniuses*

"[*Walkable City*] will change the way you see cities." —Kaid Benfield, *The Atlantic Cities*

"Refreshing, lively and engaging . . . *Walkable City* isn't a harangue, it's a fun, readable and persuasive call to arms." —Steven Litt, *The Plain Dealer* (Cleveland)

"*Walkable City* is an energetic, feisty book, one that never contents itself with polite generalities. Sometimes breezy and anecdotal yet always logical and amply researched, this is one of the best books to appear this year. Speck deserves the widest possible readership." —Philip Langdon, *Better! Cities & Towns*

"Brilliant and companionable . . . *Walkable City* is at once entertaining and enraging, its pages dotted with jaw-dropping statistics." —Carlin Rosengarten, *The Post and Courier* (Charleston, S.C.)

"Cities are the future of the human race, and Jeff Speck knows how to make them work." —David Owen, staff writer at *The New Yorker* and author of *Green Metropolis*

"It's time to add a new name to the roll call of the city gang[,] Jeff Speck . . . It turns out to be exactly the right time for a down-

and-dirty, step-by-step seminar on city repair—especially one conducted by as genial a presenter as Speck."

—Taras Grescoe, *The Globe and Mail* (Toronto)

"*Walkable City* is an eloquent ode to the livable city and to the values behind it."

—Paul Goldberger, Pulitzer Prize–winning architecture critic and author of *Why Architecture Matters*

"Jeff Speck is one of the few practitioners and writers in the field who can make a 312-page book on a basic planning concept seem too short . . . For getting planning ideas into the thinking and the daily life of U.S. cities, this is the book."

—*Planning* magazine

"If you're a professional planner or advocate, *Walkable City* is a new, essential reference. If you're new to the subject, there's no better introduction." —Angie Schmitt, *Streetsblog*

"Jeff Speck's brilliant and entertaining book reminds us that, in America, the exception could easily become the rule. Mayors, planners, and citizens need look no further for a powerful and achievable vision of how to make our ordinary cities great again."

—Joseph P. Riley, former mayor of Charleston, S.C.

"Companionable and disarmingly candid, Jeff Speck perches on your shoulder and gets you to see your community with fresh eyes. He gradually builds a compelling case for walkability as the essential distillation of a vast trove of knowledge about urbanism and placemaking. The case he makes has you both nodding at the intuitive and seemingly obvious wisdom presented, and shaking your head at why those basic principles of fixing our cities have eluded us for so long." —Harriet Tregoning, founder of the National Smart Growth Network

WALKABLE CITY

WALKABLE CITY

HOW DOWNTOWN CAN SAVE AMERICA,
ONE STEP AT A TIME

JEFF SPECK

MCD   PICADOR

FARRAR, STRAUS AND GIROUX

MCD
Picador
120 Broadway, New York 10271

Copyright © 2012 by Jeff Speck
Introduction copyright © 2022 by Janette Sadik-Khan
Part III copyright © 2022 by Jeff Speck
All rights reserved
Printed in the United States of America
Originally published in 2012 by Farrar, Straus and Giroux
First paperback edition published in 2013 by North Point Press
10th Anniversary Picador paperback edition, 2022

Grateful acknowledgment is made to Charles Marohn
for permission to use an excerpt from *Grist*.

The Library of Congress has cataloged the Farrar, Straus and Giroux
hardcover edition as follows:

Speck, Jeff.
    Walkable city : how downtown can save America, one step at a
time / Jeff Speck.
        p.   cm.
    Includes bibliographical references and index.
    ISBN 978-0-374-28581-4 (alk. paper)
    1. Central business districts—United States—Planning.
2. Pedestrian areas—United States—Planning.   3. Urban renewal—
United States.   4. City planning—United States.   I. Title.

HT175 .S64 2012
307.1'2160973—dc23

                                                    2012018934

Paperback ISBN: 978-1-250-85798-9

Designed by Jonathan D. Lippincott

Our books may be purchased in bulk for promotional, educational, or business use.
Please contact your local bookseller or the Macmillan Corporate and Premium
Sales Department at 1-800-221-7945, extension 5442, or by email
at MacmillanSpecialMarkets@macmillan.com.

Picador® is a U.S. registered trademark and is used by Macmillan Publishing Group,
LLC, under license from Pan Books Limited.

For book club information, please visit facebook.com/picadorbookclub or email
marketing@picadorusa.com.

mcdbooks.com • Follow us on Twitter, Facebook, and Instagram at @mcdbooks
picadorusa.com • Instagram: @picador • Twitter and Facebook: @picadorusa

5   7   9   10   8   6

For Alice

CONTENTS

INTRODUCTION

JANETTE SADIK-KHAN

In writing a book about the future of cities, it's tough to get everything right. *Walkable City* isn't free of error. Not everything predicted by Jeff Speck when this book first appeared ten years ago has turned out precisely as he imagined.

But there is no statement quite as mistaken as *Walkable City*'s first two sentences: "This is not the next great book on American cities. That book is not needed."

As it turns out, it was, and it was. And it still is.

America has a long history of imagining the future of cities, alternating between visions of flying cars in one telling and predictions of apocalyptic futures of disorder and decay in the other. Most of these visions have a short shelf life. When the future arrives, it often fails to meet expectations—to borrow a sardonic phrase, we wanted flying cars and instead we got 140 characters.

But just because a prediction didn't turn out right doesn't mean that the urban epidemiology it was based on was misdiagnosed.

Even the patron saint of the human-scale city, Jane Jacobs, could not have foreseen the urban economics that would one day make dense, diverse urban communities like her Greenwich Village neighborhood unaffordable to most of the denizens she defended in *The Death and Life of Great American Cities*. The civic and media tactics she skillfully employed to stymie the bulldozing of homes for a cross-Manhattan highway are today a playbook for bad-faith city residents claiming "neighborhood preservation" to fight the sort of dense, human-scale development that Jacobs herself championed.

The historian Robert Caro wrote that the damage wrought by the master builder Robert Moses signified the "death" of New York City in *The Power Broker* (1974). That death, like so many urban obituaries, proved by the 1990s to be greatly exaggerated, overtaken in New York City by an economic rebirth that can, at least in some part, be attributed to Moses's vast public works.

Yet such limitations hardly diminish these influential books, which endure not despite current events but in light of them. They are still published and widely read, and their cultural markers still frame current debates. The underlying debate in these two works in particular—who has the power to make decisions about a city, the people or the power brokers?—is still very much alive today. Great books give fresh definition to facts that people have always known, making the invisible visible and the obscure obvious. More essentially, they give the reader agency to act.

In the first edition of *Walkable City*, Speck assembled a half century of knowledge from urbanists, engineers, and social scientists, arcing from Jacobs's human-scale city to the toxic suburbanization of America, to the desiccation of the nation's downtowns in the second half of the twentieth century, distilled under a single cover through the elegant, unifying principle of walkability. Appearing in the infancy of tech-enabled mobility, *Walkable City*'s title and thesis offered a powerful, human-powered antidote to modern ills: when you design for the walkability of communities, you solve for the safety, vibrancy, health, equity, and economy of cities.

Walkable City offered readers a *Matrix*-like red pill that dissolved the nation's car mythology and exposed its structural underpinnings. In its place, it offered a choice, a walkable "neourbanism," this one based in human activity instead of a revolution in technology or engineering. Thanks to its insights but also its graceful phrasing, *Walkable City* constituted a democratizing lingua franca; it gave everyday readers and advocates a language with which to challenge a professional and political status quo that repels most attempts to change how America's public commons are designed, built, and managed.

For most Americans, save for residents of a handful of dense, typically left-leaning cities, public roads have a single use that is relentlessly reinforced: moving motor vehicles. Government agencies are set up to build more roads that bring more traffic, so that the only rational response when these lanes inevitably fill up is to build more of them. Traffic engineers have calculations for the number of lanes and signals required by cars, but no measures for reducing dependence on them nor any mandate to do so. One outcome: there are now eight parking spaces for every car in this country. More than history, culture, or civic space, American downtowns are monuments to parking, cratered with vast open lots and looming garages.

The motor vehicle alters public space and also human life. Over the course of a lifetime, the average American spends as much time in her car as she does outside breathing fresh air and being active. Even if someone wanted to walk, how could they, with no sidewalk or safe crossings nearby? And where would they walk to, with most destinations miles away? Johnny can access vast information on his smartphone but he still can't walk to school. About half of kids walked or biked to school in 1969. Today, roughly 10 percent of Americans aged five to seventeen do so.

Great writing is not automatically distinguished when it is the first word on a subject, or written by the highest authority, or based on the newest research. *Walkable City* was not Jeff Speck's first attempt at writing the story of American planning; a decade earlier, he coauthored the influential book *Suburban Nation* with his mentors Andres Duany and Elizabeth Plater-Zyberk.

Where *Suburban Nation* focused on American sprawl and its erosion of the notion of place and of civic and community values, *Walkable City* focused on what works in cities, reasserting the importance of place in urban and town centers.

These principles weren't new when Speck wrote them; much of them were known even before Jane Jacobs wrote her own treatise on cities. If Jacobs's "eyes on the street" are what's needed to look out for one another, keeping communities safe and connected, then that street must be a walkable one. And if it's easier to put slippers on one's feet than to carpet the world, Speck shows that it is better to build a city where walking is safe and attractive than it is to pave the planet.

Great streets don't build themselves. Simple changes to their design can let in the light of street life: Narrowing car lanes by a foot or two cues drivers to slow down, making streets easier to cross and sidewalks more inviting. Converting one-way streets to two-way traffic creates a complexity that similarly welcomes walking. Adjusting how and how much people pay to drive and to park—the ghost in the machine documented by the renowned parking prophet Donald Shoup—can prompt new decision points about whether and when one should drive. As car space recedes, with minimal impact on car volumes processed, new room for people emerges.

Building safe, connected networks of sidewalks and crosswalks is an obvious starting point, and something that many American cities still lack well into the twenty-first century. Where sidewalks exist, small touches can make a walk along them safe, useful, comfortable, and interesting—the four principles of Speck's General Theory of Walkability. Planting trees to shield people from the elements and creating a cozy canopy, designing diverse building faces with frequent openings to break up the blankness of drugstore window displays, hiding parking garages behind buildings, modulating the heights of buildings. It's small stuff, but small stuff can make great places.

Yet many of these seemingly simple changes are barred by antiquated municipal rules. Standards written decades ago that mandate over-wide lanes or require excessive parking have gone unchanged and unchallenged for so long that people have forgotten to ask. If too many people speed along a wide road, many cities require that the speed limit on that road be increased. It's hard to fight a system designed to defend itself, and that bars even those who want to do the right thing from doing so.

Now for the harder part: some of the positive trends Speck saw ten years ago have been paved over. Written in the wake of the 2008–2009 economic crisis, the first edition highlighted indicators suggesting that Americans wanted to live in denser, more urban communities. A historic decrease in the number of young Americans obtaining driver's licenses was an obvious symptom of driving-averse millennials. Zipcar was in its ascent, offering vehicles to car-free residents for short, on-demand rentals. Most tellingly, there was a historic decline in the average number of miles driven by Americans, the first such drop since the oil crises of the 1970s.

Once connected, these dots appeared to form an arrow pointing to an off-ramp from a half century of car-focused planning. But by the eve of the COVID-19 pandemic, Americans were less able than ever to conduct most daily activities without a car, driving more and larger cars longer distances than ever. As millennials aged and had kids, their tastes and their locations became more suburban.

Perhaps the most noticeable development on American streets in the last decade hasn't been walkability but the explosion of ride-hail companies like Uber and Lyft. Marketed as an alternative to car ownership and a means for taking cars off the road, ride-hailing ultimately added more traffic to America's cities— 5.7 billion more miles traveled in the nation's nine largest cities by 2017. The rate of national household car ownership only increased, in most cases exceeding the rate of population growth. This story hasn't gone well for people on foot, who are dying in higher numbers on America's roads today than at any point since 2006.

It's easy to think of walkability as an urban amenity, but it is also a fundamental freedom that's not equally shared. The racial justice protests of 2020 demonstrated to a national audience that streets where Black and brown people live, work, walk, and jog are places where they can just as easily be oppressed and killed. The murders of Trayvon Martin in Florida, Ahmaud Arbery in Georgia, and Elijah McClain in Colorado each commenced with a Black person walking or jogging on a neighborhood street. These events and their aftermaths challenged city leaders and planners to view transportation as an essential freedom, making it easier to reach homes, jobs, schools, services, and opportunities. A city of walkable communities is a more just city, not for walkability's sake, but to the extent that it increases the spectrum of mobility options for everyone. Chicago, Portland, and Oakland are among the prominent cities that have begun to define transportation in terms of equity—identifying neglected neighborhoods with the fewest choices for getting around, the farthest from job centers, and where transportation costs chew up household income—and allocating resources accordingly.

Walkability must guide the realignment of transportation policy as city governments become increasingly aware of their power to manage their streets—and as auto manufacturers retrench. Car companies are rebranding themselves as mobility services with a utopian promise that, through high-tech vehicles and efficient networks, they will make streets safer, free people from car ownership, and eliminate traffic. But this development won't herald more walkable cities if driverless cars put as many more miles on city streets as Uber and Lyft already have. If the last century is any guide, advances in driving technology will lead to more car-dominated roads and require new generations of infrastructure to accommodate them. As cities and towns contemplate a future of electric vehicles powering up at municipal curbside charging stations, or fleets of driverless robo-taxis trawling public streets between customers, they should recall what designing streets around cars in the twentieth century did for their walkability and for our cities.

History repeats itself, first as tragedy, then as farce, and then as the status quo. And for all of its momentum, walkability just can't keep up with drivability. Principal highways in Houston,, Phoenix, Atlanta, Portland, and dozens of other cities, built generations earlier to solve the traffic challenges of their time, have grown more engorged with vehicles to become the larger traffic, pollution, and economic challenges of today. Yet state transportation departments still ceaselessly pursue billions of federal tax dollars to build new roads and highway expansions—roads that will become just as congested, and that future generations will struggle to maintain. While the landmark 2021 infrastructure bill contained $1 billion to tear down highways that decapitated historically minority neighborhoods, the same bill contained $432 billion to build and expand highways, even as a $786 billion backlog in repairs to existing roads languishes.

This reversal of these street fortunes doesn't undermine *Walkable City*'s thesis. Update the book's key indicators, and the conclusion stands: if you want to make a change in the world, change your streets. I've devoted a career to fighting for this principle, and the lesson from the streets of dozens of cities is that you can't simultaneously prevent and prepare for more traffic . . . and that there's a better road ahead.

Arriving at the tail end of my tenure leading New York City's Department of Transportation, *Walkable City* hit the shelves after much of the paint had dried on hundreds of sweeping changes to the city's six thousand miles of streets. These streets were a laboratory, stress-testing and refining new design principles that prioritized people instead of cars. In just six and a half years, New York City reclaimed 180 acres of former street space from motor vehicles, reallocating it to bike lanes, plazas, sidewalk extensions, public seating, medians, and islands that gave people refuge while crossing the street. Mayor Michael Bloomberg authorized the reclaiming of Broadway's roadway lanes for pedestrians at Times and Herald Squares in 2009, and at seventy more locations since. Walking increased at key sites by 13 percent from 2007 to 2013 as new space invited people to places from which they'd been banned. In Times Square alone, the daily number of pedestrians increased from 356,000 to 480,000 in the ten years following the plaza's creation.

All this was accomplished without tearing down a single building or constructing a new highway, and most projects were begun for the cost of some paint, planters, and inexpensive materials sitting unused in city depots. Traffic remained the same or, on balance, a little better, as walking and biking soared. And New Yorkers? They loved the changes and are still supporting their expansion a decade later. Some may scoff that New York City's population density and transit network make it unrepresentative. But there is probably no place in the United States where street space is more contested by cars, taxis, buses, and trucks, making the politics around changing streets such an unremitting fight. If New York can restore pedestrians to their rightful place in this pressure cooker, then there is hope for cities everywhere.

In 2013 I left the transportation department to become a founding principal with Bloomberg Associates, a pro bono consultancy that collaborates with mayors around the nation and the world. Working with skilled city planners in Milan, our team helped to reclaim roadway space from parked cars to create more than thirty neighborhood piazzas. We worked with political and community leaders in Athens to restore its central Trigono commercial district to a walkable, car-free environment, replacing drive-by lanes and parking spaces with café seats, and filling empty storefronts with new businesses. In Mexico City, safety redesigns of the city's notoriously dangerous streets led to an 18 percent reduction in traffic deaths, including 24 percent fewer deaths among pedestrians in just eighteen months. In Bogotá, citywide space reclamations and pedestrian safety districts reclaimed eighty-seven thousand square feet of road space, an area equivalent to twenty playgrounds, while traffic deaths dropped by 15 percent over five years. I've also worked closely with mayors and transportation directors in Los Angeles, Chicago, Atlanta, Detroit, and Oakland to reorient their transportation operations and build transformational projects that reclaim lanes for plazas and walking and biking, showing what's possible quickly, and creating demand for more. The language of walkable streets is universal.

Facts on the ground are critical, and so are the rules of engagement. NACTO, the National Association of City Transportation Officials—a consortium of ninety-three American city agencies for which I serve as chair—has helped replace national street design standards that for the last fifty years have marginalized pedestrians and bike riders. These new standards, once considered radical, have been officially endorsed by the federal government, giving cities the authority to reimagine streets with designs that operationalize many of *Walkable City*'s tenets.

Today, most every major city can showcase streets that were foreign concepts a decade ago: hundreds of miles of new protected bike paths in the usual-suspect territories of San Francisco, Boston, and Chicago, yes; but also dozens of miles in Detroit, Salt Lake City, Indianapolis, Minneapolis, San Jose, and Austin. More than forty cities have committed to Vision Zero action plans, pledging a restructuring of city streets and policies to eliminate traffic deaths.

The pandemic briefly emptied the nation's roads, but that didn't mean they were safer. Speeding cars on vacant roads made crashes deadlier nationwide. Traffic quickly returned to cities, recovering much of its initial drop within a matter of months and exceeding pre-pandemic levels within one year of the first lockdown. As of this writing, transit ridership remains gutted, at barely 50 percent of its pre-pandemic levels. Given its climate impacts, an economic recovery where everyone drives could hardly be considered a recovery.

Yet for all of its gloom, the pandemic in 2020 glittered with walkability. As so many people around the globe began to work from home, the daily radius of life for millions of city dwellers contracted from a few miles to just a few blocks, making local streets and commercial strips more meaningful to residents than the office clusters that used to dominate their economies.

Seeing this shift, and witnessing crowded parks and sidewalks next to empty car lanes, cities from Berlin to Boise annexed street space for residents to walk and bike. New York City, Chicago, and Oakland created ambitious networks of streets closed to cars or turned into shared spaces, where people could drive only to reach local destinations, but where people had the priority. Towns that are hardly known as pedestrian meccas saw the benefit in creating car-free streets for outdoor dining, or reclaiming parking spaces, such as Tampa, Milwaukee, and Nashville.

It wasn't just walking. Boston, Austin, and Oakland responded with shared streets and pop-up bike lanes, carving out routes and street space for people who didn't have a car, or whose bus routes were discontinued due to low ridership. The Great Highway along San Francisco's Ocean Beach became a grand car-free space, connecting with walking and biking roads in Golden Gate Park to create a human-paced corridor stretching halfway across the city. Mayor London Breed, supported by the city's board of supervisors, made the people-first road in the park permanent.

At the height of the pandemic, Bloomberg Philanthropies launched the Asphalt Art Initiative, awarding grants to sixteen cities to reimagine streets as a canvas for community creativity, literally painting roads, crosswalks, and intersections with colorful place-making designs by local residents and community groups. Stretching from Reno to Pittsburgh to Glasgow to Amsterdam, these inspiring street murals will be joined by projects in twenty-six new cities in 2022, by biking and pedestrian space-making designs in Kansas City, Baltimore, Birmingham, Fairbanks, and Providence, and by new intersection murals in Billings (MT), Starkville (MS), and Huntington (WV). All of these efforts embody strategies to make the most of our streets by changing their look and feel, by elevating the pedestrian, and by giving the power to do so to the people, and they were done in the spirit of this book.

If the street is the basic unit of cities, *Walkable City* is the manual for perfecting it. Not every lane of every street is needed for cars every hour of every day. Neighborhood streets can allow local traffic and deliveries while keeping out larger trucks and speeders looking for a shortcut. What today is a parking lane along a row of storefronts could become tomorrow's restaurant, café, or public seating, alive with people and with all of the civic, social, and economic activity they generate. Even Speck in 2012 ventured that few would want to be seated for dinner near a lane of moving traffic. But dozens of cities in 2020 showed—just as we did along Broadway a decade earlier—that smart design, slower speeds, and calmer traffic can make America's streets the best seats in the house.

After the errant first two sentences of this book, Speck quickly recovers with the sage declaration that "an intellectual revolution is no longer necessary" to achieve the best in our cities. America's mobility tragedy is not that we are unaware of abject car dependence, traffic congestion, climate-threatening pollution, unsafe and uncrossable streets, and the dysfunctional policies that hinder attempts to change them. Rather, the problem lies in ourselves and our institutions, a collective failure of imagination and action to more broadly implement the vision and the strategies of *Walkable City*.

We know everything we need to know to transform our cities into walkable places. For most Americans who understand this, it is in no small part owing to the power of this book. For those who don't, it's never too late to get it right.

The best time to have read *Walkable City* was ten years ago. The second-best time is today.

WALKABLE CITY

PROLOGUE

This is not the next great book on American cities. That book is not needed. An intellectual revolution is no longer necessary. What characterizes the discussion on cities these days is not a wrongheadedness or a lack of awareness about what needs to be done, but rather a complete disconnect between that awareness and the actions of those responsible for the physical form of our communities.

We've known for three decades how to make livable cities—after forgetting for four—yet we've somehow not been able to pull it off. Jane Jacobs, who wrote in 1960, won over the planners by 1980. But the planners have yet to win over the city.

Certain large cities, yes. If you make your home in New York, Boston, Chicago, San Francisco, Portland, or in a handful of other special places, you can have some confidence that things are on the right track. But these locations are the exceptions. In the small and midsized cities where most Americans spend their lives, the daily decisions of local officials are still, more often than not, making their lives worse. This is not bad planning but the absence of planning, or rather, decision-making disconnected from planning. The planners were so wrong for so many years that now that they are mostly right, they are mostly ignored.

But this book is not about the planning profession, nor is it an argument for more planning per se. Instead, it is an attempt to simply delineate what is wrong with most American cities and how to fix it. This book is not about why cities work or how cities work, but about what works in cities. And what works best in the best cities is walkability.

Walkability is both an end and a means, as well as a measure. While the physical and social rewards of walking are many, walkability is perhaps most useful as it contributes to urban vitality and most meaningful as an indicator of that vitality. After several decades spent redesigning pieces of cities, trying to make them more livable and more successful, I have watched my focus narrow to this topic as the one issue that seems to both influence and embody most of the others. Get walkability right and so much of the rest will follow.

This discussion is necessary because, since midcentury, whether intentionally or by accident, most American cities have effectively become no-walking zones. In the absence of any larger vision or mandate, city engineers—worshiping the twin gods of Smooth Traffic and Ample Parking—have turned our downtowns into places that are easy to get to but not worth arriving at. Outdated zoning and building codes, often imported from the suburbs, have matched the uninviting streetscape with equally antisocial private buildings, completing a public realm that is unsafe, uncomfortable, and just plain boring. As growing numbers of Americans opt for more urban lifestyles, they are often met with city centers that don't welcome their return. As a result, a small number of forward-thinking cities are gobbling up the lion's share of post-teen suburbanites and empty nesters with the wherewithal to live wherever they want, while most midsized American cities go hungry.

How can Providence, Grand Rapids, and Tacoma compete with Boston, Chicago, and Portland? Or, more realistically, how can these typical cities provide their citizens a quality of life that makes them want to stay? While there are many answers to that question, perhaps none has been so thoroughly neglected as design, and how a comprehensive collection of simple design fixes can reverse decades of counterproductive policies and practices and usher in a new era of street life in America.

These fixes simply give pedestrians a fighting chance, while also embracing bikes, enhancing transit, and making downtown living attractive to a broader range of people. Most are not expensive—some require little more than yellow paint. Each one individually makes a difference; collectively, they can transform a city and the lives of its residents.

Even New York and San Francisco still get some things wrong, but they will continue to poach the country's best and brightest unless our other, more normal cities can learn from their successes while avoiding their mistakes. We planners are counting on these typical places, because America will be finally ushered into "the urban century" not by its few exceptions, but by a collective movement among its everyday cities to do once again what cities do best, which is to bring people together—on foot.

A GENERAL THEORY OF WALKABILITY

As a city planner, I make plans for new places and I make plans for making old places better. Since the late eighties, I have worked on about seventy-five plans for cities, towns, and villages, new and old. About a third of these have been built or are well under way, which sounds pretty bad, but is actually a decent batting average in this game. This means that I have had my fair share of pleasant surprises as well as many opportunities to learn from my mistakes.

In the middle of this work, I took four years off to lead the design division at the National Endowment for the Arts. In this job, I helped run a program called the Mayors' Institute on City Design, which puts city leaders together with designers for intensive planning sessions. Every two months, somewhere in the United States, we would gather eight mayors and eight designers, lock ourselves in a room for two days, and try to solve each mayor's most pressing city-planning challenge.* As might be imagined, working side by side with a couple hundred mayors, one mayor at a time, proved a greater design education than anything I have done before or since.

---

*This program, now in its twenty-sixth year, has served nearly one thousand mayors, with dramatic results. More information can be found at micd.org.

I specialize in downtowns, and when I am hired to make a downtown plan, I like to move there with my family, preferably for at least a month. There are many reasons to move to a city while you plan it. First, it's more efficient in terms of travel and setting up meetings, something that can become very expensive. Second, it allows you to truly get to know a place, to memorize every building, street, and block. It also gives you the chance to get familiar with the locals over coffee, dinners in people's homes, drinks in neighborhood pubs, and during chance encounters on the street. These nonmeeting meetings are when most of the real intelligence gets collected.

These are all great reasons. But the main reason to spend time in a city is to live the life of a citizen. Shuttling between a hotel and a meeting facility is not what citizens do. They take their kids to school, drop by the dry cleaners, make their way to work, step out for lunch, hit the gym or pick up some groceries, get themselves home, and consider an evening stroll or an after-dinner beer. Friends from out of town drop in on the weekend and get taken out for a night on the main square. These are among the many normal things that nonplanners do, and I try to do them, too.

A couple of years ago, while I was working on a plan for Lowell, Massachusetts, some old high-school friends joined us for dinner on Merrimack Street, the heart of a lovely nineteenth-century downtown. Our group consisted of four adults, one toddler in a stroller, and my wife's very pregnant belly. Across the street from our restaurant, we waited for the light to change, lost in conversation. Maybe a minute passed before we saw the push-button signal request. So we pushed it. The conversation advanced for another minute or so. Finally, we gave up and jaywalked. About the same time, a car careened around the corner at perhaps forty-five miles per hour, on a street that had been widened to ease traffic.

The resulting near-miss fortunately left no scars, but it will not be forgotten. Stroller jaywalking is a surefire way to feel like a bad parent, especially when it goes awry. The only consolation this time was that I was in a position to do something about it.

As I write these words, I am again on the road with my family, this time in Rome. Now the new baby is in a sling, and the toddler alternates between a stroller and his own two feet, depending on the terrain and his frame of mind. It is interesting to compare our experience in Rome with the one in Lowell, or, more to the point, the experience of walking in most American cities.

Rome, at first glance, seems horribly inhospitable to pedestrians. So many things are wrong. Half the streets are missing sidewalks, most intersections lack crosswalks, pavements are uneven and rutted, handicap ramps are largely absent. Hills are steep and frequent (I hear there are seven). And need I mention the drivers?

Yet here we are among so many other pedestrians—tourists and locals alike—making our way around Trastevere . . . on our toes, yes, but enjoying every minute of it. This anarchic obstacle course is somehow a magnet for walkers, recently selected by readers of *Lonely Planet* travel guides as one of the world's "Top Ten Walking Cities." Romans drive a fraction of the miles that Americans do. A friend of ours who came here to work in the U.S. embassy bought a car when he arrived, out of habit. Now it sits in his courtyard, a target for pigeons.

This tumultuous urban landscape, which fails to meet any conventional American measure of "pedestrian friendliness," is a walker's paradise. So what's going on here? Certainly, in competing for foot traffic, Anatole Broyard's "poem pressed into service as a city" began with certain advantages. The *Lonely Planet* ranking is likely more a function of spectacle than pedestrian comfort. But the same monuments, arranged in a more modern American way, would hardly compete. (Think Las Vegas, with its

Walk Score of 54*.) The main thing that makes Rome—and the other winners: Venice, Boston, San Francisco, Barcelona, Amsterdam, Prague, Paris, and New York—so walkable is what we planners call "fabric," the everyday collection of streets, blocks, and buildings that tie the monuments together. Despite its many technical failures, Rome's fabric is superb.

Yet fabric is one of several key aspects of urban design that are missing from the walkability discussion in most places. This is because that discussion has largely been about creating adequate and attractive pedestrian facilities, rather than walkable cities. There is no shortage of literature on this subject and even a fledgling field of "walkability studies" that focuses on impediments to pedestrian access and safety, mostly in the Toronto suburbs.* These efforts are helpful, but inadequate. The same goes for urban beautification programs, such as the famous "Five B's" of the eighties—bricks, banners, bandstands, bollards, and berms—that now grace many an abandoned downtown.[1]

Lots of money and muscle have gone into improving sidewalks, crossing signals, streetlights, and trash cans, but how important are these things, ultimately, in convincing people to walk? If walking was just about creating safe pedestrian zones, then why did more than 150 Main Streets pedestrianized in the sixties and seventies fail almost immediately?[2] Clearly, there is more to walking than just making safe, pretty space for it.

The pedestrian is an extremely fragile species, the canary in the coal mine of urban livability. Under the right conditions, this creature thrives and multiplies. But creating those conditions requires attention to a broad range of criteria, some more easily satisfied than others. Enumerating and understanding these criteria is a project for a lifetime—it has become mine—and is forever a work in progress. It is presumptuous to claim to have

---

*54 out of 100. See below for more on Walk Score.
*See janeswalk.net.

figured it out, but since I have spent a lot of time trying, I reckon it is worth communicating what I have learned so far. Since it tries to explain so much, I call this discussion the General Theory of Walkability.

The General Theory of Walkability explains how, to be favored, a walk has to satisfy four main conditions: it must be useful, safe, comfortable, and interesting. Each of these qualities is essential and none alone is sufficient. *Useful* means that most aspects of daily life are located close at hand and organized in a way that walking serves them well. *Safe* means that the street has been designed to give pedestrians a fighting chance against being hit by automobiles; they must not only be safe but *feel* safe, which is even tougher to satisfy. *Comfortable* means that buildings and landscape shape urban streets into "outdoor living rooms," in contrast to wide-open spaces, which usually fail to attract pedestrians. *Interesting* means that sidewalks are lined by unique buildings with friendly faces and that signs of humanity abound.

These four conditions are mostly a way of thinking about a series of specific rules that are further organized into what I call the Ten Steps of Walkability. These will be explored later. Together, I believe that they add up to a complete prescription for making our cities more walkable.

But first, we must understand that the walkable city is not just a nice, idealistic notion. Rather, it is a simple, practical-minded solution to a host of complex problems that we face as a society, problems that daily undermine our nation's economic competitiveness, public welfare, and environmental sustainability. For that reason, this book is less a design treatise than an essential call to arms. Why we need walkability so badly is the subject of the next section.

PART I

WHY WALKABILITY?

While battle was never declared, many American cities seem to have been made and remade with a mandate to defeat pedestrians. Fattened roads, emaciated sidewalks, deleted trees, fry-pit drive-thrus, and ten-acre parking lots have reduced many of our streetscapes to auto zones in which pedestrian life is but a theoretical possibility.

The causes of this transformation are sometimes surprising. In Miami, for example, people wonder why intersections in residential neighborhoods are often so fat: two relatively narrow streets will meet in a sweeping expanse of asphalt that seems to take hours to walk across. The answer is that the firefighters' union once struck a deal that no truck would ever be dispatched without a hefty number of firemen on it. That's good for safety and even better for job security, but the fire chief's response was to purchase only the heftiest trucks. So, for many years, one-story residential neighborhoods in Miami had to be designed around the lumbering turning radius of a truck built for tall-building fires.[1]

The above anecdote is far from unusual in today's landscape of disassociated professions and special interests that determine the shape of our communities. The modern world is full of experts who are paid to ignore criteria beyond their professions. The school and parks departments will push for fewer, larger facilities, since these are easier to maintain—and show off. The public works department will insist that new neighborhoods be designed principally around snow and trash removal. The department of transportation will build new roads to ease traffic generated by the very sprawl that they cause. Each of these approaches may seem correct in a vacuum, but is wrong in a city.

If they are to function properly, cities need to be planned by generalists, as they once were. Generalists understand that consolidating parks means that fewer people can walk to them. Generalists understand that infrastructure organized in service of big trucks is not always inviting to small people. And generalists, finally, are coming to understand that more lanes usually just lead to more traffic.

Most significantly, generalists—such as planners and, one hopes, mayors—ask the big-picture questions that are so often forgotten among the day-to-day shuffle of city governance. Questions like: What kind of city will help us thrive economically? What kind of city will keep our citizens not just safe, but healthy? What kind of city will be sustainable for generations to come?

These three issues—wealth, health, and sustainability—are, not coincidentally, the three principal arguments for making our cities more walkable.

WALKING, THE URBAN ADVANTAGE

The walking generation; A demographic perfect storm;
The walkability dividend

Many of my client cities ask me the same question: "How can we attract corporations, citizens, and especially young, entrepreneurial talent?" In Grand Rapids, Michigan, where I am employed by the city's leading philanthropists, they ask it differently: "How can we keep our children from leaving? How can we keep our grandchildren from leaving?"

The obvious answer is that cities need to provide the sort of environment that these people want. Surveys—as if we needed them—show how creative-class citizens, especially millennials, vastly favor communities with *street life*, the pedestrian culture that can only come from walkability.

A lack of street life was one reason why the leadership at Wolverine World Wide, the manufacturers of Merrell and Patagonia Footwear, was having trouble keeping new creative workers from jumping ship from their suburban West Michigan headquarters. The problem was not the company, but the impression among newly arrived spouses that they had no way to break into the social scene . . . even though West Michiganders are known for their openness and hospitality. So what was going on? It turns out that this social scene could only be accessed by car and thus by invitation. With no pedestrian culture, there were no opportunities for the chance encounters that turn into friendships.

When it came time to launch a new apparel division, they decided to base it in Portland, Oregon.

Since that time, Wolverine has set up a new innovation center along with three other top West Michigan companies in downtown Grand Rapids. According to Blake Krueger, Wolverine's president and CEO, the company needed "an urban hub that attracts and retains the millennial creative class. You need a vibrant city heartbeat for these people. Downtown, they're in a more creative live/work/play environment than if they are stuck out here in suburbia." This facility now includes designers and product developers across a dozen different brands.

For many companies, an urban satellite is not enough. Brand Muscle, formerly of leafy Beachwood, Ohio, recently relocated all of its 150 employees to downtown Cleveland, thanks in part to the desires of a largely twentysomething workforce. Now staffer Kristen Babjack brags about her urban lifestyle: "We can leave our apartment and walk five feet to a restaurant to get something to eat, or to go shopping. We have all of our arenas and sporting areas and concerts all in one pretty much walkable area."[*] Similar stories are making the news in Saint Louis, Buffalo, and even in beleaguered Detroit.

The economic advantage that has already begun to accrue to walkable places can be attributed to three key factors. First, for certain segments of the population, chief among them young "creatives," urban living is simply more appealing; many wouldn't be caught dead anywhere else. Second, massive demographic shifts occurring right now mean that these pro-urban segments of the population are becoming dominant, creating a spike in demand that is expected to last for decades. Third, the choice to live the walkable life generates considerable savings for these households,

---

[*] David Barnett, "A Comeback for Downtown Cleveland." United Airlines just moved thirteen hundred of its employees to downtown Chicago from suburban Elk Grove Township, Illinois (Fran Spielman, "1300 More United Jobs Downtown").

and much of these savings are spent locally. I will address each of these factors in turn.

THE WALKING GENERATION

When I worked for the town planning firm DPZ* in Miami in the nineties, everyone drove to the office, without exception. Taking transit or bicycling made no sense at all, as the buses took forever and the biking was worse than perilous. In more recent visits, I learned that a significant segment of the young designer workforce now bikes or rides the bus, even though the conditions for either are hardly better.

These are the same folks who have put a composting bin in the office kitchen . . . so are they just the exceptions to the rule?

It turns out that since the late nineties, the share of automobile miles driven by Americans in their twenties has dropped from 20.8 percent to just 13.7 percent. And if one looks at teens, future shifts seem likely to be greater. The number of nineteen-year-olds who have opted out of earning driver's licenses has almost tripled since the late seventies, from 8 percent to 23 percent.[1] This statistic is particularly meaningful when one considers how the American landscape has changed since the seventies, when most American teens could walk to school, to the store, and to the soccer field, in stark contrast to the realities of today's auto-centric sprawl.

This trend began well before the recession of 2008 and subsequent fuel spikes, and is seen as cultural, not economic. Market researchers J. D. Power—hardly part of the anticar lobby—report that "online discussions by teens indicate shifts in perceptions regarding the necessity of and desire to have cars."[2] In

---

*DPZ stands for Duany-Plater Zyberk & Company, the firm founded by Andres Duany and Elizabeth Plater-Zyberk, my coauthors on *Suburban Nation*.

"The Great Car Reset," Richard Florida observes: "Younger people today . . . no longer see the car as a necessary expense or a source of personal freedom. In fact, it is increasingly just the opposite: not owning a car and not owning a house are seen by more and more as a path to greater flexibility, choice, and personal autonomy."[3] These driving trends are only a small part of a larger picture that has less to do with cars and more to do with cities, and specifically with how young professionals today view themselves in relation to the city, especially in comparison to previous generations.

Born as the baby boom ended, I grew up watching three television shows almost daily: *Gilligan's Island*, *The Brady Bunch*, and *The Partridge Family*. While *Gilligan's Island* may have had little to say about urbanism, the other two were extremely instructive. They idealized the mid-twentieth-century suburban standard of low-slung houses on leafy lots, surrounded by more of the same. This was normal and good. As a would-be architect, I was particularly susceptible to the charms of Mike Brady's self-built split-level. This is not to say that there were no urban shows on my television set. I saw a good amount of four: *Dragnet, Mannix, The Streets of San Francisco*, and *Hawaii 5-0*—all focused on one subject: crime.•

Now, contrast my experience growing up in the seventies with that of a child growing up in or around the nineties, watching *Seinfeld, Friends*, and, eventually, *Sex and the City*. In these shows, the big city (in all cases New York) was lovingly portrayed as a largely benevolent and always interesting force, often a character and coconspirator in its own right. The most urban of American cities was the new normal, and certainly good.

The first thing that I take away from this comparison is that I watched far too much television as a child. But the real point

---

• To be fair, I also caught occasional episodes of *The Honeymooners* and *The Lucille Ball Show*, in which the city took the form of a vague, sooty presence outside the window of a cramped apartment—unthreatening but also uninviting. The only memorable exception was *The Mary Tyler Moore Show*. We'll talk about her later.

here is that today's young professionals grew up in a mass culture—of which TV was only one part—that has predisposed them
to look favorably upon cities; indeed, to aspire to live in them. I
grew up in the suburbs watching shows about the suburbs. They
grew up in the suburbs watching shows about the city. My com-
placency has been replaced by their longing.

This group, the *millennials*, represent the biggest population
bubble in fifty years. Sixty-four percent of college-educated millennials choose first where they want to live, and only then do
they look for a job.[4] Fully 77 percent of them plan to live in America's urban cores.[5]

A DEMOGRAPHIC PERFECT STORM

Meanwhile, the generation raised on *Friends* is not the only
major cohort looking for new places to live. There's a larger one:
the millennials' parents, the front-end boomers. They are citizens that every city wants—significant personal savings, no
schoolkids.

And according to Christopher Leinberger, the Brookings Institution economist who first brought my attention to the *Brady
Bunch/Friends* phenomenon, empty nesters want walkability:

> At approximately 77 million Americans, they are fully
> one-quarter of the population. With the leading edge
> of the boomers now approaching sixty-five years old, the
> group is finding that their suburban houses are too big.
> Their child-rearing days are ending, and all those empty
> rooms have to be heated, cooled, and cleaned, and the
> unused backyard maintained. Suburban houses can be
> socially isolating, especially as aging eyes and slower re-
> flexes make driving everywhere less comfortable. Free-
> dom for many in this generation means living in walkable,
> accessible communities with convenient transit linkages

and good public services like libraries, cultural activities, and health care.[6]

In the 1980s, my city-planning colleagues and I began hearing from sociologists about something called a NORC, a naturally occurring retirement community. Over the past decade, I have watched a growing number of my parents' generation abandon their large-lot houses to resettle in mixed-use urban centers. My own parents finally jumped ship last year, moving from leafy Belmont Hill, Massachusetts, to only-slightly-less-leafy but much more walkable Lexington Center. For them, that increased walkability means all the difference between an essentially housebound existence and what we all hope will be several decades of continued independence.

On the cusp of their eighties, my parents could be considered late adopters. But as pre-boomers, they represent a trickle of what is to become a torrent. Leinberger notes how, starting now, an average of 1.5 million Americans will be turning sixty-five every year, quadruple the rate of a decade ago.[7] This rate will not begin to plateau until 2020 and we will not see it return to current levels until 2033.

In combination with their independent children, these retiring boomers will numerically overwhelm those families of child-rearing age who typically prefer the suburbs. This upcoming convergence represents "the biggest demographic event since the baby boom itself."[8] Of the 101 million new households expected to take shape between now and 2025, fully 88 percent are projected to be childless. This is a dramatic change from 1970, when almost half of all households included children.* These new adults-only households won't give a hoot about the quality of

---

*Christopher B. Leinberger, *The Option of Urbanism*, 89–90. Leinberger's book is a central source for this section, as it lays out many of the arguments and statistics surrounding the demand for walkable cities. While 4 million Americans lived alone in 1950, that number now tops 31 million (Nathan Heller, "The Disconnect," 110). According to *USA Today*, there are now more households with dogs than children (Haya El Nasser, "In Many Neighborhoods, Kids Are Only a Memory").

local schools or the size of their backyards. "This fact will open up many possibilities," Leinberger observes.[9]

As that current statistical oddity, a parent of young children, I often advocate for stronger public schools and neighborhood parks to benefit families. I remind people that a community cannot fully thrive in the absence of any generational cohort, since we all support one another. I like to quote David Byrne: "If we can build a successful city for children, we can build a successful city for all people."[10] This is true enough, but I am often reminded that I lived comfortably for a full decade in one of the most extreme exceptions to that rule, Miami's South Beach, where I could easily go for a month at a time without a stroller sighting. Not one adult in my neighborhood appeared to be between thirty-five and fifty-five, and none seemed (productively) fertile. Yet South Beach was and remains a great place physically, socially, and economically. Demographically speaking, South Beach is the future of many American cities.

That seems to be the case in walkable Washington, D.C., where the past decade has seen a 23 percent uptick in the number of residents between twenty and thirty-four, simultaneous with an increased number of adults in their fifties and early sixties. Meanwhile, the number of children under fifteen has dropped by 20 percent.[11]

Clearly, Leinberger is optimistic about the larger impact of these population trends on cities. Writing in *Grist*, he concludes that "meeting the pent-up demand for walkable urban development will take a generation. It will be a boon to the real estate industry and put a foundation under the American economy for decades, just as the construction of low-density suburbs did during the last half of the 20th century."[12] Whether or not it can salvage our struggling economy, he makes a convincing case that people will be moving back to the city.

The question that remains is: Will they be moving back to your city, or to someone else's? The answer may well lie in its walkability.

Christopher Leinberger was once the owner of Robert Charles Lesser & Co., the largest real estate advisory firm in the United States, which means that he helped to build a lot of sprawl. He is now convinced that much of suburbia is poised to become "The Next Slum."[13]

In order to study real estate performance, Leinberger divides the American built environment into two categories: *walkable urbanism* and *drivable sub-urbanism*.* In the Detroit region, he finds that housing in walkable urbanism fetches a 40 percent price premium over similar housing in drivable sub-urbanism; in the Seattle region, that premium is 51 percent; in Denver, it's 150 percent. New York City, unsurprisingly, tops the list at 200 percent—that is to say, people are paying three times as much per square foot for apartments in walkable neighborhoods as for comparable suburban houses. In most markets, the demand for walkable urbanism dramatically outpaces the supply: in Atlanta, only 35 percent of poll respondents who want to live in a walkable urban place are able to find and afford it.[14]

A similar dynamic can be found at work for commercial properties. In Washington, D.C., walkable office space recently leased at a 27 percent premium over drivable suburban office space and had single-digit rather than double-digit vacancy rates. *The Wall Street Journal* has confirmed similar trends nationwide: while the suburban office vacancy rate has jumped 2.3 points since 2005, occupancy in America's downtowns has held steady.[15]

Looking at these numbers, Leinberger concludes:

The metropolitan area that does not offer walkable urbanism is probably destined to lose economic development opportunities; the creative class will gravitate to

---

* These categories are slightly misleading, since walkable urbanism is still drivable, while drivable sub-urbanism is not walkable. Or, more accurately, in walkable urbanism, driving remains a viable option for those people with disposable income and time to spend in traffic, while in drivable sub-urbanism, walking is a practice undertaken only by the least advantaged people with no choice.

those metro areas that offer multiple choices in living arrangements. . . . As consumer surveys in downtown Philadelphia and Detroit in 2006 have shown, this seems to be particularly true for the well-educated, who seem to have a predilection for living in walkable urban places.[16]

This growing demand for pedestrian-friendly places is reflected in the runaway success of Walk Score, the website that calculates neighborhood walkability.• It was started on a lark in 2007 by Matt Lerner, Mike Mathieu, and Jesse Kocher, three partners in a software company with the incongruously automotive name of Front Seat. "I had heard a story on NPR about food miles in England—labeling food with how far it had to travel to get to you," Lerner told me recently, "and I thought, why not instead measure house miles: how many miles from your house you had to go for daily errands."

Addresses are ranked in five categories, with a score of 50 needed to cross the threshold from *car dependent* to *somewhat walkable.* Seventy points earns a *very walkable* ranking, and anything above 90 qualifies as a *walker's paradise.* San Francisco's Chinatown earns a 100, as does NYC's Tribeca, while Los Angeles's Mulholland Drive rates a 9. South Beach in Miami gets a 92. Nike's headquarters in Beaverton, Oregon, comes in at a *car dependent* 42, while the street address of the nationally acclaimed "Walking Guru" Leslie Sansone, of New Castle, Pennsylvania, has a Walk Score of 37.•

•According to Lerner, once a crude version was up and running, "I emailed twenty people about the site, and we had 150,000 unique visitors the next day." Walk Score now serves up more than 4 million scores daily.

•One of the fascinating things about Walk Score is how accurate it is, despite the fact that it currently measures only one aspect of walkability: proximity to daily destinations. Specifically, the algorithm asks how far one is (as the crow flies) from nine different "amenity categories," including shopping, dining, coffee, parks, and schools. As will be discussed ahead, true walkability depends dramatically upon so many other factors that Walk Score doesn't measure—such as the size of the blocks and the speed of the cars—but its failure (so far) to measure these attributes doesn't hurt it too much due to a convenient coincidence: almost all of the places in America with many different uses

Tellingly, Walk Score has become a big hit with real estate agents. Driven by their demand, the Front Seat team has recently developed Walk Score Professional, a subscription site that already boasts links from more than ten thousand other websites, most of them belonging to realtors.

I spoke with one of these agents, Eva Otto, whose face adorns a testimonial on the Walk Score homepage. She is confident that "in a place like Seattle, walkability is the make or break for some buyers. It can add 5 to 10 percent to a person's willingness to pay for a house." For each property she handles, she places the Walk Score website amenity map inside the house in an obvious place. She comments that her buyers are increasingly aware of "how surprising and delightful your quality of life can be when you don't have to get into a car to go every place in your life besides home."

If Walk Score is so useful in helping people decide where to live, then it can also help us determine how much they value walkability. Now that it has been around for a few years, some resourceful economists have had the opportunity to study the relationship between Walk Score and real estate value, and they

---

in close proximity tend to possess smaller blocks and slower-speed traffic. Mixed uses and pedestrian-friendly streets are both part of one common model (the traditional urban neighborhood), while isolated uses and unwalkable streets constitute the other (sprawl). Where the algorithm begins to fail is in high-intensity, commercial edge cities. Here, a preponderance of retail outlets cranks up the score, despite the fact that the only walking occurs in gigantic parking lots. For this reason, sprawl poster child Tysons Corner, Virginia—straight from the cover of Joel Garreau's book *Edge City*—earns an impressive 87. This puts it two points ahead of my own U Street neighborhood in Washington, D.C., even though half my neighbors don't own cars and walk to everything. Living car-free in Tysons Corner, if not actually illegal, is still a preposterous concept.

Happily, the developers are hard at work refining the algorithm. A new version called Street Smart impressively manages to take block size, street width, and vehicle speed into account. This new version will eventually replace the original one—perhaps by the time you are reading this. But Lerner and his team are wary of moving too quickly: "When we make the change over to Street Smart, a lot of people's scores will change, so we want to have a long beta period to work out any issues."

have put a price on it: five hundred to three thousand dollars *per point*.

In his white paper for CEOs for Cities, "Walking the Walk: How Walkability Raises Home Values in U.S. Cities," Joe Cortright looked at data for ninety thousand distinct home sales in fifteen markets nationwide, places like Chicago, Dallas, and Jacksonville. After controlling for all other factors that are known to impact house price, he found a clear positive correlation in all but two of those markets.• In a typical example, Charlotte, North Carolina, Cortright found that an increase in Walk Score from the metropolitan average of 54 (*somewhat walkable*) to 71 (*very walkable*) correlated with an increase in average house price from $280,000 to $314,000.[17] That's two thousand dollars per point, or two hundred thousand dollars across the full scale. Interestingly, two hundred thousand dollars is about the minimum price you can pay for an empty buildable lot in the more walkable parts of Washington, D.C.

Of course, it's generally useful to back up the data by asking real humans what they want. The market-research firm Belden Russonello & Stewart polled several thousand American adults for the National Association of Realtors, and found the following: "When selecting a community, nearly half of the public (47 percent) would prefer to live in a city or a suburban neighborhood with a mix of houses, shops, and businesses. . . . Only one in ten say they would prefer a suburban neighborhood with houses only."[18] Given that the vast majority of the American built environment is currently the latter, it is no surprise that the demand

---

• The outliers were Las Vegas and Bakersfield, California, two cities almost entirely lacking in traditional urbanism (Cortright, "Walking the Walk," 2). In a more recent study of the Washington, D.C., region, Chris Leinberger and Mariela Alfonzo found a positive correlation across all market segments. Referring to Walk Score's five categories, they state that "each step up the walkability ladder adds $9 per square foot to annual office rents, $7 per square foot to retail rents, more than $300 per month to apartment rents, and nearly $82 per square foot to home values" (Christopher B. Leinberger, "Now Coveted: A Walkable, Convenient Place").

for walkable urbanism already outpaces the supply. This disparity is only going to get bigger.

THE WALKABILITY DIVIDEND

In 2007, Joe Cortright, the fellow responsible for the Walk Score value study cited above, published a report called "Portland's Green Dividend," in which he asked the question: What does Portland get for being walkable? Quite a lot, it turns out.

To set the stage, we should describe what makes Portland different. Clearly, it is not Manhattan. It is not particularly big or particularly small and its residential density, by American standards, is pretty normal. It has attracted a good amount of industry lately, but has shown no great historical predisposition to do so, nor is it gifted with mineral wealth. It rains a lot in Portland and, interestingly, locals pride themselves on not using umbrellas. Perhaps most fascinating is the way that Portlanders refuse to disobey DON'T WALK signs, even if it's 1:00 a.m. on a tiny two-lane street swathed in utter silence . . . and even if a blithe eastcoaster is striding happily into the intersection (I'm not naming names here).

But what really makes Portland unusual is how it has chosen to grow. While most American cities were building more highways, Portland invested in transit and biking. While most cities were reaming out their roadways to speed traffic, Portland implemented a Skinny Streets program. While most American cities were amassing a spare tire of undifferentiated sprawl, Portland instituted an urban growth boundary. These efforts and others like them, over several decades—a blink of the eye in planner time—have changed the way that Portlanders live.•

•To be accurate, Portland has not been spared its spare tire of sprawl. But thanks to the urban growth boundary, this area is smaller and more contiguous than it would have been otherwise.

This change is not dramatic—were it not for the roving hordes of bicyclists, it might be invisible—but it is significant. While almost every other American city has seen its residents drive farther and farther every year and spend more and more of their time stuck in traffic, Portland's vehicle miles traveled per person peaked in 1996. Now, compared to other major metropolitan areas, Portlanders on average drive 20 percent less.[19]

Small change? Not really: according to Cortright, this 20 percent (four miles per citizen per day) adds up to $1.1 billion of savings each year, which equals fully 1.5 percent of all personal income earned in the region. And that number ignores time not wasted in traffic: peak travel times have actually fallen from 54 minutes per day to 43 minutes per day.[20] Cortright calculates this improvement at another $1.5 billion. Add those two dollar amounts together and you're talking real money.

What happens to these savings? Portland is reputed to have the most independent bookstores per capita and the most roof racks per capita. The city is also said to have the most strip clubs per capita. These claims are all exaggerations, but they reflect a documented above-average consumption of recreation of all kinds. Portland has more restaurants per capita than all other large cities except Seattle and San Francisco. Oregonians also spend considerably more than most Americans on alcohol,[21] which could be a good thing or a bad thing, but in any case makes you glad they are driving less.

More significantly, whatever they are used for, these savings are more likely to stay local than if spent on driving. Almost 85 percent of money expended on cars and gas leaves the local economy[22]—much of it, of course, bound for the pockets of Middle Eastern princes. A significant amount of the money saved probably goes into housing, since that is a national tendency: families that spend less on transportation spend more on their homes,[23] which is, of course, about as local as it gets.

The housing and driving connection is an important one,

and has been the subject of much recent study, especially since transportation costs have skyrocketed. While transportation used to absorb only one-tenth of a typical family's budget (1960), it now consumes more than one in five dollars spent.* All told, the average American family now spends about $14,000 per year driving multiple cars.[24] By this measure, this family works from January 1 until April 13 just to pay for its cars. Remarkably, the typical "working" family, with an income of $20,000 to $50,000, pays more for transportation than for housing.[25]

This circumstance exists because the typical American working family now lives in suburbia, where the practice of drive-'til-you-qualify reigns supreme. Families of limited means move farther and farther away from city centers in order to find housing that is cheap enough to meet bank lending requirements. Unfortunately, in doing so, they often find that driving costs outweigh any housing savings.[26] This phenomenon was documented in 2006, when gasoline averaged $2.86 per gallon. At that time, households in the auto zone were devoting roughly a quarter of their income to transportation, while those in walkable neighborhoods spent well under half that amount.[27]

No surprise, then, that as gasoline broke $4.00 per gallon and the housing bubble burst, the epicenter of foreclosures occurred at the urban periphery, "places that required families to have a fleet of cars in order to participate in society, draining their mortgage carrying capacity," as Chris Leinberger notes. "Housing prices on the fringe tended to drop at twice the metropolitan average while walkable urban housing tended to maintain [its] value and [is] coming back nicely in selected markets today."[28] Not only have city centers fared better than suburbs, but walkable cities have fared better than drivable ones. Catherine Lutz and Anne Lutz Fernandez note that "the cities with the largest drops in housing value (such as Las Vegas, down

---

*Catherine Lutz and Anne Lutz Fernandez, *Carjacked*, 80. Vehicle miles traveled per household increased 70 percent from 1969 to 2001 (Chuck Kooshian and Steve Winkelman, "Growing Wealthier," 3).

37 percent) have been the most car-dependent, and the few cities with housing prices gains . . . have good transit alternatives."[29]

This is bad news for Orlando and Reno, but it's good news for Portland . . . and also for Washington, D.C., which continues to benefit from earlier investments in transit. From 2005 to 2009, as the District's population grew by 15,862 people, car registrations fell by almost 15,000 vehicles.* The National Building Museum, in its Intelligent Cities Initiative, notes that this reduction in auto use results in as much as $127,275,000 being retained in the local economy each year.■

Those are the economic benefits of not driving. Are there additional economic benefits of walking, biking, and taking transit instead? The evidence here is a little more scarce, but the indications are positive. Ignoring the health benefits, there is a clear distinction to be made in the category of job creation. Road and highway work, with its big machines and small crews, is notoriously bad at increasing employment. In contrast, the construction of transit, bikeways, and sidewalks performs 60 percent to 100 percent better. A study of President Obama's American Recovery and Reinvestment Act documented a 70 percent employment premium for transit over highways. By this measure, that job-creation program would have created fifty-eight thousand more jobs if its road-building funds had gone to transit instead.▲

* National Building Museum Intelligent Cities Initiative poster. By my estimate, this all occurred on January 20, 2009, when 15,000 Bushies were replaced by 30,000 Obamans. Many Bush staffers, as a point of pride, lived "beyond the beltway" in red-state Virginia.
■ Ibid. In Australia, a similar study determined that living in a transit-oriented neighborhood was likely to save a total of about $750,000 over a lifetime, most of which would be spent locally (Peter Newman, Timothy Beatley, and Heather Boyer, *Resilient Cities*, 120). And since each car removed from the typical household budget allows that family to afford a $135,000 larger mortgage, it's easy to see why Washington real estate prices have dropped only 20 percent from their peak, while housing beyond the beltway has lost half its value.
▲ A study of expenditures in Baltimore showed that while each million spent on roads created about seven jobs, each million spent on pedestrian facilities generated eleven jobs, and each million spent on bike lanes created more than fourteen jobs (Heidi Garrett-Peltier, "Estimating the Employment Impacts of Pedestrian, Bicycle, and Road Infrastructure," 1–2).

How does this translate at the local level? Portland has spent roughly $65 million on bicycle facilities over the past several decades. That is not a lot of money by infrastructure standards— it cost more than $140 million to rebuild just one of the city's freeway interchanges.[30] Yet, in addition to helping to boost the number of bicyclists from near normal to fifteen times the national average,* this investment can be expected to have created close to nine hundred jobs, about four hundred more than would have come from spending it on road building.

But the real Portland story is neither its transportation savings nor its bikeway employment, but something else: young, smart people are moving to Portland in droves. According to Cortright and coauthor Carol Coletta, "Over the decade of the 1990s, the number of college-educated 25 to 34 year-olds increased 50 percent in the Portland metropolitan area—five times faster than in the nation as a whole, with the fastest increase in this age group being recorded in the city's close-in neighborhoods."* There is another kind of walkability dividend, aside from resources saved and resources reinvested: resources attracted by being a place where people want to live. This has certainly been the case in San Francisco, where headhunters for companies like Yelp and Zynga (the social-gaming developers who created FarmVille) actively use urbanism as a recruiting tool. "We're able to attract creative and tech talent because we are in the city," acknowledges Colleen McCreary, Zynga's head of human resources.[31]

Ultimately, though, it would seem that urban productivity has even deeper causes. There is mounting evidence that dense,

---

*According to the census, Portland's bicycling mode share is 5.8 percent, and local studies place it at just under 8 percent. The national average is 0.4 percent.

*"The Young and the Restless," 34. As the number of college graduates in a metropolitan area increases by 10 percent, individuals' earnings increase by 7.7. This applies even to non–college graduates in the city because their productivity rises, too (David Brooks, "The Splendor of Cities").

walkable cities generate wealth by sheer virtue of the propinquity that they offer. This is a concept that is both stunningly
obvious—cities exist, after all, because people benefit from coming together—and tantalizingly challenging to prove.* This hasn't
kept it from the lips of some of our leading thinkers, including
Stewart Brand, Edward Glaeser, David Brooks, and Malcolm
Gladwell.

Speaking at the Aspen Institute, David Brooks pointed out
how most U.S. patent applications, when they list similar patents
that influenced them, point to other innovators located less than
twenty-five miles away. He also mentioned a recent experiment
at the University of Michigan, where "researchers brought groups
of people together face to face and asked them to play a difficult cooperation game. Then they organized other groups and
had them communicate electronically. The face-to-face groups
thrived. The electronic groups fractured and struggled."[32]

Face-to-face collaboration is, of course, possible in any setting. But it is easier in a walkable city. Susan Zeilinski, managing
director of the University of Michigan's SMART Center, puts
it this way: "In Europe you can get five good meetings done in a
day. In Australia, maybe three, and in Atlanta, maybe two, because you've gone way, way farther and way, way faster but you
haven't been in an accessible place that allows a lot to happen.
You've spent a lot of time sitting in traffic."[33] This discussion
raises a larger theoretical question that scientists have just begun
to take on: are there underlying universal rules that govern the
success of a place?

The theoretical physicists Geoffrey West and Luis Bettencourt believe so. They do not believe in urban theory—"a field
without principles"—they are interested only in math. "What

---

*More than twenty-five years ago, William Whyte's research tracked the stock perfor-
mance of thirty-eight New York City companies that chose to relocate to the suburbs,
and found that they appreciated at less than half the rate of thirty-five similar companies that had stayed put (Whyte, *City: Rediscovering the Center*, 294–95).

the data clearly shows," West notes, "is that when people come together they become much more productive."[34] Do the same physical laws work in reverse? Writing about West's research in *The New York Times Magazine*, Jonah Lehrer notes:

> In recent decades, though, many of the fastest-growing cities in America, like Phoenix and Riverside, Calif., have given us a very different urban model. These places have traded away public spaces for affordable single-family homes, attracting working-class families who want their own white picket fences. West and Bettencourt point out, however, that cheap suburban comforts are associated with poor performance on a variety of urban metrics. Phoenix, for instance, has been characterized by below-average levels of income and innovation (as measured by the production of patents) for the last 40 years.[35]

These findings align with a recent Environmental Protection Agency study that found, state by state, an inverse relationship between vehicle travel and productivity: the more miles that people in a given state drive, the weaker it performs economically.* Apparently, the data are beginning to support the city planners' bold contention that time wasted in traffic is unproductive.

In contrast, the Portland metro area is now home to more than twelve hundred technology companies. Like Seattle and San Francisco, it is one of the places where educated millennials are heading in disproportionate numbers. This phenomenon is what the demographer William Frey has in mind when he says:

---

* Kooshian and Winkelman, "Growing Wealthier," 2. This correlation seems especially meaningful, since wealthier people have the disposable income that would allow them to drive more.

"A new image of urban America is in the making. What used to be white flight to the suburbs is turning into 'bright flight' to cities that have become magnets for aspiring young adults who see access to knowledge-based jobs, public transportation and a new city ambiance as an attraction."[36]

The conventional wisdom used to be that creating a strong economy came first, and that increased population and a higher quality of life would follow. The converse now seems more likely: creating a higher quality of life is the first step to attracting new residents and jobs. This is why Chris Leinberger believes that "all the fancy economic development strategies, such as developing a biomedical cluster, an aerospace cluster, or whatever the current economic development 'flavor of the month' might be, do not hold a candle to the power of a great walkable urban place."[37]

WHY JOHNNY CAN'T WALK

The obesity bomb; Clearing the air; American car-nage; Tense and lonely

The best day for being a city planner in America was July 9, 2004. That's when Howard Frumkin, Lawrence Frank, and Richard Jackson published their book *Urban Sprawl and Public Health.*

Until that day, the main arguments for building walkable cities were principally aesthetic and social. More significantly, almost nobody but the planners was making them. But it turns out that while we were shouting into the wilderness about the frustrations, anomie, and sheer waste of suburban sprawl, a small platoon of physicians was quietly doing something much more useful: they were documenting how our built environment was killing us.

For Dr. Jackson, the epiphany came in 1999, when he was driving on Atlanta's Buford Highway—voted by the Congress for the New Urbanism as one of the ten "Worst Streets in America"[1]—a seven-laner flanked by low-income garden apartments, "with no sidewalks and two miles between traffic lights."[2] There, by the side of the road, in the ninety-five-degree afternoon, he saw a woman in her seventies, struggling under the burden of two shopping bags. He tried to relate her plight to his own work as an epidemiologist:

> If that poor woman had collapsed from heat stroke, we docs would have written the cause of death as heat stroke

and not lack of trees and public transportation, poor urban form, and heat-island effects. If she had been killed by a truck going by, the cause of death would have been "motor-vehicle trauma," and not lack of sidewalks and transit, poor urban planning, and failed political leadership. That was the "aha!" moment for me. Here I was focusing on remote disease risks when the biggest risks that people faced were coming from the built environment.[3]

Jackson, who has more recently served as California governor Arnold Schwarzenegger's state public health adviser, spent the next five years quantifying how so much of what ails us can be attributed directly to the demise of walkability in the auto age. The resulting book finally put some technical meat on the bones of the planning profession's admonitions against sprawl.

And the numbers are compelling. Despite spending one dollar out of six on health care, the United States has some of the worst health statistics in the developed world. According to the U.S. Centers for Disease Control (CDC), fully one-third of American children born after 2000 will become diabetics. This is due partly to diet, but partly to planning: the methodical eradication from our communities of *the useful walk* has helped to create the least active generation in American history. This insult is compounded by the very real injuries that result from car crashes—the greatest killer of children and young adults nationwide—as well as an asthma epidemic tied directly to vehicle exhaust. Comparison of walkable cities and auto-dependent suburbs yields some eye-opening statistics—for example, that transit users are more than three times as likely as drivers to achieve their CDC-recommended thirty minutes of daily physical activity.[4] Increasingly, it is becoming clear that the American healthcare crisis is largely an urban-design crisis, with walkability at the heart of the cure.

Particularly affected have been our children. While fully 50 percent walked to school in 1969, fewer than 15 percent do now.[*] And sometimes when children do walk to school, their parents are visited by the police: a Salt Lake City newspaper carried in December 2010 the story of Noah Talbot, of South Jordan, who was picked up by the police on the way to school and his mother issued a citation for child neglect.[5] Jackson and his coauthors note how "children are increasingly medicated for inattentiveness or hyperactivity, even as many are losing their opportunities for exercise at school or in the neighborhood. There are third-grade classes in which as many as a third of the boys are on Ritalin or similar medications."[6]

To summarize the findings of *Urban Sprawl and Public Health*—which are echoed by a growing number of epidemiologists nationwide—the inactivity-inducing convenience, often violent speed, and toxic exhaust of our cars have contributed mightily to the circumstance that "for the first time in history, the current generation of youth will live shorter lives than their parents."[7]

THE OBESITY BOMB

In any meaningful discussion about American health (and health care), obesity has to be front and center.[■] In the mid-1970s, only about one in ten Americans was obese, which put us where much of Europe is right now. What has happened in the intervening

---

[*] Neal Peirce, "Biking and Walking: Our Secret Weapon?" Similarly, the number of elementary school–aged children driven to school in private vehicles has risen from 12 percent in 1969 to 44 percent in 2009 (Poster, Intelligent Cities Initiative, National Building Museum).

[■] All told, obesity has been blamed for about one-eighth of the recent increase in health-care costs (Jeff Mapes, *Pedaling Revolution*, 230). Medicare reports that it pays 15 percent more expenses for obese beneficiaries. Obese employees take twelve times as many sick days as their trimmer colleagues. General Motors reports $286 million in medical expenses per year due to obesity (Thomas Gotschi and Kevin Mills, "Active Transportation for America," 29). As urban affairs writer Neal Peirce puts it, "if the fat crisis can't be dealt with, rising levels of heart disease and diabetes will assuredly swamp the nation's efforts to reduce spiraling health costs" (Peirce, "Biking and Walking: Our Secret Weapon?").

thirty years is astonishing: by 2007, that rate had risen to one in three,[8] with a second third of the population "clearly over-weight."[9] The childhood obesity rate has almost tripled since 1980 and the rate for adolescents has more than quadrupled.[10] According to the rules of the U.S. military, 25 percent of young men and 40 percent of young women are too fat to enlist.*

As recently as 1991, no states had adult obesity rates over 20 percent. By 2007, only one state, Colorado, was *under* 20 percent.[11] Projecting current trends forward, it would seem that 100 per-cent of the population will be obese by 2080, a year that my chil-dren will probably live to see—but perhaps not if they are obese.

In terms of actual weight, men are now seventeen pounds heavier than they were in the late 1970s, and women nineteen pounds heavier. This means that, independent of population growth, as a nation we have gained 5.5 billion pounds. The real problem, of course, is not obesity itself, but all the other mala-dies that obesity causes or makes worse.■ These include coronary disease, hypertension, a variety of cancers—including colorectal and endometrial—gallstones, and osteoarthritis. Excessive weight now kills more Americans than smoking.[12]

Over the past decade, there has been a series of studies that attribute obesity and its related illnesses directly to the automo-

---

*Writing for *The New Yorker*, Elizabeth Kolbert notes, "Hospitals have had to buy spe-cial wheelchairs and operating tables to accommodate the obese, and revolving doors have widened—the typical door went from about ten feet to about twelve feet across. An Indiana company called Goliath Casket has begun offering triple-wide coffins with reinforced hinges that can hold up to eleven hundred pounds. It has been estimated that Americans' extra bulk costs the airlines a quarter of a billion dollars' worth of jet fuel annually" (Kolbert, "XXXL: Why Are We So Fat?").

■Even gout, once called the "disease of kings," is staging a painful comeback among the middle class. But the biggest threat, both physically and financially, has to be diabetes, the sixth-leading cause of death in the United States. More than 21 million Americans—that's 7 percent of the population—have type 2 diabetes and it currently consumes about 2 percent of the gross national product. Obesity is the number one risk factor for diabetes, increasing one's odds of contracting the disease by as much as forty times (Howard Frumkin, Lawrence Frank, and Richard Jackson, *Urban Sprawl and Public Health*, xi).

tive lifestyle and, better yet, to the automotive landscape.* One effort found that for every additional five minutes Atlanta-area residents drove each day, they were 3 percent more likely to be obese.[13] Another showed that drivers who switch to public transit drop an average of five pounds.[14] A third, in San Diego, reported that 60 percent of residents in a "low-walkable" neighborhood were overweight, compared to only 35 percent in a "high-walkable" neighborhood.[15] Another Atlanta study found that "the proportion of obese white males declined from 23 percent to 13 percent as neighborhood residential density increased from less than two to more than eight dwellings per acre."[16] These are careful academic studies that control for age, income, and the other factors that correlate with body mass.

Finally, a six-year analysis of 100,000 Massachusetts residents found that the lowest body mass index averages were located in

---

* Much has been written, almost all of it convincing, about the absurdity of the American corn-syrup-based diet and its contribution to our national girth. Since our diets are so notoriously bad, is it fair to blame inactivity for our expanding waistlines? No American study seems to directly compare these competing factors, but the *British Medical Journal* took them on in an article that asked "gluttony or sloth?" The study compared obesity rates with data on diet and inactivity, and found a much stronger correlation with the latter. Specifically, "from 1950 to 1990, obesity steadily increased, even as gluttony peaked and declined in England. Sloth, on the other hand, increased in tandem with obesity, suggesting an important causal role" (Frumkin et al., *Urban Sprawl and Public Health*, 95).

Whatever the evidence, it is clear that our weight, independent of genetics, is a function of two primary factors: calories in and calories out. It would be wrong to ignore either of those two inputs, and the medical establishment, until recently focused principally on the former, is now giving physical activity its due. A 2007 UCLA study, investigating why so many diet regimes were unsuccessful, concluded that the "real key to slimming down appears to be not the cleverness of the food plan, but the amount of physical activity" (Mapes, *Pedaling Revolution*, 231).

Meanwhile, at the Mayo Clinic, Dr. James Levine put test subjects in motion-detecting underwear, placed them all on the same diet, and then began to stuff them with additional calories. As anticipated, some subjects gained weight while others didn't. Expecting to find a metabolic factor at work, he learned instead that the outcome was entirely attributable to physical activity. The people who got fatter made fewer unconscious motions and, indeed, spent (on average) two more hours per day sitting down (James Vlahos, "Is Sitting a Lethal Activity?").

Boston and its inner-ring suburbs, while the highest could be found in the "car-dependent" outer ring surrounding Interstate 495. *The Boston Globe* noted that "health officials suggest these higher rates are due, in part, to a lack of opportunities for everyday recreation and the time-squeezed lifestyle of many residents who have long commutes."[17]

I am wary of confusing causality with correlation, and it would be fair to say that heavier people are probably more likely to prefer driving over walking, and are therefore also more likely to prefer sprawl over urban neighborhoods. It is theoretically possible that, rather than suburbs making people fat, fat people make suburbs. But only a soulless pundit funded by the automotive industry—and there are several*—would claim that people are not more likely to be healthy in environments that invite walking.

You can tell that an idea has reached its tipping point when it makes enemies, and the sprawl-obesity connection finally has. The American Dream Coalition ("Protecting Freedom, Mobility, and Affordable Homeownership"), a consortium of automotive and sprawl-building interests, has come up with the fairly hilarious concept of the *Compactorizer*. As celebrated on their website in the (stereotypically effeminate) voice of the fictional Biff Fantastic:

> Urban planners and metrosexuals agree that suburbs make you fat! With the *Compactorizer*, you'll move out of boring and subtly racist suburban homes and into smallish apartments in high-density transit-oriented developments.

---

*Wendell Cox and Randal O'Toole. Skipping right past obesity to its outcomes, doctors have found that physical inactivity is associated with a "30 to 50 percent increase in coronary heart disease, a 30 percent increase in hypertension, and a 20 to 50 percent increase in strokes [as well as a] 30 to 40 percent increase in the risk of colon cancer and a 20 to 30 percent increase in the risk of breast cancer" (Vlahos, "Is Sitting a Lethal Activity?"). The United States' annual medical costs of physical inactivity have been estimated at between $76 billion and $117 billion, which is more than 10 percent of all medical expenses (Gotschi and Mills, "Active Transportation for America," 47–48).

> Only the *Compactorizer* uses a patented planning doctrine to create noisy nights, random crimes, and panhandler harassment, triggering the high-stress and abnormal dietary patterns so important for rapid weight loss.[18]

As both an urban planner and a purported metrosexual, I can feel my credibility tanking here. But I have to admit that this piece is more humorous than it is offensive and it appropriately pokes fun at an antisuburban snobbery that I probably share. But, ultimately, I have to ask myself: whom do I trust more: the doctors—who have nothing to gain either way—or the sprawl-builders? I'm going with the doctors.

CLEARING THE AIR

During the 1996 Olympics, more than 2 million visitors descended on the city of Atlanta, effectively increasing the city's population by 50 percent. Most of these visitors—I was among them—spent many hours huffing around the hot, crowded sports venues. Yet, during this time, asthma hospitalizations surprisingly declined by a full 30 percent.[19] What happened?

The difference was walking. Warned of the impossibility of motoring around the downtown during the games, many driving commuters took transit and walked instead. At a time when Atlanta was "one of the nation's worst violators of federal standards for ground-level ozone, with most of the problem caused by motor vehicle emissions,"[20] pollution levels dropped precipitously.*

---

*Sadly, the respite was only temporary, ending with the games' closing ceremony. Atlanta got a second breather in 1998, when the city's legendary highway-building binge was put on hold for two years thanks to its repeated violation of the federal Clean Air Act. But those were the exceptions, and by 2002, Atlanta was named "America's Unhealthiest City for Men" by *Men's Health* magazine, thanks to its forty-five days a year of "stay inside" warnings (Doug Monroe, "Taking Back the Streets," 89).

Pollution isn't what it used to be. American smog now comes principally from tailpipes, not factories. It is considerably worse than it was a generation ago, and it is unsurprisingly worst in our most auto-dependent cities, like Los Angeles and Houston. Phoenix put Atlanta to shame in 2007, with three full months of days in which it was deemed unhealthy for the general public to leave their homes.[21]

For this reason, asthma is dramatically on the rise. Almost one in fifteen Americans suffers from asthma, and the economic costs of the disease are estimated at $18.2 billion annually. About fourteen Americans die each day from asthma attacks, which is three times the rate of 1990.[22]

Of course, a community's auto dependence is not the only factor that contributes to asthma. But the 2011 WebMD list of the best and worst cities for asthma[23] speaks to a connection between walkability and breathing easier: residents of the five "worst" cities (Richmond, Knoxville, Memphis, Chattanooga, and Tulsa) drive 27 percent farther each day than residents of the five "best" (Portland, San Francisco, Colorado Springs, Des Moines, and Minneapolis).*

AMERICAN CAR-NAGE

Even if we were to dispute the notion that walking is good for you, it is indisputable that cars kill a lot of people. Car crashes have killed over 3.2 million Americans, considerably more than all of our wars combined.[24] They are the leading cause of death for all Americans between the ages of one and thirty-four,[25] and their monetary cost to the nation is estimated to be hundreds of billions of dollars annually.▪

---

* This calculation is based on data found in the Brookings Institution's ranking of U.S. metropolitan areas by vehicle miles traveled.

▪ The math used by different analysts is so varied that I hesitate to be more specific. The authors of *Carjacked* put it at "as high as $433 billion" (91).

Most people take the risks of driving for granted, as if they were some inevitable natural phenomenon. We don't bother with hand-wringing over the half-a-percent chance that our lives will end in a car crash[26] or the roughly one-in-three chance that we will eventually be seriously injured in one,* since these risks seem unavoidable. But the numbers from other developed nations tell a different story. While the United States in 2004 suffered 14.5 traffic fatalities per 100,000 population, Germany, with its no-speed-limit autobahns, suffered only 7.1. Denmark rated a 6.8, Japan a 5.8, and the U.K. hit 5.3.[27] And who beat them all? New York City, with a rate of 3.1. Indeed, since September 11, 2001, New York has saved more lives in traffic than it lost on 9/11.▪

If our entire country shared New York City's traffic statistics, we would prevent more than twenty-four thousand deaths a year.▲ San Francisco and Portland both compete with New York, with rates of 2.5 and 3.2 deaths per 100,000 population, respectively. Meanwhile, Atlanta comes in at 12.7, and anti-urban Tampa at a whopping 16.2.[28] Clearly, it's not just how much you drive, but where you drive and, more accurately, how those places were designed. Older, denser cities have much lower automobile fatality rates than newer, sprawling ones. It is the places shaped around automobiles that seem most effective at smashing them into each other.

I provide all this information to communicate the point that, while we Americans may take our great risk of automobile injury for granted, it is actually something that is well within our

* The injury statistic is calculated based on the fact that recent years have seen about seventy times as many reportable traffic injuries as traffic deaths.

▪ Richard Jackson, "We Are No Longer Creating Wellbeing." New York suffered fewer than 1 death per 30,000 population in 2004 versus the 2010 U.S. rate of more than 4 deaths per 30,000. The difference between these two rates across a city population of 8 million amounts to more than 270 deaths averted annually.

▲ Are New Yorkers (and Europeans) better drivers than the rest of us? Probably not. As you might expect, the difference in death rates comes, in part, from a difference in miles driven. But it's only in part. Here's something interesting: residents of the five control—in the long term, as a function of how we design places, and in the short term, as a function of where we choose to live. This discussion becomes particularly ironic when we consider how many people through the decades have decamped from the city into the suburbs ostensibly for the safety of their families. Dr. Jackson is famously fond of asking his audiences "In what kind of community are you most likely to end up dead in a pool of blood?"[29] He points to the work of Alan Durning, who analyzed the combined risk of dying from two causes—traffic crashes and crime—in Seattle, Portland, and Vancouver, British Columbia. He found that, on average, if you add the two factors together, you are 19 percent safer in the inner city than in the outer suburbs.*

More recently, several more thorough studies have been completed by William Lucy at the University of Virginia, looking at auto accidents and murder by strangers. In one, he found that the ten safest places in the state of Virginia were eight of its most densely populated cities and the two counties abutting Washing-

---

most dangerous states drove 64 percent more miles in 2003 than residents of the five least dangerous states. If traffic fatalities simply increased with miles traveled, then we would expect the five most dangerous states to have experienced 64 percent more traffic deaths per capita than the five safest. But, shockingly, they experienced 243 percent more traffic deaths per capita. Each mile driven in a least-safe state was more than twice as deadly as a mile in a most-safe state. (This calculation is based on state traffic fatality data collected by Drive and Stay Alive, Inc., and state VMT data from the U.S. Research and Innovative Technology Administration.)

It turns out that the four safest American states, in addition to New York, are all in the Northeast: Massachusetts (which beats New York), Connecticut, New Jersey, and Rhode Island. The four most dangerous are largely rural: Wyoming, Mississippi, Montana, and South Dakota. The principal distinction between these states, much more than miles driven, is urbanization. The five safest states average eighteen times the residential density of the five most deadly (data from U.S. Census Bureau). They are also considerably older, and were therefore extensively developed according to the more walkable pre–World War II model, rather than the higher-speed paradigm that followed. This is why a mile driven in South Dakota is about three times as likely to kill you as a mile driven in Massachusetts.

* James Gerstenang, "Cars Make Suburbs Riskier Than Cities, Study Says," A1, A20. It is worth noting that this study was completed almost two decades ago, when the murder rate in many American cities was three times what it is today (Kevin Johnson, Judy Keen, and William M. Welch, "Homicides Fall in Large American Cities").

ton, D.C., while the ten most dangerous places were all low-population counties.[30] In another, he compared crash and crime statistics in eight large American cities between 1997 and 2000. Here the data produced more subtle results. The basic theory held true: car crashes far outweighed murder by strangers as a cause of death in all locations and, in older cities like Pittsburgh, the inner cities were considerably safer overall. But in more modern places like Dallas and Houston, where the downtowns are largely unwalkable, the city car-crash statistics were almost as bad as in the suburbs. Even with its fourteen annual traffic deaths per 100,000 population, however, Dallas was still safer overall than half of its surrounding counties.*

TENSE AND LONELY

Jacqueline McFarland is a licensed clinical social worker who specializes in the driving stresses of Atlanta commuters. She teaches her patients what are called Emotional Freedom Techniques (EFT) to help them calm down in traffic. "Basically, it's

---

* Jane Ford, "Danger in Exurbia." If people knew these statistics, would it impact their choices about where to live? Probably not. The illusion of control that we have while driving gives us confidence that we are the masters of our own fate on the road. After all, in another study, 85 percent of drivers who were in the hospital recovering from accidents *that they themselves caused* rated their driving skills as "above average" (National Public Radio, July 20, 2010). But, individual drivers aside, it would be nice to see these numbers have some impact on government policy, especially at the state and federal levels. Given the tremendous economic and human cost of car crashes, and the increased death toll found in unwalkable areas, it would make tremendous sense to invest a bit in walkability. In response to September 11, we have more than doubled the size of our national intelligence apparatus; indeed, almost 1 percent of all Americans now hold confidential, secret, or top-secret security clearance (Jane Mayer, "The Secret Sharer," 48). Four hundred thousand driving deaths later, how have our leaders responded? There may be hope for a correction over time. This is of course the same federal government that in 1970 made the pronouncement that "the possible benefits of required seat belts would not justify the costs to the manufacturers and the public" (National Highway Traffic Safety Administration).

tapping on acupressure points on the body, which clears up emotional issues."[31]

Let's hope it works. A German study found that "an unusually high percentage of people having heart attacks had spent time in traffic congestion on the day they were stricken." The study concluded that an hour spent driving triples your risk of heart attack in the hours that follow.[32] A Belgian paper published in *The Lancet* found that traffic exposure accounts for more heart attacks worldwide than any other activity, even including physical exertion.[33]

Closer to home, a Miami study found that "after driving their cars across the city for forty-five minutes, university students had higher blood pressure, higher heart rates, and lower frustration tolerance." This study is mentioned in *Urban Sprawl and Public Health*, where Dr. Jackson and his colleagues go on at length about driving stress, road rage, and their significant impacts on our national well-being. And the numbers are not insignificant—but let's step back from health for a minute and talk about happiness. Is motoring around and around really how we want to be spending so much of our time?

While many of us love driving, we hate commuting. Unsurprisingly, people with longer commutes report "lower satisfaction with life" than those who drive less.[34] One study found that "a 23-minute commute had the same effect on happiness as a 19 percent reduction in income." And twenty-three minutes is hardly a long commute—it's a bit below the national average. In another poll, 5 percent of respondents said that they would be "willing to divorce their spouse if that meant they could stop commuting and work from home instead."[35]

The Princeton psychologist Daniel Kahneman reports that commuting ranks as people's least favorite regular activity, less favored than housework or child care. "Intimate relations" scored highest—big surprise there—followed closely by socializing after work.[36]

Commuting unfortunately cuts into both. In his book *Bowl-*

ing Alone, the Harvard professor Robert Putnam documents a marked decline in American social capital, and notes that commute time is more predictive than almost any other variable he measured in determining civic engagement. He states that "each ten additional minutes in daily commuting time cuts involvement in community affairs by ten percent—fewer public meetings attended, fewer committees chaired, fewer petitions signed, fewer church services attended, and so on."[37]

This finding seems perfectly logical—there's only so much time in the day, after all—but it is only one part of a much larger picture that includes not only how long it takes to get home, but also in what sort of neighborhood that home is located. Much civic engagement is physical, grown from interaction on the street. Jane Jacobs put it this way: "Lowly, unpurposeful, and random as they may appear, sidewalk contacts are the small change from which a city's wealth of public life may grow."•

About now we could use some good news, so let's turn to Dan Buettner, the charismatic National Geographic host and bestselling author responsible for *The Blue Zones: Lessons for Living Longer from the People Who've Lived the Longest*. After a tour of the world's longevity hot spots, Buettner takes us through the "*Power Nine*: the lessons from the Blue Zones, a cross cultural distillation of the world's best practices in health and longevity." Lesson One? "Move Naturally." He explains: "Be active without having to think about it. . . . Longevity all-stars don't run marathons or compete in triathlons; they don't transform themselves

---

•*The Death and Life of Great American Cities*, 72. Putnam did not measure walkability, but a 2010 University of New Hampshire study did. The researchers first did their best to determine the more and less walkable neighborhoods of two cities, Manchester and Portsmouth, New Hampshire, each of which contains a charming mixed-use downtown and a girdle of sprawl. They then surveyed seven hundred residents of twenty neighborhoods, split between more and less walkable locations. They found that "those living in more walkable neighborhoods trusted their neighbors more; participated in community projects, clubs and volunteering more; and described television as their major form of entertainment less than survey participants living in less walkable neighborhoods" (Rogers et al., "Examining Walkability," 201–203).

into weekend warriors on Saturday morning. Instead, they engage in regular, low-intensity physical activity, often as a part of a daily work routine."• Buettner quotes Robert Kane, M.D., the director of the Minnesota Geriatric Education Center, who says, "Rather than exercising for the sake of exercising, try to make changes to your lifestyle. Ride a bicycle instead of driving. Walk to the store instead of driving. . . . Build that into your lifestyle."■

Like most writers on the subject, Buettner and his sources neglect to discuss how these "lifestyle" choices are inevitably a function of the design of the built environment. They may be powerfully linked to place—the Blue Zones are zones, after all—but there is scant admission that walking to the store is more possible, more enjoyable, and more likely to become habit in some places than in others. It is those places that hold the most promise for the physical and social health of our society.

Enrique Peñalosa, the former mayor of Bogotá, Colombia, sees things in a much simpler light: "God made us walking animals—pedestrians. As a fish needs to swim, a bird to fly, a deer to run, we need to walk, not in order to survive, but to be happy."[38] That thought is beautiful, perfectly obvious, and probably impossible to prove. But we do know that we need to be active in order to be healthy and that walking is the easiest way for most humans to be usefully active. Let's make it easier.

• *The Blue Zones*, 220. It's worth noting that Lesson Four is "buy a case of high-quality red wine," which certainly adds to the book's appeal (240).
■ *The Blue Zones*, 223. According to *The New York Times*, "a recent meta-analysis of studies about exercise and mortality showed that, in general, a sedentary person's risk of dying prematurely from any cause plummeted by nearly 20 percent if he or she began brisk walking (or the equivalent) for 30 minutes five times a week" (Gretchen Reynolds, "What's the Single Best Exercise?").

THE WRONG COLOR GREEN

You can't spell carbon without CAR; Missing the forest for the trees;
Manhattan as Mecca; Happy urbanism

In 2001, Scott Bernstein, at the Center for Neighborhood Technology in inner-city Chicago, produced a set of maps that are still changing the way we think about our country. In these maps, remarkably, the red and the green switched places. This reversal, perhaps even more than the health discussion, threatens to make walkability relevant again.

By red and green, I am referring to carbon emissions. On typical carbon maps, areas with the greatest amounts of carbon output are shown in bright red, and those with the least are shown in green, with areas in between shown in orange and yellow. Basically, the hotter the color, the greater the contribution to climate change.

Historically, these maps had always looked like the night-sky satellite photos of the United States: hot around the cities, cooler in the suburbs, and coolest in the country. Wherever there are lots of people, there is lots of pollution. A typical carbon map, such as that produced in 2002 by the Vulcan Project at Purdue University, sends a very clear signal: countryside good, cities bad.

For a long time, these were the only maps of this type, and there is certainly a logic in looking at pollution from a location-by-location perspective. But this logic was based on an unconsidered assumption, which is that the most meaningful way to measure carbon is by the square mile. It isn't.

The best way to measure carbon is per person. Places should be judged not by how much carbon they emit, but by how much carbon they cause us to emit. There are only so many people in the United States at any given time, and they can be encouraged to live where they have the smallest environmental footprint. That place turns out to be the city—the denser the better.

For this reason, when Bernstein replaced carbon per square mile with carbon per household, the colors simply flipped. Now the hottest places in each American metropolitan area—and their website shows hundreds, from Abilene to Yuma—are inevitably the outer suburbs. The coolest are smack-dab in the center of town.

To be accurate: Bernstein's maps have a limitation. They do not show full carbon output; they only show CO_2 from household automobile use—data that are much easier to collect. But this limitation turns out to be useful, for several reasons: first, because it causes us to confirm that automobile use is not only the single greatest contributor to our total carbon footprint, but also a reliable predictor of that total; and second, because limiting our greenhouse gas emissions, for many, is a much less pressing issue than our dependence on foreign oil.

YOU CAN'T SPELL CARBON WITHOUT CAR

At last measure, we are sending $612,500 overseas every minute in support of our current automotive lifestyle.[1] Cumulatively, over recent decades, this has amounted to a "massive, irreversible shift in wealth and power from the United States to the petro-states of the Middle East and energy-rich Russia."[2] This cash transfer, which is quickly working its way up to a third of a trillion dollars each year, is building some truly stunning metrorail systems in Dubai and Abu Dhabi—our cars are buying their trains. Add to this amount the significant chunk of our $700 billion military budget that is used to protect these questionable foreign interests,* and it's easy to see how our oil appetite could undo us economically long before the oil begins to run dry.

Do electric cars present an answer to this challenge? Certainly hybrids don't. Their marginally improved gas mileage mostly offers a feel-good way to drive more miles in increasingly larger vehicles. I always get angry when I see a "Hybrids Only" municipal parking space, knowing that it welcomes a 21-mpg Chevy Tahoe Hybrid but not a conventional 35-mpg Ford Fiesta.* You could (theoretically) drive two 1990 Geo Metros at once and still beat the Tahoe.

In contrast, the all-electric car seems to hold some real promise for curtailing our foreign oil addiction—but at what environmental cost? In most of the United States, an electric-powered car is essentially a coal-powered car,▲ and "clean coal" is of course an oxymoron.[3] Both in its extraction and its combustion—replacing a hydrocarbon with a pure carbon—coal can make oil look positively green.*

To be perfectly accurate, electric cars are currently a bit

---

* In *Carjacked*, Catherine Lutz and Anne Lutz Fernandez suggest that "10 to 25 percent of the annual military budget should be allocated to the line item of oil resource control" (96).

■ The Tahoe data are also from *Carjacked*, whose authors note that the Tahoe costs nearly $13,000 more than its conventional twin and gets only four more miles per gallon (*Carjacked*, 88).

▲ As of 2010, almost half of all U.S. electricity was generated by burning coal, which is about twice as much as came from the next most common source, natural gas (U.S. Energy Information Administration, "Net Generation by Energy Source").

* Moreover, thanks to meager federal commitment, a significant uptick in wind, solar, hydro, tidal, or even nuclear generation seems at least a generation away. It is almost inevitable that the path to energy independence, so important to our nation's security and solvency, will take us through a sooty valley of even greater carbon expulsion. As David Owen notes in *Green Metropolis*, "sometimes the invisible hand goes for the throat" (66). See also Daniel Gros, "Coal vs. Oil: Pure Carbon vs. Hydrocarbon," achangeinthewind.com, December 28, 2007. Electricity generation is also responsible for about 20 percent of all water consumption in the United States (John F. Wasik, *The Cul-de-Sac Syndrome*, 60).

greener than gasoline cars—*per mile.* Driving one hundred miles in a Nissan Altima results in the emission of 90.5 pounds of greenhouse gases. Driving the same distance in an all-electric Nissan Leaf emits 63.6 pounds of greenhouse gases—a significant improvement. But while the Altima driver pays fourteen cents a mile for fuel, the Leaf driver pays less than three cents per mile,[4] and this difference, thanks to the law of supply and demand, causes the Leaf driver to drive more.

How much more? We don't know. But we do know what happened in Sweden, where aggressive government subsidies have led to the world's highest per-capita sales of "clean" cars. The results are in, and, shockingly, "greenhouse gas emissions from Sweden's transportation sector are up."[5] As reported by Firmin DeBrabander:

> But perhaps we should not be so surprised. What do you expect when you put people in cars they feel good (or at least less guilty) about driving, which are also cheap to buy and run? Naturally, they drive them more. So much more, in fact, that they obliterate energy gains made by increased fuel efficiency.[6]

Electric vehicles are clearly the right answer to the wrong question. This fact becomes even clearer when we note that tailpipe emissions are only one part of the footprint of motoring. As described by the strategic consultant Michael Mehaffy, this footprint includes "the emissions from the construction of the vehicles; the embodied energy of streets, bridges and other infrastructure; the operation and repair of this infrastructure; the maintenance and repair of the vehicles; the energy of refining fuel; and the energy of transporting it, together with the pipes, trucks and other infrastructure that is required to do so." These add an estimated 50 percent more pollution to the atmosphere than emissions alone.[7]

But that's just the beginning. A much larger multiplier effect comes from the way that all of our other, nonautomotive consumption patterns expand as we drive. In *Green Metropolis*, David Owen puts it this way:

> The real problem with cars is not that they don't get enough miles per gallon; it's that they make it too easy for people to spread out, encouraging forms of development that are inherently wasteful and damaging. . . . The critical energy drain in a typical American suburb is not the Hummer in the driveway; it's everything else the Hummer makes possible—the oversized houses and irrigated yards, the network of new feeder roads and residential streets, the costly and inefficient outward expansion of the power grid, the duplicated stores and schools, the two-hour solo commutes.[8]

So, while I have gone to great efforts to explain how the way we move is more important than the way we live, it turns out that the way we move largely determines the way we live.

MISSING THE FOREST FOR THE TREES

When we built our new house in Washington, we too did our best to clear the shelves of the sustainability store. We put in bamboo floors, radiant heating, double-thick insulation, dual-flush toilets, a solar water heater, and a twelve-panel 2.5-kilowatt solar photovoltaic system. A pine log crackling in our high-tech wood-burning stove supposedly contributes less pollution to the atmosphere than if it were left to decompose in the forest.

Yet all these gadgets cumulatively contribute only a fraction of what we save by living in a walkable neighborhood. It turns out that trading all of your incandescent lightbulbs for energy savers conserves as much carbon per year as living in a walkable neighborhood does each week.[9] Why, then, is the vast majority of our national conversation on sustainability about the former and not the latter? Witold Rybczynski puts it this way:

> Rather than trying to change behavior to reduce carbon emissions, politicians and entrepreneurs have sold greening to the public as a kind of accessorizing. "Keep doing what you're doing," is the message, just add another solar panel, a wind turbine, a bamboo floor, whatever. But a solar-heated house in the suburbs is still a house in the suburbs, and if you have to drive to it—even in a Prius— it's hardly green.[10]

We planners have taken to calling this phenomenon *gizmo green*: the obsession with "sustainable" products that often have a statistically insignificant impact on the carbon footprint when compared to our location. And, as already suggested, our location's greatest impact on our carbon footprint comes from how much it makes us drive.

This point was pounded home in a recent EPA study, "Location Efficiency and Building Type—Boiling It Down to BTUs,"[11] that compared four factors: drivable versus walkable location; conventional construction versus green building; single-family versus multifamily housing; and conventional versus hybrid automobiles. The study made it clear that, while every factor counts, none counts nearly as much as walkability. Specifically, it showed how, in drivable locations, transportation energy use consistently tops household energy use, in some cases by more than 2.4 to 1. As a result, the most green home (with Prius) in sprawl still loses out to the least green home in a walkable neighborhood.[12]

It is important that the EPA is doing its best to share the good news on how location trumps building design, but who is listening? Certainly not the EPA. A mere month after releasing the above study, the agency announced that it was relocating its 672-employee Region 7 Headquarters from downtown Kansas City to the new far-flung suburb of Lenexa, Kansas (Walk Score 28). Why are they moving twenty miles out of town into a former Applebee's office park? Well, because the building is LEED* (green) certified, of course.[13]

Kaid Benfield, a long-serving environmental watchdog at the Natural Resources Defense Council, did some numbers, and he found that while "an average resident in the vicinity of the current EPA Region 7 headquarters emits 0.39 metric tons of carbon dioxide per month . . . the transportation carbon emissions associated with the new location are a whopping 1.08 metric tons per person per month . . . one and a half times the regional average."[14]

These numbers are, of course, just a stand-in for the actual increased carbon footprints of the EPA's staffers, most of whom will probably not move from their current homes. Presuming these employees' houses are distributed around Kansas City in the normal manner, the vast majority will have their commutes lengthened, many by twenty miles or more each way. Those who used to take transit to work will now have to get on the highway.

This would be funny if it weren't so sad. The carbon saved by the new building's LEED status, if any, will be a small fraction of the carbon wasted by its location.* This missing the forest for the trees is what David Owen calls "LEED Brain." Many governments and corporations—and they are to be congratulated—have committed themselves to LEED-rated building construction, including the federal government, New York, Chicago, San Francisco, the District of Columbia, and a boatload of others. The list

---

*LEED refers to the now widely adopted standards of the U.S. Green Building Council, called "Leadership in Energy and Environmental Design."

*The downtown building, while not certified, is no energy hog (Kaid Benfield, "EPA Region 7: We Were Just Kidding About That Sustainability Stuff").

is getting longer every day and seems to have reached a tipping point where you can't get hired as an architect without becoming LEED accredited.

Urban location is indeed one of the factors that contributes to a LEED building rating, but it is only one of many factors, such that the overall carbon savings created by downtown locations are almost always undercounted. And because it's better than nothing, LEED—like the Prius—is a get-out-of-jail-free card that allows us to avoid thinking more deeply about our larger footprint. For most organizations and agencies, it is enough. Unfortunately, as the transportation planner Dan Malouff puts it, "LEED architecture without good urban design is like cutting down the rainforest using hybrid-powered bulldozers."[15]

MANHATTAN AS MECCA

If—in America—dense, transit-served cities are better, then New York is the best. This is the clear and convincing message of David Owen's *Green Metropolis*, certainly the most important environmental text of the past decade. This book deserves a bit more of our attention, so profound is the revolution in thinking that it represents.

As Owen himself notes, the environmental movement in the United States has historically been anti-city, as has so much American thought. This strain traces its roots back to Thomas Jefferson, who described large cities as "pestilential to the morals, the health, and the liberties of man." Not without a sense of humor, he went on: "When we get piled up upon one another in large cities, as in Europe, we shall become as corrupt as in Europe, and go to eating one another as they do there."[16]

Given that the U.S. population in 1780 was less than 1 percent of its current total, it is easy to understand why Jefferson did not see anything but good in its dispersal. With what must have seemed to be both infinite land area and resources, there was no reason not to stretch our legs, especially since the greatest by-product of transportation was fertilizer.

Unfortunately, over the next two hundred years, the American anti-urban ethos remained intact as everything else changed. The desire to be isolated in nature, adopted en masse, led to the quantities and qualities we now call sprawl, which somehow mostly manages to combine the traffic congestion of the city with the intellectual culture of the countryside.[17] Now that the full environmental impacts of suburban development are being measured, a new breed of thinkers is finally turning the old paradigm on its head. These include David Owen—like Jane Jacobs, a mere writer—and the economist Ed Glaeser, who puts it this way: "We are a destructive species, and if you love nature, stay away from it. The best means of protecting the environment is to live in the heart of a city."[18]

And no American city performs like New York. Owen's book, which was originally to be called *Green Manhattan*, is stuffed full of astounding data. The average New Yorker consumes roughly one-third the electricity of the average Dallas resident, and ultimately generates less than one-third the greenhouse gases of the average American. The average resident of Manhattan—New York at its most New Yorky—consumes gasoline "at a rate that the country as a whole hasn't matched since the mid-1920s."[19] And so on. We have already discussed the city's impressive traffic-safety record.

New York is our densest big city and, not coincidentally, the one with the best transit service. All the other subway stations in America put together would not outnumber the 468 stops of the MTA. In terms of resource efficiency, it's the best we've got. But why stop there? Other places, with a variety of densities and transit options, do much better. Sure, New York consumes half the gasoline of Atlanta (326 versus 782 gallons per person per year). But Toronto cuts *that* number in half again, as does Sydney—and most European cities use only half as much as those places. Cut Europe's number in half and you end up with Hong Kong.[20] If ten Hong Kongers were to move to New York with the goal of keeping their gasoline consumption unchanged, nine of them would have to stay at home.

These numbers become especially meaningful as we consider the impacts of peak oil prices in the years ahead. What city, or country, is likely to be the most competitive in the face of $200-per-barrel oil? Paris is one place that has determined that its future hangs upon its reducing its auto dependence. The city has recently decided to create twenty-five miles of dedicated busways, introduced twenty thousand shared "city bikes" in 1,450 locations, and committed to removing fifty-five thousand parking spaces from the city every year for the next twenty years. These changes sound pretty radical, but they are supported by 80 percent of the population.[21]

HAPPY URBANISM

Stories and numbers like these are truly intimidating, and potentially demotivating. Why even bother trying, when other countries are so far ahead?

Back in 1991, the Sierra Club's John Holtzclaw studied travel habits in twenty-eight California communities of widely varying residential density. He found, as expected, an inverse relationship between urbanity and driving miles. But, perhaps not expected, he also found his data points distributed around a pretty sharp curve, with most of the gains in efficiency occurring early on. Increasing housing density at the suburban end of the scale had a much greater impact than at the urban end, such that the vast majority of the driving reduction occurred in the switch from large-lot sprawl to densities of ten to twenty units per acre. These densities represent a traditional urbanism of apartments, row houses, and, yes, some freestanding single-family homes. In contrast, the further concentration of households at higher densities—even above one hundred per acre—while helpful, produced less dramatic results.

He subsequently conducted similar studies in New York and Los Angeles, and found the data tracking along almost identical curves. In each case, increasing density from two units per acre to twenty units per acre resulted in about the same savings as the increase from twenty to two hundred.[22] To students of urban form, these outcomes are not that surprising, because ten to twenty units per acre is the density at which drivable sub-urbanism transitions into walkable urbanism. There are of course some (rather horrid tower-in-the-parking-lot) exceptions, but most communities with these densities are also organized as traditional, mixed-use, pedestrian-friendly neighborhoods, the sort of accommodating environment that entices people out of their cars. Everything above that is icing on the cake.

That means that, while Americans might have a long way to go to match European or Asian sustainability, a little effort can get us a lot closer. But not every American is motivated by concerns about climate change or peak oil and, even among those of us who are, it is not always easy to turn that intention into action. Certainly, unless we hit a national crisis of unprecedented severity, it is hard to imagine any argument framed in the language of sustainability causing many people to modify their behavior. So what will?

The gold standard of quality-of-life rankings is the Mercer Survey, which carefully compares global cities in the ten categories of political stability, economics, social quality, health and sanitation, education, public services, recreation, consumer goods, housing, and climate.

Its rankings shift slightly from year to year, but the top ten cities always seem to include a bunch of places where they speak

German (Vienna, Zürich, Düsseldorf, etc.), along with Vancouver, Auckland, and Sydney.[23] These are all places with compact settlement patterns, good transit, and principally walkable neighborhoods. Indeed, there isn't a single auto-oriented city in the top fifty. The highest-rated American cities in 2010, which don't appear until number 31, are Honolulu, San Francisco, Boston, Chicago, Washington, New York, and Seattle.*

The Economist magazine has its own ranking that, although it uses Mercer data, tends to turn out a bit differently. It has been criticized as favoring Anglophone countries, which—although no help to the United States—means that eight of its top ten cities are in Canada, Australia, and New Zealand. But all are still places that are better for walking than driving.

Whomever you want to believe, the message is clear. Our cities, which are twice as efficient as our suburbs, burn twice the fuel of these European, Canadian, and Aussie/Kiwi places. Yet the quality of life in these foreign cities is deemed higher than ours, by a long shot. This is not to say that quality of life is directly related to sustainability, but merely that many Americans, by striving for a better life, might find themselves moving to places that are more like the winners—or better yet, might try transforming their cities to resemble the winners. This sort of transformation could include many things, but one of them would certainly be walkability.

Vancouver, British Columbia, number one in *The Economist*'s ranking, proves a useful model. By the mid-twentieth century, it was fairly indistinguishable from a typical U.S. city. Then, beginning in the late 1950s, when most American cities were building highways, planners in Vancouver began advocating for high-rise housing downtown. This strategy, which included stringent requirements for green space and transit, really hit its stride

---

*Mercer, "2010 Quality of Living Worldwide City Rankings," Mercer.com. Incidentally, the biggest loser was Baghdad.

in the mid-1990s, and the change has been profound. Since that time, the amount of walking and biking citywide has doubled, from 15 percent to 30 percent of all trips.[24] Vancouver is not ranked number one for livability because it is so sustainable; the things that make it sustainable also make it livable.

Quality of life—which includes both health and wealth—may not be a function of our ecological footprint, but the two are deeply interrelated. To wit, if we pollute so much because we are throwing away time, money, and lives on the highway, then both problems would seem to share a single solution, and that solution is to make our cities more walkable. Doing so is not easy, but it can be done, it has been done, and indeed it is being done in more than a few places at this very moment.

PART II

THE TEN STEPS OF WALKABILITY

This may seem like an odd moment to admit this, but I love cars. As a teenager, I had twin subscriptions to *Car & Driver* and *Road & Track*. My chief skill on the school bus was the ability to name the make and model of every vehicle that passed. Until recently, I have always owned the best-handling car I could reasonably afford. I especially love high-revving Japanese sports cars like the one I drove from Miami to Washington, D.C., when I moved here in 2003. I remember the trip lasting about six hours, assisted by a tailwind and a top-of-the-line radar detector.

But an interesting thing happened when I arrived in Washington. I found myself driving less and less and paying more and more per mile. Aside from trips to Home Depot and the occasional country jaunt, I had no reason to break my car out of its garage. Between walking, biking, and our extensive Metro transit system, driving was rarely the most convenient choice. And the parking lot beneath my apartment building charged a small fortune in fees. Add to that the availability of Zipcar car sharing in my neighborhood and it soon became apparent that going car-free was the most convenient option.

Back in my Miami days, the idea of selling my car would never have occurred to me. My apartment was in the heart of

South Beach's art deco district. My job was on the mainland, in Little Havana, about a twenty-minute drive away. My gym was in Coral Gables, twenty minutes further afield. Lunch, unless I wanted Cuban food every day—a decided health risk—required another twenty minutes of driving. All told, I was spending close to ninety minutes each weekday in traffic, about normal for an American. And I was OK with that.

But, in Washington, it soon became apparent that there were other benefits to my new car-free lifestyle, besides just convenience. Six months into my autoless diet, I had lost ten pounds through walking and biking, and reduced my stress levels by avoiding traffic. I had gained thousands of dollars in transportation savings and also developed a deeper understanding of my city by experiencing it at a walking and biking pace. Finally, in the ultimate mass-transit payoff, I met my future wife among the masses on a transit platform. It would be fair to say that I was healthier, wealthier, wiser—and happier—all due to what transportation engineers would call a simple mode shift.

This shift was caused by nothing more or less than the design of my city.

Washington, D.C., is one of a handful of American cities that can accurately be described as car-optional. New York, Boston, Chicago, San Francisco, and not many others, provide an equivalent or better quality of life for the carless, thanks to a combination of pre-auto-age provenance and subsequent enlightened planning. In contrast, most American cities have been designed or redesigned principally around the assumption of universal automotive use, resulting in obligatory car ownership, typically one per adult—starting at age sixteen. In these cities, and in most of our nation, the car is no longer an instrument of freedom, but rather a bulky, expensive, and dangerous prosthetic device, a prerequisite to viable citizenship.

I got rid of my car because my city invited me to and rewarded me in spades. Not everyone who is able to make a similar choice will benefit as I did—certainly not in the spouse department—but the benefits are clear. Independent of the global impacts of reduced tailpipe emissions and energy use, the personal financial and health advantages of losing the car are tremendous. They are not attractive to everyone, and a significant number of our fellow citizens will never trade their cul-de-sacs and SUVs for any other option. But, as we have seen, more Americans are desirous of vibrant urban living than are being offered that choice, and those cities that can satisfy that unmet demand will thrive.

This is already happening. More and more Americans are being attracted to places that offer the economy, excitement, and street life that cannot be found in the auto zone. To these people, malls are for teenagers, bicycles are cooler than cars, and a great night out includes being able to drink and *not* drive. Cities that have recently combined reinvestment in their downtown cores with the creation of transformative transit and biking facilities—like Portland and Denver—are the current relocation places of choice, for those who have a choice.

For those who don't, it could be said that every city has an obligation to free its residents from the burden of auto dependence. When a city does, everyone benefits, including the city. My wife and I again prove a useful example. When we built our new house in the District, we put an office where the garage was supposed to go, and a vegetable garden in place of the driveway—never mind that it took us nine months to void the city's parking requirement. Now I work from home and we eat (extremely) local produce in season. Without a car, we find ourselves spending most of our disposable income nearby, in neighborhood restaurants and at the farmers' market. When we need a lightbulb or an extension cord, we bike to Logan Circle Hardware rather than driving to Home Depot.

All these daily decisions, by us and our many carless neighbors, add up to more money retained within our community.

This is not an ideological discussion; we are not committed to an intentional pedestrian lifestyle. In fact, as of this writing, we are seriously considering buying a car. The birth of our second child has created a circumstance where a personal vehicle will contribute to our quality of life. Moving a pair of car seats in and out of the Zipcar is just becoming too big a chore for two parents with sore backs.

Disappointing? Perhaps, but perfectly in keeping with the idea of the car-optional city. We spent seven years productively without a car, two of them with child in tow. We will be able to live carless again in the future. In the meantime, it will be one convenient transportation choice among many, in a landscape that makes choice possible.

Walking is a simple and useful thing, and such a pleasure too. It is what brings planeloads of Americans to Europe on holiday, including even some of the traffic engineers who make our own cities so inhospitable. Somewhere, deep in their caveman traffic engineer brains, even they must understand the value of moving under one's own power at a relaxed pace through a public sphere that continuously rewards the senses. This same tourist experience is commonplace in Washington, Charleston, New Orleans, Santa Fe, Santa Barbara—and a few other places in America that have elevated walking to an art form. They are the cities that enjoy a higher standard of living because they provide a better quality of life. Unfortunately, they remain the exceptions when they should just be normal.

This situation need not continue indefinitely—indeed, we can't afford for it to. We need a new normal in America, one that welcomes walking. The ten steps listed ahead are designed to take us from where we are now to where we need to be.

THE TEN STEPS OF WALKABILITY

THE USEFUL WALK

Step 1: Put Cars in Their Place.

The automobile is a servant that has become a master. For sixty years, it has been the dominant factor in the shaping of our cities. Relegating the car to its proper role is essential to reclaiming our cities for pedestrians, and doing so requires an understanding of how the car and its minions have unnecessarily distorted the way that design decisions are made in American communities.

Step 2: Mix the Uses.

For people to choose to walk, the walk must serve some purpose. In planning terms, that goal is achieved through mixed use or, more accurately, placing the proper balance of activities within walking distance of each other. While there are exceptions, most downtowns have an imbalance of uses that can be overcome only by increasing the housing supply.

Step 3: Get the Parking Right.

As Andres Duany puts it, "parking is destiny." It is the not-so-hidden force determining the life or death of many a downtown. Parking requirements and pricing determine the disposition of more American urban land than any other factor, yet until recently there was not even any theory on how to use parking to a city's benefit. That theory now exists, and is just beginning to affect policy nationwide.

Step 4: Let Transit Work.

Walkable neighborhoods can thrive in the absence of transit, but walkable cities rely on it utterly. Communities that hope to become the latter must make transit-planning decisions based upon a number of factors that are routinely neglected. These include the often surprising public support for transit investment, the role of transit in the creation of real estate value, and the importance of design in the success or failure of transit systems.

THE SAFE WALK

Step 5: Protect the Pedestrian.

This is perhaps the most straightforward of the ten steps, but it also has the most moving parts, including block size, lane width, turning motions, direction of flow, signalization, roadway geometry, and a number of other factors that all determine a car's speed and a pedestrian's likelihood of getting hit. Most streets in most American cities get at least half of these things wrong.

Step 6: Welcome Bikes.
Walkable cities are also bikeable cities, because bicycles thrive in environments that support pedestrians and also because bikeability makes driving less necessary. More and more American cities are making big investments in bicycling, with impressive results.

THE COMFORTABLE WALK

Step 7: Shape the Spaces.
Perhaps the most counterintuitive discussion in planning, this may be the step that is most often gotten wrong. People enjoy open spaces and the great outdoors. But people also enjoy, and need, a sense of enclosure to feel comfortable as pedestrians. Public spaces are only as good as their edges, and too much gray or green—parking or parks—can cause a would-be walker to stay home.

Step 8: Plant Trees.
Like transit, most cities know that trees are good, but few are willing to pay properly for them. This step attempts to communicate the full value of trees and justify the greater investment that they deserve in almost every American city.

THE INTERESTING WALK

Step 9: Make Friendly and Unique Faces.
If evidence is to be believed, lively streetscapes have three main enemies: parking lots, drugstores, and star architects. All three seem to favor blank walls, repetition, and a disregard for the pedestrian's need to be entertained. City design codes, focused on use, bulk, and parking, have only begun to concern themselves with creating active facades that invite walking.

Step 10: Pick Your Winners.
With the possible exception of Venice, even the most walkable cities are not universally walkable: there are only so many interesting street edges to go around. As a result, however well designed the streets, certain among them will remain principally automotive. This is as it should be, but cities must make a conscious choice about the size and location of their walkable cores, to avoid squandering walkability resources in areas that will never invite pedestrians.

THE USEFUL WALK

■

STEP 1: PUT CARS IN THEIR PLACE

STEP 2: MIX THE USES

STEP 3: GET THE PARKING RIGHT

STEP 4: LET TRANSIT WORK

STEP 1: PUT CARS IN THEIR PLACE

Highways versus cities; Because I must: induced demand;
It's not just freeways; Kill the traffic engineers first; Remove it
and they will go; A step too far: pedestrian zones; Congestion
pricing: too smart to be easy; The long view

Cars are the lifeblood of the American city. Even in our most successful walking and transit cities, they are everywhere, contributing activity and vitality to the streetscape. Past failures have taught us that banning them outright brings with it more risk than reward. Whatever technological revolutions may transform them in the years ahead, it is a safe bet that automobiles will remain a fixture of our communities for the remainder of our lifetimes. And that's OK.

But what's not OK is the current situation, in which the automobile has mostly been given free rein to distort our cities and our lives. Long gone are the days when automobiles expanded possibility and choice for the majority of Americans. Now, thanks to its ever-increasing demands for space, speed, and time, the car has reshaped our landscape and lifestyles around its own needs. It is an instrument of freedom that has enslaved us.

This outcome is not surprising, given the wandering nature of the American spirit. The first Americans were nomads, and they were displaced by a race that had found its way across the ocean. The one characteristic that all of us share is that we come from somewhere else. Imagine two brothers eating lunch alongside a dock in Dublin, Palermo, Bombay, or Formosa and looking wistfully out to sea. One of them had the balls to get on a boat and the other one didn't. Guess whose kids are the Americans?

American mobility far precedes the automobile. Before Lewis Mumford declared that "our national flower is the concrete cloverleaf,"[1] Ralph Waldo Emerson wrote that "everything good is on the highway." Soon after him, Walt Whitman waxed: "O public road, I say back I am not afraid to leave you—yet I love you. You express me better than I can express myself."[2]

But it is an easy out to say that wayfaring is an inescapable part of our DNA, and ignore the other factors that make cities in the United States different from those in Canada or Australia— two other countries that at least started the way ours did. Neither of those nations produced anything remotely like our National Interstate and Defense Highways Act of 1956 and, not coincidentally, neither was held in thrall by a lobby as powerful as our "Road Gang," the consortium of "oil, cement, rubber, automobile, insurance, trucking, chemical, and construction industries, consumer and political groups, financial institutions, and media"[3] that, along with the military, pushed successfully for new highways.

During the greatest period of American highway construction, General Motors was the largest private company in the world[4] and the secretary of defense was Charles Erwin Wilson, the former GM chief who had famously shared his belief that "what was good for the country was good for General Motors and vice versa."[*] Whether or not it was good for America, the federal highway act and its subsequent iterations began at midcentury to distinguish American cities dramatically from their counterparts in other countries.

---

[*]Wikipedia, "History of General Motors." This comment is interesting when one considers that GM armed the Nazis even after they had declared war on the United States (Charles Higham, *Trading with the Enemy*). Adolf Hitler awarded GM CEO James D. Mooney the Order of Merit of the Golden Eagle for his services in support of the Nazi regime.

HIGHWAYS VERSUS CITIES

The most interesting article I have read on this topic is a little-known academic paper by Patrick Condon, who chairs the landscape architecture department at the University of British Columbia. Titled "Canadian Cities American Cities: Our Differences Are the Same," this study clearly shows a compelling inverse correlation between highway investment and urban property values.

The researchers expected to find a broad range of historical and cultural causes behind the differing fates of Canadian and U.S. cities. Instead, they found that these cities appeared almost identical in 1940 and then tracked in different directions based upon relative highway investment. It didn't matter whether a city was American or Canadian: the highway-investment history was all you needed to know to accurately predict the real estate–value history.

The graphs for Portland are particularly telling, with the highway and real estate lines charting almost exactly opposite one another, like an hourglass on its side. Here's what happens: In the 1960s, highway construction inflects upward while property values lie flat. In the 1970s, highway construction inflects downward, and property values rise. In the 1980s, highway construction inflects upward and property values fall. Finally, in the 1990s, highway investment inflects downward and property values rise again.[5]

Again, correlation is not cause, but the researchers could find no other data set that consistently tracked along or against urban property values. Whether American or Canadian, the inner cities with less regional highway investment fared better than those with more. Of course, most of the latter could be found in the United States, where the federal government paid ninety cents on the dollar—versus Canada's ten cents—for road building.[6]

The jury is still out on whether, on the whole, America's highway-building blitz was a completely bad idea. It seemed to work out well enough economically—at least until our domestic oil wells started to run dry. But it was clearly very bad for the central cities and it got even worse when the big-city mayors, desperate for jobs, amended the act to include an additional six thousand miles of inner-city expressways.[7] These highways, most of which gutted minority neighborhoods, were never imagined in the original measure, which was created by people who knew better.* Even Lewis Mumford, a fan of decentralization, admitted that "the right to have access to every building in the city by private motorcar, in an age when everyone possesses such a vehicle, is actually the right to destroy the city."[8]

Ironically, the city that resisted the greatest amount of federal highway spending was probably the nation's capital. Most current residents are unaware that, at one time, the Washington area was slated to receive 450 miles of interstate highways, 38 of which would have plowed through the District itself. Thanks to an epic twenty-two-year political battle, only ten miles were ever built. Instead, much of the federal funding was diverted to the 103-mile Metrorail system,[9] now considered central to the city's recent resurgence.

Bob and Jane Freundel Levey told the story this way in *The Washington Post*:

> More than 200,000 housing units were saved from destruction. So were more than 100 square miles of parkland around the metropolitan area. The city was spared from freeways bored under the Mall, freeways punched through stable middle-class black neighborhoods, free-

---

*Norman Bel Geddes, in many ways the intellectual father of the interstate system, stated in 1939 that "motorways must not be allowed to infringe upon the city" (quoted in Duany, Plater-Zyberk, and Speck, *Suburban Nation*, 86–87).

ways tunneled under K Street, freeways that would have obliterated the Georgetown waterfront and the Maryland bank of the Potomac. . . . One would [have] run in a flattened oval around the central core of the city, about half a mile north and south of the White House.[10]

Opposition to the highways was largely grassroots, spurred on by the slogan "White Men's Roads Through Black Men's Homes." People lay down in the path of bulldozers and tied themselves to trees. The protesters make it clear that the outcome could have gone either way, since the highway proposal had been warmly supported by the D.C. power structure, including *The Washington Post*, *The Evening Star*, the Board of Trade, and "leading lights on Capitol Hill." This establishment support for road building was the national norm, and, ultimately, no large East Coast city got off as lightly as Washington did.[11]

It would be a mistake to think that America's pro-highway bias has diminished markedly since the rah-rah days of the mid-twentieth century, at least at the federal and state levels. You don't have to be a conspiracy theorist to believe that, if three of the world's four largest corporations are American oil companies* and those companies make millions of dollars in campaign contributions, then roads are fairly guaranteed to remain a priority. Despite all the talk about transit—and great strides made by rail advocates—the feds are still funding highways at roughly four times the rate of public transportation. This funding, about $40 billion in 2011, is supplemented by direct and hidden subsidies to the oil industry, which former California EPA czar Terry Tamminen calculates at between $65 and $113 billion annually, "more than double the amount spent on homeland security."[12]

---

* Exxon Mobil, Chevron, and ConocoPhillips (2011 Fortune 500). The largest corporation is, of course, Walmart, whose entire business model is based on cheap driving and trucking.

Significantly, most federal transportation funds are transferred directly to state departments of transportation (DOTs), which are notoriously inbred with road builders, and typically see it as their principal mission to construct highways.[13] More on them in a minute.

As a result of its unmatched historical and contemporary commitment to automobility, the United States is full of cities that have been shaped or reshaped around the car. Because there have been so many incentives for driving, cars have behaved like water, flowing into every nook and cranny where they have been allowed. Cities with more available space (Houston, Los Angeles) got more cars, while cities with less available space (Boston, New Orleans) got fewer. The first step in reclaiming our urban centers for pedestrians is simply to acknowledge that this outcome was not inevitable, is not the global norm, and need not continue. Despite all the countervailing pressures, it is fully within the capabilities of the typical American city to alter its relationship to the automobile in subtle ways that can have a tremendous impact on walkability—to welcome cars, but on its own terms. First and foremost, this means making all transportation decisions in light of the phenomenon of induced demand.

BECAUSE I MUST: INDUCED DEMAND

About once a month, I give a talk somewhere in America, typically to a chamber of commerce, a planning association, or a bunch of people in a bookstore. Topics and approaches can vary, but I have one hard-and-fast rule: every lecture, no matter what, I will talk at length about induced demand. I do this because induced demand is the great intellectual black hole in city planning, the one professional certainty that everyone thoughtful seems to acknowledge, yet almost no one is willing to act upon. It's as if, despite all of our advances, this one (unfortunately central) aspect of how we make our cities has been entrusted to the Flat Earth Society.

Traffic studies are perhaps the most inevitable activity in planning these days. If you want to add any significant use to a neighborhood, you have to complete a traffic study. If you want to change the design of a street, you have to complete a traffic study. Once, in Davenport, Iowa, I came across a street that had lost one block of its parallel parking, turning a three-lane one-way into a four-lane one-way for just three hundred feet. I recommended bringing that one block of parking back. The city's response? "We need to do a traffic study."[•]

This circumstance is unsurprising, since traffic congestion is the main topic of civic complaint in most American communities. Since it is the only real constraint to driving, congestion is the one place where people are made to feel the pinch in their automotive lives. Were it not for congestion, we would drive enough additional miles to make congestion. So the traffic study has become the default act of planning, and more than a few large companies can thank traffic studies for the lion's share of their income. They don't want you to read the next few paragraphs.

Traffic studies are bullshit. They are bullshit for three main reasons:

First: The computer model is only as good as its inputs, and there's nothing easier than tweaking the inputs to get the outcome you want. When we were working in Oklahoma City, the local traffic engineer's "Synchro" computer model said that our pro-pedestrian proposals would cause gridlock. So we borrowed that engineer's computer model and handed it to our engineer, who tweaked the inputs, and voila: smooth sailing. By the way, the most commonly tweaked input is anticipated background growth, which typically needs tweaking anyway: most cities' traffic models presume 1 to 2 percent annual growth, even when those cities are shrinking.

Second: Traffic studies are typically performed by firms that do traffic engineering. This makes perfect sense—who else would

---

[•] Good news: upon further deliberation, the city skipped the study and added back the parking, without incident.

do them? But guess who gets the big contract for the roadway expansion that the study deems necessary? As long as engineers are in charge of traffic studies, they will predict the need for engineering.

Finally, and most essentially: The main problem with traffic studies is that they almost never consider the phenomenon of induced demand. Induced demand is the name for what happens when increasing the supply of roadways lowers the time cost of driving, causing more people to drive and obliterating any reductions in congestion. We talked about this phenomenon at length in *Suburban Nation* in 2000, and the seminal text, *The Elephant in the Bedroom: Automobile Dependence and Denial*, was published by Hart and Spivak in 1993. For this reason, I will not take the time here to address its causes, which are multifold and fascinating. Since these books were published, however, there have been additional reports, all essentially confirming what we knew then. In 2004, a meta-analysis of dozens of previous studies found that "on average, a 10 percent increase in lane miles induces an immediate 4 percent increase in vehicle miles traveled, which climbs to 10 percent—the entire new capacity—in a few years."[14]

The most comprehensive effort remains the one completed in 1998 by the Surface Transportation Policy Project, which looked at fully seventy different metropolitan areas over fifteen years. This study, which based its findings on data from the annual reports of the conservative Texas Transportation Institute, concluded as follows:

> Metro areas that invested heavily in road capacity expansion fared no better in easing congestion than metro areas that did not. Trends in congestion show that areas that exhibited greater growth in lane capacity spent roughly $22 billion more on road construction than those that didn't, yet ended up with slightly higher congestion costs per person, wasted fuel, and travel de-

lay. . . . The metro area with the highest estimated road building cost was Nashville, Tennessee with a price tag of $3,243 per family per year.[•]

Thanks to studies like this one, induced demand is by no means a professional secret. I was delighted to read the following in a 2009 article in *Newsweek*, hardly an esoteric publication: "Demand from drivers tends to quickly overwhelm the new supply; today engineers acknowledge that building new roads usually makes traffic worse."[■]

To which I must respond: "Who are these engineers and may I please meet them?" Most of the engineers that I'm forced to work with graduated from school decades ago and apparently haven't cracked a textbook—or a *Newsweek*—since.[▲] As a result, this powerful phenomenon, for which the most and best data can be found in the United States, has had virtually no impact on road building in the United States. But there is good news: it has caused great advances in Europe! In Great Britain, where planners are no longer allowed to justify new highways on the basis of reduced congestion, road construction has dropped so drastically

[•] "Does Widening Roads Cause Congestion?" Excerpted from Donald Chen, "If You Build It, They Will Come." A 2010 study by Gilles Duranton and Matthew Turner at the University of Toronto concludes that "increased provision of interstate highways and major urban roads is unlikely to relieve congestion on these roads" ("The Fundamental Law of Road Congestion: Evidence from U.S. Cities," 2616).

[■] Nick Summers, "Where the Neon Lights Are Bright—and Drivers Are No Longer Welcome." It is important to illuminate this quote with the larger discussion that induced demand applies principally to the creation and widening of highways and arterial roads, as opposed to the creation of more intricate street networks through the insertion of small local streets.

[▲] In all fairness, my comment refers principally to the municipal and DOT engineers who must approve the projects that I plan. There are now more than a handful of professional transportation engineers who do their best to share information on induced demand. I have also had good experiences recently working with municipal engineers in Carmel, Indiana; Cedar Rapids; and Fort Lauderdale. But, for most of the profession, Upton Sinclair's famous observation still holds sway: "It is difficult to get a man to understand something when his salary depends on his not understanding it."

that Alarm UK, the main freeway protest organization, disbanded itself "on the grounds that it was no longer needed."[15]

Meanwhile, back on planet Earth, Mary Peters, a recent secretary of transportation, testified before a U.S. Senate committee that "congestion must be addressed with a long-term strategy to increase capacity."[16] It would seem that Saul Bellow's Good Intentions Paving Company is still open for business.

Nowhere is this more evident than in the propaganda put forth by the current incarnation of the Road Gang. There is an engineering firm that I work with, one of the largest in the country. I won't name it here, because I would like to work with them again. They do some really top-notch city projects, are great promoters of urbanism, and are leaders in the development of new transit systems. They also build a lot of sprawl, since they do everything and the biggest part of everything is still sprawl.

Not long ago, the firm placed a full-page ad in *Planning* magazine. It shows an old highway choking on traffic. Then it shows a sparkling new cloverleaf, with cars zipping along happily. The copy reads as follows:

Vehicle miles travelled increased by 97 percent from 1980 to 1996. Infrastructure improvements could significantly reduce the $78 billion of fuel lost to congestion each year.

This ad is, to put it mildly, misleading. It is misleading on so many levels it is hard to know where to start pulling it apart. At the very least, it is misleading in what it says, what it implies, and what it assumes. It says that new roads can reduce congestion, when we know that new roads almost always increase congestion. It implies that the dramatic surge in vehicle miles traveled since 1980 was not explicitly caused by infrastructure improvements, when we know that it was. Finally, it assumes that congestion wastes fuel, when we know that congestion actually saves fuel—and ultimately is one of the only things that does.

All three of these statements are perhaps counterintuitive, which is why this promotion was not laughed off the copywriter's table at the ad agency. The first two refer, of course, to induced demand. The third statement, that congestion saves fuel, requires some evidence to be plausible.

It turns out that there is a strong correlation between a metropolitan area's average traffic speed and its fuel use. Cities with higher congestion use less fuel per capita, while cities with the least congestion use the most fuel.[17]

This strange circumstance exists not because driving in traffic is more efficient—it isn't—but because of the way we pay to drive. Whether we own or lease, most of the costs are fixed: the price of the vehicle (and/or financing), the driver's insurance, the registration fees, and most of the maintenance fees are largely the same whether we drive a little or a lot. The roads, bridges, and policing are largely paid by general taxes from drivers and nondrivers alike. Tolls, unless you are trying to enter Manhattan or San Francisco, are rarely significant, and even more rarely a deal killer. Parking, as will be discussed at length ahead, is typically priced below market rate and again is only prohibitively expensive in a few places. For most American drivers, the most meaningful variable cost is gas, and by global standards, our gas is dirt cheap—even at four dollars per gallon, it's about half the European rate. All told, the marginal costs are almost negligible compared to the fixed costs. According to the AAA, for a large sedan driven ten thousand miles per year, the operating costs total only one-fifth of the ownership costs.*

---

*AAA: "Your Driving Costs," 2010 edition, 7. The marginal operating cost of most vehicles is well below twenty cents per mile. This explains why Zipcar and the other urban car-share programs are so effective at reducing auto use. According to the company website, each "Zipcar takes at least 15 personally-owned vehicles off the road." For a Zipcar member, the fixed costs—a twenty-five-dollar application fee and a sixty-dollar annual membership fee—are negligible compared to the marginal costs of hourly rental.

This all adds up to a situation in which you are paying to drive whether you drive or not, in which the more you drive, the less each mile costs, and in which the greatest constraint to driving, then, is congestion. While the cost of the trip will rarely keep us home, the threat of being stuck in traffic often will, at least in our larger cities. Congestion saves fuel because people hate to waste their time being miserable.

That's the negative way to look at it, but there's a positive side as well. The cities with the most congestion are often the cities that provide the best alternatives to being stuck in congestion. Of the ten cities ranked worst for traffic in the 2010 Urban Mobility Report,[18] all but three—Houston, Dallas, and Atlanta—have excellent public transit and a vast collection of walkable neighborhoods. Indeed, these seven cities—Chicago, Washington, Los Angeles, San Francisco, Boston, Seattle, and New York—also appear in another list: Walk Score's ten "Most Walkable Neighborhoods" in America.*

So, with the exception of the usual Sun Belt suspects, congestion comes hand in hand with the opportunity to avoid it. And in those places like Atlanta, where congestion affects almost everyone, at least it mitigates fuel use rather than adding to it. It is certainly troubling to sit in traffic and watch the sky waver from the exhaust of a hundred tailpipes. But you can take some solace in the fact that less congestion would actually lead to more exhaust.

Nobody likes congestion, and, despite appearances, I am not arguing here for more of it. Rather, I am asking that it be better understood by those who build and rebuild our communities, so that we can stop making stupid decisions that placate angry citi-

---

*Walk Score website: "America's Most Walkable Neighborhoods." This outcome makes sense, because the best cities have often attracted the most sprawl. Footloose readers might want to relocate to one of the three cities that make it into the second list but not the first. These are Philadelphia; Long Beach, California; and Portland, Oregon.

zens while only hurting them in the long run. There is a simple answer to congestion—and it's the only answer—which is to bring the cost of driving on crowded streets closer in line with its value. That technique is the subject of the *Congestion Pricing* section ahead.

IT'S NOT JUST FREEWAYS

When I say "highway," you probably picture a limited-access six-laner with guardrails and on-ramps. But the typical American "highway" is not a freeway, but a state road running right through the middle of your town, lined by homes and businesses that are doing their best to maintain their value, often while the state DOT does its best to increase the road's volume. This is why, in the inimitable words of Andres Duany, "the Department of Transportation, in its single-minded pursuit of traffic flow, has destroyed more American towns than General Sherman."[19]

Depending on what state you live in, a few or many of your streets are the responsibility of the Department of Transportation. In Virginia, whose DOT is famous for calling street trees "FHOs"—Fixed and Hazardous Objects[20]—almost every street is state property. In most states, however, it is just the ones that carry a lot of traffic. Unfortunately, this means that many American Main Streets are not controlled by the communities that rely on them, but by state engineers. Main Streets are main streets, after all, and the state relies on them to keep traffic counts up.

This is the worst of news. Whenever I am asked to help resuscitate a city or town center, before doing anything else, I run in a panic to Google Maps to see which, if any, of the downtown streets are state property. Then, if there are many, I adjust my fee up and their expectations down. Because dealing with the state DOT almost always means that the outcome will be a disappointment.*

While all traffic engineers can be trouble, state engineers are the toughest because they have no obligation to listen to a local mayor or citizens. They answer to a higher authority, which is ultimately the god Traffic Flow. They will typically claim a concern for walkability and "context-sensitive design," but everything is still viewed through the lens of "level of service," and level of service means smooth flow. Incidentally, state DOTs are also a huge source of work for planning consultants, which is a big reason why few planners are willing to stand up to them.

The same is true of county engineers in places like New York State, where many communities are held hostage by Main Streets that are also county highways. In both cases, fighting the DOT is always a struggle, but there is a way to win, and it's called leadership. The communities that prevail are those whose elected officials confront the DOT head-on and publicly demand a more walkable solution. This approach is admittedly easier for bigger cities, but even small towns can come out on top if they make enough noise.

This is what happened in the Village of Hamburg, New York (population roughly ten thousand), where Mayor John Thomas was being told by NYDOT to accept three major road widenings that would have removed parallel parking, increased travel speeds, and generally trashed his town center. Working with the nationally known pedestrian advocate Dan Burden,* the mayor

---

*A few disclaimers: Some states are better than others; I have had good experiences in Massachusetts and Michigan, and the District of Columbia (almost a state) is ahead of most cities in its pro-pedestrian policies. Also, most state traffic engineers are very nice people. Despite *The New York Times*' 2010 exposé about engineers' proclivities for terror—"in the ranks of captured and confessed terrorists, engineers and engineering students are significantly overrepresented" (David Berreby, "Engineering Terror")—I have always found them pleasant enough to work with. Of course, they haven't seen this book yet.

*Dan Burden is profiled nicely in Jeff Mapes, *Pedaling Revolution*.

refused the DOT "improvement" until a new design could be produced with public participation. Now Hamburg's Main Street is a delicate two-laner with bikeways and parking, and the DOT proudly showcases its award-winning design at transportation conferences.[21]

Beating the DOT is often the most important thing that a community can do to reclaim its center, and battles of this epic nature must be fought on occasion if cities are to thrive. But I would be protecting you from the truth if I were to suggest that the Boogieman always comes from out of town. In most communities, there are also daily battles to be fought within city administration, where, in the absence of mayoral leadership, traffic trumps livability.

As mentioned earlier, I spent four years working with the Mayors' Institute on City Design, a program that convenes mayors for intensive city-planning workshops. As the ranking representative of the program's main funder, I was always given a chance to speak, and my message was always the same: "Stop letting your traffic engineer design your city!"

The need for this message became all the more clear after I had attended a handful of Mayors' Institute sessions. In city after city, left to their own devices, traffic engineers were widening streets, removing trees, and generally reaming out downtowns to improve traffic flow. Much of this was happening below the mayor's radar. In the absence of any design leadership from above, the city engineer, simply by doing his job, was redesigning the city—badly.

It seems a bit unfair to blame the city engineer for this situation. Because most of the public complaints one hears in cities are about traffic, it stands to reason that any good public servant would work to reduce traffic congestion. This would be acceptable if efforts to reduce traffic congestion didn't wreck cities and perhaps also if they worked. But they don't work, because of induced demand. Most city engineers don't understand induced demand. They might say that they do, but, if so, they don't act upon that understanding.

I say this because it would seem that almost no traffic engineers in America possess the necessary combination of insight and political will that would allow them to take the induced demand discussion to its logical conclusion, which is this: Stop doing traffic studies. Stop trying to improve flow. Stop spending people's tax dollars giving them false hope that you can cure congestion, while mutilating their cities in the process.

I understand that it might be difficult to tell the public that you can't satisfy their biggest complaint. But there is a happier way to frame the message, and it goes like this: We can have the kind of city we want. We can tell the car where to go and how fast. We can be a place not just for driving through, but for arriving at. This is the story that traffic engineers should be sharing, rather than spending their careers running scared from congestion. Until they do, it will be necessary for mayors, Main Street merchants, and concerned citizens to discredit them. Toward that end, I provide the following short interlude.

KILL THE TRAFFIC ENGINEERS FIRST

Everybody likes Jane Jacobs, right? She was famous for fighting traffic engineers, and took them to task repeatedly and effectively in her masterpiece, *The Death and Life of Great American Cities*. Most planners and many public servants swear by that book, but few have read *Dark Age Ahead*, in which, forty years later, she took off the gloves. Until traffic engineers change their tune on induced demand, here is the statement from Jane Jacobs that every public official and planner needs to tape prominently above his or her desk:

It is popularly assumed that when universities give science degrees in traffic engineering, as they do, they are recognizing aboveboard expert knowledge. But they aren't. They are perpetrating a fraud upon students and upon the public when they award credentials in this supposed expertise.[22]

And a bit more:

> I thought sadly: "Here they are, another generation of nice, miseducated young men, about to waste their careers in a fake science that cares nothing about evidence; that doesn't ask a fruitful question in the first place and that, when unexpected evidence turns up anyhow, doesn't pursue it. . . . This incurious profession pulls its conclusions about the meaning of evidence out of thin air—sheer guesswork—even when it does deign to notice evidence. . . . In the meantime, each year students have poured forth from universities, a clear, harmful case of education surrendered to credentialism. One wonders at the docility of the students who evidently must be satisfied enough with the credentials to be uncaring about the lack of education.[23]

Perhaps inspired by Jane, a few brave, young, credentialed traffic engineers have recently had the nerve to come out of the closet. Foremost among them is probably Charles Marohn, who published the following piece in *Grist*. It is so powerful, and important, that it deserves quoting at length:

> ### CONFESSIONS OF A RECOVERING ENGINEER
> After graduating from college with a civil engineering degree, I found myself working in my home town for a local engineering firm doing mostly municipal engineering (roads, sewer pipe, water pipe, stormwater). A fair percentage of my time was spent convincing people that, when it came to their road, I knew more than they did.

And of course I should know more. First, I had a technical degree from a top university. Second, I was in a path towards getting a state license . . . which required me to pass a pretty tough test just to get started and another, more difficult, exam to conclude. Third, I was in a profession that is one of the oldest and most respected in human history, responsible for some of the greatest achievements of mankind. Fourth—and most important—I had books and books of standards to follow.

When people would tell me that they did not want a wider street, I would tell them that they had to have it for safety reasons.

When they answered that a wider street would make people drive faster and that would seem to be less safe, especially in front of their house where their kids were playing, I would confidently tell them that the wider road was more safe, especially when combined with the other safety enhancements the standards called for.

When people objected to those other "enhancements," like removing all of the trees near the road, I told them that for safety reasons we needed to improve the sight distances and ensure that the recovery zone was free of obstacles.

When they pointed out that the "recovery zone" was also their "yard" and that their kids played kickball and hopscotch there, I recommended that they put up a fence, so long as the fence was outside of the right-of-way. When they objected to the cost of the wider, faster, treeless road that would turn their peaceful front yard into the viewing area for a drag strip unless they built a concrete barricade along their front property line, I informed them that progress was sometimes expensive, but these standards have been shown to work across the

state, the country, and the world, and I could not compromise with their safety.

In retrospect I understand that this was utter insanity.
Wider, faster, treeless roads not only ruin our public places,
they kill people. Taking highway standards and applying
them to urban and suburban streets, and even county
roads, costs us thousands of lives every year. There is no
earthly reason why an engineer would ever design a 14-
foot lane for a city block, yet we do it continually. Why?

The answer is utterly shameful: Because that is the
standard.*

The two above selections are offered to help cities defend themselves against abuse by traffic engineers. It gives me no great
pleasure to share them, and I wish it were unnecessary. But the
profession of traffic planning is so desperately in need of a course
correction that the most productive approach would seem to be
to shame them mercilessly. That said, Marohn's essay is ultimately
cause for hope. He is, after all, a traffic engineer, and he clearly
gets it. He is actually only one of a growing number of traffic
experts—both professional consultants and city staffers—who
have been leading the charge in recent years toward a new paradigm. Because cities demand them, these engineers still do traffic studies. But these studies, like the British ones, finally take
induced demand into account.

REMOVE IT AND THEY WILL GO

If more and bigger highways mean more traffic, does the same
logic work in reverse? The latest twist in the induced demand

---

* "Confessions of a Recovering Engineer." More about Charles Marohn and his work
can be found at strongtowns.org.

story might be called *reduced demand*, which seems to be what happens when "vital" arteries are removed from cities. The traffic just goes away.

The two best-known American examples remain New York's West Side Highway and San Francisco's Embarcadero Freeway, which collapsed in 1973 and in 1989, respectively. In both cases, contrary to the apocalyptic warnings of traffic engineers, most of the car trips simply disappeared. They did not pop up elsewhere, clogging surface streets; people just found other ways to get around, or felt less compelled to be mobile.* The Embarcadero was replaced by a lovely boulevard, whose cute little streetcars actually transport more riders per day than the freeway once did.

People's dawning awareness of these successes has led to a growing list of highway teardowns, both domestically and around the world. These include Harbor Drive in Portland, Milwaukee's Park East Freeway, and another elevated road in San Francisco: the Central Freeway, now replaced by the attractive Octavia Boulevard.[24] Beyond giving new life to the areas previously blighted by the highways, these road removals have actually been found to reduce overall travel times within their cities. The most celebrated, and properly so, has got to be the Cheonggyecheon (pronounced *chung-yay-chun*) Freeway in Seoul, where a traffic-choked elevated expressway was hauled down in the mid-2000s, daylighting the river that it had obscured for half a century.[25]

The Cheonggyecheon story is so intriguing that it deserves its own book. It began as a grassroots effort, with no political support whatsoever—after all, who advocates for removing a road that carries 168,000 cars per day? Since nobody in office would back it, proponents shopped the idea around to mayoral candidates, in the hope that someone would make it their platform.

---

*One British study of worldwide data found that road removals generally improve local economies, while new roads increase urban unemployment (Jill Kruse, "Remove It and They Will Disappear," 5, 7).

The one candidate who bit—ironically, the former president of the company that built the freeway—was elected on that promise. As mayor, Lee Myung-bak commenced the teardown project on inauguration day.

Mayhem ensued. Opponents mounted huge protests, including the three thousand street vendors whose livelihoods depended on hawking wares to the highway's gridlocked travelers. Some threatened suicide unless the project was stopped. Through all of that, a two-year design process was shortened to six months, and the entire effort was completed within thirty months. A sixteen-lane highway was replaced by an urban boulevard and a spectacular 3.6-mile river park.[26]

A few years later, the river's ecosystem had been significantly restored, an urban heat island had its temperature reduced by more than five degrees, and traffic congestion had dropped sharply—thanks in part to simultaneous investments in transit. As of this writing, property values surrounding the former highway have risen 300 percent. And Lee Myung-bak has been elected president of South Korea.[27]

I wish we had known about this effort in September 2004, when Seattle's Mayor Greg Nickels came to the Mayors' Institute on City Design, and brought along the Alaskan Way Viaduct as his planning challenge. Like the Embarcadero, the two-deck, six-lane viaduct had been damaged in an earthquake and needed replacement. The state DOT proposed replacing the highway with an elegant surface boulevard . . . and a $4.2 billion highway tunnel.

"That sounds perfect—just cut the tunnel!" the planners around the table shouted in unison. "But where will all the traffic go?" asked the mayor. "Not to worry!" we responded.• But we apparently weren't very convincing, as Mayor Nickels returned

---

• This exchange is obviously paraphrased from a longer and more broad-ranging discussion.

to Seattle still committed to the tunnel. Even this Democratic leader of a progressive left-coast city—and an environmentalist so devout that he didn't allow salt for snow removal—couldn't be sold on induced demand.

How did that work out for him? Well, first, Seattle's citizens voted in a referendum to reject plans to replace the Viaduct with either a tunnel or a new elevated expressway. Then, as Nickels continued to support the tunnel, Mike McGinn, a relatively un-known Sierra Clubber, announced a run for mayor centered on a no-tunnel platform. Despite raising only $80,000 to Nickels's $560,000, McGinn beat Nickels handily in the primary and is now mayor.[28]

So Lee Myung-bak is president and Greg Nickels is out of politics. . . . Is there a lesson here about induced demand? It would seem that the people are in front of the politicians as usual, except that they aren't: in a more recent referendum, the tunnel won, and now seems imminent. But that doesn't make it right.

Ultimately, this discussion is more about fiscal restraint than traffic theory. The most beautiful tree-lined boulevard can be built for a fraction of the cost of either a tunnel or a viaduct. The current (and likely permanent) cash-strapped status of our cities and states suggests that all elevated urban expressways should be replaced by surface streets when they become decrepit—although perhaps not any sooner.

But this final caveat requires more thought. Elevated ex-pressways are a blight on cities and depress surrounding prop-erty values drastically—not only immediately adjacent, but sometimes for several blocks on both flanks. Tree-lined boule-vards, of course, do the opposite. The Embarcadero boulevard project cost $171 million, but raised property values by 300 percent—the same as in Seoul—for a full 1.2-mile stretch.[29] You don't need a real estate degree to understand that a threefold increase in property taxes for 1.2 miles of downtown San Francisco has probably paid for the boulevard several times over since 2000. Some cities, if they care to do the math, might find ample economic justification for tearing down an expressway or two, even before they begin to crumble.

A STEP TOO FAR: PEDESTRIAN ZONES

Jan Gehl, the legendary Danish city planner, elegantly sums up the traffic discussion this way:

> The connections between invitations and behavior came to a head for cities in the 20th century. . . . In every case, attempts to relieve traffic pressure by building more roads and parking garages have generated more traffic and more congestion. The volume of car traffic almost everywhere is more or less arbitrary, depending on the available transportation infrastructure.[30]

This assessment, to my mind, properly conveys the noninevitable nature of the auto-dominated city, and how communities, by making concerted choices about their infrastructure, can fully dictate the quality of their landscapes and lives. In his work in Copenhagen, Gehl has presided over a gradual removal of cars from the heart of the city. From 1962 to 2005, a central zone dedicated to pedestrians and bicycles has grown sevenfold in size, from about four acres to over twenty-five acres.[31] In concert with this effort, the city has been eliminating 2 percent of its downtown parking spaces every year, for the past thirty years.[32]

Gehl has recently been consulting to the City of New York, which turned a stretch of Broadway in Times Square into a pedestrian park with great results. The city has also completed about twenty blocks of the spectacular High Line project, a former elevated railway that has been converted to a linear park, perhaps the most delightful piece of civic art to have been created since midcentury. You've probably seen the pictures, and they don't lie: these public amenities are a real boon to the livability of their neighborhoods and are well used in all but the worst weather.

These car-free successes provide a powerful lesson that unfortunately does not apply to most American cities. It is a mistake to think that similar designs will produce similar results in vastly dissimilar places. Face it: you aren't Copenhagen, where cyclists outnumber motorists.[33] You aren't New York, where pedestrian congestion can actually make it almost impossible to walk south along Seventh Avenue near Penn Station at 9:00 a.m. Unless you have similar residential and pedestrian density and stores that can thrive in the absence of car traffic—a rarity—to consign a commercial area to pedestrians only, in America, is to condemn it to death.

When I arrived at the NEA in 2003, my office was stocked with a collection of publications describing past NEA successes. One of them, in quaint 1970s lettering, celebrated dozens of Main Streets across America that had been pedestrianized using NEA funds. As I flipped through it, I was treated to page after page of failure. From Baltimore to Buffalo, from Louisville to Little Rock, from Tampa to Tulsa, from Greenville, North Carolina, to Greenville, South Carolina, almost every Main Street that was closed to car traffic in the sixties and seventies failed almost as soon as the NEA book hit the presses.

In all, of the two hundred or so pedestrian malls created in the United States, only about thirty remain.[34] Of those, most are moribund low-rent districts like Main Street in Memphis where, despite the presence of an appealing streetcar line, empty storefronts abound. The exceptions are almost all in college towns like Boulder, Colorado, and Burlington, Vermont, or in resorts like Aspen and Miami Beach. Other outliers, like Santa Monica's Third Street Promenade and Denver's 16th Street, show that successful pedestrianization is indeed possible. It's just very, very unlikely.

It would seem that only one thing is more destructive to the health of our downtowns than welcoming cars unconditionally and that is getting rid of them entirely. The proper response to obesity is not to stop eating, and most stores need car traffic to survive. With autos reintroduced, most failed pedestrian malls, like Monroe Place in Grand Rapids, have come back at least partway. The key is to welcome cars in the proper number and at the proper speed.

It is easy to catch the Broadway bug and hope to create pedestrian refuges in your city. New York could handle a lot more of them—I advised its planning commission in 2010 to add one new one every year.[35] Certain other cities with great residential densities downtown, like Boston and Chicago, could produce some successes in the years ahead and should perhaps try. But the main lesson here is to not do it the way they did last time, with the construction of expensive and expensive-to-remove streetscapes that make driving impossible. Instead, put up some temporary bollards and bring in a few potted trees and movable chairs, like they did in Times Square. Try it on a weekend and, if it works, expand the days. Don't spend a penny on gorgeous car barricades, because if a pedestrian zone is going to be successful, it will thrive due to its location, demographics, and organization—not its streetscape.

CONGESTION PRICING: TOO SMART TO BE EASY

No chapter on cars and cities would be complete without a discussion of congestion pricing, a vastly underutilized tool that communities can use to protect themselves from the automotive hordes. We have already celebrated congestion, reluctantly, as a dominant factor in limiting people's time on the road. Most cities need congestion to keep driving in check, because driving costs drivers so much less than it costs society.* But what if motorists were asked to pay something closer to the real cost of driving, so that they were once again allowed to make market-based choices about when to drive where? The result would be a solution to both excessive driving and excessive congestion. That's the idea behind congestion pricing.

In the early 2000s, London was choking on traffic, and people were desperate for a solution. Having exhausted the alternatives, Mayor Ken Livingstone proposed the only known cure, economics. Against "a massive and sustained media campaign,"[36] he introduced a roughly fifteen-dollar fee for any driver who wanted to enter the congested heart of the city on weekdays, with the revenue to be used to support a progressive transportation agenda.

Here's what happened: Congestion dropped 30 percent in the toll zone, and typical journey times went down by 14 percent. Cycling among Londoners jumped 20 percent and air pollution fell about 12 percent. The fee has already generated over a billion dollars in revenue, much of which has been invested in mass transit. London now has hundreds of new buses, providing almost thirty thousand more daily trips than before the charge. Bus reliability has jumped by 30 percent and bus delays have dropped by 60 percent.[37]

Before introduction of the congestion charge, Londoners were evenly divided on the concept. When last polled, pros beat cons by 35 percent.[38] And in the subsequent mayoral election, largely a referendum on the pricing scheme, Livingstone was reelected by a broad margin.

London is not alone in its embrace of congestion pricing. São

---

*This is a fact even ignoring externalities like pollution and time wasted. For example, general taxes in New Jersey transfer approximately $700 million from the general population to drivers every year (Charles Siegel, *Unplanning*, 29).

Paulo, Shanghai, Singapore, Stockholm, and Sydney[39] have all introduced similar measures, with varying, but all generally positive, results. San Francisco is now working on its own scheme. Not beginning with the letter *S* like all the others, New York City was apparently at a distinct disadvantage when Mayor Michael Bloomberg hatched a congestion-pricing scheme on Earth Day 2007. His proposal would have raised about half a billion dollars annually, and was additionally slated to receive $354 million off the bat from the federal government. To the surprise of many, it was killed by the State Assembly in Albany,[40] which is disproportionately composed of suburban commuters. Well, as a New Yorker would say, "Screw you, too."

Ironically, four-dollar gasoline quickly accomplished the better part of what Mayor Bloomberg hoped to do[41]—minus the revenues to the city—demonstrating the effectiveness of using price to control congestion. But gas prices are a much blunter instrument than congestion pricing, which allows cities to specifically attack problem locations, and make a lot of money in the bargain. Most cities are not beholden to their state legislatures in the same way New York is, and the more congested ones should consider pilot projects in the manner of London's. After all, Mayor Bloomberg's proposal was supported locally by 67 percent of voters.[42]

THE LONG VIEW

"Americans are in the habit of never walking if they can ride." So commented the duke of Orléans, Louis Philippe, as early as 1798 (he became king of the French in 1830).[43] This tendency, apparently established in our nation's earliest days, has had a profound impact on both our physical landscape and our physical selves. Considerably more recently, the French philosopher Bernard-Henry Lévy described our autocentric lifestyle as "a global, total obesity that spares no realm of life, public or private. An entire society that, from the top down, from one end to the other, seems prey to this obscure derangement that slowly causes an organism to swell, overflow, explode."[44] These two comments, made two centuries apart, are more connected than they at first may seem.

Lévy was not talking explicitly about our bodies, but about our society as a whole, and how we live so large on the land. To figure out what happened in the time between these two French pronouncements, we need to take a brief detour through the writings of Ivan Illich, the multinational intellectual who in 1973 wrote the smartest thing that I have yet to read about transportation: "Beyond a certain speed, motorized vehicles create remoteness which they alone can shrink. They create distances for all and shrink them for only a few."[45]

Illich was essentially making an equity argument and, if he had stopped there, his message might not have been compelling to many. Sure, it's not fair that "an elite packs unlimited distance into a lifetime of pampered travel, while the majority spend a bigger slice of their existence on unwanted trips,"[46] but since when is life fair? Statements like "extremes of privilege are created at the cost of universal enslavement"• don't win votes today the way they might have in the seventies. However, beyond discussing equity, Illich actually uncovered a vast mother lode of American waste:

> The model American male devotes more than 1600 hours a year to his car. He sits in it while it goes and while it stands idling. He parks it and searches for it. He earns the money to put down to meet the monthly installments. He works to pay for gasoline, tolls, insurance,

---

• *Toward a History of Needs*, 127, 119. It gives us little comfort to learn that Illich was no great fan of railways either: "From our limited information it appears that everywhere in the world, after some vehicle broke the speed barrier of 15 mph, time scarcity related to traffic began to grow" (ibid., 119).

taxes, and tickets. He spends four of his sixteen waking hours on the road or gathering the resources for it. . . . The model American puts in 1600 hours to get 7500 miles: less than five miles per hour. In countries deprived of transportation industry, people manage to do the same, walking wherever they want to go, and they allocate only 3 to 8 percent of their society's budget to traffic instead of 28 percent.•

This is remarkable. Compared to our colonial ancestors, we throw 25 percent more of our national and personal resources into transportation and we ultimately move no faster. But we do move farther, and Illich might as well have been speaking about contemporary Atlanta when he wrote that "everybody's daily radius expands at the expense of being able to drop in on an acquaintance or walk through the park on the way to work."▪

Illich discovered a hidden physical law: the faster a society moves, the more it spreads out and the more time it must spend moving. And he hadn't seen the half of it. Since 1983, when the American sprawl machine really kicked in, the number of miles driven has grown at eight times the population rate.[47] While almost one in ten commuters walked to work in Illich's day, fewer than one in forty do now.[48]

As disturbing as this transformation is, we must remember that it is not irreversible and—more to the point—not the current experience of every American. Walkable cities, with their

---

•Illich, *Toward a History of Needs*, 120. He adds: "And this figure does not take into account the time consumed by other activities dictated by transport: time spent in hospitals, traffic courts, and garages; time spent watching automobile commercials or attending consumer education meetings to improve the quality of the next buy." And let's not forget that Illich's data were from roughly 1970, when we drove considerably less and spent considerably less of our income on driving.

▪Illich, 119. For the sake of accuracy, I should note that my friend Phil Harrison walks through the park on the way to work in Atlanta. But he is the only one.

dense, vibrant, mixed-use neighborhoods, offer residents a life-style that combines superior economic and social opportunity with a transportation cost, in both time and money, that is not necessarily any higher than in Illich's "countries deprived of transportation industry." This is particularly true when more citizens are able to live right in the center of town, a subject for the next chapter.

STEP 2: MIX THE USES

It's usually housing; Invisible affordability; The rest of the picture

Cities were created to bring things together. The better they do this job, the more successful they become. This has always been the case, but there was a time when what was good for cities was not good for citizens. The belching fumes of the "dark satanic mills" and the rampant spread of epidemics through tenement housing shortened urban life spans dramatically. By 1900, a typical New Yorker enjoyed seven fewer years aboveground than his cousin on the farm.*

City Planning to the rescue! Before it had a name, the planning profession scored its first great victory, by reducing urban overcrowding and moving housing and factories away from each other. Life expectancies shot upward, the planners were hailed as heroes, and thus began the century of separating everything from everything else.[1] This dismantling of the city into its constituent parts became known, appropriately enough, as zoning, and zoning still rules the day in most American communities. Cities are organized not according to "planning regulations" but by "zoning codes," and different land uses still tend to be kept

---

* Edward Glaeser, comments to the Congress for the New Urbanism, June 3, 2011. For reasons already discussed, New Yorkers born in 2010 are expected to live two years longer than the national average.

apart much more than health, safety, or common sense would dictate. Most small-scale urban industry no longer pollutes and, last we checked, cholera was under control.

The zoning tendency finds its apotheosis, of course, in suburban sprawl, where an elephantine regime of separated activities enforces the bankrupting hyper-mobility that has been so destructive to our national civic life. That story has been well told. Less often discussed are the ways that zoning has undermined, and continues to damage, our inner cities. So profound was its impact that it is now not enough to just abolish zoning and let the free market run its course. Cities, if they are to become whole again, must not only reform their codes—to be discussed in Step 9—but must also earnestly labor to reestablish a proper balance of activities downtown.

IT'S USUALLY HOUSING

What is that balance? Better to ask: what do humans do? Work, shop, eat, drink, learn, recreate, convene, worship, heal, visit, celebrate, sleep: these are all activities that people should not have to leave downtown to accomplish. While there are exceptions, most large and midsized American downtowns possess a good supply of all of the above except places to sleep, lost to the twentieth-century suburban exodus. Moreover, thanks to the paucity of housing, many of the other categories are unable to thrive. Specialty shopping may remain, but food markets are rare. Restaurants do their best to survive on only a lunchtime service. Historic churches struggle to hang on to suburban parishioners who used to live nearby.

As we have discussed, the demand for downtown housing is significant and it is about to skyrocket. But supply will have a hard time meeting demand unless cities become politically committed to its provision and lend a hand. Building new housing downtown is an expensive and punishing process: unlike the suburban greenfield sites that most developers are accustomed to, city properties often come burdened with a whole range of utility issues, easements, and access challenges, not to mention pesky neighbors. Local banks, until recently all too willing to finance condo clusters on the periphery, shy away from investing in new apartments downtown.

This continues to be the situation in Davenport, Iowa, where the big local lenders have long been unwilling to support the construction of housing on the very streets surrounding their offices—this despite the fact that the three residential developments to come downtown in the last decade have all rented up or sold out almost immediately. No *It's a Wonderful Life* here: the investors have had to come in from Minneapolis, Madison, and Saint Louis. This contemporary version of redlining is a significant reason that downtown housing often cannot be built without municipal support.

What does this support look like? A great example is Lowell, Massachusetts, which is quickly transforming its downtown through a focus on new housing. I grew up not far from Lowell, and it was known as a place to avoid. Once an industrial mecca, Jack Kerouac's hometown had lost most of its vitality by the sixties, along with most of its market-rate downtown housing. As recently as 2000, the heart of the city held only about seventeen hundred housing units, of which an astounding 79 percent were subsidized and income restricted. Eleven years later, the number of units has almost doubled and, more significantly, almost 85 percent of the new housing is market rate. That means that the number of non–income-restricted homes has more than quadrupled.

According to Adam Baacke, Lowell's assistant city manager for planning and development, achieving this transformation was essentially a three-step process that could perhaps be best described as *politics*, *permitting*, and *pathfinding*.

Politics refers to changing attitudes (and people) on the city council, where most members shunned downtown housing because "only commercial development was considered good." Eventually, the city's new outlook motivated it to sell one of its underutilized parcels for the express purpose of creating artists' housing downtown.

Permitting refers to sidestepping the city's conventional zoning code, which, for example, caused this new artists' housing to require fourteen distinct variances just to get built. In its place, the city treated each new residential proposal as a "special permit," and then these permits were "given out like candy" to qualified applicants. Next, the city replaced its stringent requirements for parking with the new rule that developers needed only to identify one parking space per unit, anywhere nearby, that could be leased to their residents. Most of these were spaces in municipal garages that were busy from nine to five but empty at night.

Finally, *pathfinding* refers to setting up an extensive regime of hand-holding from city staff, to walk developers through the tricky process of winning every available federal and state subsidy, including historic preservation tax credits and community renewal block grants. Some of these awards are quite competitive, and the city went so far as to package all the required letters of support from the community. And, yes, this help even included cash, with the city finding ways to put money into some of the projects.[2]

To be accurate, Baacke cites one other essential step to the process of attracting downtown residents, what he describes as "a citywide commitment to creating an environment that people want to live in"—which I would call walkability. In a virtuous circle, more walkability begets more housing downtown, which begets more walkability. This chicken-and-egg relationship raises the question of which item to invest in first. The answer, of course, is both.

INVISIBLE AFFORDABILITY

Lowell raises an interesting point, which is that most American cities do not need more affordable housing in their downtowns. Most American cities have too much affordable housing downtown. Or, more accurately, too much of their downtown housing is affordable, since everyone but the poor was able to join the suburban exodus. The typical midsized American city center now contains a few market-rate apartment houses, a smattering of raw urban lofts occupied by people in black, one or two Corten-steel-walled fortress row houses of the type featured in *Dwell* magazine, and a ton of poor people, many of them in projects. These downtowns need more housing, but that housing should contribute to a more normal distribution of incomes downtown. This has been the effort in Lowell.

But not every city is like Lowell. A lucky few, larger cities—some of the heroes of this book—have already attracted so many well-off people into their downtowns and close-in neighborhoods that these places are in danger of becoming social monocultures. Despite their wealth, these can also be detrimental to street life, since yuppie overachievers tend to spend less time in the public sphere, and also because sidewalks, like communities, thrive on diversity: different types of people use the streets at different times of day, keeping them active around the clock.•

For these gentrified and gentrifying communities, two powerful remedies exist for increasing and maintaining affordability. One is well known and the other hardly so. They are *inclusionary zoning* and *granny flats*.

Inclusionary zoning—requiring a set percentage of all new

•Incidentally, monocultures also aren't very good for society. Jane Jacobs put it this way: "Does anyone suppose that, in real life, answers to any of the great questions that worry us today are going to come out of homogeneous settlements?" (Jacobs, *The Death and Life of Great American Cities*, 448).

housing developments to meet affordability criteria—hardly requires a mention, except to say that it works and it is always the right thing to do. Every city should have an inclusionary-zoning ordinance in place, and few currently do, because it has gotten the reputation of being a hidden tax on developers and an impediment to the free market. While these criticisms are technically true, they ignore the real experience of inclusionary-zoning programs in action, which is that they have never stifled development. In some cases, they have been shown to accelerate it.[3]

And while the libertarians may hate inclusionary zoning, sophisticated developers seem to be just fine with it.* This is probably because the affordable component can qualify a development for federal or state subsidies that make projects more profitable. Some of the biggest inclusionary-zoning programs are in Denver, San Francisco, San Diego, and Boston. The program in wealthy Montgomery County, Maryland, in force since 1974, has built more than ten thousand units of affordable housing. In today's moribund homebuilding climate, the "pro-business" lobby will no doubt redouble its efforts against inclusionary zoning, but it will do so with scant evidence and ultimately against its own best interests.

Granny flats, on the other hand, have yet to gain much traction in America's cities. Called "accessory dwelling units (ADUs)" by planners, and "backyard cottages" by clever marketers, these apartments are as intelligent as they are illegal. The few ADU ordinances that have been passed in the United States allow single-family houses to place a small apartment in their backyard—often atop a garage on a rear lane—that can be rented in the free market. They are typically opposed by neighbors who are worried about property values. An old college roommate of mine from

---

*I use the word *sophisticated* in order to rule out the National Association of Home-builders, who continue to advocate incessantly for sprawl despite the fact that it has bankrupted their membership.

Los Angeles put it succinctly: "We are afraid that nine illegals will move in."

Happily, there is no evidence that granny flats lower property values and it's easy to see why. First, they are almost invisible. Second, they provide the homeowners with an income stream that allows them to live in their own home more comfortably. Third, they are of course carefully regulated to avoid the tenement-style use contemplated by my Angeleno friend. (Indeed, the tenant is often a homeowner's parent or college-age child.) Fourth, they introduce affordability in a dispersed rather than a concentrated way, avoiding the pathologies that sometimes arise from the latter. Finally, they are inevitably well supervised by their landlords, who live just a few feet away.

And they are great for walkability, as they increase neighborhood density, putting more feet on the sidewalks, and making transit service and local shopping more viable. They are ideal in those older single-family neighborhoods that can often be found on the edges of downtown, where bungalows and larger homes line walkable streets. Indeed, that's where they can still be found in places like Charleston and West Hollywood. Granny flats are also big in Canada, where NIMBYs generally hold less influence over local planning matters. Vancouver decriminalized them in 2008 as part of the city's EcoDensity initiative, and hundreds have already been built and rented.•

Despite all this, even some of America's most progressive city councils have found it a struggle to make granny flats legal again. Seattle finally succeeded after a lengthy fight, with critics claiming that the cottages would double the city's density. Others suggested that neighbors would lose the privacy they required to "barbecue, entertain guests, or walk around naked if they're

•Incidentally, this country's densest collection of granny flats probably can be found in the new village of Rosemary Beach, Florida, which I helped DPZ design in the late 1990s. As of last count, there are 214 "carriage house" apartments there.

kinky."[4] Now about a hundred granny flats are receiving building permits in Seattle each year.[5] As of this writing, the cottages have just been legalized in Portland, Miami, Berkeley, Denver, and Burlington, Vermont.[6] If you make one of these cities home, you can build one for maybe seventy-five thousand dollars. If you live elsewhere, take heart: there are at least six working ADU ordinances that you can show to your city council.

THE REST OF THE PICTURE

This chapter about mixed use has quickly become a chapter about housing, because that is the activity most often underrepresented in American downtowns, and also because that is the activity most American downtowns have a decent shot at attracting right now. As more and more American industry is either outsourced overseas or executed by laptoppers who can live wherever they please, most city centers will struggle to maintain their current stock of dedicated work space. There will of course be exceptions, but this situation will continue for some time, until enough people have moved back downtown that the workplace follows them there, just as it followed them to the suburbs in the sixties.

For this reason, the best strategy for attracting business to your city is no longer the conventional zero-sum game of luring corporations away from other places with tax breaks, land deals, and other door prizes. Too many cities still think that economic development can occur in a vacuum of golf and giveaways, ignoring the fact that such victories are increasingly rare and don't always last. After all, the corporation that dumps Philly for Indy thanks to a 5 percent tax cut will happily run off to Cincy for 7.5—and perhaps to Tijuana soon thereafter.

Cities whose economic-development strategy is a corporate-capture strategy are typically those whose economic development director and planning director don't talk to each other. The smart cities, like Lowell, hire a director of planning and development, who is first charged with creating a city where people want to be. Rather than trying to land new office tenants in a shrinking office market, this person understands that future economic growth will take place where the creative people are, and then works to lure more residents downtown.

As Adam Baacke suggested, this strategy means building more market-rate housing while also promoting those things that residents want and need: parks and playgrounds, supermarkets and farmers' markets, cafés and restaurants—and, eventually, good schools—all embraced in a framework of top-notch walkability. Each of these items is a book in its own right, and well beyond this discussion. Suffice it to say that they are necessary, and that the first step to attracting them is to reorient economic development around creating a downtown that has them all.

STEP 3: GET THE PARKING RIGHT

What parking costs and what it costs us; Induced demand redux;
Addiction made law; The cost of required parking; Some smarter places;
The problem with cheap curbside parking; The right price; A tale of two
cities; What should we do with all this money?; A bargain at $1.2 billion

This chapter exists because of one man. He is in his mid-
seventies, green-eyed, gray-bearded, and often pictured riding
a bicycle. He holds four degrees from Yale in engineering and
economics, and teaches at UCLA, where he was chair of the
Department of Urban Planning and ran the Institute of Transportation Studies. His name is Donald Shoup and, inside an
admittedly small circle, he is a rock star. He is alternately
hailed as the "Jane Jacobs of parking policy" and the "prophet
of parking." There is even a Facebook group called "The
Shoupistas."[1]

Shoup has earned his exalted status by being perhaps
the first person to really think about how parking works in cities. This effort has led him to some conclusions that have now
been backed up with decades of evidence, and he is just beginning to get the attention he deserves. In the words of a former Ventura, California, mayor, Bill Fulton, "Don has been
saying the exact same thing for 40 years, and finally the world
is listening to him."[2] That doesn't mean that the world is yet
doing what he says, but, with a little luck, that is about to
change.

Parking covers more acres of urban America than any other
one thing[3]—just look at an aerial photo of downtown Houston—

yet, until Shoup, nobody seems to have made any effort to fig-ure it out; certainly not the planners, who happily institute and enforce outdated parking requirements nationwide like a barn-yard of headless chickens. Shoup himself notes how the "bible" of city planning, F. Stuart Chapin's *Urban Land Use Planning*, doesn't even mention parking once.* We did better than that in *Suburban Nation*, but our focus was more on the *what* than the *why*, which Shoup has refined to the level of science.

What Shoup has discovered about parking—using both an economist's cold logic and the careful, sustained observation of reality—is that every city in America handles it wrong. Rather than parking working in the service of cities, cities have been working in the service of parking, almost entirely to their detri-ment. He has also determined, and demonstrated, that this problem can be fixed fairly easily and with great rewards for all involved. And he is just beginning to see his ideas bear fruit in places like San Francisco, which we will discuss below.

WHAT PARKING COSTS AND WHAT IT COSTS US

The first step to understanding how parking works is to get a grasp of how much it costs and who pays for it. Because it is so plentiful and often free to use, it is easy to imagine that it costs very little. But this is not the case. The cheapest urban parking space in America, an 8½-by-18-foot piece of asphalt on relatively worthless land, costs about four thousand dollars to create—and not much urban land is worthless. The most expensive parking space, in an underground parking garage, can cost forty thou-

---

*Donald Shoup, *The High Cost of Free Parking*, 25. Shoup's book is 751 pages long and weighs three and a quarter pounds, but after we are done, you will want to read it. Not everything in this chapter is from that book, but so much of it comes from there that I am happy if its author gets credit for the whole chapter.

sand dollars or more to build. Parking spaces under Seattle's Pacific Place Shopping Center, built by the city, cost over sixty thousand dollars each.* In between those extremes is the standard aboveground urban parking structure, which can usually be built for between twenty and thirty thousand dollars per space.

Given the size of most parking lots, these numbers add up quickly. The twelve-hundred-space Pacific Place garage cost $73 million. Shoup calculates that "the cost of all parking spaces in the U.S. exceeds the value of all cars and may even exceed the value of all roads."[4] There are also the ongoing costs of taxes, management, and maintenance. If the journal *Parking Professional* is to be believed, more than a million Americans make their living in some aspect of the "parking profession."[5] These people have to be paid. Somewhat conservatively, and based on the study of hundreds of parking lots, Shoup estimates the monthly cost of a structured parking space to be at least $125 per month,[6] or roughly $4 per day.

This amount seems reasonable, and actually quite easy to pay for. Presuming a conservative 50 percent occupancy from nine to five, that's only a dollar per hour. So, do most parking structures cover their costs? Far from it. One study of parking garages in the Mid-Atlantic region determined that annual operating revenue per space ranged between 26 and 36 percent of annual cost.[7]

I found a similar circumstance in Lowell, where I was told that the revenue from the city's six public garages was paying all the debt service on those garages. Digging a bit deeper, I learned that five of those garages, from the eighties, had already paid off their bonds—with considerable taxpayer help. So, in

* Shoup, *The High Cost of Free Parking*, 190. Shoup notes that the world record holders are in Japan, with one underground structure in Kawasaki costing $414,000 per space. The entire garage cost over $157 million.

actuality, the revenue from all six of the city's garages was covering only the debt service on the city's one new garage.

This circumstance exists all over the United States, principally because cities and other sponsors keep parking prices artificially low. Because there are so many parking spaces, this cumulative subsidy was calculated a decade ago at between $127 billion and $374 billion a year,[8] which puts it in the range of our national defense budget. This number seems preposterous, until you consider that the typical parking space in the United States is not in a pay-to-park garage at all, but alongside a condo cluster, inside an office park, or in front of a Walmart, where admission is free.

If parking is "free" or underpriced in so much of the United States, who is actually paying for it? The answer is: we all are, whether we use it or not. Shoup puts it this way:

> Initially, the developer pays for the required parking, but soon the tenants do, and then their customers, and so on, until the price of parking has diffused everywhere in the economy. When we shop in a store, eat in a restaurant, or see a movie, we pay for parking indirectly, because its cost is included in the price of merchandise, meals, and theater tickets. We unknowingly support our cars with almost every commercial transaction we make, because a small share of the money changing hands pays for parking.[9]

The ramifications of this situation are disturbing. Nobody can opt out of paying for parking. People who walk, bike, or take transit are bankrolling those who drive. In so doing, they are making driving cheaper and thus more prevalent, which in turn undermines the quality of walking, biking, and transit.

INDUCED DEMAND REDUX

Is this beginning to sound familiar? Like roadways in general, all this free and underpriced parking contributes to a circumstance in which a massive segment of our national economy has been disconnected from the free market, such that individuals are no longer able to act rationally. Or, more accurately, in acting rationally, individuals are acting against their own self-interest.

All in all, Shoup calculates that the subsidy for employer-paid parking amounts to twenty-two cents per mile driven to work, and thus reduces the price of automotive commuting by a remarkable 71 percent. Eliminating this subsidy would have the same impact as an additional gasoline tax of between $1.27 and $3.74 a gallon.[10] That is a price hike that would change many people's driving habits.

This subsidy could perhaps be justified if it produced some greater good for society, but it only produces one benefit: cheaper parking. How does it perform in terms of other important measures? Well, it worsens air and water quality, speeds global warming, increases energy consumption, raises the cost of housing, decreases public revenue, undermines public transportation, increases traffic congestion, damages the quality of the public realm, escalates suburban sprawl, threatens historic buildings, weakens social capital, and worsens public health, to name a few things.*
And you wanted free parking why?

ADDICTION MADE LAW

But businesses should be allowed to provide parking to lure customers, you might protest. Fair enough. But in America, such parking is not just allowed; it's required. Some cities, like Monterey

---

*Shoup, 585. All these criteria except the final three are listed by Shoup.

Park, California, not only require on-site parking, but insist that it be provided to visitors free of charge.[11]

These requirements are powerfully disruptive to the way cities function. A true master of the long-form analogy, Shoup describes the situation this way:

> If cities required restaurants to offer a free dessert with each dinner, the price of every dinner would soon increase to include the cost of dessert. To ensure that restaurants didn't skimp on the size of the required desserts, cities would have to set precise "minimum calorie requirements." Some diners would pay for desserts they didn't eat, and others would eat sugary desserts they wouldn't have ordered had they paid for them separately. The consequences would undoubtedly include an epidemic of obesity, diabetes, and heart disease. A few food-conscious cities like New York and San Francisco might prohibit free desserts, but most cities would continue to require them. Many people would get angry at even the thought of paying for the desserts they had eaten free for so long.[12]

Look at any city, suburban, or rural zoning code, and you will see page after page of rules about parking. Of the six hundred or so land uses that we planners have managed to identify, each has its own minimum parking requirement.[13] Shoup documents how these requirements have often been generated from a bare minimum of data and can bear little resemblance to reality.[14] A gas station requires 1.5 spaces per nozzle. A bowling alley requires 1 space per employee, plus 5 spaces per lane. A swimming pool requires 1 space per twenty-five hundred gallons of water.* These

---

*Shoup, 80. I am particularly enamored of this requirement, which apparently supposes that a ten-foot-deep pool holds twice as many swimmers as a five-foot-deep pool, presumably stacked in two layers like a deluxe assortment of chocolates.

requirements are then passed from city to city and town to town,[15] almost always resulting in the same outcome: too much parking.

How much? In 2010, the first nationwide count determined that there are half a billion empty parking spaces in America at any given time.[16] More to our purposes, a 2002 survey of Seattle's Central Business District found that, during times of peak demand, almost four out of ten parking spaces were empty.[17] This condition of oversupply occurs most often in central cities, and is typically the result of downtowns importing zoning standards from the suburbs, where no alternatives to driving exist.

Even Washington, D.C., suffers from this phenomenon. When my wife and I built our house in the District, we were required to provide an on-site parking space, even though we didn't own a car, our property was three blocks from a subway stop, and none of our neighbors had one; ample parking was available on the street. Ironically, parking on our lot would have required removing an on-street parking space—replacing a public good with a private one—trashing a granite curb, and violating a public sidewalk with our driveway. Not owning a car, I designed a carless house, and threw our fate to the Board of Zoning Appeals. Eventually, reason prevailed, but it took nine months and a public battle that was written up in *USA Today*.[18] I think it is accurate to say that almost no other designer would have bothered. Four years later, the code has yet to be fixed.

Whenever I feel like complaining about our own Washington parking struggle, I remind myself of the story of DC USA. In the mid-2000s, construction began on what was to become the District's largest retail complex, a $145 million, 500,000-square-foot colossus anchored by Target, Best Buy, and Bed Bath & Beyond. Because the development was located at a Metro stop in the heart of Columbia Heights, with thirty-six thousand residents within a ten-minute walk,[19] the city generously modified its parking requirements. Rather than insisting on its obligatory four spaces per one thousand square feet—a truly suburban standard—the

District allowed the number to be cut in half.[20] Despite the designers' predictions that this was still way too much parking, the project went ahead with a $40 million, taxpayer-funded underground garage holding one thousand cars.

Fast-forward to 2008: DC USA has become a resounding success, having brought new life to a struggling neighborhood, thanks in part to its pedestrian-oriented design. Shops are doing even more business than expected. And the parking garage is empty—so empty that its managers routinely shut off one of its two levels completely, an unvisited $20 million underground air museum. From February through July, average peak use never rises above three hundred cars, and at no time does occupancy top 47 percent.[21]

This was an expensive lesson, a $100,000/month *I told you so* for the District and its taxpayers—now in its fifth year—as parking revenues fail to cover debt service on the garage. It was just the kick in the pants the city needed to finally rewrite its fifty-year-old regulations to eliminate parking minimums for new shops, offices, and apartments near Metro stations.[22] They have decided to leave commercial parking provision to the free market, as Donald Shoup recommends.

Even smaller suburban cities are beginning to find that their parking requirements are routinely too high. A useful experiment was conducted in progressive Palo Alto, California. Real estate developers were allowed to cheat on their parking requirements by as much as 50 percent if the land area saved was turned into a natural "landscape reserve" that could be converted to parking if the need arose. Not one such reserve has yet to make that conversion.[23]

THE COST OF REQUIRED PARKING

Even in cities with high residential densities and great transit systems, ample parking encourages driving that would not occur without it. As Shoup likes to say, "Off-street parking requirements are a fertility drug for cars."[24] We have already discussed most of driving's attendant woes, from global warming to obesity, but it would be useful here to focus briefly on some of the specific social and personal costs inflicted by the on-site parking requirement in particular.

In *Suburban Nation*, we coined the term "Pensacola Parking Syndrome" to describe the fate of so many historic cities that had eventually managed to satisfy their parking demand. They achieved this condition by replacing beautiful old buildings with ugly parking lots—in such number that nobody wanted to go downtown anymore.[25]

Certainly, the destruction of architectural masterpieces is one of the most obvious and upsetting manifestations of modern parking pressures. In Detroit, a parking garage even sits beneath the rococo vaults of the reamed-out 1926 Michigan Theatre— built, ironically, on the site where Henry Ford invented his automobile. In Buffalo, where 50 percent of the historic city center has become parking lots, one commenter wryly observed, "if our master plan is to demolish all of downtown, then we're only halfway there."[26]

These days, however, with preservationists wielding greater power, the harm perpetrated by parking demands is often more subtle, taking the form not of destruction, but of obstruction: things failing to happen. Most empty urban buildings—historic or otherwise—sit on properties of limited size, with limited opportunities for increasing their parking supply. Yet many changes in use bring with them an uptick in the parking requirement. Shoup notes how replacing a defunct furniture store with a new bicycle shop would typically require tripling the size of the parking lot.* Where are those spaces supposed to come from?

---

* Shoup, 153. Shoup also tells the story of an entrepreneur in South Berkeley who wanted to replace a failed guitar shop with a restaurant, but was defeated by a twelve-space increase in the parking requirement.

The result, of course, is that nothing gets done and old buildings stay empty. Similarly, a thriving restaurant that wants to add sidewalk dining—something every city now says it wants—can't do so without increasing its parking supply, often an impossibility.[27] The only path to providing more parking in urban areas is typically to replace surface parking lots with multistory decks, at tremendous cost. That money is increasingly difficult to come by.

This parking-induced commercial stasis is only half the story. The other half is the great burden that parking minimums place on affordability, especially for housing, and most especially in those communities that most need it. Developers in San Francisco estimate that the city's one-space-per-unit requirement adds 20 percent to the cost of affordable housing. Shoup calculates that eliminating this requirement would allow 24 percent more San Franciscans to buy homes. Even the city's chief comprehensive planner, Amit Ghosh, admits that "we're forcing people to build parking that people cannot afford."[28]

Similarly, a study in Oakland found that requiring one parking space per home "increased housing costs by 18 percent and reduced density by 30 percent."[29] Back in Palo Alto, Alma Place, a nonprofit 107-unit single-room occupancy hotel, was granted a reduced parking requirement of 0.67 spaces per unit. It was later determined that this scant requirement still increased construction costs by a whopping 38 percent.[30]

The larger question is why the future residents of Alma Place—Walk Score 95, for God's sake—should need parking at all. Does a household located three blocks from a train station in one of America's most walkable and employment-loaded communities need to own a car? Did I mention that the train station is flanked by more than three hundred commuter parking spaces that all sit empty overnight?[31]

The answer is not that future residents would come with cars, but that current residents were worried about spillover parking on their streets. Even more troubling was the city's refusal to allow the developer to charge for parking. The housing corporation was prohibited from charging a parking fee of one hundred dollars per month, which would have reduced non-drivers' rents by about 10 percent.* So, even among the city's poorest citizens, the pedestrians are subsidizing the drivers. So much for "progressive" Palo Alto.

But before we beat that city up too badly, let's turn our accusing gaze back to the Green Metropolis itself, where the New York City Housing Authority still maintains parking minimums for its publicly assisted housing stock. These minimums have caused the city to abandon plans to add much-needed street-edge buildings to several of its 1960s "tower in the park" projects. Currently, one such project, in Brownsville, Brooklyn, hangs in the balance. It would replace surface parking lots with housing, shops, schools, and gardens, but it is being held up by parking minimums—despite being directly adjacent to two stops of the 2, 3, 4, and 5 subway lines straight to Manhattan. The chairman of the housing authority admits sheepishly that "certain zoning rules may need to be reconsidered."[32]

SOME SMARTER PLACES

If you've been to the former artists' colony of Carmel-by-the-Sea, California, you've probably enjoyed strolling its picturesque main street, Ocean Avenue. This would have been due not to the smooth quality of the pavement—spike heels require a city permit, thanks to a spate of trip-and-fall lawsuits in the twenties[33]—but rather to all its other positive pedestrian qualities, including an absence of visible parking lots.

Ocean Avenue is free of off-street parking because it is

---

* Shoup, *The High Cost of Free Parking*, 150. Rent reduction was predicted at fifty dollars, with initial average rents in the five-hundred-dollar range.

illegal. Instead of providing parking lots for their customers and employees, businesses pay in-lieu fees that help finance shared city parking spaces located a few blocks away. This strategy has helped to create a unique collection of midblock courtyards and walkways, as well as ensuring a maximum amount of sidewalk activity, since nobody arrives at their destination from the rear. Carmel is now one of dozens of American cities that handle downtown parking this way, including Orlando, Chapel Hill, and Lake Forest, Illinois. In-lieu fees in these cities typically range from about seven to ten thousand dollars per space not provided, which is roughly in line with the cost of building a space in an asphalt surface lot. In Beverly Hills, where land is more valuable and most parking is structured, developers pay over $20,000 per space. In the more lefty Carmel, it's $27,520.[34]

What's most interesting—and perhaps a bit frustrating—about this solution is that it does not address the parking supply directly. Every one of these cities still has a downtown parking requirement, some quite high.[35] But instead of providing parking, businesses are only required to pay for it, which allows the parking to be located in the right place and, importantly, shared. When parking is no longer the exclusive property of an individual business, it becomes much more efficient. A space that serves an office during the day can serve a restaurant in the evening and a resident overnight. So, by simultaneously setting parking minimums and outlawing private parking lots, cities are able to indirectly reduce the amount of parking that has to be provided. Eventually, as real life determines the number of shared spaces that are actually needed, a city can adjust its in-lieu fees downward. Or it can keep them steady and pocket the difference.

For large employers, California has pioneered a second powerful strategy for managing parking, called "parking cash-out." The California Health and Safety Code requires many businesses that offer free employee parking to give their workers the option of trading that parking space for its cash equivalent. This is an ingenious law, because it is all carrot and no stick. Cities are required to reduce each business's parking requirement by the number of employees who cash out, thus placing no greater burden on the employer, while providing a great incentive for alternative transportation. On average, businesses that offered the cash-out option saw their number of driving commuters drop by 11 percent. In downtown Los Angeles, one employer saw its parking demand drop by 24 percent.[36]

These two strategies, in-lieu payments and parking cash-out, are a great start at decoupling the cost of parking from all the other activities in which it has become imbedded—that is, hidden—so that parking demand can once again behave according to the principles of the free market. This concept of decoupling makes so much sense that one would expect it to have become commonplace. Instead, it is rare, because residents of places like Palo Alto fear that costly off-street parking will cause bargain seekers to overwhelm their precious curbside parking. And they are correct in this fear, because most cities lack a comprehensive parking policy that deals with off-street and on-street parking together. Until this mandate is met, in-lieu payments and parking cash-out can serve as good transitional strategies toward a more ambitious goal, which is the elimination of off-street parking requirements entirely.

Abolishing the off-street parking requirement is one of the three cornerstones of Shoup's theory, because it would allow the market to determine how much parking is needed. He notes that "removing off-street parking requirements will not eliminate off-street parking, but will instead stimulate an active commercial market for it."[37] This would bring U.S. policy more in line with that of Western Europe. Shoup describes the situation as follows:

> American cities put a floor under the parking supply to satisfy the peak demand for free parking, and then cap development density to limit vehicle trips. European cities,

in contrast, often cap the number of parking spaces to avoid congesting the roads and combine this strategy with a floor on allowed development density to encourage walking, cycling, and public transport. That is, Americans require parking and limit density, while Europeans require density and limit parking.[38]

Such a concept seems unlikely to win many followers on this side of the pond, but it is exactly what the free market creates all by itself in America's most walkable communities. In Manhattan, developers do not feel any need to provide parking for their apartments, stores, and offices, so the outcome is more Düsseldorf than Dallas. That outcome would be unimaginable with a parking requirement in place. Eliminating parking minimums simply allows developers to give their customers what they want. But, as we will discuss ahead, it is only politically viable when combined with a safety net that protects current residents' status quo.

THE PROBLEM WITH CHEAP CURBSIDE PARKING

Cheap and plentiful off-street parking is only half the problem. The other half is what happens on the streets, and here even New York City gets it dead wrong. Because if curbside parking is not priced properly, the resulting perversity of the overall parking regime creates vast inefficiencies that are costly for drivers and nondrivers alike.

Let's take Manhattan. Off-street parking is roughly $15 for the first hour in most locations, while curbside parking costs just $3. Is it any wonder that the city's streets are choked with double-parked cars and people hunting for parking? Underpriced curb parking is no fairer than giving random discounts on other municipal services like water or electricity based upon who circles the block the longest, and just as counterproductive.

A study of six different urban sites found that roughly a third of all traffic congestion was made up of people trying to find a parking spot. In one Los Angeles neighborhood, Westwood Village, it was twice that amount—and between 1:00 and 2:00 p.m., an astounding 96 percent of cars on the road were circling for parking.[39]

Some version of this condition exists in most American cities. In downtown Chicago, curbside parking costs one-thirteenth as much as off-street parking.[40] The outcome of this market inefficiency is not just congestion and all its attendant woes—pollution, time wasted, slow emergency response—but also reduced revenue to area businesses. This counterintuitive fact can be surprising to the businesses themselves, who routinely fight bitterly against any effort to raise meter rates. These merchants forget the origin of the parking meter, in Oklahoma City, as a tool to improve business revenue. Shoup quotes an *American City* reporter from 1937:

> Merchants and shoppers are both in favor of them. When one side of the street has them, merchants on the other side demand them. When one town has them, the merchants of nearby towns demand them, showing that they draw out-of-town shoppers rather than driving them away.[41]

Why were these first meters so popular? Because they reduced overcrowding and hassle, but also because they increased turnover, ensuring more customers per hour. The result was more sales and dramatically higher downtown property values.[42] The same calculus holds true today, as underpriced curbside parking scares away potential customers who believe that there is no place to park, even as nearby parking lots sit half empty. As Shoup notes, "If it takes only five minutes to drive somewhere else, why spend fifteen cruising for parking?"[43]

I encountered just this condition in Lowell, where on-street parking became free at 6:00 p.m., while parking structures still charged admission. The result was that residents coming home from work would rush into the parking spaces on restaurant row, leaving no room for the dinner crowd.

THE RIGHT PRICE

Which leads us to Shoup's second key recommendation, that on-street parking be priced at a level that results in an 85 percent occupancy rate at all times.[44] This number may seem a bit low, but it corresponds with roughly one empty space per block face, just the right amount to ensure Daddy Warbucks a spot near the furrier. Because it is precisely the shoppers with dollars to spare who have the most to offer your Main Street merchants.

In its most sophisticated form, this approach means true variable congestion pricing, which we will discuss in a minute. But for many cities, a perfectly adequate outcome can be achieved simply by raising meter rates a notch, especially if they are currently set at zero. This was the case in both Aspen in the nineties and, more recently, Ventura, California.

Shoup reports on how, by 1990, Aspen's downtown merchants were suffering from overcrowded curbside parking. The city responded by building an expensive parking garage, but that structure sat half empty as the parking crush continued. Finally, the city proposed charging one dollar per hour on-street, and all hell broke loose.[45]

Opponents, mostly local employees, mounted a noisy "Honk if You Hate Paid Parking" campaign. This was quickly met by a rogue "Honk if You Love Dirty Air" campaign, in reference to all the cruising and double parking that had become the norm. Paid parking eventually prevailed and the new rates took effect in 1995. Almost immediately, the opponents realized that they had been wrong. Now the municipal parking structure is well used, the on-street parking and cruising are under control, the businesses are thriving, and the city receives over half a million dollars a year in new parking revenue, most of it from tourists.[46]

In Ventura, Shoupista Mayor Bill Fulton introduced on-street parking rates of one dollar per hour, aiming toward 85 percent occupancy.[47] In addition to being mayor, Fulton is a city planner, and his blog is worth following. On the momentous morning of September 14, 2010, he posted that "only 30 minutes after we instituted the parking management program, it is working." The employee vehicles that had previously crowded the curbs were happily stowed away in nearby lots.[48] Fulton went on to add:

> Some shoppers have complained over the past few months that parking at the mall is free, so why should they pay to park downtown? The answer . . . is that you're paying for access to a few hundred premium spaces. . . . After all, all the mall parking spaces are far away from the stores— farther than even the most remote free lot downtown. If it was possible to drive right inside the mall and park in front of your favorite store, don't you think the mall would charge for that space? And don't you think some people who think it's worth it would pay the price?[49]

The city plans to adjust rates as necessary: if parking use falls below 80 percent, the prices will be lowered until occupancy hits the exalted 85.[50] It's important to stress that the math works both ways. In Davenport, Iowa, the combination of free parking lots and curbside meters caused a ghost-town effect: nobody parked at the curb, the place felt dead, and drivers sped recklessly along empty streets. Our planning team convinced the city to reprice the on-street parking at zero, a regime that will remain in effect until scarcity sets in. That change immediately improved activity downtown. It also made us some friends, but perhaps for the wrong reasons. Unfortunately, we were unable to stop the mayor from decapitating a meter with the Jaws of Life, which may have sent the misleading message of *free parking forever.*

Neither Aspen, Ventura, nor Davenport has been fully studied, but the great investigation on right-priced curb parking occurred in central London in 1965. It was found that a fourfold increase in parking price shortened the average park-and-visit time by 66 percent, vastly increasing turnover for merchants. The average time spent searching for parking dropped from 6.1 minutes per trip to a mere 62 seconds.[51]

For a twenty-first-century version, we turn to San Francisco, which, thanks to Shoup, has recently introduced a true congestion-pricing regime. For seven thousand spaces in eight key neighborhoods—25 percent of the city's metered parking—prices are being adjusted block by block and hour by hour to achieve a goal of 80 percent maximum occupancy.* This means rates ranging from as little as twenty-five cents to as much as six dollars per hour. The system also includes the fourteen city-owned garages in the pilot area, as it must, since their pricing needs to be coordinated if drivers are to make wise choices. As you might expect, this being San Francisco, the project is fully supported by online real-time data, including a smartphone app that tells you how many spaces are available on any given street, and how much they cost.[52] The sfpark.org website is really quite a marvel.

Such a parking system, which includes thousands of newly embedded car sensors, does not come cheap. It was supported largely by a $20 million U.S. Department of Transportation grant[53]—one wonders what it would have cost without federal funding—and we will soon know how well it works. If it performs anywhere near as well as expected, it will earn back its huge

---

* The current SFPark on-street pricing policy (as of April 11, 2011) causes prices to rise or fall whenever occupancy rises above 80 percent or below 60 percent. Why these numbers are below Shoup's 85 percent is not explained.

price tag in short order, through increased meter receipts. This income is not the goal of the exercise, but it's nice to know it's there. Indeed, it is only because these systems pay for themselves that we can expect them to catch on.

If there are no surprises in San Francisco, full-fledged congestion-priced parking is something that many cities will want to try. But, given its novelty and significant start-up cost, smaller cities may elect not to spend millions chasing perfection, when *good enough* is close at hand. A simple repricing of downtown spaces and parking lots may solve 90 percent of most cities' parking problems. That said, since the start-up costs are easily bondable and the potential income so great, opting out of a full-fledged congestion-pricing regime could turn out to be a pound-foolish choice.

A TALE OF TWO CITIES

As if we weren't convinced, Shoup has a final morality lesson to teach, and that is the story of the two Southern California shopping districts of Old Pasadena and Westwood Village. In the late eighties, these two downtowns were fairly similar. They were roughly the same size, both were in historic sections of larger cities (Pasadena and Los Angeles), and both had the standard collection of review boards and business-improvement districts. Both had limited on-street parking and ample off-street parking. Both were challenged economically, but by no means in trouble. If anything, Westwood Village was in better shape, as it was surrounded by both a higher density of housing and a wealthier customer base. In fact, Shoup describes how residents of Pasadena used to drive twenty minutes in order to shop in Westwood Village.[54]

Then, in the early nineties, the two districts went in dramatically different directions. While both were struggling with overcrowded on-street parking, only Old Pasadena raised its parking rates, installing 690 new meters. While both maintained a conventional off-street parking requirement, only Old Pasadena allowed in-lieu fees, so that developers could pay cash in support of municipal lots rather than build additional parking themselves.[55]

What happened over the next decade was as shocking in reality as it was predictable in theory. Old Pasadena staged a brilliant revival, while Westwood Village entered a steady economic decline that continues to this day. Now residents of Westwood drive to Old Pasadena to shop. Westwood's curbs are crumbling, while the sidewalks of Old Pasadena boast new tree grates, fancy lighting, and street furniture. Not only does each parking meter in Pasadena generate an average of $1,712 in annual revenue for the city, but sales tax receipts are way up. Indeed, the city's sales-tax revenue tripled in the first six years after the meters were installed.[56]

While it is always easy to park in Old Pasadena, the average shopper in Westwood Village circles for 8.3 minutes before either finding a spot or giving up. Shoup delights in telling us how Westwood cruisers cumulatively log a total of 426 vehicle hours per day, covering more distance than a trip across the United States. Over a year, this adds up to thirty-eight trips around the globe.[57]

In the interest of telling the whole story, it is worth spending another minute describing exactly how boneheaded Westwood Village was. Faced with the perception that a parking shortage was to blame for their economic woes, community leaders responded by cutting the price of on-street parking in half. ("Adam Smith, please call your office!") Meanwhile, the city continued to enforce its draconian off-street "replacement parking" requirement, which effectively made redevelopment impossible. Even though the village's vast supply of asphalt parking lots typically held 1,250 unused spaces at peak hour, any developers who wanted to build on these lots were required to both meet their parking quota and replace half of the removed spaces.[58] This rule, still in force, effectively amounts to a requirement for expensive parking decks where there is already an oversupply of off-street parking.

Westwood's ineptitude calls attention to the fact that parking decisions are never made in a vacuum and political pressures from an uninformed public can often sway the outcome. Indeed, in Old Pasadena, things almost went the other way. When the city first proposed installing meters, it was fought vehemently by downtown merchants, who were convinced that they would lose all their business to the mall. This battle dragged on for two years before a compromise was reached.[59] Interestingly, it was this compromise that gave the new parking regime what may be its most powerful feature.

WHAT SHOULD WE DO WITH ALL THIS MONEY?

The final bone that the city threw to its reluctant merchants was this: all the net revenue from the parking meters would pay for physical improvements and new public services in Old Pasadena. And why not? This was free money, over a million dollars a year, and it was easy to identify where it was coming from. It wasn't like anybody else deserved it.

This creative leap leads us to Shoup's third cornerstone, the institution of "parking benefit districts" that put meter revenues to work locally.[60] In addition to improving sidewalks, trees, lighting, and street furniture, these districts can bury overhead wires, renovate storefronts, hire public service officers, and of course keep everything spic-and-span. They can also construct the public parking lots a block away that serve employees and shopper overflow. In Pasadena, meter revenues even paid for converting a collection of run-down rear alleys into an intricate network of pedestrian spaces.[61]

Since most of the parkers are from out of town and pricing is based on what they are willing to pay, there are few losers in this bargain, as long as employees can find parking within a reasonable walking distance. As Shoup puts it, "If nonresidents pay for curb parking, and the city spends its money to benefit the residents, charging for curb parking can become a popular policy rather than the political third rail it often is today."[62]

This is true enough for retail areas, but what about principally residential streets that have become overcrowded? What about the residents of Palo Alto who, fearing competition for on-street spaces, fought against reduced off-street parking requirements? The third rail that threatens to kill Shoup's two main proposals is not about where the money goes, but about the fact that it is just so hard to take away anybody's free anything. This is the reason that on-street parking remains free of charge in much of New York City, of all places.

Shoup is not ignorant of this fact, quoting George Costanza's famous rant: "My father didn't pay for parking, my mother, my brother, nobody. It's like going to a prostitute. Why should I pay when, if I apply myself, maybe I can get it for free."[63] It is one thing to put parking meters in front of a bunch of stores and quite another to put them on a street of houses. That is why, where theory meets reality, we may need to bend the rules a little, by using residential parking permits. These, too, can be priced at market value for maximum efficiency, but they must sometimes be deployed at a low cost to win over residents who stand in the way of a larger public benefit, like keeping affordable housing affordable. And, you didn't hear it from me, but once residents get used to the idea of paying for a coveted parking pass—even just a "processing fee" of twenty bucks a year—you would be surprised how quickly they are willing to pay considerably more.

Not having been involved in the Palo Alto fiasco, I am reluctant to suggest that there was an easy solution, but it is likely that a properly managed parking pass proposal might have turned the tide. What was certainly missing, among all the parking policy, was a parking plan, and such a comprehensive plan is ultimately what every "over-parked" place in America needs. This plan must include on-street pricing, off-street pricing, in-lieu payments supporting a collective supply, parking benefit districts, and residential permits where needed. Above all, it must be managed comprehensively with an eye toward community success, not just meter revenue. Parking is a public good, and it must be managed for the public good. Such management takes full advantage of the free market but—this is important—it is not the free market.[64] The single largest land use in every American city is very much that city's business.

A BARGAIN AT $1.2 BILLION

So, if parking is a public good, why did Mayor Richard M. Daley sell it off? This is a question many of us asked when the otherwise heroic Daley presided over the lease of Chicago's thirty-six thousand meters to Morgan Stanley for the next seventy-five years. The answer probably lies in the date—December 2008, the depths of the city's financial crisis—and the price tag—$1,200,000,000.[65]

This $1.2 billion tells us a number of things. One of them is that $20 million for a congestion-pricing regime in San Francisco is chump change. Another is that there is obviously a lot of money in privately managed parking, and, that as Chicago goes, so may go the nation. As of this writing, New Haven is one of several cash-strapped cities working toward a deal. Many have already privatized their public garages.

Unsurprisingly, Chicago's sale brought with it a dramatic hike in on-street parking rates. Neighborhood spots previously available at 25 cents an hour are on their way up to $2.00. Prices inside the Loop, already high, will more than double, to $6.50 an hour.[66]

In the short term, this strategy could perhaps be described as the wrong path to the right result. Greedy investors are pulling off what the city couldn't do, which is to bring the price of curbside parking in line with its value. As demand falls closer to supply, Shoup's 85 percent ideal may be achieved. But who's to say it will stop there? As any purveyor of private parking lots will tell you, an 85 percent–occupied lot at ten dollars a pop is less profitable than a half-empty lot at twenty dollars—and few parking-lot owners have a citywide monopoly. Morgan Stanley maximizing its return on the street does not necessarily bear any relationship to the city getting the most out of its parking in terms of all the other things that parking affects, including drivers' speed, retail profitability, and property values.

That's the scary part. The more practical frustration brought on by the Chicago sale concerns our larger discussion about neighborhood parking as a comprehensive system. Communities can only be their best if on-street parking, off-street parking, parking permits, and parking regulations are all managed collectively. In the past, this has hardly ever happened, but things are beginning to change. Places like Old Pasadena are showing us that well-managed parking is both possible and profitable. The Shoupistas are ready for their day in the sun. It would be a pity if, on the cusp of this parking revolution, cities were to sell away to the highest bidder their ability to make use of this powerful tool.

STEP 4: LET TRANSIT WORK

Where America sits; It's the neighborhoods, stupid; Don't mess with Dallas; The other kind of transit; What streetcars do; Transit for drivers; Trains versus buses; Zip it if you can

If I had to pick one word that best describes why good public transportation is a vital part of walkable cities, it would be this: dating. When I lived in Miami in my thirties, it would have been possible for me to live, work, and play all in the same neighborhood. That neighborhood could have been South Beach, Coconut Grove, downtown Coral Gables, or a few other walkable places. But I was single and looking to meet someone, and I wasn't willing to limit the gene pool to a neighborhood the size of a small town when an entire city was theoretically at my disposal. Given the sorry state of public transit in Miami, this meant buying a car.

I wasn't the only one. Put in more universal terms, it could be said that people who live in a city want to have access to everything that city has to offer. If the vast majority of those things cannot be reached conveniently via transit, then people of means buy cars and you end up with a driving city. As the city grows, it grows around the car. Its neighborhood structure dissolves and its streets widen. Walking becomes less useful or pleasant and, soon, less likely or even imaginable.

This relationship between transit and walking is borne out by the data, which clearly show that American cities with larger numbers of rail and bus commuters also have more pedestrian commuters. When more than a quarter of workers take transit, more than 10 percent go on foot. When fewer than 5 percent take transit, fewer than 3 percent go on foot.[1] It isn't just that transit users walk more, but that *non*transit users also walk more in cities that are shaped around transit. For the most part, cities support either driving or everything else.

Most American cities are driving cities and will remain so for years to come. For these cities, transit can still play an important role, by enhancing the walkability of the few walkable places and by connecting these places—more on that below. In contrast, a number of American cities, like Boston, Chicago, and San Francisco, are resolutely car-optional, and more than a few others may be on the verge of becoming so. Baltimore, Minneapolis, Denver, Seattle . . . as these cities and others invest in well-planned transit, and as younger populations make a conscious effort to drive less, it is possible to imagine a future of more comprehensive transit-based walkability.

As vastly different as these types of cities are, they all share one thing, which is that somebody in them is probably laboring feverishly to dramatically transform their transit system. From the Coalition for Alternative Transportation in Bethlehem, Pennsylvania, whose leaders steadfastly refuse to drive, to John Schneider of Protransit, who is single-handedly bringing streetcars to Cincinnati, someone out there is hunting down federal and state dollars, leading fact-finding junkets, and otherwise fighting the good fight for mass transit. And half of these people are wasting their time, because their efforts are not sufficiently informed by the relationship between transit and walking.

With rare exceptions, every transit trip begins and ends with a walk. As a result, while walkability benefits from good transit, good transit relies absolutely on walkability.

WHERE AMERICA SITS

Currently, only 1.5 percent of all trips in the United States are made on public transportation.[2] In our star cities of Washington, Chicago, and San Francisco, that number is closer to 5 percent, and the New York region, unsurprisingly, tops the list at 9 percent. But what happens when you cross the border? Toronto, with a residential density roughly a third of New York's, has a 14 percent transit share. Across the Atlantic, Barcelona and Rome hit 35 percent. Tokyo tops 60 and Hong Kong, the global leader, has reached 73 percent.[3]

The American numbers are misleading, however, as they are measured over entire metropolitan areas, and nobody in the world can match America's sprawl. Zoom in to the central cities themselves, and you find a more encouraging picture. Roughly a third of Washingtonians and San Franciscans take transit to work, and the majority of New Yorkers do. Perennial sprawl stars like Jacksonville and Nashville, on the other hand, hover below 2 percent, no matter how you measure them.[4]

These numbers are principally the result of how each city has chosen to grow, or not grow, around the automobile. European and East Asian countries, lacking America's wealth and oil reserves, chose to maintain and expand existing rail infrastructure throughout the twentieth century, while America threw most of its trains away. In 1902, every U.S. city with a population of ten thousand or more had its own streetcar system.[5] At mid-century, Los Angeles was served by more than a thousand electric trolleys a day.[6] These were torn out in a vast criminal conspiracy that is as well documented* as it was inevitable. It's

*This conspiracy is best summarized in Terry Tamminen's *Lives per Gallon*. As related by Tamminen, GM's Alfred Sloan, Jr., faced in 1922 with record losses, teamed up with Standard Oil, Phillips Petroleum, Firestone Tire and Rubber, and Mack Truck to create a shell company, National City Lines, "to quietly buy up the nation's mass-transit agencies and scrap the electric trains they operated. National City Lines could then replace easy to get mad at General Motors and forget that, at the time, most cities and citizens delighted over the change from old-fashioned streetcars to streamlined buses. The real transition, of course, was from dependence on a public system to liberation via the private automobile, albeit subsidized formidably with public dollars. We trashed our trains because we wanted to and nobody said we couldn't. As David Owen comments, "There was no public force in the United States, in those days, that could have held back the death of the streetcar, even if anyone had had the will to try."[7]

Now that we have begun to understand the true costs of that choice—including watching our automotive liberation obliterated by congestion—most Americans are ready for something different. According to America's Finest News Source, *The Onion*, "98 percent of U.S. commuters favor public transportation for others." This fictional article described a campaign mounted by the American Public Transportation Association—slogan: "Take the Bus . . . I'll Be Glad You Did"—that was remarkably insightful in its recognition of the impacts of one person's transit on another's traffic, known as the "multiplier effect." In San Francisco, for example, every passenger mile traveled by rail replaces nine miles traveled by car.[8] I can also recommend *The Onion's* video report: "Tired of traffic? A new DOT report urges drivers 'honk.'"

More seriously, a national poll funded by Transportation for America found that the average respondent would allocate 41 percent of transportation funding for public transit versus 37 percent for roads. In another poll, the devoutly nonideological Consumer Preference Survey, respondents favored public trans-

---

the trains with buses made and fueled by the conspirators. In the process, it could reduce mass-transit service and promote automobile sales as a more convenient option to millions of consumers." Also, although "the conspiracy was proven in court . . . the corporations involved were fined only $5,000 and the executives fined just $1 apiece because the judge determined that there wasn't much anyone could do about the lost mass transit" (110–11).

portation over road building as a solution to congestion by almost three to one.* The actual funding allocation currently favors roads four to one over transit,[9] so it would seem that a major correction is in order.

If only our governments were as responsive to public opinion as they seem to be in Western Australia. Emboldened by a poll that showed strong support for transferring road funds to nonautomotive transportation, the state government reversed a five-to-one roads-to-transit spending ratio to one to five. This change paid for a new rail system that has increased patronage since the early nineties from 7 million to an astounding 50 million riders per year.[10] Since the shift, a pro-rail platform has led to victory in four state elections.

When American governments do give the people a choice, they tend to invest in transit. Since 2000, over 70 percent of public transportation ballot measures have passed, creating more than $100 billion in transit funding.[11] According to the National Association of Realtors, "Light rail is popular in the communities that have it and voters have shown a remarkable willingness to raise their taxes to pay for it."[12]

Perhaps the voters understand instinctively what the data are now telling us, which is that the typical household savings accrued from good public transit service clearly outpaces the cost of that service. In his study "Raise My Taxes, Please!" Todd Litman of the Victoria Transport Policy Institute compared the fifty largest U.S. cities, of which seven were deemed to have "high-quality" transit service and forty-three were found wanting. He determined that each resident of the seven high-quality cities paid roughly $370 more per year for public transportation than a resident of the other forty-three, but saved $1,040 in vehicle, parking, and road costs. These costs were measured in terms

---

* Thomas Gotschi and Kevin Mills, "Active Transportation for America," 18. Incidentally, respondents also recommended allocating 22 percent for biking and walking versus the 1 percent currently allocated.

of actual dollars spent on goods, services, and taxes, and ignored all the additional indirect savings surrounding congestion, safety, pollution, and health.[13]

The lesson from these data seems clear: big investments in comprehensive citywide transit systems pay off in spades. But it's not that simple, because the study compared cities that were different in many respects beyond transit. Its conclusions imply that building a new transit system can be expected to transform all these other factors as well. But adding trains to Miami does not make it Minneapolis.

IT'S THE NEIGHBORHOODS, STUPID

What are these other factors? Principally, they are *local density* and *neighborhood structure*. I say *local density*, because city-wide density can be misleading when a city includes its suburbs or large areas of parkland; what matters is how many people live near the transit line. The transit discussion has of course included density since it began, but, until recently, it has been largely silent on neighborhood structure. This has been a huge mistake.

Neighborhood structure refers to the presence or absence of real neighborhoods, which are technically defined as being com-pact, diverse, and walkable. A true neighborhood has a center and an edge, and contains a wide variety of activities in close proximity within an armature of pedestrian-friendly streets and public spaces. A traditional city is composed principally of these neighborhoods, interspersed periodically with districts like uni-versities and airports, and corridors like rivers and railways. If you live in an older city, you can probably identify its neighbor-hoods, like New York's West Village, Tribeca, and SoHo.*

---

*This paragraph and the next restate one of the principal arguments to be found in Andres Duany, Elizabeth Plater-Zyberk, and Jeff Speck's *Suburban Nation*, where the discussion is made in much greater detail.

Compact, diverse, walkable neighborhoods were the basic building blocks of cities from the first nonnomadic settlements over ten thousand years ago until the height of the auto age. What took shape around the measure of the human stride flourished with the advent of rail transport, since the distance between rail stops reinforced the nodal structure of the neighborhood pattern. Only the hegemony of the automobile, with its unprecedented capacity to equalize the entire landscape, allowed the abandonment of the neighborhood in favor of sprawl, which is defined as being vast, homogeneous, and unwalkable. And since it is organized around the automobile, sprawl has no use for transit. As the administrator of any suburban transit agency will tell you, running buses in sprawl is a lose-lose scenario, in which heavy subsidy yields inadequate service.

Even in areas of high density, public transportation cannot thrive in the absence of a neighborhood structure, since it is the nodal and pedestrian-friendly nature of neighborhoods that allows riders to walk to the transit stop. For this reason, the cities that are best poised to put new transit systems to good use are those that grew up around trains in the first place.

This is essentially what happened in northern Virginia, where Metro's western Orange Line extension took the new subway through an area that had originally developed around streetcars. By any measure, that investment has paid off. Indeed, over the last decade, a full 70 percent of the population growth in Arlington County occurred in less than 6 percent of the county's land area, that being the census blocks in closest proximity to the five Orange Line Metro stops. Now 40 percent of the residents in these census blocks use transit to get to work.[14]

DON'T MESS WITH DALLAS

Based on the above logic, many of the low-quality-transit cities studied in Litman's report are perfectly poised to waste transit dollars. Dallas presents an instructive example. In 1983, residents of fifteen Dallas-area cities voted to levy a 1 percent sales tax to create what has become the largest light-rail system in the United States. The multibillion-dollar system currently includes 72 miles of track, on its way to 91 miles and 63 stations by 2013.[15] Service began in 1996 with an 11-mile stretch linking the downtown to its close-in neighborhoods. Within four years, public transit ridership, formerly all on buses, had surprisingly *dropped* 8 percent below 1990 levels.[16]

Through the 2000s, the Dallas Area Rapid Transit (DART) system has continued to grow, and transit ridership has continued to drop.[17] A few billion dollars later, despite escalating gasoline costs, a greater percentage of Dallas residents are driving to work than at any time in the past quarter century.

That is not to say that DART has not produced benefits. According to a 2007 report from the University of North Texas, over $4 billion in new development has sprung up around DART stations. While this growth is currently stalled with the economy, we can expect it to continue. Additionally, the UNT study found that homes near rail stations had appreciated almost 40 percent more than homes elsewhere in the metropolitan region.[18] These figures are impressive, but they don't begin to address the original motivation for the rail system, which was to reduce highway congestion. Nor do they suggest that increased economic development will eventually pay for the system.

Were there other benefits? It is very possible that much of the new growth around DART stations would have happened elsewhere without it, which throws into question the system's economic impact. However, it is likely that this development would have occurred at lower densities, and probably at greater distance from downtown. Some Texas scrubland was saved, and some gasoline, too. But there is no getting around the fact that all this new transit-oriented development has not increased the percentage of people taking transit. Even the biggest transit fan—me, perhaps?—would have a hard time considering the DART system anything but a failure.

Which raises the question: What is Dallas doing wrong? For an answer, we turn to Yonah Freemark, the sagacious blogger behind *The Transport Politic* and probably the best-informed source on transit today. His answer, paraphrased, is "just about everything," which includes: lacking sufficient residential densities; encouraging ample parking downtown; placing the rail alignments in the least costly rights-of-way rather than in the busiest areas; locating stations next to highways and with huge parking garages; reducing frequencies to afford farther-flung service; and, finally, forgetting about neighborhoods. He suggests: "If people are going to be living in apartments anyway, have them do so in mixed-use, walkable neighborhoods within easy distance of light rail stops."[19]

All these mistakes matter—some will be addressed in detail below—but, with his final point, Freemark is nibbling around the edges of the biggest problem of all. The simple fact is that Dallas and its suburbs are almost completely lacking in neighborhood structure. As a result, you get off the train, and . . . ? The likelihood that you can then walk to any destination of utility is preposterously slim. This might be expected in the system's more exurban locations, where a park-and-ride commute is the norm. But park-and-ride only works—when it does work*—if you don't need a car at both ends. Downtown, only a few of the system's

---

*Park-and-ride thrives only in cities where driving downtown is prohibitively expensive in terms of money or time, since people who begin their commutes in a car are loath to make the dreaded *intermodal shift* unless punishment awaits (Duany, Plater-Zyberk, and Speck, *Suburban Nation*, 138–39).

stations could be said to provide anything resembling a quality pedestrian experience, and that experience doesn't last long, because very little of downtown Dallas is truly walkable. Simply too much of it consists of over-wide streets carrying high-speed traffic along treeless sidewalks flanked by blank walls and parking lots. Like so many American downtowns, Dallas's passes the Litman test of having been designed before the auto age, but it has been so transformed around the demands of the automobile that pedestrians appear to be more of a parasitic species, an appendage to the dominant creatures they inhabit.

Without much walkability on either end of the line, DART can hardly be expected to have changed people's driving habits. But, as astute readers of Step 1 have perhaps already reasoned, nothing was going to reduce the amount of driving in Dallas. Not a transit system, not walkability, not neighborhoods: Texas drivers will continue to fill the roads they have, and if America's largest light-rail system takes sixty thousand drivers off the highway—the current total—sixty thousand more will take their place. Because in Dallas, where parking is as ubiquitous as it is cheap,* the only significant constraint to driving is the very congestion that DART hopes to relieve.

This is the part of the story that the train boosters don't want you to hear: investments in transit may be investments in mobility or investments in real estate, but they are not investments in reduced traffic.* The only way to reduce traffic is to reduce roads or to increase the cost of using them, and that is a bitter pill that few pro-transit cities are ready to swallow. Civic leaders insist that driving remain as cheap and convenient as ever and new systems

---

*No quick Shoupista pricing fix here: Dallas is so overpaved that its super-cheap parking—typically a dollar per hour—is actually the free-market rate.

*This conclusion was supported by the study "The Fundamental Law of Road Congestion: Evidence from U.S. Cities," published by Gilles Duranton and Matthew Turner at the University of Toronto, which finds that "extensions to public transit are not appropriate policies with which to combat traffic congestion" (34).

like DART go hungry for riders. Why take the train when you can drive there just as quickly and park for a dollar an hour?

So how can Dallas make good on its billions of dollars in transit investment? There is a short answer and a long answer. The short answer is to congestion price the freeways for maximum efficiency—making the most of current road investment—and use the bounteous revenue to buy down transit fares to zero while shortening wait times. That will never happen, so let's look at the long answer.

We have already discussed how, to benefit from the presence of transit, a metropolis has to take shape around that transit. It is not too late for this to happen in Dallas. The city and its surrounding municipalities must make a commitment to focus development more assiduously at DART stations, including making plans for walkable neighborhoods around every one.[*] They must focus especially on downtown stations, creating truly pedestrian-friendly precincts with high housing densities within them. They must eliminate the on-site parking requirement near all stations, and prohibit new parking lots near stations downtown. Then they must wait . . . for gasoline to hit ten dollars per gallon.

As we have already seen in New York, oil prices can accomplish in short order what defeated congestion-pricing schemes fail to do. At some point, sooner or later, it will become much more expensive to drive around every American city, especially those like Dallas. When this happens, the cities that remain competitive will be the ones with comprehensive transit networks surrounded by high-density neighborhoods. Suddenly, a 1 percent sales tax does not seem like such a high price to pay. But without the neighborhoods—as yet lacking in Dallas—there is

[*] Yonah Freemark, "An Extensive New Addition to Dallas's Light Rail Makes It America's Longest." While some of the new station-area developments contain high density, not one of them has taken the form of a walkable neighborhood. Most are the conventional edge-city conglomerations of towers and parking lots, with nary an intimate street in sight.

no future scenario in which the city's transit investment makes sense.

THE OTHER KIND OF TRANSIT

Only big, fast transit systems have the potential to fundamentally transform cities. But that does not mean that smaller systems can't be worthwhile. When effective, these systems take one of two forms: either nodal, to connect several walkable districts together, or linear, to enhance and extend a walkable corridor.

The former, such as the gondola connecting the town of Telluride, Colorado, with Telluride Mountain Village, can be powerfully effective at both reducing car trips and improving walkability. "What, a gondola??" you ask. Yes, a gondola that carries more than 2 million riders a year[20]—roughly 10 percent of the number served by the entire Dallas system—at one-fifth the cost per passenger of local bus service. Many of these riders are tourists in jaunty moon-boots, but a significant number are low-wage workers. Small nodal systems like these are perhaps the easiest to make work: all they need is a great interface with urbanism at each stop, frequent headways, and an expedited path. They are also useful for surmounting geographical obstacles, such as Pittsburgh's famous Duquesne and Monongahela inclines, the latter of which does a pretty good job of connecting urbanism to urbanism. These systems need not be unusual machines; sometimes they are just the shuttle bus that connects a university to its downtown.

Far more common are linear corridor systems, also known as streetcars, trolleys, or trams. These distinguish themselves from conventional light-rail systems by their slower speed and frequent stops; they are not rapid transit, but "pedestrian accelerators," in the words of Portland's Charlie Hales, who helped create that city's modern streetcar. If done properly, they are also "place makers," which is another way of saying "land-appreciation tools." Hales reminds us that most old U.S. streetcar lines were short-term value-creation strategies by real estate developers with property to sell.[21] The same economics still hold sway and need to be pondered deeply by cities considering new streetcar lines.

Which, these days, seems to be everybody. I don't think I've worked for a city in the past few years which was not conducting some sort of streetcar study. These studies generally come out positive—for the same reason that roadway expansion studies by road builders generally come out positive—and they need to be supplemented, or supplanted, by a simple question: "Why do you want one?"

On the rare occasion that this question is asked, typical answers include "We want to increase walking"; "We want to enliven Main Street"; "We want to get people out of their cars"; and, my favorite, "We want to be like Portland." These are all wrong answers and here's why: Charlie Hales is careful to call streetcars pedestrian accelerators and not pedestrian creators, because they do not have any record of filling empty sidewalks. If anything, it's the other way around: it is the presence of heavy pedestrian activity that indicates a potential for streetcar success. In places like Memphis, Tampa, and Little Rock, streetcars put in place between 1993 and 2004 have done little to add pedestrian life to the sleepy Main Streets they inhabit, and their ridership is paltry at best. Memphis, the star of the bunch, attracts only 343 daily boardings per mile, which is one-eighth of what Portland logs and one-twentieth of Boston's Green Line.[22]

None of these small systems—what ArtPlace CEO Carol Coletta calls "toy transit"—connect to a larger rail network, so they don't offer the regional mobility that allows people to leave the car at home. Portland's streetcar line is roughly half the length of Memphis's seven-mile system, but it connects to fifty-three miles of MAX light rail. And, importantly, Portland's system was instituted hand in hand with a commitment to "a host of other strategies and policies, including higher density, neighborhood-based urban design, elimination of minimum parking require-ments, and basically the whole list of things that add up to walkability," says Hales. "You can't just drop in a streetcar."[*]

WHAT STREETCARS DO

So why should a city want a streetcar? Successes like Portland teach us that streetcars make the most sense when a large area of vacant or underutilized land sits just beyond walking distance from a walkable downtown. In these cases, a streetcar may rep-resent the best opportunity to connect that area to the down-town in a way that it has never been connected before, spurring its development. In Portland, both the city and the development community identified the Hoyt Rail Yards, north of downtown, as just such an area. They prepared a design that was both a streetcar plan and a neighborhood plan, and included an eight-fold up-zoning in exchange for parks, affordable housing, and the removal of a freeway ramp. The new streetcar opened in 2001 at a total cost of $54.5 million.[23]

Since then, over $3.5 billion of new investment has sprung up around the trolley line—an astounding sixty-four times the initial investment. According to a Brookings Institution report, ad-jacent property values have risen by 44 to well over 400 percent, compared to the city's baseline appreciation of 34 percent. Several thousand people have moved in, and they, in turn, have caused a revolution in street life. The Brookings report notes that "pe-destrian counts in front of Powell's Books, a major retailer sited along the line, went from three people per hour to over 933."[24]

[*] Charles Hales's presentation at Rail-Volution, October 18, 2011. The "host of strate-gies" included Portland's famous urban-growth boundary, which had contributed to a pent-up demand for real estate.

Portland's streetcar succeeded as a tool for increasing urban vibrancy because it was first a tool for neighborhood development. This fact is important for two reasons: first, because it is a mistake to promote a streetcar in the absence of a major real estate opportunity and, second, because such an opportunity suggests the presence of private parties who stand to benefit tremendously from the investment. And these parties should want to help pay for it.

This was precisely the case in Seattle, where landowners in the city's South Lake Union district, led by Microsoft cofounder Paul Allen, contributed fully half the cost of a new $52 million trolley line connecting their property to downtown. With another third of the money coming from federal and state sources, this left only $8.5 million unaccounted for, which the city obtained by selling surplus property along the line.[25] Only five years old, this trolley is now serving four times as many passengers as Tampa's,[26] thanks in part to the relocation of Amazon .com and the Bill & Melinda Gates Foundation. During the period of its planning and construction, property values along the line appreciated at more than twice the city average,[27] amply repaying the private investors.

The experiences of Portland and Seattle may seem a bit chastening to other cities, and rightly so—not everyone has huge housing demand or Amazon. But even the duds of Memphis, Tampa, and Little Rock produced positive outcomes, namely new development around the line averaging seventeen times the value of the rail systems.[28] The tax revenue that this construction represents is promising news in terms of finding ways to finance future streetcar lines,[29] but it still doesn't address most cities' stated goal in chasing a trolley, which is to enliven their downtown. Principally, streetcars enliven not the downtown, but the new area opened up for development. Downtown only benefits as a secondary impact, if and when thousands of people move into the previously underdeveloped area.

Indeed, more careful study of Tampa may show the opposite effect. While property values have soared where the trolley passes through former industrial land, the city's already established neighborhoods have fared less well. In Ybor City, Tampa's most walkable district, properties actually appreciated at rates from 24 to 36 percent *below* the rest of the surrounding county.[30] The lesson here is that trolleys, unless integrated into a robust citywide transit network, are first and foremost a tool for creating new urban districts, and are not necessarily the mobility-enhancing, street-enlivening walkability bomb that their promoters would have us believe. By all means build one, if you can get someone else to pay for it.

TRANSIT FOR DRIVERS

Most Americans live not in big cities with big transit systems, but in smaller places that face a dramatically different landscape when it comes to public transportation. In most American cities, everyone still drives, traffic is relatively light, and parking is cheap. What is the role of transit in these places? Or more to the point, how do you create a transit-and-walking culture in a place where driving is so easy?

It may not be possible. In some of these locations, the bus is destined to remain the "loser cruiser," the mode of choice for those who have no choice: the elderly, poor, and infirm. As such, it will always be underfunded and struggling for survival, like any social service.

If it is to become widely used, transit has to be ruthlessly reconceptualized as a convenience, not just a rescue vehicle. Or, more accurately, while certain rescue routes must remain—from the old-age home to the health center, for example—the system needs to focus on those rare opportunities where it can offer a superior experience to driving. These few lines should be earmarked for a higher level of service, and indeed only provided with service if certain conditions can be met. These conditions are what is lacking in much of transit today: *urbanity*, *clarity*, *frequency*, and *pleasure*.

Urbanity means locating all significant stops right in the heart of the action, not a block away and, God forbid, not across a parking lot. This is the *problem of the last one hundred yards* that haunts so many a bus or train station. Riders should be able to fall into the bus from a stool at a coffee shop.[31] If the dimensional requirements of your vehicle do not allow this, then you need a different vehicle. And without true walkability on both ends of the line, your system is a nonstarter.

Clarity means a route that is a simple line or loop, with as few diversions as possible. This not only expedites travel—and limits frustration—but also allows riders to form a mental image of the path, so important to their comfort. Sometimes, when I ride another city's bus for the first time, I am reminded of the one-day bus strike I encountered in Florence, Italy: the drivers showed up for work but, once the passengers boarded, they cruised wherever the heck they wanted. We got the message.

Frequency is the thing that most transit service gets wrong. People hate to look at schedules almost as much as they hate waiting, so ten-minute headways are the standard for any line that hopes to attract a crowd. If you can't fill a bus at that rate, then get a van. GPS-enabled time-to-arrival clocks at stations (and smartphone apps) are also essential, and particularly helpful after hours. What *after hours* means depends on the circumstances, but staying popular may require short headways all evening. The byword here is to provide service frequently or not at all. Limiting service due to limited ridership is a death spiral that few transit lines survive.

Pleasure is the mandate that is most often overlooked by transit officials, yet the search for its attainment is at the heart of so many human choices. As Darrin Nordahl argues convincingly in *My Kind of Transit*, public transportation is "a mobile form of public space,"[32] and can provide so many of the benefits we seek from our time spent out of the house. When I first read Nordahl's book, I was ready to dismiss this concept as so much sentimental prattle, but then I was reminded that I owe my own marriage to a train ride. What does a social, fun, *pleasurable* experience mean for transit design? Seats that face inward rather than at the back of someone's head. Big, nontinted windows that open wide—or no glass at all, as in San Diego. Wifi. And, yes, even novel vehicles, like double-decker buses, that add capacity and charm while reducing turning radii.[33]

In short, the imperative of competitive transit has a hard side and a soft side. The hard side is all about not wasting people's time and the soft side is about making them happy. If you can commit to doing both, then you can get people out of their cars.

TRAINS VERSUS BUSES

If your goals are efficiency and pleasure, rail beats bus hands down. With expedited paths, trains are almost always faster, and most trains are way cuter than your average diesel-belching bus. Even the latest zero-emissions buses are typically an intimidating presence in the streetscape compared to a delicate tram car. That's why trains cost more.

Or do they? Hartford is now building a Bus Rapid Transit (BRT) system that costs over $60 million per mile.[34] That's almost twice the cost of the average American light-rail project.[*] But Hartford is an exception that proves the rule, and points to the sometimes high costs of doing BRT properly, which means

---

[*] Light Rail Now, "Status of North American Light Rail Projects," 2002. The average cost of such projects is approximately $35 million per mile, excluding Seattle's unusual system.

giving the bus its own dedicated pathway, much like a train. I'm not sure what went wrong in Hartford, as the typical BRT costs about half as much as light rail, roughly $15 million per mile.[35]

This typically lower cost is drawing a lot of cities to BRT. If done properly, BRT is indeed a legitimate alternative to regional light rail. Just don't forget the R. True BRT systems include not only a separated path, but also signal priority at intersections, level boarding at raised pay-to-enter stations, ten-minute headways, and GPS-enabled wait-time indicators. If you can't do most of those things, don't call it Rapid. Oregon's popular Eugene-to-Springfield BRT even has its own artwork and landscaping program, not just at stations, but along the whole line.

These surface investments are often cited by BRT advocates when responding to the biggest criticism of bus systems, that they lack rail's permanence: how can you drive real estate investment around transit if the transit might leave? Well, we've already learned in America that trolleys can leave, too, but BRT infrastructure has a long way to go to match the sense of permanence that rail provides. That's half the story. The other half, rarely discussed, is that the more permanent the BRT infrastructure feels, the more ugly it usually looks. BRT buses, and the constructions that support them, just don't evoke many feelings of comfort in the fragile human bodies they serve. Sure, BRT has done great things for pedestrians in Bogotá . . . but how many Americans want to be pedestrians in Bogotá?

It would seem that everyone in this argument, except Darrin Nordahl, has forgotten just how darn adorable trolleys really are. They also last twice as long as buses and, unlike buses, the old ones often look even better than the new ones. Buses might stay in service for twenty years but, after ten, they start to make a place feel run down. Because they are not only a "form of public space," but also very often a *part* of public space, this fact deserves greater weight in the train-versus-bus calculus that many cities undertake.

That said, not all bus systems are duds—far from it. The most remarkable one nationally may be Boulder's, an inexpensive network that confounds conventional transit wisdom in a number of important ways. Thanks to its system of cleverly branded routes—including the Hop, Skip, and Jump, with each route getting its own color—the city is living up to its motto of "Breathing Required, Driving Optional." Despite gaining ten thousand new residents and twelve thousand new jobs since 1994, the city has seen zero increase in its total vehicle miles driven. Much of the system's success comes from the way that it is marketed. Households buy a $120 EcoPass that gives all members free rides all year—and also gives them special treatment at local stores, restaurants, and bars. As a result, an entire EcoPass culture has evolved, in which driving just isn't as cool.

Finally, many cities that are considering trolleys for the standard set of wrong reasons may want instead to purchase small electric shuttles like the ones that have brought increased life to places like Chattanooga and San Diego. These don't need rails, but they function as pedestrian accelerators in already-populated corridors, and each one costs less than the cheapest Ferrari.* Although technically buses, they are also cute, and can serve as an effective gateway drug to more hard-core rail transit in the future.

ZIP IT IF YOU CAN

Every city wants Zipcar. Does Zipcar want them back? Probably not. By all means, invite them to dinner, give them the key to your city, and offer them all of the concessions they usually ask, including dedicated parking spaces in the best locations—as many as they want. But understand that this superficially pro-

---

*Chattanooga's cost between $160,000 and $180,000 apiece.

driving enterprise cannot thrive in your city unless you have already moved beyond the pro-driving paradigm. Because if everybody has a car, nobody needs one. If the design of your city still makes daily driving a prerequisite to viable citizenship, then you are not yet ready for urban car-share.

Some people worry that car-share might undermine public transportation, taxis, walking, or biking, but the opposite is true. It is only in the driving-optional cities with good public transportation, taxis, walking, and biking that car-share can thrive. It is also in these same cities that car-share might push someone over the tipping point into ditching their car, as it did me. So, here's one good test: Go downtown. Stick out your hand. Does a taxi stop? If so, you are probably ready for Zipcar.

And then go for it, as the benefits are tremendous. After a year of service, Zipcar Baltimore polled its members and found that they were walking 21 percent more, biking 14 percent more, and taking transit 11 percent more than before joining. Only 12 percent of members had taken more than five driving trips in the previous month, compared to 38 percent before joining Zipcar. About a fifth of members had sold their cars, and almost half claimed that Zipcar had saved them from having to buy a car.[36] There is only one challenge to Zipcar, which is that they are too smart to locate in unwalkable cities.

THE SAFE WALK

∎

STEP 5: PROTECT THE PEDESTRIAN
STEP 6: WELCOME BIKES

STEP 5: PROTECT THE PEDESTRIAN

Size matters; A turn too far; Fat lanes; Keep it complicated; The safety apotheosis; The one-way epidemic; Sacred sidewalks; Senseless signals

Will the pedestrian survive? Or, more precisely: Will potential walkers feel adequately protected against being run over, enough so that they make the choice to walk?

This is clearly the central question of any discussion of walkable cities. As all the other steps make clear, pedestrian safety is not enough. But it is essential, and also so often needlessly botched by the people who build our cities. These failures stem from two principal sources: a lack of concern for the pedestrian and a fundamental misunderstanding within the professions about what makes streets safe. The first cause is political, and can be overcome through advocacy. The second cause is technical, and can be overcome by setting the record straight.

SIZE MATTERS

In his landmark book *Great Streets*, the urbanist Alan Jacobs (no relation to Jane) lays out figure-ground maps, each a mile square, of more than forty world cities. With streets in white and blocks in black, these drawings allow us to understand and compare the patterns underlying some of the planet's most walkable and unwalkable places. The lessons that emerge are unmistakable, especially as you compare cities that you have had the pleasure or misfortune to visit. The most obvious of these lessons pertains to block size.

Generally speaking, the cities with the smallest blocks are the ones best known for walkability, while those with the largest blocks are known as places without street life—if they are known at all. The preindustrial neighborhoods of downtown Boston and lower Manhattan, like their European counterparts, have blocks that average less than two hundred feet long (and the cranky medieval street patterns to match). The most walkable grids, like Philadelphia's and San Francisco's, have blocks that average less than four hundred feet in length. And then there are the pedestrian-free zones, like Irvine, California, where many blocks are one thousand feet long or longer.

There are, as always, exceptions. Much of Berlin has surprisingly large blocks. But its street maps are effectively a lie, since so many Berlin blocks are rife with interior passages and courtyards that create a hidden network of pedestrian life. The blocks of Los Angeles aren't much bigger than Barcelona's, but the latter's streets aren't engineered for high speeds. Los Angeles demonstrates that it is possible to make a small-block city unwalkable, but the larger pool of evidence confirms that it is much harder to make a big-block city walkable.

I remember the first time I visited Las Vegas, which, aside from the Strip and the old main street (Fremont Street) is a place where nobody walks. Driving into town in my rented Mustang, I checked the Hertz map for the path to my hotel. In those days, rental-car maps typically showed only a city's major roads, skipping the fine-grained network in between for simplicity. As I entered the city, I was astounded to learn that there wasn't a fine-grained network in between: the dumbed-down rental-car map *was* the city. This explained a lot.

There are two main reasons why smaller blocks make for better cities. The first has less to do with safety and more with convenience: the more blocks per square mile, the more choices a pedestrian can make and the more opportunities there are to alter your path to visit a useful address such as a coffee shop or dry cleaner. These choices also make walking more interesting, while shortening the distances between destinations.

The second, more important, reason is that bigger blocks mean fewer streets and thus bigger streets. Presuming a similar traffic volume, a city with twice the block size requires each street to hold twice as many driving lanes. The typical street in downtown Portland, with its two-hundred-foot-per-side blocks, holds two lanes of traffic.* The typical street in downtown Salt Lake City, with blocks over six hundred feet per side, holds six lanes of traffic.■ And six-lane streets are much more dangerous than two-lane streets.

The definitive study on this topic was completed by Wesley Marshall and Norman Garrick at the University of Connecticut, who compared data from twenty-four medium-sized California cities. They looked at more than 130,000 car crashes that occurred over nine years, and were able to divide the subjects into twelve "safer" cities and twelve "less safe" cities. Among these two groups, they found no single variable to be more predictive of injury and death than block size. Blocks in the dozen safer cities averaged eighteen acres in size, while blocks in the dozen less safe cities averaged thirty-four acres in size. All told, a doubling of block size corresponded with a tripling of fatalities.[1]

---

*Portland's fine-grained network contains a remarkable six hundred intersections per square mile. You can fit nine typical Portland blocks in a typical Salt Lake City block. The block-size versus street-width math is not exact for a number of interesting reasons. Portland's blocks are generally taller than Salt Lake City's, but this factor is counterbalanced somewhat by the vicious circle that occurs in big-blocked cities, where an automotive environment causes many potential pedestrians to drive instead.

■Each Salt Lake City street is famously 132 feet wide, thanks to the dictate by Brigham Young that streets be wide enough to turn a wagon team around without "resorting to profanity" (Mark Haddock, "Salt Lake Streets Have Seen Many Changes over Past 150 Years"). This 132 feet now includes sidewalks, but that still leaves room for a lot of lanes.

Big-block, multilane systems result in streets that are both harder to cross and easier to speed on. Here, the most significant threshold is between one lane and two lanes in any given direction, since that second lane offers the opportunity to pass and thus allows drivers to slip into a "road racer" frame of mind. Whichever lane you are in, the other one looks faster.[2] It is possible to make an eminently walkable multilane boulevard— picture Paris—but few big-block cities have the budget or the desire to buy that many trees. And even the Champs Élysées is a nightmare to cross.

Multilane streets are much more dangerous for drivers as well, thanks to the "killed by kindness" scenario. As it typically unfolds, this story line involves a motorist signaling left and an approaching car in the adjacent lane slowing down to allow the turn. As the motorist crosses the centerline, a speeding car in the far lane, hidden by the kind driver, T-bones the turning vehicle.

The good news is that four-lane streets can be as inefficient as they are deadly, because the fast lane is also the left-hand turn lane, and maintaining speed often means jockeying from lane to lane. Thanks to this inefficiency, many cities across the country are finding it politically possible to introduce something called a "road diet." In a road diet, a standard four-lane street is replaced by a three-lane street: one lane in each direction and a center lane reserved for left turns.

What is remarkable about road diets is not that they save lives—that is to be expected. In a typical road-diet conversion, Orlando's Edgewater Drive, the number of crashes fell by 34 percent and, because the crashes were slower, the number of injuries fell by an impressive 68 percent: from one per nine days to one per month. Rather, the surprising thing is that they do not reduce a street's carrying capacity. Thanks to the inherent efficiency of maintaining a dedicated turning lane, the typical road diet does nothing to lower the traffic volume on a street. Comparison of seventeen different road diets conducted by the engineering firm AECOM found that only two streets lost capacity, while five stayed the same, and ten actually handled more cars per day after the conversion.

These numbers are important, because most road-diet opponents are fearful of increased congestion. In the 1980s, 95 percent of the residents of Lewistown, Pennsylvania, came out against a road diet proposed by some progressive engineers at PennDOT, citing concerns over increased travel times. PennDOT built the conversion anyway—as DOTs will do—and travel times remained unchanged as crashes dropped to nearly zero.[3]

This story and the dozens since then represent a great opportunity for almost every American city. There is hardly a downtown in the United States that does not have a four-laner that would benefit from a road diet tomorrow. A happy by-product of the road diet is the additional ten to twelve feet of roadway freed up by the eliminated lane. This space can be used to expand sidewalks, plant trees, create a missing parking lane, or replace parallel parking with angled parking in a business district. Since most urban four-laners already have sidewalks, trees, and parking, this pavement is often redeployed as two ample bicycle lanes, further humanizing the street. This solution presents the additional benefit of avoiding the expense of rebuilding any curbs.*

A TURN TOO FAR

Now that I've fully sung the praises of turn lanes, let me attack them. Road diets aside, left-hand turn lanes have done more

---

*One powerful example of this type of road diet is San Francisco's Valencia Street, which in 1999 was converted from four driving lanes into three driving lanes plus two ample bike lanes. As a result, the number of commute-time cyclists rose from 88 to 215 per hour. There were no negative spillover effects on traffic, as car volumes on parallel roads remained largely unchanged. (Michael Rankin, presentation at New Partners for Smart Growth, February 10, 2007).

than their share to wreck a good number of American downtowns. Why? Because, by inserting them where they are not needed, or making them much longer than needed, engineering departments have caused many Main Streets to become a lane too wide.

This wouldn't be as big a problem if it were only a matter of ten feet. Unfortunately, the big problem is where those ten feet are found, in what used to be a parking lane. This is the situation in Bethlehem, Pennsylvania, where the once-bustling Wyandotte Street has the misfortune of also being State Route 378. Here, the same enlightened DOT engineers who brought us Lewistown's road diet decided that a two-laner needed a center turn lane, and they scraped an entire block face of its parallel parking to get it. Without convenience parking for their customers, the stores that line Wyandotte Street are all dead or dying; those that remain will not last long. And here's the kicker: the DOT's turn lane—four hundred feet long, enough for a stack of two dozen cars—serves a minor side street containing a mere eleven houses.

This is highway engineering perversity at its most wasteful . . . were it only an isolated incident! Most American downtowns suffer from unnecessary and overlong left-hand turn lanes that eliminate parking, broaden streets, speed up traffic, and otherwise detract from the pedestrian experience. While most can't be eliminated without a negative impact on traffic flow, most can be shortened. A three-car-long turn lane that eliminates three parking spaces at a corner is a vast improvement over the block-long monsters that most cities install without a second thought.

FAT LANES

Contrary to perceptions, the greatest threat to pedestrian safety is not crime, but the very real danger of automobiles moving quickly. Yet most traffic engineers, often in the name of safety, continually redesign city streets to support higher-speed driving. This approach is so counterintuitive that it strains credulity: engineers design streets for speeds well above the posted limit, so that speeding drivers will be safe—a practice that, of course, causes the very speeding it hopes to protect against.

Even my old South Beach neighborhood, known for its walkability, was not immune to this sort of thinking. If you have seen the remake of *La Cage aux Folles,* you might remember the lively streetscape of Espanola Way, where Robin Williams buys a birthday cake for his partner. Follow that street two blocks west and you will find that already-narrow sidewalks have been cut in half in order to widen a roadway that functioned perfectly well before. Why? Because *the standards had changed*—from walkable to not.

I have never heard a proper explanation for the creeping expansion of America's street standards. All I know is that it is very real and that it has a profound impact on the work that city planners do every day. In the late nineties, I was helping to design Mount Laurel, a new town outside of Birmingham, Alabama, that was modeled on that city's most successful prewar neighborhoods. We had measured the streets of Homewood, Mountain Brook, and the city's other best addresses, and planned our thoroughfares with the same dimensions. We were then told that our streets did not meet the standard, and our engineering firm was unwilling to stamp the drawings for fear of legal liability.

I remember one particular afternoon, when we convinced the county engineer to tour these great neighborhoods with us in our van. Perhaps anticipating our consternation, he gripped the door handle with white knuckles and shouted "We're gonna die!" as we motored calmly around the narrow, leafy streets of Mountain Brook. I'm pretty sure he was joking, but his ultimate pronouncement was clear: we had to reengineer our streets with a higher design speed.

This logic—that higher design speeds make for safer

streets—coupled with the typical city engineer's desire for un-impeded traffic—has caused many American cities to rebuild their streets with lanes that are twelve, thirteen, and sometimes even fourteen feet wide. Now cars are only six feet wide—a Ford Excursion is 6'6"—and most Main Streets were historically made of ten-foot lanes. That dimension persists on many of the best, such as ritzy Worth Avenue in Palm Beach, Florida. Yet many cities I visit have their fair share of twelve-footers, and that is where much of the speeding occurs.

For me writing this and you reading it, it is undoubtedly clear that building wider lanes would cause drivers to speed. After all, if highways have twelve-foot lanes, and we are comfort-able negotiating them at seventy miles per hour, wouldn't we feel the same way on a city street of the same dimension? Yet in the bizarre parallel universe of the traffic engineer, no such relation-ship exists: motorists will drive at the speed limit, or slightly above, no matter what sort of drag strip we lay in their path.

As with induced demand, the engineers have once again failed to comprehend that the way they design streets will have any impact on the way that people use them. By their logic, just as more lanes can't cause more driving, high-speed lanes can't cause high speeds. Ladies and gentlemen, allow me to introduce you to the second great misunderstanding that lies at the root of most urban degradation today: widening a city's streets in the name of safety is like distributing handguns to deter crime.

Just in case you think I am making this up, let's turn to the calm analysis of Reid Ewing and Eric Dumbaugh, professors at the University of Maryland and Texas A&M, respectively. In their 2009 study, "The Built Environment and Traffic Safety: A Review of Empirical Evidence," they assess the situation this way:

> Considered broadly, the fundamental shortcoming of conventional traffic safety theory is that it fails to ac-count for the moderating role of human behavior on

crash incidence. Decisions to . . . widen specific roadways to make them more forgiving are based on the assumption that in so doing, human behavior will remain
unchanged. And it is precisely this assumption—that human behavior can be treated as a constant, regardless of
design—that accounts for the failure of conventional
safety practice.[4]

How costly is this failure? In another study, presented at the
eightieth annual meeting of the Transportation Research Board,
Rutgers professor Robert Noland calculated that increased lane
widths could be blamed for approximately nine hundred additional traffic fatalities per year.[5]

We can only hope that these studies eventually have an impact on thoroughfare engineering as it is practiced in the typical
American city. Currently, engineers still deny their stamp of
approval to streets configured without "adequately" high design
speeds. "We're afraid of being sued," they say. Someday, I might
get up the nerve to respond as follows: "Afraid? You should be.
Now that we've publicly presented to you that narrower roads save
lives, we are going to sue you when people die on your fat streets."

There is some good news. Thanks to the labors of the Congress for the New Urbanism, a nonprofit focused on making
more livable cities,[*] we have made a start in changing the standards. The CNU teamed up with the Institute of Traffic Engineers to create a new manual, *Designing Walkable Urban
Thoroughfares*, that recommends street lanes of ten and eleven
feet wide.[6] With the imprimatur of the ITE, this book can now
be waved at planning meetings in support of more reasonable
standards. I just wish that "eleven" wasn't in there.

---

[*]Full disclosure: I am a charter member of this organization, which over the past two
decades has been laboring arduously in support of the ideals presented in this book.
You can join us at cnu.org.

Another cause for hope is the growing "20's Plenty for Us" movement that, having taken the United Kingdom by storm, is just beginning to win followers in the United States. Recognizing that only 5 percent of pedestrian collisions at twenty miles per hour result in death, versus 85 percent at forty mph,[7] the British have introduced twenty-mph speed limits in many of their cities. There are currently more than eighty "20's Plenty" campaigns in the UK, and about twenty-five British jurisdictions, with a combined population of over 6 million, have committed to a twenty-mph speed limit in residential areas. In June 2011, the European Union Transport Committee recommended such a rule for the entire continent.[8] It is easy to imagine twenty mph becoming a standard throughout Europe in the near future.

On this side of the pond, Hoboken, New Jersey, may be the first city to have instituted a "20's Plenty" campaign. Unfortunately, in true Jersey fashion, the twenty is just a suggestion, while higher official speed limits remain in place. As I write this, New York City is pioneering some legitimate twenty-mph zones. These developments are important—but not as an end in themselves. As any London pedestrian will tell you, a twenty-mph sign does not a twenty-mph driver make. Most motorists drive the speed at which they feel comfortable, which is the speed to which the road has been engineered. "20's Plenty" is most useful as a first step to slower design speeds. Once twenty-mph zones become more common, we may finally be able to convince the engineers to design twenty-mph streets.•

KEEP IT COMPLICATED

Narrower lanes are not the only way to slow traffic down. Each and every aspect of the built environment sends its own cue to

---

• As you might expect, this is far from likely, for the reasons already discussed. Most engineers would insist that streets posted with a twenty-mph speed limit be laid out according to a design speed of twenty-five or thirty mph so that speeders are "safe."

drivers and too many of those cues say "speed up." Most of them, unfortunately, are the law. Two more that deserve our attention are intersection geometry and sight triangles.

Recently, my wife and I took a road trip to Philadelphia. It was our first weekend alone without the two kids, and we were determined to make it count. The first stop, about a mile south of the Liberty Bell, was the intersection of Ninth Street and Passyunk Avenue. Fast-food aficionados will recognize this address as the location of Geno's Steaks and Pat's King of Steaks, the two oversized food stands that have been duking it out for decades over the title of Best Philly Cheesesteak.

I had heard about the cheesesteak duel, but I was not aware of the odd urban condition that surrounds it. As befits their embattled circumstances, the two restaurants sit nose-to-nose on opposing flatiron lots, like two skinny slices of pie, framed by two streets that cross in a sharp thirty-degree X. Pat's points north, directly at Geno's pointing south. With all their flashy signage, they look like two casino yachts playing a game of chicken.

For me, the question wasn't which sandwich was better (my vote goes to Pat's*). Rather, the question was: After all the cheesesteaks these two establishments had undoubtedly served to traffic engineers throughout the years, why is it still illegal in most of America to intersect two streets at a thirty-degree angle?

Observing the intersection at work, it would be hard to imagine a safer scene. First, there were the snaking lines of customers that made their way right into the street. We planners call this "human traffic calming"—as opposed to "human speed bumps," another common phenomenon—and the traffic was further slowed by all the cars pulling in for curbside pickups. But even without this confusion—we returned when the crowds had abated—the simple fact was that nobody drove dangerously through this intersection, precisely because the intersection felt dangerous.

---

*Thanks mostly to Geno's xenophobic political displays.

Welcome to the world of *risk homeostasis*, a very real place that exists well outside the blinkered gaze of the traffic engineering profession. Risk homeostasis describes how people automatically adjust their behavior to maintain a comfortable level of risk. It explains why poisoning deaths went up after childproof caps were introduced—people stopped hiding their medicines—and why the deadliest intersections in America are typically the ones you can navigate with one finger on the steering wheel and a cellphone at your ear.[9]

The best risk-homeostasis story comes from Sweden, a nation that is obsessed with traffic safety. If you look at the bar chart of Swedish traffic fatalities through the years, most of what you see is not surprising. There is the rise in deaths into the sixties, the decline as seatbelts are introduced, the leveling off in the eighties, and then a further decline as airbags become standard equipment. But, wait a minute, what happened in 1967? In a single year, fatalities dropped from more than thirteen hundred to fewer than eleven hundred, a decline of 17 percent. It turns out that, on March 9, 1967, Sweden switched from driving on the left-hand side of the road to driving on the right-hand side of the road.[10]

As might be expected, everyone was quite worried about this transition. The steering wheels were on the wrong side of the cars, a ton of signals and signs all had to be moved at once, and the government feared a bloodbath. But, precisely because people were scared, car crashes dropped precipitously, and didn't return to the prior level until 1970.

The lesson from this experience is clear: if you value the lives of your countrymen, you should switch sides of the road every three years. Since that is unlikely to win popular support, let's turn to the larger lesson: the safest roads are those that feel the least safe, demanding more attention from drivers.

This lesson has yet to crack through the ossified shell of the mainstream traffic engineering profession. In most cities, intersections are required to meet at ninety degrees or close to it.

Staggered intersections, great for slowing speeds, are strictly forbidden. Five-ways, common in older places, are also off the table. My house sits on just such a crazy intersection, and in three years we have yet to witness a crash. Actually, we have: about once a season, on the perfect ninety-degree intersection a block away.

The shape of the intersection is half the story. The other half is the visibility at that intersection, and the second rule that foils the best attempts of city planners to make memorable places: the sight-triangle requirement. This standard mandates that all vertical objects such as buildings and trees maintain a minimum distance from street corners, so that drivers can see around them. Such a requirement makes perfect sense in a world in which design can't affect behavior. But on planet Earth, it causes speeding at intersections.

Many of the best places in America, with leafy, well-shaped public spaces, violate the sight-triangle requirement.* Many of these places are located in those very cities that enforce sight triangles on all new construction. Luckily, each jurisdiction has the right to enforce its own sight-triangle rules. While they are hard to throw out entirely, they can often be rejiggered to the point where they do no harm. Hint: it all comes down to how you measure the triangle.

THE SAFETY APOTHEOSIS

If greater perceived danger leads to safer driving, how do you make the safest streets in the world? That question was probably best answered by Hans Monderman (1945–2008), the Dutch traffic engineer who pioneered two wonderful and interrelated

---

*See *The Boulevard Book* by Alan Jacobs for a thorough discussion of how sight-triangle requirements make great streets illegal. In one trenchant drawing, Jacobs demonstrates how applying the American standard would wipe out one-third of the trees on Barcelona's gorgeous Passeig de Gràcia (118–19).

concepts: *naked streets* and *shared space.* While not appropriate everywhere, these techniques have a lot to teach us as we work to improve our cities.

Naked streets refers to the concept of stripping a roadway of its signage—all of it, including stop signs, signals, and even stripes. Far from creating mayhem, this approach appears to have lowered crash rates wherever it has been tried. Following Monderman's advice, the Danish town of Christiansfeld removed all signs and signals from its main intersection, and watched the number of serious accidents each year fall from three to zero. The British county of Wiltshire, home to Stonehenge, pulled the centerline off a narrow street, and witnessed a 35 percent drop in the number of collisions.[11] Drivers passed oncoming cars at a 40 percent greater distance than on a striped street, even though the striped roadway was wider.[12]

Monderman described his approach this way: "The trouble with traffic engineers is that when there's a problem with a road, they always try to add something. To my mind, it's much better to remove things."[13] This makes particular sense in the Netherlands, where there is a tradition of reticent roadways—you are unlikely to see a stop sign there[14]—but the idea has also spread to Austria, France, Germany, Spain, and Sweden.[15]

Naked streets are also beginning to appear in the United States, typically in conjunction with Monderman's other big idea, *shared space.* In some ways, shared space is simply the extension of the naked streets concept to include the elimination of physical cues and barriers as well, such as curbs and distinct materials for streets and sidewalks. The goal is to create an environment of such utter ambiguity that cars, bicyclists, and pedestrians all come together in one big mixing bowl of humanity.

As David Owen notes, "This sounds to many people like a formula for disaster." Not so: "The clear experience in the (mainly) European cities that have tried it has been that increasing the ambiguity of urban road spaces actually lowers car speeds, reduces accident rates, and improves the lives of pedestrians."[16] In Monderman's terms, "Chaos equals cooperation."[17]

Monderman was a man with the courage of his convictions. One of his favorite tricks with television reporters was to speak to them while standing in front of a shared-space intersection he had built in the Dutch village of Oosterwolde. Without missing a beat, he would blindly walk backward into the flow of traffic, parting it like the Red Sea.[18]

America has no shared-space examples as pure as Monderman's, but one of the first attempts can be found on Espanola Way in Miami Beach—just two blocks from the street that was unnecessarily widened a few pages ago. In good political fashion, the city asked the street's neighbors to participate in the redesign of one of its key intersections, unaware that the neighborhood was infested with urban designers just back from Europe. "No curbs," we said. "Just pave it with bricks from building face to building face." Completed around 2000, Espanola Plaza works just fine, albeit with fairly low car counts. When the traffic engineers come to their senses, we will see Shared Streets begin to proliferate in the United States.

THE ONE-WAY EPIDEMIC

In 1918, a flu pandemic killed more than 75 million people worldwide. Almost exactly fifty years later, the United States was hit by another epidemic that, while less harmful to humans, laid waste to city after city from coast to coast. I am talking, of course, about the wholesale replacement in downtowns of two-way traffic with one-way traffic, a plight that few American cities escaped. Its impacts were profound, and haunt us to this day.

The logic was simple enough: to stay competitive in the face of suburban out-migration, cities needed to retool themselves around the goal of moving suburbanites in and out of the downtown quickly. One part of this effort—the obvious part—involved building elevated interstates, with the near-suicidal outcomes that have been well documented. The other part, less discussed, involved the remaking of downtown street networks around free-flowing systems of one-way pairs. By replacing two-ways with one-ways, cities were able to introduce synchronized signals and eliminate the slowdowns caused by left turns across traffic.

Like the interstates, these retrofitted streets were indeed effective at speeding commuters, enough so that there was no longer any reason to live downtown. They also turned what had once been a great urban asset—the public realm—into little more than a collection of surface freeways. Thoroughfares that once held cars, pedestrians, businesses, and street trees became toxic to all but the first. Freed of other uses, they effectively turned into automotive sewers.[19]

We have already discussed how multilane streets contribute to antipedestrian driving. Add to that the elimination of all friction from cars headed in the opposite direction and the sheer momentum represented by two to four columns of unopposed traffic, and you can see why these streets quickly depopulated. It is difficult to name a midsized or larger American city that was not damaged by this technique, whether it takes the form of a largely one-way network—Saint Louis, San Diego—or just a single one-way pair—Alexandria, Virginia; Cornelius, Oregon. Indeed, driving west from Portland to the Oregon coast, I witnessed how a single DOT had managed to send a good number of a state's Main Streets onto life support with this one trick.

One-ways wreck downtown retail districts for reasons beyond noxious driving, principally because they distribute vitality unevenly, and often in unexpected ways. They have been known to kill stores consigned to the morning path to work, since people do most of their shopping on the evening path home.* They also

---

*Just such a numbskull move devastated Calle Ocho, the main drag of Miami's Little Havana, in the seventies (Andres Duany, Elizabeth Plater-Zyberk, and Jeff Speck, *Suburban Nation*, 161n).

create a situation in which half the stores on cross-streets lose their retail visibility, being located over the shoulders of passing drivers. They intimidate out-of-towners, who are afraid of becoming lost, and they frustrate locals, who are annoyed by all the circular motions and additional traffic lights they must pass through to reach their destinations.

Indeed, these looping motions call deeply into question the presumed greater efficiency of one-way systems. Sure, they move vehicles faster, but does that greater speed make up for the additional distances that motorists have to travel . . . especially lost motorists? While there are plenty of studies documenting the congestion-busting efficacy of one-ways, I have yet to see one that factors in the marginal congestion caused by circling.

I was reminded of this fact on my first visit to Lowell, Massachusetts, on the day I was hired to work on their downtown. After twenty minutes spent lost—despite Google Maps—I finally had to call the deputy city manager, who talked me in for a landing. For a city planner with what I thought was a well-calibrated internal compass, this was a profound embarrassment. Later, as I got to know the city, I began to feel a bit better. The superimposition of a one-way network on Lowell's cranky preindustrial grid, interrupted by canals and rivers, had created one of the most discombobulating street networks in America. In my eventual report, I took great pleasure in documenting how the drive from the Memorial Auditorium to its designated parking lot, a mere two hundred yards away, required a looping five-turn odyssey of more than a mile.

At this point, some astute readers will be asking about Portland: it has a one-way grid and it's doing great. What gives? Portland adds a major caveat to this discussion: if the grids are simple and the blocks small, corresponding to a dense network of fairly tiny streets, then one-way systems can function quite well—picture most of the residential cross-streets in Manhattan. But Portland has a number of one-ways that are simply too big to invite walking, and so does Seattle, another small-block gem.

When the streets get more than two lanes wide, it takes some pretty tall buildings to make them feel comfortable, buildings that most American cities don't have.

Take Savannah. In 1969, a one-way system was applied to many of the north-south streets in Oglethorpe's delicate grid. Most still remain, and create perhaps the only significant impediment to pleasurably strolling this otherwise eminently walkable city. Recognizing this problem, the city government commissioned the architect Christian Sottile to study what happened to just one thoroughfare, East Broad Street, when it became a speedway. He dug into the tax rolls and counted the number of active (taxpaying) addresses located along the street in 1968 and then a few years later. He learned that, as a result of its conversion, the street lost almost two-thirds of these addresses.[20]

Happily, there's a flip side to that story. Worried about speeding as it built a new elementary school, the city returned East Broad Street to two-way. In short order, the number of active addresses shot up by 50 percent.[21]

Savannah's experience is not alone. Based on a few well-publicized successes, dozens of American cities are beginning to revert their one-way systems back to two-way traffic. These include Oklahoma City, Miami, Dallas, Minneapolis, Charleston, Berkeley[22] . . . and, soon, Lowell. Perhaps the best documented of recent reversions was accomplished in Vancouver, Washington. As told by Alan Ehrenhalt in *Governing* magazine, Vancouver had "spent millions of dollars trying to revitalize its downtown," but these investments "did nothing for Main Street itself. Through most of this decade the street remained as dreary as ever."[23] He continues:

> Then, a year ago, the city council tried a new strategy. Rather than wait for the $14 million more in state and federal money it was planning to spend on projects on and around Main Street, it opted for something much simpler. It painted yellow lines in the middle of the road,

took down some signs and put up others, and installed some new traffic lights. In other words, it took a one-way street and opened it up to two-way traffic. The merchants on Main Street had high hopes for this change. But none of them were prepared for what actually happened following the changeover on November 16, 2008. In the midst of a severe recession, Main Street in Vancouver seemed to come back to life almost overnight.[24]

The success has continued, and business owners remain ecstatic. Twice as many cars drive past their businesses each day and the once-feared traffic congestion has never occurred. Now the head of Vancouver's Downtown Association, Rebecca Ocken, has some planning advice for other cities: "One-way streets should not be allowed in prime downtown retail areas. We've proven that."[25]

For small and midsized cities like Vancouver (population 162,000), she is almost certainly right. For larger cities, it depends. I, for one, am not about to revert Manhattan's Columbus and Amsterdam Avenues back to two-way traffic, but it's fair to say that New York would be an even more walkable place if that change were made. Bottom line: if your downtown lacks vitality and it's got one-ways, it's probably time for a change.

SACRED SIDEWALKS

Now that we are almost done talking about pedestrian safety, maybe it is time to actually discuss where pedestrians spend most of their time. I have avoided the subject until now, because sidewalk design has almost nothing to do with pedestrian safety. Pedestrian advocates always fight for wider sidewalks, but that's largely irrelevant. Some of America's most walkable cities have some of the narrowest sidewalks—picture Charleston, Cambridge, or Georgetown. In New Orleans's French Quarter, sidewalks are seven feet across.

What makes a sidewalk safe is not its width, but whether it is protected by a line of parked cars that form a barrier of steel between the pedestrian and the roadway. Have you ever tried sidewalk dining on a sidewalk without curbside parking? Those sorry little table installations rarely last long. Whether they are two feet away or ten feet away, nobody wants to sit—or walk— directly against a line of cars traveling at sixty feet per second. On-street parking also slows traffic down, since drivers are wary of other cars potentially pulling into the roadway.[26]

Few sidewalks without parking entice walking, yet cities routinely eliminate it in the name of traffic flow, beautification, and, more recently, security. Many curbs in Oklahoma City have lost their parking spaces based on the assumption that terrorist bombers are afraid of getting a parking ticket. This line of reasoning is so patently ridiculous that it has been embraced by the federal government.* Fortunately, at least local leadership has shown a capacity for reform: our new plan for OKC's central business district more than doubles the number of on-street parking spaces—from fewer than eight hundred to more than sixteen hundred. According to the National Trust's Main Street Center program, each eliminated on-street parking space costs an adjacent business ten thousand dollars each year in sales. If the inverse is true, we've just made Oklahoma City merchants $9 million richer every year.

The latest enemies of on-street parking to make the scene are two erstwhile friends: bikeways and transit lines. Stripping a sidewalk of its protection in order to add bike lanes is just sacrificing one form of nonmotorized transportation for another. And since transit depends on walkability for its success, any trolley system that undermines pedestrian comfort is shooting itself in the foot. If they are truly to offer an alternative to the automobile, bikes and trolleys must displace moving cars, not parked ones.

---

*As in many American cities, it is the curbs in front of federally owned buildings that have seen the greatest application of antiterrorist parking bans.

Can trees and landscape make up for an absence of curb parking? Not completely, unless you are willing to build big, chunky planter boxes like those found on Chicago's State Street—and, even then, cars are likely to drive too fast. Trees are typically essential, however, for pedestrian comfort, as I will cover in Step 8, and they do slow drivers down a bit. They can also stop a car that has hopped the curb. For that reason, the safest sidewalks are lined by both parked cars *and* trees.*

The other great threat to pedestrians on sidewalks, beyond cars that jump the curb, is cars that are welcomed across it by drop-offs and drive-thrus. In the interest of driver convenience, most American cities handed out curb cuts in the seventies like candy at Halloween, to banks, restaurants, dry cleaners, hotels . . . anyone who asked. These now send a very clear message to pedestrians that the sidewalk does not belong to them.

Many of these can now be eliminated. If a city has rear alleys, there is no justification for providing businesses additional access at the curb. Without alleys, there are still remedies. Most bank drive-thrus—often three and four lanes wide—can be necked down at the sidewalk, to widen beyond it. Indeed, with

---

* One fun battle that has been raging lately is the dispute between head-in and back-in angled parking. Many cities include business districts where the width of pavement is appropriate for angled parking. The recent tradition has been for this parking to be nose-to-the-curb although, historically, many Main Streets did it the other way around. Enter the traffic engineers, and somebody's discovery that back-in parking is actually safer than head-in, and a new movement is born. Now dozens of Main Streets nationwide have reintroduced back-in parking—including Charlotte, Honolulu, Indianapolis, New York, Seattle, Tucson, and Washington—and accidents are down, especially those involving bikes. Tucson, for example, averaged about one bicycle-car crash per week before converting from head-in to rear-in parking. Now, more than four years into implementation, no such crashes have been reported (see brunswickme.org/backinparking.pdf).

It is easy to see why. With back-in parking, the reverse motion is into the curb, while head-in parking requires drivers to back into moving traffic. Back-in parking is also more convenient for loading and unloading. The only major problem with back-in parking is that almost everybody hates it, mostly because they are not used to it. This was the case in Cedar Rapids, Iowa, where the typical public reaction was summed up in the online comment of one Brent B.: "Amazing, it only took the dum-dums on the city council three years to realize what an idiotic idea while those of us with common sense the rise of online banking, many drive-thru lanes can just be eliminated. Whether or not businesses can be made to give up their current curb cuts, the best strategy now is to simply not allow any new ones. Even hotels, unless they are quite large, should be able to handle drop-offs easily at the curb, in the parking lane. In Philadelphia, we stayed at the 230-room Hotel Palomar, which welcomes all its cars this way. To be stingy with curb cuts, cities must be generous with small no-parking zones at places like hotels, where drop-offs occur continuously.

SENSELESS SIGNALS

In the last step, I mentioned the visible presence of taxis as one indicator of a city's walkability. Another reliable bellwether is the visible absence of push-button traffic signals. In my travels, it is almost always the cities with push-button crossings that need the most help. I remember when these were introduced during my

---

knew it was stupid to begin with" (comment to Rick Smith, "Cedar Rapids Phasing Out Back-In Angle Parking," *The Gazette*, June 9, 2011). To his credit, one council member, Jerry McGrane, said that he had voted in support of back-in parking "for the entertainment value if nothing else" (ibid.).

Back-in parking has also been implemented in some communities that are simply not ready for it. I mean this not intellectually, but urbanistically. If residents are not accustomed to parallel parking—which is more difficult than back-in—and if almost all local parking is head-in at strip malls, then reverse parking may just be too big a stretch. That was the case in Fremont, California, where back-in parking was discontinued after one year when 70 percent of poll respondents said they would be "less likely to stop" at retail shops with back-in parking (City of Fremont, City Council Agenda and Report, May 3, 2011). But take a look at Fremont: it's pure sprawl—217,000 residents without a single block of urban walkability.

The best argument I have heard against back-in parking is that the exhaust fumes can be noxious to sidewalk dining. This point makes sense and needs to be taken into account when back-in parking districts are located. As suggested by Tucson, bike routes need to be considered as well, as cycle lanes behind head-in parking are basically suicidal. With those two cautions, I am happy leaving it up to the citizens. When asked, I usually put it this way: "Back-in parking works just fine in Washington. Are you better or worse drivers than we are?"

childhood, and they seemed at the time like a gift. Wow, I can actually control the traffic light. What power! But the truth is quite the opposite. Push-buttons almost always mean that the automobile dominates, as they are typically installed in conjunction with a new signal timing in which crossing times are shorter and less frequent. Far from empowering walkers, the push button turns them into second-class citizens; pedestrians should never have to ask for a light.

It is fascinating to talk to blind people about push-button walk signals. They push the button and wait for a lull in the noise. But then they can't tell if what they hear is a red light, or just a gap in the speedy traffic. The alternative are those annoying chirping signals that now mark the pace of daily life in crunchy towns like Northampton, Massachusetts. These are unnecessary in a standard (non–push-button) crosswalk, where the visually impaired can hear and predict the direction of traffic.

Another recent favorite among traffic planners is the "Barnes Dance" intersection, popularized in the United States by Denver's Henry Barnes, in which all pedestrians wait a full cycle for all cars to stop and then are briefly given free rein over the entire intersection—including diagonally. The Barnes Dance is a sexier version of the generic "dedicated-cycle" intersection, which lacks the diagonal paint job, but functions the same way. This system was introduced to avoid conflicts between turning vehicles and pedestrians in crosswalks, another example of "pedestrian safety" being used as an excuse to limit pedestrian convenience in the service of traffic flow. There are more than three hundred of these intersections in Japan, and they do make sense in places with pedestrian crowding, like Manhattan's Union Square. But there is no pedestrian crowding in Bethlehem, Pennsylvania, which is why I have an impressive photo collection of dedicated-cycle jaywalkers. Smaller cities need to be aware that some big-city best practices just aren't made for them.

What makes dedicated-cycle intersections so frustrating to

pedestrians is the likelihood that they will have to stand still at almost every street they cross. Experienced Manhattan walkers will confirm that, in a true grid with standard signals, it is possible to cover huge swaths of a city without stopping once. Most pedestrian routes are not due north-south or east-west, but diagonal, and every intersection provides the opportunity to cross in one direction at all times. Walkers like to keep walking and dedicated signals kill the momentum.

Denver has recently eliminated its diagonal Barnes Dances due to the introduction of streetcars, but it has kept its dedicated-crossing cycles and—in a horrible move—increased the length of each cycle from an already-too-long seventy-five seconds to ninety seconds.* The city claims that this change is partly due to a federal recalibration of pedestrian speed downwards from 4 feet per second to 3.5 feet per second (as Americans become fatter and slower targets). But do the math: it takes 9 seconds to cross three driving lanes at the old, fast speed, and 10.3 seconds at the new, slow one. And you need 15 more seconds why? The clear winners, as usual, are the automobiles, which the city is afraid of inconveniencing with trolleys. Let's hope that the high altitude bestows superhuman patience on Denver's pedestrians.

The other way that cities increase traffic flow at the expense of pedestrians is with the "right on red" rule. God knows, I love this as a driver, but, as Jan Gehl puts it, "the widespread American practice of allowing cars to 'turn right on red' at intersections is unthinkable in cities that want to invite people to walk and bicycle."[27] It is banned in the Netherlands.[28]

Of course, the obligatory right-on-green is even more dangerous to pedestrians—and left-on-green worse than that[29]—

---

* The ideal signal cycle timing is almost always sixty seconds or less. Longer signal cycles have long been favored by traffic engineers, who calculate that these contribute to system throughput. However, their calculations ignore the associated negative impacts of the speeding and road rage that result from drivers having to wait inordinately long times at stoplights, not to mention the jaywalking accidents.

since the driver is being told to go. One recent safety innovation, just implemented in Washington, D.C., is the leading pedestrian interval, or LPI, better known as the "pedestrian head start." With the LPI, the "walk" signal appears about three seconds prior to the green light, allowing pedestrians to claim the intersection before cars do. This is the ideal form of walkability enhancer, since it improves both pedestrian safety and pedestrian convenience, rather than pitting the two against each other. Meanwhile, in Los Angeles, the city's bright idea for improving pedestrian safety is to remove crosswalks.[30]

Finally, though, with signals as with road design, the safest approach may turn out to be "less is more," as embodied in the four-way stop sign. What if, instead of simply telling drivers when to go, we asked them to think for themselves? Four-way stop signs, which require motorists to approach each intersection as a negotiation, turn out to be much safer than signals.[31] Drivers slow down, but never have to wait for more than a few seconds, and pedestrians and bicyclists are generally waved through first.* Clearly, these are not possible on the busiest streets, but most cities have many intersections that would benefit from the removal of their signals in favor of stop signs.

If stop signs are so much better than signals, why do signals still proliferate on local low-traffic streets? Indeed, why does the typical corner include not just a signal in each direction, but a distinct signal in each direction over every single lane of traffic, such that the typical urban four-lane intersection now bristles with a good dozen lights? In the sixties, one signal hanging over the middle of the crossing was enough.

The answer may lie in who makes the rules. As director of the Davenport, Iowa, Design Center, Darrin Nordahl did a little

---

*Indeed, four-way stops are in most cases a biker's dream, as they generally allow confident bikers to blow through intersection after intersection without even having to slow down.

digging, and found out that the firm the city hired to design its signalization regime was the same firm who then sold the city its signals. Enough said.

Would most intersections be safer with one traffic signal rather than twelve? Maybe, maybe not. But many streets would be safer with four-way stop signs. And we could sure use the savings.

STEP 6: WELCOME BIKES

A better way to go; Amsterdam, Copenhagen, Portland, and other foreign cities; Hey! I'm bikin' here!; How safe is safe?; I run afoul of the vehicular cyclists; Bike lanes, separated paths, and shared routes; Advanced cycling; Don't get greedy

Perhaps the greatest revolution currently under way in—only some—American cities is the dramatic rise in biking. This has not happened by accident. New York City recently saw a 35 percent jump in ridership in one year alone, thanks specifically to its strong commitment to an ever-improving bicycle network. Almost every American city is currently well stocked with would-be bike riders who are only waiting for an invitation to hop on the saddle, and it is likely that those cities that invest now in (relatively inexpensive) biking infrastructure will have a meaningful advantage in attracting the next generation of new residents. Millennials routinely cite biking as an important motivator in location choice, and today's seventeen-year-old is a third less likely to have a driver's license than a baby boomer was at that age.

To anyone who lived in New York during the eighties, it might seem a bit odd to advocate for bicycles in a discussion of pedestrian safety. The only cyclists at that time were reckless messengers who broke every traffic law and took out pedestrians with alarming frequency. But visit the city now and it's hard to spot the messengers among the throngs of civilians, most of whom do a pretty good job of sticking to their newly minted bike lanes.

Not that there aren't exceptions.* In a heart-stopping aerial video, "3-Way Street," by Ron Gabriel,[1] one can witness some more adventurous Manhattan cyclists weaving through multiple lanes of oncoming traffic to surprise hapless pedestrians in crosswalks. Clearly, some people have yet to get with the program. After a few minutes of the video, it becomes apparent that these bikers probably pose the greatest danger to themselves, so we can only assume that Darwinism will cull the herd. Every evolution involves growing pains, and these daredevils hide a deeper truth, which is that cities with more bicyclists are considerably safer for both bicyclists and pedestrians.

Take a step back and it's easy to see why. A street with bikes, once the drivers get used to them, is a place where cars proceed more cautiously. And a city with bikes everywhere is a different kind of city. As bike lanes have been added along New York's avenues, injuries to pedestrians have dropped by about a third. Indeed, on Broadway and on Ninth Avenue, reported accidents and injuries to all users were cut in half,[2] outpacing even the advocates' expectations.

A BETTER WAY TO GO

Safety is but one of many reasons why our cities need more bicycles. As anyone who has taken advantage of a good biking city will tell you, cycling has got to be the most efficient, healthful, empowering, and sustainable form of transportation there is. Using the same amount of energy as walking, a bicycle will take you three times farther.[3] Bicycle commuters enjoy about double the

---

*Indeed, it is in some of the most advanced biking cities, like Amsterdam and Berlin, where I have had my closest calls with speeding bicyclists. In both cases, though, I was firmly at fault, strolling mindlessly in well-marked bike lanes, just off the plane and not yet adjusted to the eminently logical and well-marked street divisions. And one close brush was all it took to correct my course for the remainder of my visit.

amount of daily physical activity of drivers.[4] Bikes are cheap, and the fuel is free. And it's fun. As one happy biker put it, "It's like being able to golf to work."[5]

I have friends who bike to and from their offices instead of joining a gym, saving time and money and generally having a great time of it. (Yes, they have showers at work.) As Robert Hurst says in *The Cyclist's Manifesto*, "If you need to exercise, and you need to get around, why not do both at the same time?"[6]

Compared to the car, the bicycle's spatial demands are minimal. Ten bikes can park in the space of a single car, and the typical bike lane handles five to ten times the traffic volume of a car lane twice its width.[7] As already mentioned, money spent on bike lanes generates more than twice the jobs of money spent on car lanes. And if every American biked an hour per day instead of driving, the United States would cut its gasoline consumption by 38 percent and its greenhouse gas emissions by 12 percent, meeting the Kyoto Accords instantly.[8]

In Washington, I have found that there is simply no faster, easier, or more convenient way to get around. If I have an appointment almost anywhere in the city, I just set my alarm for fifteen minutes prior and I will be there on time. Were I to take transit or drive and park, that would require twice as long. Just the other morning, I biked the two miles to my doctor's office, had a checkup, and biked home, all in half an hour. Two caveats: I have America's only on-time doctor and I had to take a shower when I got home—it's August.

As one compares different biking and nonbiking places, it is interesting to see that climate plays a surprisingly small role. Canada's Yukon Territory—up there next to Alaska—has twice the rate of bicycle commuters as California.[9] In October 2011, icy Minneapolis was named "America's #1 Bike City" by *Bicycling* magazine, with 4 percent of all work trips being made by bike.[10] Nor is topography a significant factor: San Francisco has three times the ridership of relatively flat Denver.[11]

Rather than environmental or cultural, it seems that the biggest factors in establishing a biking city are strictly physical, and of two different types. First, there needs to be urbanism. As John Pucher and Ralph Buehler suggest in their report to the Institute of Transport and Logistic Studies, the main reasons that Canadians "cycle about three times more than Americans" are "Canada's higher urban densities and mixed-use development, shorter trip distances . . . [and] higher costs of owning, driving and parking a car"[12]—all conditions associated with city living. Second, and also cited by the authors, are "safer cycling conditions and more extensive cycling infrastructure"•—in other words, streets that have been designed to welcome bikes.

Of these two categories, the former equates with walkability. The conditions that support pedestrians are also needed to entice bikers. Once they are in place, the further provision of a truly useful biking network should be enough to allow a cycling culture to grow. Build it and they will come.

AMSTERDAM, COPENHAGEN, PORTLAND, AND OTHER FOREIGN CITIES

Since Americans are not constitutionally prohibited from embracing cycling in the same way that so many other nations do, it might be useful to look at some of the societies in which biking is a mainstay to see what is possible. Any such investigation probably has to begin with the Netherlands, which has the planet's highest percentage of people cycling. The Dutch statistics are staggering. Fully 27 percent of all trips are made on bicycle. School buses are uncommon, as the vast majority of high schoolers

---

• "Why Canadians Cycle More Than Americans," 265. The authors conclude that "most of these factors result from differences between Canada and the United States in their transport and land-use policies, and not from intrinsic differences in history, culture or resource availability."

bike to class.[13] Indeed, 95 percent of ten-to-twelve-year-olds bi-cycle to school at least some of the time.[14] Women take more bike trips than men, and roughly a fourth of all trips made by the elderly are on a bicycle.[15] In Amsterdam, a city of 783,000, about 400,000 people are out riding their bikes on any given day.[16] In a telling detail, spandex sightings are exceedingly rare; nobody wears anything special to bicycle, certainly not a helmet.

Bike safety, etiquette, and respect for bikers are taught from an early age. Drivers learn to reach for the door handle with their opposite hand, so that they cannot exit the car without checking for bikes. Food shopping is more likely to occur daily than weekly, to fit it in the bike basket. As Russell Shorto notes in *The New York Times*, biking means that the Dutch eat fresher bread.[17]

Biking in the Netherlands is a virtuous circle, in which more bike paths—the most in the world—has led to more biking, which has led to more bike paths. It is empowering to know that things were not always this way. Amsterdam's chief planner, Zef Hemel, told Shorto that "back in the 1960s, we were doing the same thing as America, making cities car-friendly." He credits Jane Jacobs, of all people, with the transformation of Dutch think-ing.[18] It's nice to know that *somebody* was listening to her back then.

Like the Netherlands, Denmark has also seen a revolution in cycling, much of it recent, and most of it spearheaded by gov-ernment investment in bike infrastructure. In Copenhagen, most of the city's major four-lane streets have been converted to two lanes plus two bike paths. As a sign of the city's priorities, these bike lanes are always cleared of snow before the driving lanes are. The minimum recommended bike path width is over eight feet,[19] which makes America's five-footers look pretty dinky.

The impact of this investment has been profound. Forty years ago, peak-hour motorists in Copenhagen outnumbered bicyclists by three to one. In 2003, the two modes reached parity, and now cycling is the most popular way around town.[20] Forty percent more people bike to work than drive.[21]

Closer to home, and supposedly part of America, the most bike friendly of our sizeable cities has got to be Portland. Although no match for Europe, Portland has accomplished something remarkable. A mere fifteen years ago, only 1 percent of Portlanders biked to work; today, that number tops 8 percent.[22] Between 1993 and 2008, peak-season bike traffic across the Willamette River climbed from about 3,600 trips per day to more than 16,700.[23]

This change is palpable. I was recently e-mailed some photos of the city's morning commute and I had to ask the sender: "What was this, Bike to Work Day?" No, he said, it was just Tuesday.

As in Europe, this change was led by an investment in bicycle infrastructure, but at a limited cost. According to Mia Birk, the city's bicycle coordinator at the time, "For less than one percent of Portland's transportation budget, we've increased bicycling from negligible to significant. For the cost of one mile of freeway— about $50 million—we've built 275 of bikeways."[24] Spending 1 percent of transportation funds on a network serving 8 percent of commuters sounds like a good deal, even better when you consider the indirect economic benefits. In contrast to widened roads and other highway "improvements," new bikeways actually increase the value of nearby real estate.

It's not for nothing that Portland even has a woman called "the Bike Realtor," Kirsten Kaufman, who specializes in selling overpriced homes next to bike routes. Her website, bikerealtor .com, lays it out simply enough: "I get it. I specialize in helping people who want to drive less and enjoy life more. I know from personal experience that the less time my family spends in the car, the happier and healthier we are."[25]

If bikeways make houses more valuable, some of that value accrues back to the city in higher property taxes—undoubtedly enough to pay for the bikeways. Of course, these dollars are only a fraction of the savings that result from time and money not spent in traffic, as Joe Cortright says (see page 29).

And then there are the noneconomic benefits to a community that has reshaped itself around bicycles. In *Pedaling Revolution*—the seminal book on urban cycling—Jeff Mapes describes one popular local activity, "bike moving," in which people literally help each other change homes through the exclusive use of pedal power. It sounds like a great way to meet people, although perhaps not as effective as North America's largest annual naked bike ride, also claimed by Portland.[26] (Don't forget the baby wipes.)

Before turning to New York's recent transformation, it is worth mentioning one other American city, Boulder, Colorado. In a mere three years, from 2000 to 2003, the percentage of residents' commute trips by bike tripled, from an already hefty 7 percent to an epic 21 percent, thanks to investment in biking and transit.[27] Ninety-five percent of Boulder's arterial streets—the type usually most dangerous to cyclists—have been made bike friendly, with what can now be described as the expected results. Similar things are happening in Seattle, Chicago, Madison, Minneapolis, and elsewhere.* It can now be said with some confidence that any urban road investment that ignores bicyclists is money that could be better spent.

HEY! I'M BIKIN' HERE!

Street space in New York has always been contested, so you can imagine the furor that erupted when Janette Sadik-Khan, Mayor

---

* "America's Top-50 Bike Friendly Cities," bicycling.com. For example, Chicago's Rahm Emanuel has committed to adding twenty-five miles of bike lanes during each year of his first term. Seattle is executing a ten-year, $240 million bike plan that will add 450 miles of bike paths.

Michael Bloomberg's transportation chief, started taking lanes away from cars and giving them to bicycles. Manhattan was one thing, but Brooklyn? That's looking for trouble.

Here's what happened: The city converted one lane of Prospect Park West from driving to biking. As a result, the number of weekday cyclists tripled, and the percentage of speeders dropped from about 75 percent of all cars to less than 17 percent. Injury crashes went down by 63 percent from prior years. Interestingly, car volume and travel times stayed almost exactly the same—the typical southbound trip became five seconds faster—and there were no negative impacts on streets nearby.[28]

Sounds pretty good, right? Well, as of this writing, Sadik-Khan has personally been subpoenaed by the ironically named Neighbors for Better Bike Lanes (just replace "Better" with "No," and you'll get the picture) for trying to turn this successful and popular trial project into a permanent installation. Other opponents include Borough President Marty Markowitz, who calls bike lanes "discrimination to those who prefer to own or need their cars for their livelihood or convenience."[29] Not without a sense of humor, Mr. Markowitz put a cartoon of the bike lane on his annual Christmas card, flanked by additional crowded lanes for sitting, walking, holiday revelry, and, yes, driving—the narrowest lane of all. The cartoon was accompanied by a song, to the tune of "My Favorite Things":

> Strollers and schleppers and skaters and joggers
> Holiday lanes just for egg-noggers
> But let's not forget cars—it's getting insane
> Welcome to Brooklyn, "The Borough of Lanes."[30]

If this opposition fails, which is likely given its lack of supporting data, Prospect Park West will continue to serve close to 10 percent more commuters than it did before, with greatly reduced risk to life and limb. One can only hope that Markowitz, unde-

terred by the facts, will be swayed by the constituents he supposedly serves, who support more bike lanes at a ratio of almost two
to one.[31]

The Prospect Park West controversy is just one part of a
much larger and happier picture of New York City that includes
225 miles of bike lanes added since 2006, with more to come.
These lane miles have contributed to a massive rise in commuter cycling, from 8,650 riders recorded in 2006 to 18,800
today. In the past year alone, biking has risen by 14 percent.[32]
According to a Quinnipiac University poll, support for bike lanes
across the city has also been growing every year, hitting 59 percent in 2011.* The remaining New Yorkers, of course, are still
pissed off.

HOW SAFE IS SAFE?

We know that biking cities are safer cities. But is biking really
worth the risk? The numbers could be more encouraging. The
safety expert Ken Kifer found that "bicycling was nineteen to
thirty-three times more likely to result in injury than driving
a car the same distance." Shortly after publishing his research,
Kifer was killed by an automobile while biking.[33]

I try to stay mindful of Kifer's story as I bike around Washington, as there is always a temptation to cut corners to avoid
slowing down. Like many cyclists, I treat red lights as yield signs
and blow through stop signs when I can. Using this method, my
only close call in nine years has been at a four-way stop, with
another bicyclist of similar bent. This experience made me wonder whether the much-advertised salubrious benefits of "active

*Andrea Bernstein, "NYC Biking Is Up 14% from 2010; Overall Support Rises," trans-
portationnation.org, July 28, 2011. This 59 percent is up from 56 percent in 2010, which
matched the percentage of New Yorkers who don't own cars (U.S. Census, 2010).

transportation" get canceled out by the occasional tumble. Did I really want to be ten pounds slimmer with a broken wrist?

I am aware of only one study that addresses this, by the British researcher Mayer Hillman. From his study of British factory workers, he concluded that the health benefits of biking outweigh the risks by twenty to one. In Hillman's estimation, the regular cyclists were as fit as the noncyclists ten years younger[34] and enjoyed such better health that their few biking injuries were almost statistically insignificant. This conclusion is comforting, but one does have to remember that it is British, from a town that is likely to have developed a prominent biking culture.

This presence of an established cycling population, as it makes for more aware drivers, seems to be the biggest factor in bike safety. From city to city, the "strength in numbers" theory holds sway. In New York, with bicycling up 262 percent since 2000, injury risk has declined by 72 percent.[35] In Portland, a fourfold increase in cycling has brought with it a 69 percent reduction in the crash rate.[36] Davis, California, "America's Bicycle Capital"— where one trip out of seven is by bike—has the lowest bicycle fatality rates of sixteen similarly sized California cities.*

Of course, we have a long way to go to equal the Netherlands, whose fatality rate is less than a third of ours, despite the lack of helmets.[37] This evidence has prompted some American cyclists to stop wearing helmets, as if the wind blowing through your hair somehow magically turns your city into Amsterdam. This is a bad idea, even though it is bolstered by the recent discovery that passing cars give more elbow room to bikers without helmets—and, incidentally, even more space to bikers wearing blond wigs.[38] This latest episode of risk homeostasis threatens to

---

*Jeff Mapes, *Pedaling Revolution*, 23, 128. Referred to as "ten square miles surrounded by reality" (135), Davis also has the lowest rates of pedestrian and vehicular deaths of the sixteen cities studied.

camouflage the larger fact that 63 percent of bicycle fatalities are the result of head injuries.[39]

Bottom line: it would seem that we are presented with two statistics that could potentially cancel each other out. If biking is nineteen to thirty-three times more dangerous than driving, but the health benefits of biking (in bikeable cities) are twenty times greater than the risks, then maybe we can call it a wash. Most important to this discussion is the fact that bicycle safety seems to depend largely on how many people are biking, and that the resulting mandate—to create as many cyclists as possible—needs to drive the design of our urban bicycle networks. As we shall see ahead, this mandate leads to some counterintuitive conclusions.

I RUN AFOUL OF THE VEHICULAR CYCLISTS

Not very long ago, I was against bike lanes in downtown areas, mostly because they can widen streets that are already too wide, encouraging cars to speed. More recently, for reasons that will become evident, I changed my mind. I hardly ever change my mind about anything, and I had every reason to expect that my revised position might win me some friends in the cycling community. Imagine my surprise, then, when I released my proposals for Davenport, Iowa, and was soon directed to the following (excerpted) e-mail message: "This is the same 'solution' he's trashing downtown Oklahoma City with. . . . He defines the problem without seeing it. Because he's only looking in his own lane. . . . Snake oil!" Yikes, what gives? I thought you people *liked* bike lanes! Utterly confused, I forwarded the exchange to Mike Lydon, a consultant who specializes in urban biking. It was then that I learned about the fascinating technique called *vehicular cycling* and the waning but still significant influence of its ardent practitioners.

In many cities, if you take a lesson in bicycle safety, there is a good chance it will be taught by a vehicular cyclist. You will be instructed essentially to drive your bike as if it were a car, albeit a slow one. This includes "claiming your lane," staying near its center and only allowing cars to pass when there is ample room. In the words of the movement's founder, John Forester: "The vehicular-style cyclist not only acts outwardly like a driver, he knows inwardly that he is one. Instead of feeling like a trespasser on roads owned by cars he feels like just another driver with a slightly different vehicle."[40]

Forester is motivated principally by rider safety and by what he earnestly believes is the best way to stay safe: visibly claiming the proper amount of roadway at all times. But he is also driven, as it were, by a conviction that cyclists should not be assigned second-class status to motorists. For this reason, as Robert Hurst puts it, "Forester's crusade has always been directed primarily at bike lanes and the idea that bicyclists should be 'shoved over to the side' [as he puts it] to make way for motor traffic."[41] For Forester and his disciples, bike lanes are worse than "separate but equal," and must be eradicated from the landscape. As a result, he has become a darling of the libertarian American Dream Coalition, where he sits on the Speakers' Bureau with the rest of the Road Gang, making sure that not a single transportation dollar gets diverted from highways.

The biggest problem with vehicular cycling is neither its politics nor its relative safety—which has not been discredited—but whom it serves. John Pucher and Ralph Buehler summed up the predicament in their important paper, "Cycling for Few or for Everyone":

> In the vehicular cycling model, cyclists must constantly evaluate traffic, looking back, signaling, adjusting lateral position and speed, sometimes blocking a lane and sometimes yielding, always trying to fit into the "dance"

that is traffic. Research shows that most people feel very unsafe engaging in this kind of dance, in which a single mistake could be fatal. Children as well as many women and elders are excluded. While some people, especially young men, may find the challenge stimulating, it is stressful and unpleasant for the vast majority. It is no wonder that the model of vehicular cycling, which the USA has followed de facto for the past forty years, has led to extremely low levels of bicycling use.[42]

And there's the rub. Vehicular cycling may indeed be the safest way to bike, but it is also the most exclusive. Perhaps the ideal candidate for vehicular cycling was the fellow I met in Davenport, who was so aggressive a cyclist that he had dispensed with his bike saddle. I suspect that the next step in this evolution is to wear a thong and to tattoo "Hard Core" on your buttocks.

If bike safety is largely a factor of the number of cyclists, as the studies insist, then any technique that works against their proliferation can hardly be considered safe. Jeff Mapes notes that Forester "didn't think that cycling would ever become a mass form of transportation in America, and that was fine with him."[43] Now, as that outcome is already happening, it's time to show the vehicular cyclists the bike path out of town. More important, it's time to create bicycle facilities that not only allow for cyclists, but actively and boisterously invite them to share the road.

BIKE LANES, SEPARATED PATHS, AND SHARED ROUTES

That said, there is a good argument against bike lanes. Because narrower streets are safer streets, and because the perception of potential conflict is what makes all road users act with caution, it is likely that adding bike lanes to a street makes it less safe. This conjecture is supported by several studies in different countries, cited in Tom Vanderbilt's book *Traffic*, that found that "drivers tend to give cyclists more space as they pass when they are on a street without a bicycle lane. The white marking seems to work as a subliminal signal to drivers that they need to act less cautiously—that it's the edge of the lane, and not the cyclist, that they need to worry about."[44]

This experience suggests that most bike routes should be unmarked. However, unmarked bike routes do not attract bikers and most cities do not have enough bikers to make biking safe. For that reason, I believe that it often is wiser to include bike lanes anyway—not everywhere, but in locations where they make sense.

And where is that? That tricky question can be answered by working through a series of simpler questions. The first is whether bike lanes can be used to take up excess street space. As seen in Brooklyn, trading driving lanes for biking lanes need not make a street less efficient for automobiles. The same goes for the "road diets" of the previous chapter: trading four lanes for three lanes plus cycling rarely reduces car capacity when it introduces a center turn lane.

However, in some cases, turning driving lanes into bike lanes will indeed slow down drivers. That trade-off may well be worthwhile, especially if a street sits along an important cycling trajectory. It is important to remember that, in a robust street network, traffic redistributes itself intelligently, with parallel roads able to pick up the slack. For that reason, any analysis of likely impacts needs to look not just at the street in question, but at the larger system. Of course, you already know that reducing capacity reduces traffic, so the real challenge here is not technical, but political.

Another good way—and good reason—to add bike lanes is to right-size existing lanes that are too fat. We did that in Lowell, where a street misdesigned as a highway, with (four) twelve-foot driving lanes and eight-foot parking lanes, will be remade with ten-foot and seven-foot lanes, yielding ten extra feet for biking. Since a standard bike lane is five feet wide, we were able to add a bike lane in each direction. This change will have no impact on the road's car capacity, but it will encourage safer speeds.

But five-foot bike lanes up against car doors are nobody's favorite, so the next question is whether there is enough room to build a *separated path*. These typically claim at least eleven feet of roadway, to allow for two adjacent four-foot paths protected by a three-foot buffer. If you haven't seen them, these paths—the type employed in Brooklyn—take some getting used to. They are located between one curb and that curb's parallel parking aisle, which gets pushed out into the street. The buffer is marked with striping and often holds vertical posts. Once you get the hang of these paths, however, it's hard to go back to a plain old bike lane. My wife will go three blocks out of her way to take the new separated path in our neighborhood. It goes down one side of a formerly four-lane one-way street, a street that now operates perfectly well with one fewer eleven-foot lane. D.C. planning czar Harriet Tregoning, a master communicator, shrewdly refers to streets with this much pavement as having "extra lanes."

The final question to ask is whether a bike lane is in keeping with the nature of the street. While carving bike lanes out of existing retail Main Streets can sometimes make sense, they should not be allowed to replace curbside parking, nor can they be allowed to create an impediment between cars and shops. For this reason, separated paths rarely belong in a retail environment. All those stripes and posts may send a message of sustainable transportation, but it is still a message of motion, not of the stasis appropriate to a Main Street. The design objective for this type of street should be to create an environment of such slow driving that bikes and cars can mix comfortably at biking speeds. The technical term for this sort of facility is a *shared route*, and the vast majority of bikeways must remain unmarked streets that belong to everyone. To use an extreme example, a residential cul-de-sac is no place for a bike lane. Only when car speeds get well into the thirties does the need for lanes kick in.

ADVANCED CYCLING

As long as we're getting technical, let's mention some of the more sophisticated bikeways that have recently hit the streets. If you are not a cycling nut, feel free to skip this bit.

One technique that's been getting a lot of play lately is the *sharrow*, which is a wide lane shared by cars and bicyclists, indicated by a prominent biker decal in the right-center of the pavement. In *The Cyclist's Manifesto*, Robert Hurst comes out strongly in favor of sharrows over bike lanes, noting that "the sharrow doesn't really tell the bicyclist or the driver to do anything specifically, and therein lies much of its beauty. It's art that conjures awareness, and that, as we've seen, is what traffic safety is all about."[45]

He is, of course, right, but the problem is that all things fade, and those sharrow markings seem to disappear faster than almost any other type of road decal. In many northern cities, where they effectively sandblast the streets every winter, a townful of sharrows can disappear in two seasons. And then all you're left with is a super-fat lane. For this reason, sharrows are best used to encourage and announce the presence of bikes in streets that are a bit too wide, but not wide enough to hold a dedicated lane instead. In my experience, if a driving lane is approaching fifteen feet wide, a bike lane is far better than a sharrow.

Another interesting development is something called the *bi-*

cycle boulevard, which has taken Portland by storm and can also be found in Madison, Tucson, Minneapolis, Albuquerque, and a handful of California cities. To create a bicycle boulevard, you take a street that is long enough to be of regional significance and hobble its intersections so that only bicycles can flow quickly from block to block. Residents can enter with their cars, but diverters at the cross-streets quickly free the street of cut-through traffic. Then, if you're really serious, you time the signals at each intersection to match the twelve-mph speed of the average cyclist,* and you end up with what is called a *green wave*. Green waves on bicycle boulevards contribute mightily to Portland's bike commute and cycling culture. Clearly, they are best limited to residential areas where, indeed, they contribute to property values, as the Bike Realtor will tell you.

Finally, investment in a different kind of cycling infrastructure, pioneered in Europe, has begun to take root in American soil: urban bike share. After some small and mostly failed attempts in prior decades, this concept is finally catching on, thanks largely to new technologies that remove some earlier inconveniences. The best-known bike share is the twenty-thousand-bike Vélib system in France, which is considered a resounding success despite the fact that more than 80 percent of its bikes have been damaged, dumped in the Seine, or shipped off to Africa.[46] The French program is actually dwarfed by one in Hangzhou, China, where bike stations are located only 330 feet apart, and where not one of the system's 60,600 bikes has yet to be stolen.[47]

Recently, Washington, D.C., pioneered large-scale bike sharing in the United States, and our bright red Capital Bikeshare cycles have become a fixture of urban life in the District. Here's how it works: you check your smartphone for the location of a

---

*Mapes, *Pedaling Revolution*, 81. Since the timing only enhances travel in one direction, these are paced to ease the inbound and outbound rush-hour commutes.

bike docking station near you, and make sure that there are bikes available. The city currently has 1,100 bikes distributed among 114 stations. Show up, stick in your key, take a bike, and go. The first half hour is free—that's enough time to get almost any-where in the District—and then you start paying a nickel a min-ute. This price escalates to discourage all-day rentals, to the point that each hour after ninety minutes costs twelve dollars. Near your destination, you locate another docking station—again, you can check your phone for open docks—and you're done.

Given the system's convenience, and the continually improv-ing bikeability of the District, public buy-in has been huge.* After one year, the program had amassed fourteen thousand annual riders, as well as over forty thousand day memberships.[48] In Au-gust 2010, Capital Bikeshare members logged almost 150,000 trips, and that was during the most sweltering four weeks in D.C. history.■ In response to the program's success, its sponsors hope to create a regional system of more than five thousand bikes within a few years.[49] Across the Potomac, Arlington, Vir-ginia, already has fourteen docking stations, with sixteen more on the way.[50]

Washington was first out of the gate, but similar programs are now in place—or will be soon—in a dozen other American cities, including the usual sustainable suspects (New York, San Francisco, etc.) as well as some surprises (San Antonio, Des Moines).[51] These bike-sharing programs are not cheap. Washing-ton's took about $5 million to start, and costs a couple million to operate each year. This means that the District has paid more than six thousand dollars so far for each bicycle in service, which seems awfully steep, even though almost all of it has been other

---

*While some local bike shops initially feared the competition, they are now celebrating a major uptick in sales, fueled by Capital Bikeshare renters who decide that they want to own.

■One can only assume that they were principally downhill—the bike-share staff use vans to redistribute the bikes, which tend to settle at lower altitudes.

people's money. Some of that cash has been recouped by selling advertising space, but the system will never break even—nor should it be asked to. Just like highways and transit, bicycle transportation will require public investment to succeed. Given the environmental and health benefits of turning drivers and riders into bikers—and the very real public savings associated with those benefits—that six thousand dollars is a better deal than it looks. All the more so when you consider the free publicity these systems bring.

DON'T GET GREEDY

There is no doubt in my mind that many bicycle advocates will find this chapter's prescriptions woefully inadequate. What, five feet for a bike lane? They will remind me of Copenhagen's eight-footers, and quote Bogotá's Enrique Peñalosa, "If a bike lane isn't safe for an eight-year-old child, it isn't really a bike lane."[52] Some will bemoan my suggestion that separated paths and bike boulevards are best kept out of commercial areas. These complaints are certainly valid, and also correct—from the perspective of a bicycle advocate.

But bicycle advocates are specialists. Like the highway specialists who reamed out our cities with freeways, they are often focused myopically on the one aspect of the public realm that concerns them, sometimes at the expense of all the others. It is for this reason that specialists are the enemy of the city, which is by definition a general enterprise. Let's consider for a minute what would happen to the typical American Main Street if we were to redesign it to keep all of the specialists happy.

First, we would need at least four travel lanes and a center turn lane, to keep the transportation engineers happy. These would need to be eleven feet wide—no, wait, make that twelve feet, because the fire chief might want to pass a bus without slowing down. To satisfy the business owners, we would need angle parking on both sides (another forty feet), and eight-foot separated bike paths against each curb for you-know-who. Then we would have to add two ten-foot continuous tree trenches to satisfy the urban forester, and two twenty-foot-minimum sidewalks for the pedestrian advocates. Have you been doing the math? We now have a Main Street over 175 feet wide. This is more than twice the normal width and about as efficacious an urban environment as a large-jet runway—and just as conducive to shopping.

The moral of this story is that everyone has to compromise if our cities are going to be any good and also if they are going to be affordable. Greediness costs too much, and can also cause you to end up shortchanging yourself. In New York City, they have built a stunning "cycle track" along Sands Street in Brooklyn. This massive center-road facility cost taxpayers $13 million per mile. That's almost ten times the cost of a signal-protected bike path, and *one hundred times* the cost of a standard separated path.[53] Presuming that budgets have limits, could it possibly be worth losing one hundred miles of separated path to build one mile of cycle track?

The goal of an intelligent cycling plan should be to allow bikes access to every address in the city. Some of those trips will be on separated paths, others on bike lanes, and most will be mixing with traffic on slower streets. Some may even be on sidewalks, which surprisingly is still legal in many places. The dream is to get bicyclists where they need to go, not to apportion them a slice of every road, tied up with a bow.

That said, there is reason to go a bit overboard, especially when it comes to lane markings. If the evidence is to be believed, bike lanes—especially separated lanes—basically mint cyclists. But, beyond that, they also send a message. A bold green stripe down the side of a street—or many streets—tells residents and potential residents that a city supports alternative transportation, healthy lifestyles, and cycling culture, and that it welcomes the sort of people who get around on bikes. For the most part, those people are the millennials and creatives who will help a city thrive. For that reason, even if nobody in town even owns a bike, a few snazzy new lanes are probably a good idea. Or you can just skip right to the Naked Ride and see how that goes.

THE COMFORTABLE WALK

■

STEP 7: SHAPE THE SPACES
STEP 8: PLANT TREES

STEP 7: SHAPE THE SPACES

Embrace me; Object fetishism; Tiny is tastier; Weather or not

Do snakes disturb you? Don't be embarrassed, it's not your fault. Thousands of years of your ancestors' being bitten by snakes have planted that fear in your unconscious mind. Without it, your bloodline may never have lasted long enough to create the crowning achievement that is you.

The same sort of process explains why, contrary to common perception, people need to be spatially contained by the walls of buildings. Most of us enjoy open spaces, long views, and the great outdoors. But we also enjoy—and need—a sense of enclosure to feel comfortable as pedestrians. Evolutionary psychologists tell us how all animals seek two things: prospect and refuge. The first allows you to see your prey and predators. The second allows you to know that your flanks are protected from attack. Prospect and refuge explain why, when I first moved into my new apartment in Washington, my cats ended up on top of the refrigerator in the corner of the (open) kitchen.

For Homo sapiens, the need for prospect and refuge may have an even more specific source. The ecologist E. P. Odum argued that it was not grassland or forest that provided the ideal early habitat for humans, but rather the boundary between the two, the "forest edge," where both distant views and physical enclosure were present. Thomas Campanella of the University of

North Carolina notes that the "recollection of the forest edge may explain why architectural and urbanistic elements evocative of this space—colonnades, loggias, arcades, verandas, even porches—are so appealing and comfortable."[1]

EMBRACE ME

From an ecological perspective, then, most U.S. cities offer too much grassland and too little forest. The need for refuge, deep in our DNA from millennia of survival, has led us to feel most comfortable in spaces with well-defined edges, and those edges have gone missing. Forget that emblematic image of Madison Avenue, where the craggy towers turn the streets into canyons. The typical American urban experience is a profound lack of spatial enclosure. I am not talking just about the parking lot at the mall, but also about the centers of our cities, where once-substantial buildings have been torn down and replaced, almost always, by surface parking.

I remember in 1998, when I was helping Andres Duany redesign downtown Baton Rouge and we were taken to the top floor of the tallest banking tower for a bird's-eye view, that a tremendous amount of development was on display—the city had abolished its downtown height limits—but every block of construction was surrounded by at least three blocks of parking. The result was a checkerboard city, almost completely devoid of two-sided streets in which a pedestrian could feel comfortable.

In towns and cities of every size, with buildings of every height, otherwise promising pedestrian environments have been rendered uninviting by these empty lots—what planners call "missing teeth." It takes only one of them to wreck a place for walking. Akron, for example, has spent millions improving its Main Street area, building a minor-league baseball stadium and a canal park along it, in what by all rights should be the walkable heart of the city. They paid extra money for a Camden Yards–style stadium, complete with storefronts facing brick sidewalks and historic streetlamps. But someone forgot about the piece of property directly across the street, where almost a full mile of continuous building fronts is interrupted by a single, three-hundred-foot-long stretch of parking. This one relatively tiny tear in the downtown's urban fabric, which could be repaired with a single building, provides remarkably convenient game-day parking for sixty lucky baseball fans . . . at the expense of a Main Street that people would want to use.•

Most city-planning offices are aware of these missing teeth and know that they are a problem. But what are they doing about them? In Akron, the city clearly has not made a priority of getting something built there, when a mere half-acre of construction would transform what, for many, is the central experience of visiting downtown. This oversight is sadly typical, as most cities undervalue the role of spatial definition in urban vitality.

Indeed, many cities actively work against spatial definition with the requirement for shadow studies, which are often used to chop the tops off tall buildings in urban centers. These make sense against public greens and in dark, northern cities like Boston, where light and air are at a premium, but what are they doing in Miami Beach, where shadows are what make summer walking possible? Where they are necessary, shadow studies need to be supplemented by "shaping studies" that show how well buildings make streets into spaces. When the two are combined properly, you get Vancouver: elegant point towers sitting atop lower sidewalk-hugging bases . . . and another great city to move to.

•What is so heartbreaking about Akron's Main Street neighborhood is how far it has come—with great adaptive reuse of historic properties, a sexy new art museum, and some delightful restaurants and cafés—and how easily it could be brought to the next level if energy were only directed at a few problem sites that nobody seems to care about.

OBJECT FETISHISM

The success of "Vancouver urbanism" shows us one path toward the happy resolution of a great war that has been raging in city planning for decades: figural space versus figural object. Traditional, walkable urbanism is grounded in figural space. It believes that the shape of the spaces between buildings is what matters, because this is the public realm—the place where civic life plays out. In traditional urbanism, buildings often take on odd, unsatisfying shapes in order to surround extremely satisfying streets and squares, what can be called outdoor living rooms. Figural space is one of the things that allows traditional cities to so generously support pedestrian life. Look at an aerial photo of Paris and you will be astounded by how contorted some of the buildings become in order to shape the delightful spaces they frame.

In contrast, modern urbanism was founded on the cult of the figural object. It became the role of the hero architect to create buildings as three-dimensional sculptures akin to a Brancusi or a Calder, floating freely in space. The shape of this space became residual and meaningless—and inhospitable to pedestrians. Most urban designers now consider this evolution to have been a horrible mistake. Most architects also agree with this assessment publicly, even as they hope against hope for their chance to design the figural object building that will land them on the cover of a hero architect magazine. And then there are the starchitects, most of whom don't care about figural space at all.

A fairly typical battle in this war was fought at the Mayors' Institute on City Design, when Mayor Frank Cownie presented a plan for a piece of Des Moines that was based on the Vancouver model. A collection of quirky, expressionistic towers were shown in red, sitting atop a series of block-filling bases, shown in blue, that shaped the streets beautifully. "That's a really interesting plan," said the one starchitect at the table. "Just get rid of the blue bits and you'll have something special."

Wow. First of all, when a designer says something is "interesting," it's time to get your guard up. Now that both beauty and truth are considered subjective among the intellectual class, "interesting" has become the new term of highest praise, which can lead to all manner of architectural mischief in the hands of aging *enfants terribles* like Rem Koolhaas. Second, and more to the point, I was surprised to learn that, despite all that I had read about the utter failure of the modernist spatial program (code name: Pruitt Igoe*), there were still ardent advocates for object urbanism on the loose among us.

This was the 2000s, and I was tempted to take a plaster cast of the offending architect for my fossil collection. But fast-forward a decade and, at least in the academy, tower-in-the-park city planning is once again ascendant. This time it has taken the guise of "landscape urbanism," the dominant ideology at Harvard and elsewhere, where the ostensibly overriding objective of enhancing each site's natural ecology has led to a newfound disregard for creating well-shaped public spaces. We are being banished to the grasslands once again—but at least this time the grasslands are made of grass. Starchitects of course adore landscape urbanism, as the vast distances between buildings allow each sculptural object to be seen to best effect.

We can give the last word on this topic to Jan Gehl: "If a team of planners was asked to radically reduce the life between buildings, they could not find a more effective method than using modernist planning principles."[2] Gehl obviously has not seen Monty Python's hilarious abattoir-designer-as-architect sketch,* but his point is hard to discredit. The evidence suggests that any environmental benefits that accrue from landscape urbanism

---

*For the uninitiated, Pruitt Igoe was Minoru Yamasaki's award-winning tower-in-the-park housing project in Saint Louis that had to be abandoned and demolished due to its complete social collapse. Most people agree that this failure, while caused in part by improper management, was also the result of an urban design that failed to provide physical spaces for which tenants could feel a sense of ownership.
*Just Google "Monty Python Architect."

will quickly be outweighed by the increased car trips of residents who refuse to walk.

TINY IS TASTIER

Jan Gehl may be the world's leading observer of how people use places. In *Cities for People*, he notes how we walk just under 3 miles per hour in warm weather, and just over 3.5 miles per hour in cold weather; how we bow our heads ten degrees while walking; how we can see a person's movement at one hundred yards and recognize and hear them at about fifty.[3] These sorts of observations have powerful implications for how we should design public streets and squares and, more often than not, the lesson is to make them smaller. He shares the aphorism "When in doubt, leave some meters [yards] out," and reminds us that "if a dinner party is held at narrow tables, a festive mood quickly catches on because everyone can talk in several directions across the table."[4]

This analogy is apt. It is often surprising to measure some of America's favorite and most successful public spaces—New York's Rockefeller Center, San Antonio's Riverwalk, San Francisco's Ghirardelli Square—and discover how small they actually are. Few are much broader than sixty yards across.* And let's not forget Disney's Main Street, famously built at three-quarters scale. Large public spaces, increasingly demanded of developers by citizens' committees and planning boards, can often end up offering less of an amenity than smaller ones, especially if the buildings surrounding them are not very tall. Since the key measure of a place's spatial definition is its height-to-width ratio, wide spaces only feel enclosed when flanked by buildings of considerable height.*

---

*Times Square? Sixty yards across. Rome's Piazza Navona? Sixty yards across.
*As discussed in Andres Duany, Elizabeth Plater-Zyberk, and Jeff Speck's *Suburban Nation* (78), a width-to-height ratio above 6:1 is generally agreed to exceed the limits of spatial definition, with a 1:1 ratio historically considered the ideal.

Yet Gehl's well-earned distaste for large things extends to building heights as well. This stance puts him in the company of some of our most prominent urban thinkers while alienating him from others. In *A Pattern Language*, the bestselling design book of all time, Christopher Alexander drew the limit at four stories, noting that "there is abundant evidence to show that high buildings make people crazy."[5] The fertile-minded Leon Krier, Luxembourger godfather of the New Urbanist movement, is likewise adamant in his dismissal of skyscrapers, which he terms "vertical cul-de-sacs," arguing instead for cities limited to four stories, the convenient height for a walk-up. This position is embraced by peak-oilers like Jim Kunstler, who worry—or celebrate—that escalating energy costs will eventually put all our elevators out of service.

Gehl's beef with tall buildings comes from his concern for the public realm, and the fact that only people in the lower stories of a building can interact with people on the street. He wryly comments that "above the fifth floor, offices and housing should logically be the province of the air-traffic authorities."[6] He also notes that tall buildings capture the air currents that circulate around the ten-story level, which "can cause wind speed at the foot of tall buildings to be up to four times greater than in the surrounding open landscape." He observes that, in Amsterdam, umbrellas protect people, while in (high-rise) Rotterdam, people protect umbrellas.[7]

Gehl and Krier are probably right that the most pleasant and livable cities are those like Amsterdam and Paris that were principally built before elevators. This outcome is, of course, more dependent on the fact that they were also built before cars, but the human scale of the buildings contributes as well. The more important discussion, however, concerns whether taller buildings degrade walkability by their presence as much as they improve it with their capacity. The more people a building can hold, the more people on the street, and the superlative pedestrianism of Manhattan and Hong Kong suggests that inhumane, vortex-generating skyscrapers have little negative effect on street life. Indeed, it is essential to recognize that, in Manhattan, it is precisely the continuous presence of tall buildings along the avenues that allows them to support a continuous array of shopfronts for block after block after block.

It is for this reason, among others, that while some urban designers rail against tall buildings, most economists clamor for more. Ed Glaeser, today's noisiest advocate for skyscrapers, insists that they are necessary for preserving affordability in our blossoming urban cores, and Chris Leinberger has notoriously dared to question Washington, D.C.'s century-old height limit. This position is right in theory, but the economists don't seem to have fully processed one thing the designers know, which is how tremendously dense a city can become at moderate heights. Boston's North End, in Jane Jacobs's day, achieved 275 dwelling units per acre with hardly an elevator in sight.[8] A ten-story city like Washington simply does not need towers to achieve great walking density. Indeed, outside of Midtown and the Financial District, most of Manhattan's lively avenues are lined by buildings closer to ten stories tall.

Ultimately, since most cities are not New York, there is a much more important argument to be made for height limits than Gehl's call for sociability and calm winds. The typical American downtown is not faced with the volume of development, even in good times, that needs tall buildings to contain it. In most places, the challenge is the exact opposite: a preponderance of vacant properties and parking lots, the missing teeth that make walking so unpleasant. Raising or abolishing the height limit, as occurred in Baton Rouge, creates the outcome of Baton Rouge, where a single skyscraper lands on an empty block and sucks up an entire year's worth of development activity, while all the surrounding blocks stay empty—or fill up with skyscraper parking.

Meanwhile, witnessing the success of the skyscraper developer, the surrounding landowners begin to speculate. They won't build a midrise on their lot, because that's not the most the lot can hold. And they won't sell it for a reasonable price, because it's "worth" building a skyscraper on.[9] The next thing you know, all the would-be urban developers have fled to the beltway.

In this context, it is tempting to do a bit of our own speculation, on how tremendous the District of Columbia's height limit has been for the city and its walkability. That limit, set at twenty feet taller than the width of each building's enfronting street, has caused new development to fill many more blocks than it would have otherwise. This strategy has created street after street of excellent urbanism, even in places where the architecture could be better. (The running joke is that Washington is the place where the best architects go to do their worst work.) A case in point would be the K Street neighborhood, northeast of the Watergate, where hardly a single building is worth a second look, but where every boring glass-and-steel-lined sidewalk is perfectly hospitable to its promenading lobbyists.

Does this experience suggest that skyscrapers are always a bad idea in typical American cities? Not necessarily, as long as they follow the Vancouver model of a skinny tower atop a broad base. While a bit more expensive than fat slabs, narrow towers create a skyline instead of blocking out the sky, and don't cause the same wind problems. They can also satisfy the developers who, far from chasing Leinberger's density or Glaeser's affordability, are most often hoping to sell luxury condos.

WEATHER OR NOT

Talking to audiences across the United States, I am always surprised to hear that—no matter where I am—their city's weather makes it somehow less capable of supporting pedestrian life than the rest of planet Earth. Never mind the crowds of happy visitors who flock to New Orleans in the summer, Quebec City in the winter, Seattle in the rain, and Chicago in the wind . . . "people won't walk here because it's just too hot/cold/wet/blustery!"

There is no doubt that climate exerts some influence on walking, but the evidence suggests that this factor is not half as impactful as street design. In that regard, I have always found these three questions to be especially useful: What North American city has the most linear feet of successful retail-fronted sidewalks? Toronto. What developed country has the highest share of urban trips going to walking instead of driving? Sweden.* How many months out of the year do sidewalk cafés stay open in Copenhagen? Twelve.[10]

The lesson we learn from these places is that walking down a narrow, shop-lined street in icy Boston or sweltering Savannah is a vastly superior experience to walking down an arterial between parking lots and car dealerships on San Diego's best day. Get the design right and people will walk in almost any climate.

---

*29 percent versus 6 percent in the United States (Pucher and Dijkstra, "Making Walking and Cycling Safer," 27).

STEP 8: PLANT TREES

Trees for life; The greenest of green products; Trees pay;
What tree where?

I used to work in Little Havana, the heart of Cuban Miami, where the main drag, Calle Ocho, is flanked by literally hundreds of blocks of one-story houses. As I would drive from street to street, I developed first impressions about which places were richer or poorer, safer or more dangerous. One day, the landscape architect Douglas Duany suggested that I take the same tour while thinking about trees. Not sure what he was getting at, I tried it . . . and found that all my "rich" and "safe" streets had good tree cover, and all my "poor" and "dangerous" streets did not.

It's best not to pick favorites in the walkability discussion—every individual point counts—but the humble American street tree might win my vote. Often the first item in the budget to be cut, street trees are key to pedestrian comfort and urban livability in so many ways. In addition to offering shade, they reduce ambient temperatures in hot weather, absorb rainwater and tailpipe emissions, provide UV protection, and limit the effects of wind. Trees also slow cars and improve the sense of enclosure by "necking down" the street space with their canopies. A consistent cover of trees can go a long way toward making up for an otherwise nasty walk.

Because they have such a powerful impact on walkability, street trees have been associated with significant improvements in both property values and retail viability. Since this enhancement translates directly into increased local tax revenue, it could be considered financially irresponsible for a community to *not* invest heavily in trees.

TREES FOR LIFE

We already know that trees are good for us. This is something most of us understand intuitively, but it doesn't hurt to have studies. The most famous such investigation, conducted in a suburban Pennsylvania hospital between 1972 and 1981, tracked the recovery patterns of surgical patients in a single wing of rooms. Half of these rooms faced (at some distance) a brick wall, while the other half faced a row of trees. All other factors were held constant. Under these conditions, those patients with tree views had fewer negative evaluations, required many fewer doses of potent narcotics, had a lower likelihood of postsurgical complications, and were discharged from the hospital, on average, a day earlier.[1]

This evidence aligns with the work of Dr. Roger Ulrich at Texas A&M University, who has found that "in laboratory research, visual exposure to settings with trees has produced significant recovery from stress within five minutes, as indicated by changes in blood pressure and muscle tension."[2] Given the stress that so many commuters complain of, this phenomenon might help explain the engineer Walter Kulash's finding that a drive on a treeless street is perceived to be significantly longer than an equal-length drive on a street lined with trees.[3]

If trees are so good for us, and indeed make driving less stressful, it would stand to reason that they are encouraged along our roadways. But of course, they are not, because the traffic engineers are quite reasonably worried about people smashing into them. The Georgia DOT outlaws placing trees within eight feet of a state-owned street because, in the words of one reporter, "sidewalks are auto recovery zones where drivers have space to correct course if they've veered off."[4] And only recently did the Virginia regulations stop referring to street trees as "Fixed and Hazardous Objects."

Clearly, this approach bodes ill for walkability, as it presumes that only drivers' lives are at risk. This makes good enough sense along truly rural highways, but not along streets with sidewalks, where it has also been indiscriminately applied. As a result, soft pedestrians have proved a much lesser threat to moving vehicles than hard trees.

In the face of this challenge, there are two complementary tactics for convincing transportation engineers to advocate for street trees. The first is to shame them into placing pedestrian safety on par with driver safety. But since this approach is not always effective, the larger strategy would be to convince them that street trees make roadways safer for drivers as well as pedestrians. This counterintuitive supposition has one important argument on its side, which is that it appears to be true. Thanks to risk homeostasis, drivers respond to the presence of broad "recovery zones" by speeding, and crashes become both more frequent and more deadly.

This was the case in an investigation of arterial streets in Toronto, which found that the presence of street trees and other vertical objects along the road edge correlated with a 5 to 20 percent decline in midblock crashes. (Accidents at intersections were relatively unaffected.) A University of Connecticut study of two-lane roadways found that although broad shoulders "were associated with reductions in single-vehicle, fixed-object crashes, they were also associated with a statistically significant increase in total crashes." Most recently, the researcher Eric Dumbaugh compared four years of crash statistics from two different sections of Colonial Drive in Orlando and found that the section without trees or other vertical features experienced 12 percent more midblock crashes, 45 percent more injurious crashes, and a dramatically higher number of fatal crashes: six versus zero.[5]

THE GREENEST OF GREEN PRODUCTS

As always, car crashes remain the greatest individual threat to our physical health, but we shouldn't underestimate the additional nuisance of heat waves, which are unsurprisingly on the rise and kill dozens of Americans annually. Before long, many of our cities could begin to experience scorchers like the one that hit Moscow in 2010, killing more than seven hundred people every day. When this happens, we will wish we had planted more street trees. Measurements of ambient temperatures taken on exposed versus canopied streets around the United States document temperature differentials ranging from five to fifteen degrees (Fahrenheit) between the two,[6] which can make a big difference when temperatures hit the triple digits. The relevant term here is "urban heat island," a downside of city living that can largely be eliminated by proper tree cover. According to the U.S. Department of Agriculture, the cooling impact of a single healthy tree "is equivalent to ten room-size air conditioners operating 24 hours a day."[7]

Our reliance on air conditioners means that the ambient temperature of our treeless cities exerts a global warming double whammy, complete with feedback loop. Not only do shade-deprived neighborhoods make the world hotter, but they require much more electricity to cool, most of which is still sourced from coal. A properly shaded neighborhood is said to require 15 to 35 percent less air conditioning than a treeless one.[8] Climate change begets air conditioning begets carbon pollution begets climate change. Denser urban canopies could help short-circuit this vicious circle.

But even this factor pales next to the astoundingly large role that trees perform simply as a carbon sink. In what economists call an "ecosystem service," trees are unsurpassed in the landscape at gobbling up CO_2. And urban trees, located as they are in close proximity to roadways, are ten times more effective than more distant vegetation at hijacking car exhaust before it hits the stratosphere.[9] All greenery absorbs CO_2, but trees are by far the most effective. A study in Leicester, England, found that aboveground vegetation stores more than 200,000 tons of the city's carbon, of which over 97 percent is stored by trees rather than in groundcover—even counting those ample British gardens.[10]

That's just the air. What about water? One of the biggest and costliest problems facing many cities is the pollution caused by combined sewage overflows (CSOs). More than nine hundred American communities, many of them large cities like mine, have old collection systems that combine stormwater with sanitary sewage. When it rains hard—something that has been happening with increasing frequency—the commingled waste surges into local waterways. A rainstorm in the summer of 2010 caused the city of Milwaukee to dump more than a billion gallons of raw sewage into Lake Michigan. All told, the EPA estimates such overflows to surpass more than 1.2 trillion gallons annually— "enough to keep Niagara Falls roaring for eighteen days."[11]

Here in Washington, where CSOs are a regular occurrence, we are seeing some unnerving impacts. Male smallmouth bass in the Potomac River are growing eggs in their sex organs. These involuntarily transgendered fish are being blamed in part on pharmaceuticals, including birth control pills, that have been dumped down toilets (or transported through urine) and then discharged due to CSOs. We get our drinking water from the Potomac, so this concerns us. In Maryland, cancer rates of the people who drink this water are markedly above the state average.[12]

What does this have to do with street trees? Well, here's what happens when an inch of rain falls on a tree: the first 30 percent of the precipitation is typically absorbed directly by the leaves and never even touches the ground.[13] Once the leaves are saturated, up to 30 percent more of the rain seeps into the soil, made more porous by the tree's root structure. This root structure then slurps the water back up into the tree, from which it is eventually transpired back into the air. This process allows a mature tree to absorb about half an inch of water from every rainfall.[14] As a result, communities that add 25 percent additional tree cover will reduce their stormwater by 10 percent.[15] In many American cities, this 10 percent would be enough to eliminate most CSOs.

Lacking these trees, and the public will to plant them, we are faced with a huge financial challenge. New York State anticipates a bill of $36 billion over the next twenty years to solve this problem. Philadelphia alone is currently collecting $1.6 billion to prevent CSOs.[16] In Wheeling, West Virginia, where median income is eighteen thousand dollars, residents are anticipating a sewer repair bill that could top fifteen thousand dollars per household.[17] How much better things would be if, in the 1990s, each household had planted a $150 tree!

The several-decade time lag between planting and maturity is the obvious hitch here. Our water systems are in crisis now, and you want to plant trees? Obviously, there are a lot of sewer repairs and upgrades that need to be made immediately, but many more are simply anticipated. A twenty-year window, for water systems planning, is not a long stretch of time. Any sensible analysis of present and future costs would conclude that we should plant trees now.* But since asking a sewer specialist to plant trees is like asking a pig to fly, we need to make the case to the generalists who are hopefully in charge, like mayors, to make

---

*On a recent visit to the Kentlands—a new community in Gaithersburg, Maryland, designed by DPZ in 1989—I was thrilled to discover that the trees we planted twenty years ago are already forming a complete canopy over many of the streets.

trees a priority. Fortunately, there are even greater financial rewards that can be reaped by doing so.

TREES PAY

"The first duty of the inhabitant of forlorn neighborhoods is to use all possible influence to have the *streets planted with trees.*"[18] So intoned the dominant landscape architect of the antebellum period, Andrew Jackson Downing. In *Republic of Shade*, Thomas Campanella's masterful history of the elm tree, an editorial taken from the 1835 *New England Farmer* shares that sentiment:

> Would it not be a regulation well deserving of the attention of the General Court to require every town to plant the sides of the public roads with forest trees? . . . The value of most farms would be raised ten or fifteen per cent by the addition of shade trees about the buildings and along the public road. [Moreover, trees] give the country an appearance of wealth, that nothing else can supply. . . . The most spacious and princely establishments without them appear covered with the most prison-like gloom. . . . A bald head is not comely, neither is a street seemly which is not well set with trees.[19]

It is hard to know whether the editorialist's calculation regarding real estate value was supported by economic studies, but we have them now and he wasn't too far off. According to a study conducted by the University of Pennsylvania's Wharton School of Business, trees planted within fifty feet of houses in one Philadelphia neighborhood caused home prices to increase by 9 percent.[20]

A more comprehensive study, this time of Portland's east side, reached conclusions that were less dramatic but, taken as a whole, no less compelling. Comparing houses with and without nearby street trees, it found that an adjacent tree added 3 percent to the median sale price of a house, an uptick of $8,870— the equivalent of an additional small bedroom. Interestingly, since there are more houses than street trees, each individual tree was deemed responsible for almost $20,000 in increased real estate value. Taken across the entire east side, the benefit from street trees was calculated at a whopping $1.12 billion.[21]

How does that increased value affect the city's bottom line? Extrapolating to Portland as a whole, the study's authors found that the presence of healthy street trees likely adds $15.3 million to annual property tax revenues. Meanwhile, the city pays $1.28 million each year for tree planting and maintenance, resulting in a payoff of almost exactly twelve to one.[22]

That powerful ratio should become the mantra of urban foresters everywhere, but it is probably an underestimation. Focused strictly on housing, it ignores the benefits that accrue to cities when their businesses are more profitable: one recent study shows 12 percent higher income streams accruing to shops on tree-lined streets.[*] I am a bit suspicious of this study, because its outcomes depend on so many other factors that are difficult to hold constant, but few would argue that a healthy tree canopy doesn't contribute mightily to establishing both the cachet and the comfort of a walkable shopping district.

In any case, the residential numbers should be enough. Absent a sophisticated carbon tax, it is difficult to monetize the environmental benefits of planting more street trees; even the stormwater savings can be a tough sell, given the time lag. But a clear outcome in which city revenues dramatically outpace city investment seems a sturdy foundation on which to build policy.

---

[*] Dan Burden, "22 Benefits of Urban Street Trees." In another six-city study conducted by the University of Washington, polled consumers interestingly rated products 30 percent higher for quality when those products were purchased on streets with good tree cover ("Trees and Commercial Business," coloradotrees.org).

For this reason, it would be wise for other cities to pursue their own Portland-style investigations in order to help justify the multimillion-dollar investment in street trees that they invariably need.* I call such an investment a Continuous Canopy Campaign and, while I have yet to convince a city to commit to such a lofty goal, this means that the catchy moniker is yours for the taking.

It is astounding to me, given the vast and multifarious advantages of a continuous urban canopy, that most American cities care so little about their trees. This philistine disregard is not a universal condition; in Melbourne, for example, five hundred new street trees have been planted every year for the past seventeen years.[23] New York City, where one can walk entire neighborhoods without a single tree sighting, has recently set a goal of planting a million trees over the next decade, including 220,000 street trees.[24] But this campaign is the exception. Most progressive American cities only go so far as to become a "Tree City USA," a status achieved through the faint-hearted commitment to spend two dollars per capita on trees. Apparently, every citizen gets a handful of acorns to scatter.

Here in Washington, the District plants trees and abandons them for the residents to tend, a common strategy in the United States, and one that would be more effective if it were actually known to the residents. It took me three years to learn that I was my street tree's keeper, and that was by accident. Now I water my tree when I water my garden, but I'm the rare tree hugger who cares. Clearly, letting trees loose in the world without designated caregivers is a pound-foolish strategy. Particularly in distressed neighborhoods, where trees can mean so much but residents are not conditioned to take charge, a commitment to planting trees

---

* To assist in this effort, the USDA's Forest Service has created a software package called i-Tree Streets, which can be downloaded at www.itreetools.org/streets/index .php.

has to be matched with a commitment to keeping them alive. This takes more than two dollars per capita, which is why mayors need to both embrace and celebrate the fact that trees may be the best investment a city can make.

WHAT TREE WHERE?

Now that you're committed to a continuous canopy, there are a few things you should know. The first, for my southern friends, is to stop planting palm trees. Correction: only three cities in America should be planting palm trees: Palm Beach, Palm Springs, and Hollywood—and there, only along Sunset Boulevard. The point is: if you've got great, palm-lined avenues, by all means, keep them. But understand that palm trees are merely decorative, and don't begin to offer the same environmental benefits as deciduous trees. The last time I checked, most Florida cities had not learned this lesson.* The same goes for crepe myrtles, spruce pines, and those other bushes masquerading as trees that somehow grace many a city's tree list.

My second suggestion is to abolish the current practice of refusing to plant more than a few of the same tree in a row. Too many American cities are held hostage by urban foresters who, fearing the next Dutch elm disease, require that every street be planted with a tutti-frutti species mélange, so that no single blight can denude a whole street. While based on sound logic, this proscription typically prevents cities from doing what they once did, which was to create streets of distinct character based upon their consistent use of a single tree species. Many of us grew up in towns with an Elm Street, a Maple Street, a Beech Street, and a Walnut Street. In contrast to the current tradition of streets named after the developer's daughters, these streets

---

*Incidentally, we had another term for palms in Miami: hurricane missiles.

were actually planted according to their name, and each had its own unique landscape. Residents of Philadelphia will find this discussion familiar.

The tutti-frutti rule makes most of America's best streets illegal. As many observers have commented, a street with consistent, mature trees is like a cathedral, with the trunks serving as columns and the branches forming the vaults. This happy outcome is only truly possible when a single species of tree is planted at a consistent spacing distance.*

Moreover, when the next blight comes, better that it wipe out one street out of ten than one-tenth of every street, because, in most cities, nobody gets a phone call unless the die-off is pronounced and localized. A mandate for replanting often only arises when a street is impacted dramatically. When this happens, that street can be reforested with trees that will once again reach skyward in unison.

---

*One compromise position is worth mentioning here: in the hands of a truly skilled forester, streets can be planted with two or three species that appear almost identical yet have a distinct genetic makeup.

THE INTERESTING WALK

■

STEP 9: MAKE FRIENDLY AND UNIQUE FACES

STEP 10: PICK YOUR WINNERS

STEP 9: MAKE FRIENDLY AND UNIQUE FACES

Invisible parking; Sticky versus slippery edges; Attack of the starchitects;
Too much of a thing; Boring nature

If only safety and comfort were enough. More Americans would stay in their marriages, we would eat the same dinner every night, and we could limit ourselves to Eight Steps of Walkability. But we are humans, after all, and our motivations are more complex. Among other things, we demand almost constant stimulation. Pedestrians need to feel safe and comfortable, but they also need to be entertained, or else those with a choice will choose to drive.

And what could be more boring than a parking lot? Whether the windblown tarmac of a surface lot or the incommunicative blank walls of a parking garage, there is little appeal to walking when faced with such an unrewarding view.

But it is not only parking that contributes to a blight of boredom in many American downtowns. Almost every city that has witnessed construction since 1950 has its share of cold, uninviting buildings fronting the sidewalk with rough concrete, tinted glass, or other such nastiness. Most architects have moved on from this style of building, but that is not to say that they are any more motivated to engage the pedestrian. Evidence would suggest that, among the leading starchitects, *creating street life* still ranks low on the list of priorities, somewhere down there with *staying on budget* and *keeping the rain out*.

In most cities, however, the culprit is less likely to be a starchitect than a Rite Aid, as pharmacies and other national chains refuse to put windows where shelves can go. These standards can be overcome, but only by cities that throw off the beggar mentality and outlaw the practice.

Finally, in their quest to become more sustainable, cities need to remember that, for the typical pedestrian, the most mundane storefront is still more interesting than the most luxuriant landscape. A determination to increase walking means not allowing the greening impulse to undermine the core qualities of urbanity that draw people downtown in the first place.

INVISIBLE PARKING

Mayor Joe Riley of Charleston, South Carolina, now in his tenth term, tells the story of when he tried to convince a local architect to make a new parking garage look instead like a traditional Charleston building. "We learned in school that form follows function," the architect said, "so this building needs to look like a garage." "Yes, I learned that too," replied the mayor. "We're just not going to do that in Charleston."

That building now graces East Bay Street, where it does three important things right. First, it places high-ceilinged commercial space on the ground floor directly against the sidewalk, giving it windows, doors, and human activity. Second, it hides its tilted car ramps away from the edges of the building, so that it doesn't shout "I am a garage." Placing the flat parking areas at the building's perimeter also allows for its eventual transformation to nonautomotive use.* Third, it details its upper floors as if they were inhabited, with window-sized openings equipped with

---

* Most parking structures, with ramping perimeter floors, can never serve any use other than parking. When the ramps are instead placed at the center of the garage, they can eventually be removed to create a light court surrounded by flat floors that can become offices or housing. Garages served by lateral spiral ramps, while a bit more expensive, are even more easily converted to nonautomotive uses.

Charleston-style shutters. The shutters are closed, which limits the building's gregariousness but also hides the cars behind them. Upon closer inspection, this building clearly serves cars more than humans, but you have to look hard to see it.

Five blocks west of this garage can be found another essay in urban parking. This newer, bigger structure sits twenty-five feet back from Market Street. At its corners, this setback is occupied by two mixed-use buildings that hide the parking lot from view. At the ground floor, these attractive structures—one of them historic—contain a beauty salon and a pet-oriented gift store. Between them, the setback is occupied by a shallow urban plaza that holds outdoor dining for Chucktown Tavern, located at grade under four stories of parking.

The main lesson from this garage is that it only takes 25 feet of occupied building edge to hide 250 feet of parking lot. Indeed, thanks to sight angles from the sidewalk, three stories of building can hide four or five stories of garage. On Market Street, three hundred cars have effectively disappeared into thin air. The same technique can be practiced even more cheaply with surface parking lots, where a thin crust of wood-frame structures can conceal acres of tarmac. At Mashpee Commons, a strip mall on Cape Cod that was retrofitted into a new downtown, this feat is accomplished by tiny one-story shops, each about the size of a two-car garage.

Enlightened developers like the ones at Mashpee know that hidden parking boosts retail sales and property values. Enlightened mayors like Joe Riley know that hidden parking boosts downtown appeal and livability. The rest of us need to be kept in check by building codes, the everyday city ordinances that determine what can be built where. It is fairly easy to gauge the intelligence of a city's planning department by asking a simple question: in downtowns and other areas of potential pedestrian life, do your rules require that all parking lots be hidden behind a habitable building edge?

STICKY VERSUS SLIPPERY EDGES

In America, most advanced city codes go that far when it comes to attracting street life. Few go much farther. This fact can be demonstrated by a walk down almost any Main Street, where drugstores, banks, and other businesses either place blank walls to the sidewalk or fill up their windows with signs designed to obscure the shelving and other *stuff* located behind them. This common activity runs exactly counter to what we know about making pedestrians happy. Jan Gehl puts it this way: "No single topic has greater impact on the life and attractiveness of city space than active, open, and lively edges."[1]

In *Cities for People*, Gehl talks about the "edge effect": how "wherever people stay for a while, they seek out places along the edges of the space."[2] He photographs Siena's famous Piazza del Campo, where the main pavement is surrounded by chunky man-size bollards, each one having accumulated the appendage of a standing or sitting man. These simple stone posts serve as anchors in a sea of activity, inviting people to tether themselves and stay a while. Most often, this job is performed by the fronts of buildings which, if adequately porous and deep, attract both walkers and lingerers. By *porous*, I refer to windows and doors, proper interior lighting, and any other measure that better connects the interior of the store to the sidewalk. By *deep*, I mean the degree to which the facade provides opportunities for shelter, leaning, sitting, and other physical engagement, and also how effective the design is at blurring the distinction between public and private while drawing out the experience of entering and exiting.

Outdoor dining and sidewalk displays are perhaps the most common and impactful contributions to a deep facade. Awnings also help, as they can give a potential shopper the feeling of already being inside the store. In the early 1990s, Andres Duany and I had lunch with a fellow who was the retail expert for one of Canada's largest real estate developers. His employers had spent untold thousands of dollars sending him around the globe for a full year, visiting dozens of successful shopping districts. We asked him: "Is there anything that all of the best places shared in common?" His immediate reply: "Awnings you can touch."

Deep facades are also thick facades. Do columns stick out beyond the front wall? Is the front door recessed? Are the windowsills substantial enough to sit on? Or maybe there's a bench built in? All of these things help. As an art history student, I was always impressed that the Palazzo Medici in Florence was constructed with a stone bench surrounding its entire perimeter. In Renaissance Florence, there were knife fights in the streets— and bars on the windows—but still the Medici saw fit to invite passers-by to rest their *posteriori*. When we built our house, I put a sitting-height wall on both sides, and a prominent sidewalk-hugging bench by the front door. You would be surprised how often someone sits there. Never mind that on occasion that person is a homeless crack-smoking schizophrenic . . . it was the right thing to do.

Jan Gehl's observations of successful downtowns even extend to facade geometries, noting that a more vertical orientation, such as that provided by columns, makes for a seemingly shorter walk. "In contrast," he says, "facades designed with long horizontal lines make distances seem longer and more tiring." He adds: "It is interesting to note that shops and booths in active, thriving commercial streets all over the world often have a façade length of 16–20 feet, which . . . means that there are new activities and sights to see about every five seconds."[3]

Unfortunately, most cities' building codes, while maddeningly specific on certain statistical measures like *floor area ratio*, say little to nothing about those things that matter to pedestrians, like the window-to-wall ratio and the presence of awnings. This is fairly easy to change, but cities need to ask. A bit ahead of the curve, both Melbourne and Stockholm have adopted active facade policies. Melbourne's code, for example, requires that "60 percent of street facades in new buildings along major streets must be open and inviting."[4] While many new communities have recently been designed with such rules in place, few older cities have adopted equally prescriptive guidelines requiring friendly building fronts on new buildings.

A dozen years ago in *Suburban Nation*, Andres Duany, Elizabeth Plater-Zyberk, and I advocated for the replacement of conventional city zoning codes with a new type of instrument that we called the Traditional Neighborhood Development Ordinance.[5] First created by my coauthors in the 1980s, this ordinance was notable for how it supplanted the land-use and statistical orientation of conventional coding with a focus on the physical form of buildings: how they met the ground, the street, and the sky; how they handled the transition from public to private realms; and how they hid their parking.

Since that writing, this type of ordinance has come to be known as a "form-based" code and hundreds of cities and towns have enacted them, most notably the City of Miami in 2009. The most prominent version of this ordinance, called the SmartCode, is a piece of open-source shareware available for free download.• This document is a comprehensive tool for making better places, and almost every growing city would benefit from throwing out its current zoning in favor of the SmartCode or something similar. However, replacing an entire code is a big job. In the short term, a few simple rules, like Melbourne's open-facade law, can make a big difference.

In most cases, fixing a code is a two-part process: adding a few new rules and deleting a few old ones. In 1993, I was working with Andres Duany on the resuscitation of 5th Avenue South, the main street of Naples, Florida. One of the things we noticed

---

•The SmartCode can be downloaded from the Center for Advanced Transect Studies at www.transect.org/codes.html.

was that most of the shops had awnings no bigger than umbrellas, little semicircular zits that didn't begin to shade the street's parched sidewalks. We looked into the building code, and found that, unbelievably, any awning larger than a certain tiny size had to be sprinkled for fire suppression. We got rid of that rule first.

ATTACK OF THE STARCHITECTS

We've come a long way since the seventies, when every city endeavored to build its own version of Boston's fortress-like City Hall, a structure that only architects love (yes, I love it). This style of architecture was called brutalism, supposedly after Le Corbusier's *béton brut*—rough concrete—but the name stuck for other reasons. It was characterized by walls so abrasive they could rip your arm open. Happily, this technique is no longer in vogue, but many architects, especially the starchitects, still build blank walls where they least belong. The Spaniard Rafael Moneo, my old professor, is probably the leading blank wall composer, a veritable Copland of Concrete. In his studios, like all my architecture-school studios, nobody ever talked about how buildings need to give life to the sidewalk. We did discuss such things as a facade's thickness and depth—"sickness and death," in Moneo's formidable accent—but these were architectonic qualities, not practical ones. Most architecture schools still promote an intellectual and artistic sensibility that has little patience for such mundane questions as whether a building will sustain pedestrian activity.

This issue was the subject of a now famous exchange that took place at the 2009 Aspen Ideas Festival between Frank Gehry and a prominent audience member, Fred Kent. Kent, who runs the Project for Public Spaces, pointedly asked Gehry why so many "iconic" buildings by star architects fail to give life to the streets and sidewalks around them. Gehry, who was once quoted as saying "I don't do context,"[6] claimed to be above this criticism, but Kent didn't buy it. I wasn't there, so we'll let *The Atlantic*'s James Fallows tell the rest:

> But the questioner asked one more time, and Gehry did something I found simply incredible and unforgettable. "You are a pompous man," he said—and waved his hand in a dismissive gesture, much as Louis XIV might have used to wave away some offending underling. He was unmistakably shooing or waving the questioner away from the microphone, as an inferior—again, in a gesture hardly ever seen in post-feudal times.[7]

Gehry was clearly having a bad day, but his imperiousness is worth recounting as a metaphor for some of his work—not all, but some. Kent was no doubt recalling his son Ethan's visit to Gehry's masterpiece, the Guggenheim Bilbao, an experience he describes in the Project for Public Spaces website's "Hall of Shame." After failing to find the front door and taking note of the treeless, depopulated plaza, Ethan observed a mugging, something he later learned was common there. He adds, "In the span of 10 minutes that we spent around the museum, I witnessed the first mugging of my life—and I've lived my entire life in New York City."[8]

Robberies are no longer very common in New York, but the same goes for Bilbao—except for certain problem places. That one of these places enfronts the Guggenheim is partly Gehry's fault, the outcome of a landscape (more of a *landscrape*) conceived as a tabula rasa to show off the building to its best effect.* Gehry is actually perfectly capable of contributing to attractive, engaging landscapes—as he has done in Chicago's Millennium

---

* Equally at fault are the city planners who worked with Gehry to so completely disengage the museum from the adjacent neighborhood.

Park—but he rarely does so with his buildings, most of which do not reward proximity. His Disney Hall, in Los Angeles, has about fifteen hundred feet of perimeter, perhaps one thousand feet of which is blank wall of the most slippery sort.

But it's a concert hall, you say . . . it needs to have blank walls. Well, take a stroll around the Paris Opera, or even Boston's Symphony Hall, and let's talk again. These older buildings' facades are awash in engaging detail, so that even their blank walls don't feel blank. Walking next to them is a pleasure.

This discussion reminds me of a wonderful set of drawings by Leon Krier in which he shows two buildings side by side from three different distances. From far away, we can see that one is a classical palace, the other a modernist glass cube. The palace has its base, middle, and top, while the glass cube is articulated with the horizontal and vertical lines of its large, reflective windows. As we get closer, the palace reveals its doors, windows, and cornice, while the glass cube remains the same as before: horizontal and vertical lines. Zooming in to just a few paces away, we now observe the palace's decorative string course, the window frames, and the rafter tails supporting the eaves. Our view of the glass cube is unchanged and mute. We have walked a great distance to its front door but received no reward.[9]

Krier presents these drawings as a powerful argument against modernism. But this is not merely a question of style. Any architectural style—except minimalism, I suppose—is capable of providing those medium- and small-scale details that engage people as they approach and walk by. The high-tech Pompidou Center, by celebrating its mechanical systems on its exterior, gives life to one of the most successful public spaces in Paris. What matters is not whether the details were crafted by a stone carver or a cold extruder, but whether they exist at all. Too many contemporary architects fail to understand this point, or understand it but don't care.

TOO MUCH OF A THING

But a preponderance of human-scaled detail is still not enough if a streetscape lacks variety. However delicate and lovely a building facade, there is little to entice a walker past five hundred feet of it. As Jane Jacobs noted, "Almost nobody travels willingly from sameness to sameness and repetition to repetition, even if the physical effort required is trivial."* Getting the scale of the detail right is only half the battle; what matters even more is getting the scale of the buildings right, so that each block contains as many different buildings as reasonably possible. Only in this way will the pedestrian be rewarded with the continuously unfolding panorama that comes from many hands at work.

This fact seems to be lost on the vast majority of architects, especially the big names, whose unspoken goal is to claim as much territory as possible for their trademarked signature, even if it means a numbingly repetitive streetscape. It is rarely taught in architecture schools, where there persists a deep misunderstanding of the difference between city planning and architecture, such that most urban-design projects are seen as an opportunity to create a single humongous building. Design superstars like Rem Koolhaas, in their giddy celebration of "bigness," have adopted this confusion as doctrine.*

---

*The Death and Life of Great American Cities, 129. She adds: "No special form of city blight is nearly so devastating as the Great Blight of Dullness" (234), and "in architecture as in literature and drama, it is the richness of human variation that gives vitality and color to the human setting" (229).

*Koolhaas, who is a commanding presence and writes beautifully, has by now mesmerized two full generations of architecture students with his compelling dogma. In the essay "What Ever Happened to Urbanism?" he sums up his larger agenda this way: "The seeming failure of the urban offers an exceptional opportunity, a pretext for Nietzschean frivolity. We have to imagine 1,001 other concepts of city; we have to take insane risks; we have to dare to be utterly uncritical; we have to swallow deeply and bestow forgiveness left and right. The certainty of failure has to be our laughing gas/oxygen; modernization our most potent drug. Since we are not responsible, we have to become irresponsible" (Koolhaas, Werlemann, and Mau, S,M,L,XL, 959–71). Surely this quote is something to keep in mind before giving him the key to your city.

To be fair, egotism and the desire for celebrity are only partly responsible for this orientation. It also comes from an insistence on intellectual honesty. Just as a building supposedly bears the obligation to be "of its time," it must also be "of its author." For the designer of a large structure to pretend to be many different designers is to falsify the historical record, especially since the modern myth of the genius architect insists that every designer's personal style is as unique as his fingerprint. I still remember (how could I not) the critic at my architectural-school-thesis final review who said, "I don't understand: your two buildings seem to have been designed by two different architects." My fantasy-world response, twenty years after the fact: "Why, thank you, sir."

There is of course an easier way to solve this problem: give some of the project away. When presented with a "building" that is rightly the size of a bunch of buildings, call up your friends and share the wealth. . . . And exactly how many architects, particularly in these slim times, do you expect are willing to take that leap? Only those rare few that consider city planning as important as architecture itself.

That's exactly what happened in early 2000, when DPZ entered an international competition to redesign the Piazza dei Navigatori, a prominent site on the main southern road out of Rome. The program brief called for half a million square feet of building on roughly a dozen acres. The other invited architects were Rem Koolhaas, Rafael Moneo, Rafael Viñoly, and three leading Italian firms. Each designer came forward with a single megabuilding in his inimitable style. Our strategy was a bit different. We proposed dividing the large site into seven distinct building blocks, and assigning each block to one of the competitors, ourselves included. We wrote a one-page form-based code that controlled the volume and placement of each building, and admonished the judges that, rather than sponsoring a single monument, they could build a diverse neighborhood.

The next part was the most fun. I went to the Harvard design library and got pictures of each of our competitors' most famous building. I handed these to our renderer, with the instruction to reshape them into their assigned locations in our plan, and brought the resulting artwork to Rome for the final judging. We did not win, but the look on our competitors' faces when they saw their buildings in our renderings was well worth the trip. When they learned that we wanted to beat them in order to share the job with them, they seemed equal parts angry, grateful, and embarrassed.[*]

Since so few architects are willing to give away design to others, or to pretend, Sybil-like, to possess multiple design personalities, the responsibility lies with cities to force them into it. Most of the design codes that I write for governments include a paragraph that goes something like this: "While even smaller units of design are encouraged, no more than 200 feet of continuous street frontage may appear to have been designed by a single architect." Along with an active facade policy, such a rule can help save a street from succumbing to Jane Jacobs's "Great Blight of Dullness."

Ultimately, however, this is as much a business discussion as a design discussion. Too much of real estate practice in this era has been about faking variety, about creating the impression of multiple actors when control has unwisely been concentrated in the hands of too few powerful players. As in the new suburbs, individual developers are invited into cities and given control over huge swaths of land, such that the future of those parcels ends up depending entirely on the skill and magnanimousness of those developers.

This common approach is certainly expeditious, and may be the only way to get something built quickly in blighted neighbor-

---

[*]We came in second to the one Roman architect in the bunch, an outcome that, given local politics, felt like a victory. His winning proposal, a gravity-defying megabuilding, has yet to be built. (Of those invited, Moneo and Koolhaas ultimately decided not to submit.)

hoods. But that redevelopment comes at a price, which typically includes the sense of character and variety engendered by the outcome. It also presents a greater risk, which is that the whole deal falls apart, leaving you nowhere or—sometimes worse— that construction produces such drastic change that a place loses all of its original character, not to mention its population. This is what Jacobs referred to as "cataclysmic money" versus "gradual money."[10]

On large projects, the path to avoiding this sort of outcome is straightforward and involves naming a master developer who oversees the project but who is not the developer of the individual buildings. That role can be played by the city, by a public authority, or even by a private developer in certain cases.* What matters is that different buildings are built by different people. The result, in true *Small Is Beautiful* practice, is the city of chipmunks, not of gorillas. Happily, while gorillas usually come in from out of town, chipmunks are mostly homegrown and have a greater vested interest in the outcome.

BORING NATURE

In *Green Metropolis*, David Owen tells the story of how he used to take long walks around Manhattan, running errands with his baby daughter in a Snugli. She would never complain and, planning a move to Vermont, Owen was anticipating how much more she would enjoy walks in the country. Here's what happened instead: "The first time we walked to the village green to buy the

---

*Probably the best-known example of such an approach is Manhattan's Battery Park City, which was developed and remains owned by a public-benefit corporation. As described by Witold Rybczynski, "It was designed to grow piecemeal, building by building, with individual projects financed and built by different developers, in response to changing market demands, but following the architectural guidelines of the master plan" (Rybczynski, *Makeshift Metropolis*, 151).

morning newspaper, on a spectacular autumn morning, she fussed and squirmed in her backpack almost the whole way. As far as she was concerned there was nothing to look at."[11]

Green spaces in cities are a lovely, salubrious, necessary thing. But they are also dull, at least in comparison to shopfronts and street vendors. Our kids may be suffering from nature deficit disorder, but they also know instinctively what we have been taught to ignore, which is that verdant landscapes do not entertain. As Owen further notes, large open areas "can encourage some people to *take walks*. But if the goal is to get people to embrace walking as a form of practical transportation, oversized greenways can actually be counterproductive."[12]

This critical outlook toward open space puts Owen in the company of Jane Jacobs, who had this to say fifty years prior:

> The first necessity in understanding how cities and their parks influence each other is to jettison confusion between real uses and mythical uses—for example, the science-fiction nonsense that parks are "the lungs of the city." It takes about three acres of woods to absorb as much carbon dioxide as four people exude in breathing, cooking, and heating. The oceans of air circulating about us, not our parks, keep cities from suffocating.[13]

Like Owen, Jacobs was fighting a dominant ethos that more green spaces make cities more healthy, when in truth their microcosmic appearance belies their macrocosmic impact. By separating useful things from each other, they can contribute to an automotive culture that exacerbates pollution. Jacobs's case in point was Los Angeles, with the most open space and the most smog of any contemporary American city.[14]

This doesn't mean that we should stop building parks—Chicago and Seattle are two cities with new, big, expensive waterfront parks that nobody regrets—but rather that we shouldn't allow open space to rip apart the urban fabric of our walkable city centers. Every city, particularly if it is to attract millennials, needs to provide easy access to nature, including regionally scaled trails for hiking and biking. Likewise, frequent small pocket parks and playgrounds are key for retaining citizens into their parenting years. But meeting these needs is a very different brief from turning the city into a garden. Current impulses to make our downtowns more sustainable by filling them with pervious surfaces, prairie grass, and the latest craze—"rain gardens"*— threaten to erase one of the key characteristics that distinguishes cities from the suburbs that remain their principal competition.

Indeed, it was desire to somehow magically merge city with country that created the environmental, social, and economic disaster that is sprawl. Still, it is common to come across architecture-school proposals and design-competition entries that have us questing for "a new and unprecedented relationship between man and nature,"■ as if there is some undiscovered way to improve the city by diluting its best qualities. We know better. And we know that central among these qualities is the street life that is only possible in a truly urban environment, where there are more buildings than bushes.

* Rain gardens, which allow streets in certain climates to drain naturally, are a worthy alternative to conventional stormwater systems. They can be provided in ways that do not enlarge the street space or impede pedestrian access.

■ This quote is paraphrased from the winning entry in a 2000 competition to remake the site of the Fornebu Airport in Oslo. (We lost that one, too.)

STEP 10: PICK YOUR WINNERS

Urban triage; Anchors and paths; The lesson of LoDo; Downtowns first

The previous nine steps embody a comprehensive strategy for creating walkable places. As I have stressed throughout, following all these steps, rather than just a few of them, is essential if we are to convert a large segment of drivers into walkers. But following these steps everywhere would bankrupt most cities. Moreover, the universal application of walkability criteria is simply not in keeping with the way that cities actually work: great swaths of any significant metropolis are necessarily dedicated to activities that don't and shouldn't attract street life. To give an obvious example, a container depot is not a place to encourage sidewalk dining.

URBAN TRIAGE

But it is the less obvious examples of this phenomenon that require our attention, or rather, our concerted disregard. A shockingly large amount of money is currently being spent adding walkability enhancements to streets that will never attract more than the occasional stranded motorist hiking for gasoline. In half the cities I visit, I am given a tour of some newly rebuilt street, often the main corridor out of downtown, that has been dolled up with the latest streetlights, tree grates, and multicolored pavers, as if these modifications will create walking in a place where there is almost nothing to walk to. The corridor has been made more attractive for driving, certainly, but at a much greater cost than if that had been the goal.

This error points the way to the first question to ask before investing in walkability: where can spending the least money make the most difference? The answer, as obvious as it is ignored, is on streets that are already framed by buildings that have the potential to attract and sustain street life. In other words, places where an accommodating private realm already exists to give comfort and interest to an improved public realm. Most cities have their fair share of streets like this, where historic shopfronts and other attractive buildings line sidewalks that are blighted only by a high-speed, treeless roadway. Fix the street, and you've got the whole package, or close to it.

In contrast, there is little to be gained in livability by improving the design of a street that is lined by muffler shops and fast-food drive-thrus. When you're done, it's still the auto zone and not worthy of our attention. Let it go.

This more mercenary approach to urban revitalization is what we have come to call *urban triage*, an apt moniker for a technique initiated in the battlefields of World War I.* In pedestrian crises, as in combat, the worst off must sometimes be sacrificed for the greater good. Here, the categories of patient are slightly different: first to receive care are the "A" streets that are best poised to benefit from it. Second are the "B" streets that might present a bit of a tougher win, but are needed to tie the best streets together into a proper network—more on that in a minute.

*Andres Duany, Elizabeth Plater-Zyberk, and Jeff Speck, *Suburban Nation*, 162. The phrase was coined, like so many, by Andres. Battlefield triage involves withholding care from those patients very likely to either live or die and focusing resources principally on those whose fate could go either way.

Third, and off the table, is what remains: the automotive city. These "C" streets should not be allowed to go to seed; by all means, fill the potholes and pick up the trash. But don't worry about sidewalk widths, street trees, or bike lanes—at least, not in this decade.

ANCHORS AND PATHS

The second category above, streets that connect, requires the greatest amount of thought, along with—dare I say it—some design. Because, in any city's downtown, there is a network of walkability, sometimes hidden, that is waiting to emerge. Coaxing it to the surface requires some careful observation and then a decisive design effort. At its heart is the concept of anchors and paths.

Say what you will about shopping malls, you have to admit that in their heyday they did certain things very well. One of these was the almost scientifically determined placement of stores in relationship to each other to encourage maximum spending, which included separating the anchor tenants by a certain distance in order to get people walking past the smaller shops in between. Creating pedestrians in front of the in-line stores was so important to the design of the mall that the anchor tenants were often welcomed rent-free.[1]

In a downtown, the anchors are few and fairly easy to identify: major retailers, large parking structures, movie theaters, and any other use that generates significant foot traffic on a regular basis, such as a performance hall or a baseball stadium.* An already-walkable street network is also a type of anchor, as it creates pedestrians who are willing to stroll farther afield if that walk is rewarded. Sometimes these anchors are quite close to

---

*Baseball needs to be distinguished from football, in which games happen so rarely that a stadium is much less effective at spurring revitalization.

each other, but almost nobody walks between them because of the poor quality of the connection. Beyond the conditions of the roadway itself, this street may suffer from a lack of well-defined, active edges that puts it firmly in "B" or even "C" territory. If this stretch is short enough and opportunities exist for its development, it might make sense for the city to spend money to fix it quickly.

Let's say we are faced with a situation in which two walkable neighborhoods are located a few blocks away from each other. One holds a convention center, hotels, and an arena. It is full of people but few walk very far. The other neighborhood contains restaurants, bars, galleries, and is surrounded by working-class housing. It has tremendous character but needs a bit of a lift. Conventioneers and arena visitors would love to visit it, but few ever do, because the short distance between the two neighborhoods is utterly uninviting. What's a city to do?

This was precisely the scenario in Columbus, Ohio, where the city's convention center and arena were cut off from the gritty Short North neighborhood by a below-grade interstate highway, reamed through in the sixties. Getting from one side to the other meant crossing a barren, windswept bridge, complete with chain-link suicide screen. When it became necessary in 2003 to reconstruct this bridge, the city and state did an unusually smart thing: instead of building a one-hundred-foot-wide bridge, they built a two-hundred-foot-wide bridge, creating two retail pads on its flanks. They gave these pads to an enlightened developer, who built a modern-day Ponte Vecchio, lining the sidewalks with shops and restaurants.

For an additional public cost of $1.9 million, this novel bridge performed an act of magic: it made a highway disappear. Now conventioneers regularly visit the Short North, and the difference to businesses there is described as "night and day."[2] Two walkable districts have been unified into one, and an entire sector of the city has changed its character.

Many cities contain depressed highways and railways, and some of these places are contemplating caps like the one in Columbus. But these are an obvious example of what can be a much subtler situation, in which a few parking lots or lube joints sever what would otherwise be a walkable connection between anchors. Stitching this fabric back together can be even less expensive than the Columbus effort, and just as impactful, but doing so requires an explicit act of identification.

For this reason, when I do a walkability plan, it is a multistep process. First, I study every street that has a chance of being walkable and I grade it in terms of its urban qualities. I ignore the street's traffic characteristics, since they are simple to fix, and look only at comfort and interest: spatial definition and the presence of friendly faces. This effort produces a map in which the streets are colored from green through yellow to red based on their potential to attract pedestrian life. From this map, a pattern emerges, in which certain streets that are good enough come together to form a clear network of walkability. I then supplement this network with the additional streets that are necessary to connect it to the key anchors that it almost reaches, including other pieces of itself.

The result is an urban triage plan: streets are either in or out. This plan mandates the pattern for both public and private investment over the next decade. Only the "in" streets are to receive walkability improvements like safer traffic patterns, street trees, and better sidewalks. Only the "in" street properties are to receive city redevelopment support, whether that means money or just expedited permitting. And the "missing teeth" within this network—especially along the key severed connections—get the full front-burner treatment. Ideally, the entirety of the city leadership, both public sector and private sector, comes together around a simple understanding: Build These Sites First.

THE LESSON OF LoDo

The plans that emerge from this process can have some surprising features. For example, a neighborhood can be eminently walkable and still contain many unwalkable streets. In fact, many great downtowns alternate good streets with bad ones. All that matters is that the good streets connect into a continuous network so that, while you may have to walk across a "C" street, you never have to walk along one.[3] This phenomenon occurs in every American city that is graced with rear alleys.

Even more surprising is how small a network of walkability can be while still giving the impression of a walkable city. Some smaller cities that are known for their walkability, like Greenville, South Carolina, owe much of their reputation to just one great street. Less important than the size of a walkable district is its quality. This was a lesson that we were taught most convincingly by Denver.

In 1993, the city-planning world was abuzz with stories about Denver. "You've got to get to Denver," people kept telling us. "It's amazing what they're doing there."

So we went to Denver, and what we found there was not Denver, but Denver's Lower Downtown, LoDo. In fact, it wasn't LoDo, really; it was just a few blocks of LoDo, blocks that happened to hold John Hickenlooper's Wynkoop brewery, pool hall, and comedy club, across the street from the (empty) beaux arts Union Station, surrounded by some industrial lofts that had just begun to attract urban pioneers. The urbanism wasn't perfect, but it was close enough, although only a few acres of it showed much promise at all. Most of the district was unchanged from decades prior when, according to sportswriter Rick Reilly, "it was full of druggies and brutes and three-toothed thieves. And those were the women."[4]

But those few almost-perfect blocks were enough. Like us, other people were hearing these stories and had begun investing in LoDo and in Denver at large. Within ten years, the whole city was experiencing a powerful renaissance. Denver's population has grown 28 percent since 1990.

Did all those people come to Denver because of the Wynkoop brewery? Clearly not. But it only takes a few blocks to create a reputation. The lesson of LoDo is to start small with something that is as good as you can make it. That is the beauty of urban triage.

DOWNTOWNS FIRST

As much sense as it makes logically, urban triage can be a challenge politically. First, there is the name, which aptly conveys the presence of winners and losers and, for that reason, requires a lot of explanation. I am always quick to point out how the automotive strip can actually demand higher rents than Main Street, and that this is merely a discussion about walkability, not property value. That said, maybe the name *urban triage* needs to be replaced by something less trenchant.

Second, and a bigger problem, is the way that public servants think about distributing resources. Most mayors, city managers, and municipal planners feel a responsibility to their entire city. As a result, they tend to sprinkle the walkability fairy dust indiscriminately. They are also optimists—they wouldn't be in government otherwise—so they want to believe that they can someday attain a city that is universally excellent. This is lovely, but it is counterproductive. By trying to be universally excellent, most cities end up universally mediocre. Walkability is likely only in those places where all the best of what a city has to offer is focused in one area. Concentration, not dispersion, is the elixir of urbanity.

This discussion is a loaded one, as it quickly raises questions of equity, and not just from street to street, but from neighborhood to neighborhood. In most American cities, realistic planning for walkability starts downtown, where most of the key ingredients are already in place. But not many people may actually live there yet. So, who are the efforts for, and are they justified? This is one of the toughest questions a city planner can face. In Baton Rouge, it was phrased this way: "Why are you working on downtown, when it's in such better shape than where we live? Why aren't you doing a plan for our community instead?"

The answer to this question is simple. The downtown is the only part of the city that belongs to everybody. It doesn't matter where you may find your home; the downtown is yours, too. Investing in the downtown of a city is the only place-based way to benefit all of its citizens at once.

And there's more. Every relocation decision, be it a college graduate's or a corporation's, is made with an image of place in mind. That image is palpable and it is powerful. It is resolutely physical: a picture of buildings, streets, squares, cafés, and the social life that those places engender. Whether good or bad, that image is hard to shake. And, with rare exception, that image is downtown.

Each city's reputation therefore rests in large part on its downtown's physical attributes. If the downtown doesn't look good, the city doesn't look good. People won't want to move there, and it will be that much harder for citizens to feel good about the place where they have chosen to live. A beautiful and vibrant downtown, in contrast, can be the rising tide that lifts all ships. As in LoDo, a little bit of great downtown can help push a whole city into the great category. That is the place to begin.

As I ponder the concept of city image, there is one image in particular that I can't get out of my head. I am ten years old, gathered in front of the television with my parents and brother, and we are watching the title credits to *The Mary Tyler Moore Show*. In stark distinction to most American cities portrayed on TV at the time, Mary's Minneapolis is sparkling, lively, and brimming with opportunity. A thirty-year-old woman has broken off her engagement and moved to the big city to start afresh. We don't know what awaits her, but share in her wide-eyed embrace of the infinite possibility of urban life. Surrounded by fellow pedestrians, she pirouettes joyfully in the street and lofts her wool cap into the air. We never see it come down.

PART III

UPDATE TO THE 10TH ANNIVERSARY EDITION

PREFACE TO THE
10TH ANNIVERSARY UPDATE

As the turtle said after being mugged by snails, "It all happened so fast." The last decade has unfolded with a combination of breakneck speed and moments—two years in particular—when time seemed to stand still. We watched long-ago-predicted crises occur unimpeded in slow motion while somehow lacking the agility to prepare for even greater threats on the horizon. Nobody will be able to say we were not warned.

Still, amid all the negative feedback loops and mounting evidence of the shortcomings of our shared race, cities and towns have given us cause for hope. At least from my vantage point, the conversation about what makes for healthy community has fundamentally changed. Walkability, once not even a word, and then an outré concept—an "alternative transportation"—has entered the mainstream. Cities and citizens have stopped asking "What is it?" and are now simply asking for it. Some are even getting it. Neighborhoods from coast to coast are adding bike lanes, removing parking minimums, fighting highway expansions, and, most important, copying one another's successes. Bloodied but not beaten by COVID, the mass movement on behalf of life outside of automobiles is expanding geometrically.

Given these advances, I ardently want this book to keep doing its job. But it is literally old news. Most of its stories—and it is made up mostly of stories—are now becoming histories. Happily, nearly all of them are still relevant, having grown from principles that some people believe to be timeless. But they are getting old, which prompts two questions: Did they all prove out? And what has happened since? This update tries to give answers.

Sorry to say, it is really long. Actually, I'm sorry only to my publisher, who was expecting half as many words. But the answer to the second question is so vast—including COVID, Uber, self-driving cars, mass protests, the weaponization of motor vehicles, a nationwide housing shortage, an escalating climate crisis, and a 50 percent increase in annual pedestrian fatalities—that another hundred pages was inevitable.

There is also a lot more to know. Much of *Walkable City* was an attempt to synthesize a pile of important one-subject titles of the preceding decade. Were the book to be reconceived now, it would make a similar effort with a tremendous collection of intervening works including *Happy City*, *Human Transit*, *Street Fight*, *Right of Way*, *Confessions of a Recovering Engineer*, *There Are No Accidents*, *Policing the Open Road*, *Evicted*, *How to Be an Antiracist*, *The Color of Law*, and, dare I say, *Walkable City Rules*, my effort of 2018. The pages that follow are written by someone who has learned something from all of those books but is unable to do them justice here. Please read them next.

Jeff Speck
Brookline, Massachusetts
August 28, 2022

DO I NEED TO REMIND YOU WHY?

Urban fundamentals; Soft targets; Hidden scourges; The walking cure;
Not changing the climate; Infra-structural racism; Walking while Black

Ten years ago, before lecturing cities on how they could become more walkable, I was often asked to explain why it was so important. Most lecture clients now tell me I can skip that bit. "We're already sold."

Still, the evidence keeps piling in, and it's tempting to pile on. I recently reviewed a deeply researched technical report from the engineering giant Arup. It documented how walkability improves, among other things, traffic safety, community identity, tourism, stormwater management, transit effectiveness, urban competitiveness, and connection to cultural heritage; it reduces obesity, other chronic diseases, health-care costs, crime, traffic congestion, maintenance costs, fossil fuel dependence, air pollution, ambient noise, and microclimates; and it increases life spans, neighborhood vitality, worker creativity, social interaction, intergenerational connectedness, community inclusivity, employment rates, economic productivity, local investment, property values, efficiency of land use, public engagement, civic responsibility, urban resiliency, beauty, and happiness.[1] Anything missing?

I have found that it is still useful to organize all of these benefits under the tripartite headings of wealth, health, and sustainability, except that I missed one: equity. Bringing this book up to date means correcting both for ten years of history and for a lifetime of insufficient awareness of how car culture disproportionately punishes people of color and other marginalized populations.

URBAN FUNDAMENTALS

As will be discussed ahead, COVID-19 caused a lot of city dwellers to head for the hills. Many are now coming back, and the long-term outlook is strong. But, even before COVID, it became clear that the millennial urban invasion was losing steam, for reasons I should have expected.[2] Young adults kept flocking to cities, but millennials stopped being young adults. The average millennial is now—brace yourself—thirty-six years old. That puts them in that small window of life when their housing location is going to be driven mostly by school choice. Urban schools may be getting better, but they are not the best, so the parents who are able will continue to flock to the suburbs, abandoning inner-city schools to those without choice.

Ignoring the immorality of this situation, we can still say that downtown and other walkable urban neighborhoods, post-COVID, will remain popular, thanks to nothing more than the law of supply and demand. Demographers and real estate economists will continue to grab headlines with stories about one group or another "swarming into" cities or "flocking out" of them—parenthood apparently making birds of bees—but the fundamental American mismatch between the desire for and the availability of walkable places is not about to change. Depending on who you listen to and when they conduct their polls, somewhere between 45 and 55 percent of the American public would prefer a home in a walkable neighborhood to one with a big yard. Meanwhile, the number of Americans who live in walkable communities has been estimated at one in ten. That means that most of the half of us who want walkable places aren't getting them, so we can be confident that the "urban advantage" persists.

The desire for authentic urbanism is still impacting shopping as well, only reinforced by COVID. While many struggling Main Street stores eventually regained their footing by taking advantage of sidewalk space, this option wasn't available to merchants trapped in retail malls. As things reopened, retailers noticed that their mall-based stores were underperforming, and started abandoning them. Joan Hilson, the CEO of Signet Jewelers (owner of Kay and Zales), observed that "the foot traffic for off-mall locations is better than what we're seeing in the mall . . . and we see that shift continuing." Similarly The Gap, that suburban mainstay, plans to pull all but 20 percent of its stores out of enclosed centers.[3] Fully a quarter of U.S. malls aren't expected to hang on through 2025.[4]

By goosing telework, COVID and Zoom have allowed many Americans to decamp for greener pastures. For some, that has meant the country or the suburbs. But many others have moved to smaller cities and towns with less overblown real estate markets, places with decent Main Streets that just needed a little more juice. These relocations—from New York City to Hudson, and from San Francisco to Truckee—will help bring walkability faster to a lot of places that were lagging.[5]

What will a dispersing workforce mean for the American economy? As discussed ahead, there are reasons to be worried about Zoom. The creative benefits of human propinquity measured by West and Bettencourt have not gone away, and are now supported by additional data. A three-year University of Pennsylvania study of 3,445 inventors commuting to 1,180 different firms found that "for every [6.2 miles] of added travel distance, the firm employing those inventors registered 5 percent fewer patents. The quality of the patents took an even bigger dive, dropping 7 percent with every 6.2 miles added to the inventors' commute."[6]

In other words, for every additional mile your inventors commute, they are likely to produce 1 percent fewer inventions of 1 percent worse quality. Acknowledging how lengthy commutes hurt productivity, Facebook offered ten-thousand-dollar bonuses to workers who moved closer to their Menlo Park campus.[7]

Is it the lack of proximity that enfeebles suburban inventors, or the time wasted driving? Likely both. Whether the solution is urbanism or Zoom, we can be confident that more suburbanization is not a path to success. Even the Mafia is struggling from sprawl. An October 2021 *Wall Street Journal* article noted how "bumbling suburban-bred mobsters kneecap a storied New York clan":

> Older members complain that the millennials—who grew up in the suburbs instead of city streets—are softer, dumber, and not as loyal as mobsters of the past. Plus, they're always texting. "Everything is on the phones with them," said a former made member of the Colombo family.[8]

SOFT TARGETS

What our gangster meant by "soft" could be interpreted several ways, but suburbanization continues to contribute to an obesity epidemic that has grown unabated. The percentage of obese Americans rose a solid 24 percent from 2008 to 2018,[9] and our driving lifestyle deserves much of the blame. How do we know? Evidence comes from many sources, but my favorite is an accidentally randomized experiment conducted in China. I know of no other study that has been able to isolate the impacts of car ownership while holding all other variables constant.

Beijing is like the Soviet Union used to be: if you want to own a car, you have to win a lottery. Fewer than one in fifty applicants are allowed to buy cars. Researchers from China and California tracked 937 "winners" and "losers" over five years. They found that the winners walked twenty-four minutes less each day than the losers, and that, for people over fifty, winning the car lottery meant gaining an average of 22.7 pounds.[10] In a nation as fit as China, that's a lot of weight.

While the clear causality can't be mistaken, it is difficult to know exactly how much of our current obesity crisis can be pinned on the automobile. Not so for the other epidemic discussed in this book, the roughly 40,000 of our fellow citizens killed each year by traffic violence—up to 42,915 in 2021.[11] That's like a 737 crashing every single day. The most shocking thing about this number is how we continue to take it for granted. If some communities' response to the COVID crisis conveyed the impression that life is cheap in America, we need look no further to understand why.

And the injuries! Two million Americans are "permanently injured" in car crashes each year. That's 228 life-changing injuries per hour, every hour. Every day. Every year. It is a strange collective psychosis indeed that blinds us to this rolling disaster. Only opioids and guns are worse, and guns just barely.

I guess this is old news, and, thanks to evolving technologies, the risks of driving a car have been falling each decade. Also on a steady decline were pedestrian fatalities—until 2009. What has happened since then *is* news, and is expertly covered in Angie Schmitt's important book, *Right of Way*: pedestrian fatalities have been rising on average almost 5 percent a year, every year.[12] Pedestrian fatalities were 6,700 in 2020, up 63 percent from 2009.

I have never seen a group of professionals as demoralized as the people who track American pedestrian safety. They've stopped keeping up any pretense of hopefulness. In the latest edition of *Dangerous by Design*—the annual assessment of pedestrian carnage—the authors at Smart Growth America and the National Complete Streets Coalition seem ready to throw in the towel:

> We are tired and saddened to produce yet another edition of this report without any positive change to show for it. . . . Our current approach to addressing the rising number of people struck and killed while walking has been a total failure. It needs to be reconsidered or dropped altogether.[13]

Why the sudden rise? There appear to be two main causes, and they do not include cell phones, which have proliferated in Europe without causing similar bloodshed. The first is that more Americans have been forced to live in suburbia, especially low-income Americans. As cities become less affordable, more carless citizens find themselves living and working in places never intended for walking. With bus stops located on seven-lane arterials and crosswalks a half mile apart, it's a killing zone out there, and one that discriminates ruthlessly, as will be covered ahead.

The second factor affects all Americans, and is likely dominant: the rise of the sport utility vehicle. SUVs have been around for decades, but through the course of the 2010s they took over. By 2018, they captured 48 percent of the U.S. new car market, as sedans dropped below 30 percent. According to the National Highway Traffic Safety Administration (NHTSA), SUVs are two to three times more likely than sedans to kill pedestrians when they hit them, and four times more likely to kill children.[14]

SUVs, ever growing in size, are much heavier than cars, so they take longer to stop, and hit harder. Just as important is their high stance, which causes people struck by SUVs to fall under the vehicle, where they are crushed. When hit straight on by a sedan, adult pedestrians end up on the hood, with mostly lower-body injuries; SUVs aim for the chest—or the head, if it's a child. A study of crashes in Michigan found that 100 percent of pedestrians struck by SUVs traveling more than forty miles per hour died, compared to 54 percent of pedestrians struck by cars.[15]

SUV hoods are taller because SUVs are taller, but also due to the aggressive styles preferred by their designers. General Motors wunderkind Karan Moorjani, the hand behind the 2020 GMC Sierra, could barely mix enough metaphors to convey his violent intent:

> We spent a lot of time making sure that when you stand in front of this thing it looks like it's going to come get you. It's got that pissed-off feel. . . . My first week in Detroit, I was driving through downtown and seeing the fist of Joe Louis, and remember thinking that's what this truck should look like—a massive fist moving through the air. . . . If you look at the body, it's like the barrel of a gun.[16]

The newer the SUV—or pickup truck—the taller the grille, with some unintended consequences. An Indianapolis television news exposé discovered that the owner of a Cadillac Escalade was unable to see twelve children seated in a row in front of her bumper. Only the thirteenth child was slightly visible to this normal-height woman sitting upright.[17] No wonder the number of annual "frontover" fatalities rose from 5 in the late nineties to 72 a decade later and 366 in 2020. Eighty percent of frontovers involve larger vehicles, and, tragically, the majority are parents killing their own children.[18]

Why are so many Americans buying SUVs? One reason is fear of SUVs. That fear is justified: when a sedan and an SUV hit head-on, the passengers in the sedan are four to ten times as likely to die as those in the SUV.[19] The result has been an arms race the likes of which our roads have never seen. The NHTSA could reverse this trend in a week—especially when it comes to "pissed-off" grilles—but don't hold your breath.

Can I admit to you that I owned a sport utility vehicle? My parental car-buying saga, initiated in these pages, rapidly escalated through the 2010s, and my wife and I ended up with a used seven-seat SUV. Then I read Angie Schmitt, and I traded it in for a sleek, low-lying station wagon. Now I just have to dodge the Durangos.

HIDDEN SCOURGES

Walkable City described an American asthma epidemic that continues unabated, but it neglected to discuss the larger health impacts of tailpipe emissions and vehicle noise, which have both been discovered to be staggering.

According to a 2013 MIT study, emissions from road transportation are responsible for approximately fifty-three thousand annual "early deaths" in the United States, more than doubling the carnage that comes from crashes.[20] A separate study placed fourteen hundred of those annual deaths in New York City alone, where the health-care costs attributed to vehicle emissions surpassed $21 billion annually.[21] Electric cars won't fix this: "85 to 90 percent of toxic vehicle emissions in traffic come from tire wear and other non-tailpipe sources."[22]

Meanwhile, what you do hear can kill you. Scientists have discovered that being subjected to traffic noise "results in altered blood chemistry and meddles with blood vessel function."[23] The result is a greater risk of diabetes, heart attacks, and strokes.[24]

A recent study linked road noise to dementia as well, especially Alzheimer's. This remarkable effort spent thirteen years tracking the health outcomes of 2 million people—a third of all Danes—living in every residential building in the country. By comparing sides of buildings exposed to traffic noise with more sheltered sides, researchers found that fully 15 percent of dementia cases could be attributed to transport noise.[25]

THE WALKING CURE

Finally, proof that driving makes you crazy. Can walking make you sane? As reported in *Fast Company*:

> People who walk 8.6 minutes a day are 33 percent more likely to report better mental health. . . . On the other hand, researchers found that if someone shifts from a long commute to a walk, their happiness increases as much as if they'd fallen in love.[26]

Heading back to Denmark, we can find the same understanding in the words of Søren Kierkegaard:

> Above all, do not lose your desire to walk. Every day I walk myself into a state of well-being and walk away from every illness. I have walked myself into my best thoughts and I know of no thought so burdensome that one cannot walk away from it.[27]

Kierkegaard was not the first to connect regular walking not just with happiness, but with wisdom. As early as the fifth century, St. Augustine wrote *"solvitur ambulando"*: it is solved by walking.[28] To this, Friedrich Nietzsche added "only thoughts reached by walking have value."[29] He walked six to eight hours a day,[30] which may explain why I have heard him referred to as "the last man to know everything."

Researchers are beginning to parse the connection between thinking and walking, and it's more foundational than we expected. The Irish neuroscientist Shane O'Mara is one of many who promote a "motor-centric" concept of the brain, that it "evolved to support movement and, therefore, if we stop moving, it won't work very well." He believes that "the activation that occurs across the whole of the brain during problem-solving becomes much greater almost as an accident of walking demanding lots of neural resources."[31] His experiments found, through brainwave analysis, that rats who were wheeled around instead of walking became measurably more stupid.[32]

One other justification for more walkable cities appears in this book's second chapter: social capital. In *Bowling Alone* (2000), Robert Putnam blamed a decline in social capital nationwide, in part, on people's long commutes. In *Suburban Nation* (also 2000), my coauthors and I talked about how the grave danger and spatial competition of driving turns normal people into sociopaths. If driving is so bad for community, could walking and biking produce better results? That question was answered in a 2021 study by Jessica Stroope of Louisiana State University. She found that, aside from age and education, no other factor was as great a predictor of community participation than "active transportation." Subjects who got around more on foot or by bicycle were demonstrably more likely to engage in policy change efforts through writing letters, making phone calls, and/or attending community meetings.[33] These findings were a nice complement to the classic research of Donald Appleyard, who in 1981 compared the social lives of people who lived on streets with and without heavy car traffic. He found that while people on lightly traveled streets counted an average of 3 friends, people on busy streets averaged 0.9 friends.[34]

That's hardly the best ad copy: "Heavy traffic: for those times you want slightly less than one friend."

NOT CHANGING THE CLIMATE

Since I wrote about climate change a decade ago, what we knew about climate change three decades ago has become all the more compelling. Yet this knowledge remains consistently unable to motivate meaningful action, even as the first impacts are being experienced regularly.

This past summer, some 719 deaths in a single week were attributed to a "heat dome" that toppled temperature records, including hitting 121 degrees in—wait for it—Canada.[35] The previous summer, a "derecho" windstorm destroyed two-thirds of the tree canopy in Cedar Rapids, Iowa, in one hour.[36] This year began with a wildfire in Boulder, Colorado, that leveled an estimated 1,084 structures, including homes, a hotel, and a shopping center.[37] As the casualties continue to mount, it has become impossible to deny Naomi Klein's assertion that the world's neoliberal economic order simply lacks any mechanism for averting catastrophe. But its capacity for rearranging deck chairs has been a wonder to behold.

Since the publication of *Walkable City*, transportation has surpassed electricity production to become the largest source of greenhouse gas emissions in the United States. Most of this comes from light-duty vehicles, including cars, SUVs, vans, and pickup trucks, which produce more than 1.1 billion metric tons of carbon dioxide equivalents each year. As noted by the Center for American Progress, "If the U.S. light-duty vehicle fleet were a country, it would be the sixth largest emitter on earth, ahead of Germany."[38]

On the face of it, this might sound like good news. If the problem is cars, we can solve it with cars. Except we can't, at least not in time to make a difference. Electric cars are greener than gasoline cars, but they are simply not arriving fast enough.

The data on electric-car performance is better than we thought, and getting better every year, as electrical grids become cleaner. It's true that adding the battery almost doubles the carbon impacts of manufacture, but that impact is typically offset within six to eighteen months of driving. Currently, a typical gasoline car emits about five hundred grams of carbon per mile over its lifetime, while a typical electric car emits less than two hundred. And while getting an electric car may cause you to drive more, it won't cause you to drive 2.5 times more.

If everyone were to trade in their gas-powered clunker for a

Tesla today, that might make a difference. Certainly, everyone who can, should. But most won't, and nobody is making them. Currently, fewer than 1 percent of the 250 million light-duty vehicles on the road are electric. General Motors does not plan to transition fully to electric vehicles until 2035, and the average age of the U.S. auto fleet is twelve years. Do the math: *The New York Times* predicts that, even by 2050, most American cars and trucks will still be running on gasoline. And let's not forget about Mexico and points south, where our cars will keep polluting well after we're done with them.[39]

Bottom line, gasoline cars will gradually disappear from our roads over the next four decades, exactly four decades too late.

Meanwhile, what are our leaders doing to reduce transport emissions? Well, for one, they are funding new roads. As documented in this book and elsewhere, there is likely no other tool as effective at increasing vehicle miles traveled as road building. The recently passed $1.2 trillion infrastructure bill dedicates $110 billion to highways, roads, and bridges, almost three times what it invests in public transit.[40] While much of this money is supposedly dedicated to "fix it first" projects, experience has shown that state DOTs are expert at redefining repair as expansion. For his part, Transportation Secretary Pete Buttigieg, reportedly a *Walkable City* fan, is reduced to playing dumb on this issue. Confronted this January with my critique, he told NPR, "Sometimes, the roads legitimately need to be expanded. This is the United States of America."[41]

And he's one of the good guys. A similar blind spot afflicts John Kerry, our "climate ambassador." He is a real hero who is doing his best to repair the planet, but with a strangely small toolbox. I had the thrill of sitting ten feet away from him in the summer of 2021 as he gave a blistering speech at the Château de Chantilly outside Paris.[42] Every minute of that inspiring half-hour sermon was about one thing: cleaning the power grid. No mention of transportation alternatives like transit or biking, and certainly no mention of giving people more choices about how to live.

My issue with clean electricity and electric cars is not that they won't help save the planet. My issue is that they are not enough to save the planet, and yet they get all the attention, at the expense of our having a national conversation on the alloca- tion of our transportation investment and the shape of our com- munities, both of which are still driving us off the cliff's edge.

And this second item—how the presumption of universal car ownership has remade our cities—remains a dominant force in our profligate lives. Echoing David Owen in these pages, Far- had Manjoo had this to say in *The New York Times*:

> [The] problem isn't just gas-fueled cars but car-fueled lives—a view of the world in which huge private automo- biles are the default method of getting around. In this way E.V.s represent a very American answer to climate change: To deal with an expensive, dangerous, extremely resource-intensive machine that has helped bring about the destruction of the planet, let's all buy this new ver- sion, which runs on a different fuel.[43]

Like Owen, Manjoo understands that the real problem with cars is that they cause us to live so large on the land, expanding all of our consumptive patterns. Can we reshape the American-built environment fast enough to slow climate change? No. But people can be encouraged to move, and we can stop incentivizing sub- urban lifestyles at every level of government.

These incentives are huge and perverse. Highway building and a miniscule gas tax—unchanged since 1993—keep the cost of driving well below its value. The mortgage interest deduction, that most American of boondoggles, effectively transfers wealth from working-class renters to the landed gentry. Purchasers of an electric Audi Q4 receive a federal income tax credit of $7,500. As Gregory Shill asks in *The Atlantic*, "Why are we taxing bus riders to pay rich people to buy McMansions and luxury electric SUVs?"[44]

A more climate-savvy approach would look like Heidelberg, Germany, where Oberbürgermeister Eckart Würzner sees electric cars as but one rung on the ladder to carbon neutrality, along with a hydrogen-powered bus fleet, a network of "bicycle superhighways," and a mile-long downtown pedestrian-only zone. Buying an electric car in Heidelberg earns you a moderate cash reward. But giving up your car entirely gets you unlimited free transit for a year.[45]

Meanwhile, back in the United States, Joe Biden is gleefully putting the three-ton Ford F-150 Lightning through its paces, and Farhad Manjoo is test-driving luxury SUVs:

> I found myself driving more, longer, because driving the Escalade was so totally easy. If most cars become as comfortable, convenient and luxurious as this one—while growing ever larger—what hope is there that we might ever reduce our dependence on these monstrous machines? Also, should I plan to lease or to buy?[46]

He knows better. But that's what we're up against. Our leaders aren't truly leading, and human nature has shown itself to be deeply allergic to short-term sacrifice in the name of long-term benefit . . . or even mere survival.

Against these odds, I've decided to adopt a "yes, and" approach to climate change resistance. There is no reason to pit solutions against one another. We need everything, all at once. I'm sick of electric cars sucking all the air out of the room, but we need electric cars. We also need everything else, especially electric bikes, bike lanes everywhere, urban housing, transit-oriented development, development-oriented transit, incentives for people to live in more walkable places, and the removal of hidden subsidies for sprawl. Everything needs to be on the table, and I'll work with anyone: Greta, Mayor Pete, Ambassador Kerry, Elon, even the assholes at Davos. Let's do this together.

But, just an FYI, if your solution involves more driving, you're on the wrong team.

INFRA-STRUCTURAL RACISM

In February 2019, when I arrived to give a lecture in Houston, I was met by protesters holding signs. This had never happened to me before. Happily, it turns out we were on the same side: they had come to the theater for the same reason I had, to stop the ill-conceived $7 billion expansion of U.S. Interstate 45 through their city. Their motivation was mostly personal: a desire not to have their homes destroyed, their air polluted, and their tax dollars wasted. Mine was more professional: the hope of bringing to a major metropolis some basic concepts about city-building that, so far, had seemed to elude it. The Texas Department of Transportation (TxDOT) was trying to sell the I-45 expansion to Houston with the usual false promises: reduced traffic congestion, improved driver safety, and cleaner air quality. These are three promises that no highway expansion in America has ever delivered on.

I was prepared to attack the expansion on these terms, but what I learned during my visit was even more compelling. By TxDOT's own admission, the plan to widen I-45 was on track to destroy no fewer than 1,235 units of housing, home to about five thousand people.[47] It would also plow through 331 existing businesses that provide almost twenty-five thousand permanent jobs.[48] Together, these residential and business losses were predicted to cost the City of Houston about $135 million in forgone property and sales taxes each year. But these financial deficits paled next to the very real human cost of breaking communities apart. If the plan proceeds, 40 percent of the young students at Bruce Elementary are set to lose their homes and end up at different schools. The historic Mount Olive Baptist Church, the heart of Independence Heights, is set to be demolished, along with forty-three other properties there. Remarkably, the first town incorporated by African Americans in Texas was completely omitted from TxDOT's Historical Resources Survey for this project.

And let's talk air quality. Black families with children suffer from asthma at roughly twice the average rate,[49] and most of that comes from living within five hundred meters of highways.[50] Currently, a dozen daycare facilities and two dozen schools sit within a mere 150 meters of the highway. More cars and trucks on I-45 will mean more particulate matter, more asthma, and more environmental inequity for Houston.

Stories like this are well documented in Robert Caro's *The Power Broker*, one of those books you read while thinking, "Well this could never happen today." But it may very well happen in Houston. Three years later, this project hangs in the balance, wisely tied up with an environmental lawsuit. If it moves forward—which still seems likely—it will be just one of many similar efforts nationwide. According to a *Los Angeles Times* investigation, more than two hundred thousand people have lost their homes to federal highway projects since 1990. These include 750 families in Tampa, 850 in Los Angeles and Orange Counties, and thousands more in between. These families have been mostly Black and Latino.[51] This is what the planner Destiny Thomas calls "*infra*-structural racism."[52]

WALKING WHILE BLACK

Communities destroyed by highways and children sickened by asthma are only two ways in which minority and other marginalized communities have disproportionally borne the brunt of

American car culture. A recent study of twenty-four years of data found that lower-income neighborhoods experienced road fatality rates more than 3.6 times higher than wealthier places. Research also shows that Blacks and Latinos are at considerably higher risk on the road—especially as pedestrians and bicyclists—than white populations.[53] African Americans and Native Americans make up 12.9 percent of the population but they represent 22 percent of pedestrian deaths. In all, people of color are 54 percent more likely to be struck and killed while walking in the United States.[54]

Meanwhile, an analysis of jaywalking tickets in Jacksonville, Florida, which typically result in a sixty-five-dollar fine, found that ticketing did not correlate with the most dangerous walking areas. Rather, they were focused in communities of color, with African Americans nearly three times as likely as whites to be ticketed.[55] Just as with driving violations, police are targeting minority populations with jaywalking tickets as a way to troll for other offenses. For this reason, the Commonwealth of Virginia has decriminalized jaywalking throughout the state,[56] and others will likely follow.

One state over, Maryland Representative Robbyn Lewis is one of a new breed of legislators who make a point of recognizing walking as a fundamental American freedom in need of protection, whether it be from police harassment or from the threat of traffic violence:

> Walkability is a human right, like any other—the right to self-determination, bodily autonomy, or privacy. And as an elected official who swore to defend the Constitution and protect human rights, it is my duty to ensure that every person—no matter where they were born, what color they are, or what language they speak at home—has the right to walk, to get where they want or need to go, in comfort and safety.[57]

As this sort of advocacy implies, public investments in walkability disproportionally benefit the most disadvantaged Americans. Blacks are three times as likely as whites to take transit. Latinos are twice as likely as whites to have no access to a car.[58] People who earn less than twenty-five thousand dollars annually are three times as likely to walk to work as people who earn three times that much.[59] Every single investment in walkability also makes a community safer and more accessible to people in wheelchairs, as it benefits the young, the old, and the rest of the 103 million Americans who can't drive.

One of the reasons it has been so hard to knock driving off its pedestal in the United States is that, despite its populist image, driving trends rich and therefore powerful. Walking trends poor. Cities that hope to improve social equity should start there.

LONG COVID

Cities are safer; COVID cars; The COVID workplace;
COVID-safe streets

What is the future of cities post-COVID? That is the question that has been on the lips of every journalist, urbanist, and real estate analyst whose apparition has graced my Zoom screen over the past two years. My quick answer is that, when you take the long view, the future of cities will look a lot like the past of cities. More on that in a minute; for now, it is useful to observe some of the events that have played out in our downtown areas over this strange and calamitous moment in history.

First, it was impossible to ignore how quickly cities were pegged as villainous coconspirators in the spread of disease, and abandoned by many who had the means. True, the coronavirus struck first in cities, for the obvious reason. Just as Willie Sutton robbed banks "because that's where the money is," COVID initially hit hardest where the people were.

"There is a density level in NYC that is destructive. It has to stop and it has to stop now. NYC must develop an immediate plan to reduce density."[1] So tweeted Governor Andrew Cuomo when the state of New York went into lockdown in March of 2020. Certainly, early indications and common sense led naturally to the conclusion that avoiding other people's germs would be easier in less urban places. So, like the Florentine nobles fleeing the Black Death in Bocaccio's *Decameron*, a better part of

America's nattering classes decamped to their countryside villas, or the suburban equivalent.

CITIES ARE SAFER

But it didn't take long for the data to begin to tell another story. Even before the availability of vaccines, it was clear that some of the densest places on earth, like Singapore, Seoul, and Shanghai, were experiencing the lowest rates of infection and death. Singapore, which holds twice the population of Chicago in about the same land area, currently enjoys a COVID death rate one seventeenth as high.[2]

But comparisons between the United States and civilized nations are not convincing, so let's stay domestic. America's Singapore is Washington, D.C., a state that is also a city. Its COVID deaths are 26 percent below the national average. The states with the highest death rates are among the most rural.

A team at Johns Hopkins studied 913 U.S. counties. They found that, after adjusting for additional factors like city size, race, age, and education, "denser counties, as opposed to more rural, sprawling areas with smaller populations, were associated with lower death rates." Doubling the density cut the death rate by 11.3 percent. Interestingly, the impact of city density on infection rates was negligible.[3]

As studies show no greater infection rate but a considerably lower COVID death rate from higher-density places, it is natural to attribute that outcome to better urban hospitals and more educated urban populations. But other experts point to another cause, the reduced obesity rates in cities that come from less driving and more walking. As noted by Chris Webster at the University of Hong Kong, "Higher density areas are more likely to be well served by public transport, and public transport travel always involves a walking component."[4]

Wouldn't you know it, there's that walking thing again. Just in case any other panicked governors aren't paying full attention, the Johns Hopkins study's lead author, Shima Hamidi, PhD, notes: "These findings suggest that urban planners should continue to practice and advocate for compact places rather than sprawling ones, due to the myriad well-established benefits of the former, including health benefits."[5] As one reporter concluded, "Potential mass exoduses from densely populated U.S. cities may actually be a bad idea for everyone."[6]

Of course, postvaccine, the distinction between urban and rural places has become more stark, as vaccine compliance does indeed track alongside educational attainment, and a significant portion of the exurban Fox News audience has lined up for what Dan Savage calls "the Rapture for idiots." Here we can't help but empathize with the words of the comedian Jimmy Carr: "The spread of COVID was directly linked to how dense the population is, and some of the population are really quite fucking dense."[7]

COVID CARS

It's wonderful to hear that you are safer in cities during COVID, but that fact matters little if most people don't know it, won't know it, and act upon the opposite understanding. Certainly, when faced with a potentially deadly disease that is spread by people, it's only natural to pack up and go where there are fewer of them. COVID spurred a rural and suburban real estate boom. The number of suburban home shoppers surged upward 41.2 percent with the onset of the pandemic, and the suburban inventory dropped by 55 percent over a single year.[8] Rents and home prices in the centers of large U.S. cities tanked. The good news (for owners) is that they quickly rebounded, long before the pandemic waned. That speaks well to the evergreen appeal of walkable places, but it doesn't negate the fact that COVID was a sprawl bomb. With climate imperatives ideally coaxing more Americans out of their cars, the pandemic could not have come at a worse time.

Indeed, car sales, new and used, shot upward, as mass transit was immediately abandoned by everyone who had the option. This makes sense both practically and metaphorically. As Tom Vanderbilt noted:

> The single-occupancy car itself is the original social-distancing machine. [Hermann] Knoflacher has likened it to a virus—a pathogen that has infiltrated its host (the city) and hijacked its molecular infrastructure to create a more welcoming environment for its own replication.[9]

Knoflacher is the Austrian civil engineer who, well before CO-VID, invented the "walkmobile," a sedan-shaped lightweight wooden frame that pedestrians can suspend from their shoulders to approximate the space-hogging size of a car.[10] This device was a prescient antecedent to the six-foot-radius Hula-Hoops that a few witty public health advocates donned to demonstrate coronavirus protocols, a coincidence that cannot be ignored. And, as Knoflacher notes, the worst thing about cars is the way they change cities to welcome only more of the same.

Can the virus metaphor fruitfully be taken further? Let's try. A traditional vaccine is a weak little version of a deadly disease that makes its host immune to the damage that disease can inflict. Well, what could be more of a weak little car than a bicycle, and is there anything better for cities? Happily, bike sales also soared in 2020, and, judging from the cycling I witnessed in my neighborhood, some people turned to bikes who had never biked before. But most folks fell into cars, which they then piloted around the city with the most extreme abandon.

Or so the experts would have us believe: in some Jekyll-and-

Hyde transmogrification, normally calm and peaceable motorists, confronted with a pandemic, metamorphized into road-raging speed demons. The picture painted by highway agencies and road builders was of panicked motorists screaming "AIEEEEEEE COVID!!!!," throwing off their seatbelts, and punching the accelerators through the floorboards.

I bought into this misleading narrative until quite recently, when I realized that it was a convenient smokescreen deployed between us and the more obvious conclusion, something we already knew: traffic congestion saves lives. With rush-hour traffic down by three-quarters in the early pandemic, empty streets were finally available to be used at the high speeds for which they were designed. The result was the largest one-year increase in motor vehicle deaths since the earliest days of motordom.[11] As the number of miles driven dropped by more than an eighth, driving deaths rose by a quarter.[12] For all the state highway departments that advocate for road expansions on the basis of saving lives—and it's most of them—that's an important statistic to remember.

Traffic congestion in most larger cities is now returning to historical highs, which are likely to be surpassed as people only slowly return to transit. It is fair to expect that, while congestion represents an equilibrium as discussed in this volume, COVID has adjusted people's tolerance for it upward. So, as you creep along on your interminable morning commute, perhaps take some comfort in the many lives saved.

THE COVID WORKPLACE

Meanwhile, midsized and smaller cities are a mixed bag. Those with office-heavy downtowns, like Des Moines and Omaha, made expendable by Zoom, are remarkably free of traffic, both in cars and on foot. I recently biked through downtown Des

Moines at rush hour, and the city looked like it had been hit by a neutron bomb. It was heartbreaking. For those of us who labor daily to bring downtowns to life, witnessing the short-term impacts of the coronavirus feels downright Sisyphean.

Will these places come back? Somewhat. How much, and how fast, will depend partly on Zoom, and partly on each city's commitment to building new housing downtown. Each deserves brief consideration.

It is very difficult to convert empty office space to housing. Washington, D.C., for one, has created a special program to incentivize it,[13] but most office floor plates are too fat, and the desire for operable windows adds an expense that can be prohibitive. What *is* easily convertible to housing are surface parking lots, which most midsized cities possess in abundance. A large portion of Des Moines's 1.33 million surface parking spaces[14] can be found downtown, and many of them are now empty around the clock. Most of them used to also be empty overnight, due to the lack of housing nearby. Single-use parking is always wasteful; unused parking, during a housing crisis, is inexcusable. Given the unlikelihood that Des Moines offices will ever reach full capacity again, it makes sense to start converting blocks of parking to housing, which will find more than ample overnight parking in adjacent empty blocks. The same goes for most midsized cities. With this new housing nearby, and the other activities and amenities that housing attracts, the remaining offices will be revalued. Now that people can work from anywhere, offices need a competitive advantage to thrive; being within an easy walk of apartments, restaurants, and the gym is one such advantage.

The demand for office space was already shrinking before Zoom, with greater workplace flexibility making offices smaller. Now, the future seems clear. The pandemic tripped a wire, and deeply flawed but deeply convenient teleconferencing is here to stay. Our time in the physical presence of our collaborators is dwindling. Five years hence, this fact may be the most pronounced impact of the virus, and it's not encouraging. Here's Walter Isaacson's take:

> One of the transformations wrought by the coronavirus pandemic is that more meetings in the future will be done virtually. It's a shame. If COVID doesn't kill us, Zoom will. As Steve Jobs emphasized when he built a headquarters for Pixar and planned a new Apple campus, new ideas are born out of serendipitous encounters. In-person interactions are especially important in the initial brainstorming of new ideas and the forging of personal bonds. As Aristotle taught, we are a social animal, an instinct that cannot fully be satisfied online.[15]

My own social life on Zoom would seem to bear this out. If you are like me, you spent the first month or two of the pandemic reconnecting with close friends. My wife and I would make cocktails and arrange video dates with the people we would otherwise be hoping to see in person. It was nice to catch up. Each call ended with a promise to reconnect in a week or a month. Some of those reconnections happened, once. Then they stopped. As much as we enjoyed our friends, there was no compulsion to keep the effort going; it had started to feel like work.

We've learned from many studies of cognition that, below our conscious brain, there lies a much more powerful unconscious brain that is really in charge, determining our actions and our happiness. Jonathan Haidt describes it as a monkey riding an elephant. The monkey thinks it's in charge, but much of its intellection surrounds rationalizing choices that the elephant has already made.

Scientists report that one of the first things most people do after shaking hands is to find a way to smell their own hand.[16] While Zoom may be satisfying our conscious need to connect with one another, it is certainly not satisfying our deeper unconscious need to connect with one another in ways that we do not fully understand.

Ultimately, this is good news for cities. As long as we are human, their special sauce of physical propinquity will continue to draw us to them. Urban density will always cause cities to be centers of energy and growth. Ten thousand years of history give us little reason to fear that COVID or any other factor—even those that stigmatize density—is going to bring our cities down.

COVID-SAFE STREETS

Aside from Zoom—and, of course, mRNA vaccines—the most impactful technology to evolve thanks to COVID was the one at the very heart of this book: street design. This story has been well told and does not need much elaboration here. Reduced car traffic, increased walking and biking, social-distancing protocols, and a restaurant attrition crisis all combined to accomplish in weeks what many urbanists had been clamoring for, mostly unsuccessfully, for decades. Streets were closed to vehicular traffic. Driving and parking lanes were converted to bike facilities and broader sidewalks. Elaborate roadside "streateries" gave life support to bars and restaurants while bringing new and in some cases unprecedented energy to the public realm. Lots of neighbors complained, but, hey, it was a global health crisis, and bold measures were needed.

Cities and their leaders embraced these changes with different attitudes and aptitudes. My town of Brookline, Massachusetts, was fast out of the gate, turning four-lane Beacon Street into a two-laner, pushing the parking lanes into the street to create a protected bike/stroll zone along the curb; my younger son christened it on a pogo stick. Cambridge, New York City, Milwaukee, Minneapolis, Denver, Seattle, San Francisco, and others also moved quickly. Boston's mayor, pressured by the city council, eventually made similar changes, to dramatic effect. Hanover Street through the North End—our "Little Italy"—was transformed into the outdoor-dining mecca it always should have been. Other cities did much less, but most saw the need to keep their merchants alive. One survey of U.S. mayors found that 92 percent had initiated some sort of outdoor-dining program in response to COVID, while almost half had closed some streets to pass-through traffic.[17]

I was one of many planners who sold these Main Street makeovers to cities, pro bono. While I acknowledged other motivations beyond the pandemic for making our streets more livable, I saw the fastest path to the end zone and took it. My line to public officials was that "this public-health crisis is at its heart a *spatial* crisis: the way that space has been allocated in our communities is increasing the spread of the disease."[18] It mostly worked.

Or did it? Now, as the pandemic is waning, most of these interventions are being ripped out. Brookline's are long gone. Parking is back on Hanover Street. Some of this is just winter, but most such spaces nationwide are not coming back. Live by the sword, die by the sword: pandemic-justified transformations have no value postplague. This, despite some surprising data. Research conducted by the City of Yarra, just east of Melbourne, Australia, found that a typical parking spot that had generated $1,050 per month in meter fees was generating $8,940 monthly in additional business revenue when converted into a dining parklet.[19]

Other advocates were more forthright than I. I was afraid of being seen as using a pandemic to push my own agenda. Not so for Paris mayor Anne Hidalgo, who pointed to the cleaner air of a city under lockdown as inspiration for making the changes demanded by the climate crisis. "We could breathe," she said. "We heard birds. If it could be like this, how pleasant it would be."[20]

Upon reelection in June 2020, she doubled down on her 870

miles of new bike lanes, removing cars from the Rive Droite and the rue de Rivoli, eliminating tens of thousands of parking spaces, and backing a $300 million plan to turn the Champs-Élysées into a multimodal linear garden.[21] Ah, to be in Paris in the springtime!

Hidalgo, London's Sadiq Khan, even New York's (former DOT Commissioner) Janette Sadik-Khan (no relation) made no bones about COVID being a dry run for climate change. "For cities to return to the pre-pandemic status quo would be a historic blunder," she and Seth Solomonow wrote in *The Atlantic*.[22] Yet, return we mostly have.

This relapse is cause for frustration and regret. But it should also be cause for anger and action, because it is not what the people want. Back here in Massachusetts, an independent pollster found that, among registered voters, 59 percent favored closing some streets to traffic post-COVID. The poll asked: Would you do these things even if it would result in "less space for cars"? Fully 67 percent of respondents favored giving buses their own lanes; 71 percent favored wider sidewalks; 75 percent favored bike lanes separated from traffic; and 83 percent favored more space for sidewalk dining. Again, post-COVID, instead of space for cars.[23]

If past pandemics are any indication, the coronavirus will release its grip before very long. It's seemed like forever, and there are many friends to mourn, but we will move on. Meanwhile, global warming remains an epoch-ending existential threat, and traffic violence still kills forty-three thousand and seriously injures 4.4 million Americans each and every year. Most people want change, and we are learning that the only way to get it is to make it ourselves.

AMERICAN HOUSING: PICK YOUR CRISIS

Thinking like a state; Attack of the fourplexes; What about the homeless?;
I've seen the future, and it's called Culdesac

A decade ago, *Walkable City* concerned itself with a shortage of housing in walkable places. Most apartment developers were not interested in investing downtown, or at least their bankers weren't. That has all changed. Now, every developer and bank wants to invest downtown; they just can't get the permits.

It has become apparent that we have a shortage of housing not just downtown, but almost everywhere. By one estimate, the United States needs to build 7.3 million homes to meet current demand.[1] A lot of ink and airtime are being thrown at this crisis, and also at an equally alarming crisis around housing equity. While the housing supply crisis has been mounting slowly, the housing equity crisis has been a permanent feature of American life; the only thing that changed was that the city planning profession—which helped create it—suddenly became aware of it, thanks mostly to a book by Richard Rothstein.

The Color of Law: A Forgotten History of How Our Government Segregated America lays out in excruciating detail the careful government-level planning that kept whites and Blacks from sharing the same neighborhoods as it also kept Blacks from accumulating wealth. If you haven't bought this book, you should, but today you can read a wonderful summary in a *Boston Globe* article by Noah Y. Kim, "A Test of White Support for Black Lives."

The article begins with a description of three yard signs arrayed on a Newton, Massachusetts, lawn. Newton is a wealthy Boston suburb with a fairly progressive population, of which 2.5 percent are African American. Almost everyone lives in single-family homes, but developers have been struggling for many years to build a dense, mixed-use village on a ten-acre parking lot at Riverside, a terminus of Boston's Green Line subway. This proposal, in the spirit of the city's clear-sighted comprehensive plan, included 675 apartments, 17.5 percent of which were directed through an inclusionary zoning ordinance to lower-income renters. Full disclosure, my firm designed it.

The first two yard signs said RIGHT SIZE RIVERSIDE and RIGHT SIZE NEWTON. The third said, BLACK LIVES MATTER. Noah Kim observes the irony inherent in this juxtaposition:

> Increasing the housing supply for Black Americans would be one of the quickest and most effective ways to bring about a more just society. Even now, the legacies of "red-lining" and other forms of segregation, predatory lending, and housing discrimination continue to push many Black Americans away from wealthier, better-schooled neighborhoods. But efforts to fix this problem by building affordable housing in suburban communities and affluent parts of cities have often been met with anger from white residents worried about "density" and "crowding." White progressives in particular have a long history of refusing to integrate their communities, even as they vocally support civil rights movements.[2]

This irony was lost on these Newton homeowners because, like most people, they were unaware of the sordid history of the single-family zoning ordinances underlying their suburban Shangri-la. As Rothstein documents ruthlessly, single-family zoning was invented as a way to preserve race-based zoning after segregation was ruled unconstitutional by the Supreme Court. Much of this was accomplished under the expert guidance of the much-revered city planner Harland Bartholomew, who lived from 1889 to 1989 and therefore ostensibly spent an entire century being a racist prick.

Before he became chairman of the National Capital Planning Commission, Bartholomew was the first full-time planner for the city of St. Louis. Here is some of Rothstein's account of his work there:

> According to Bartholomew, an important goal of St. Louis zoning was to prevent movement into "finer residential districts . . . by colored people." . . . The survey Bartholomew supervised before drafting the zoning ordinance listed the race of each building's occupants. Bartholomew attempted to estimate where African Americans might encroach so the commission could respond with restrictions to control their spread. . . . The St. Louis zoning ordinance was eventually adopted in 1919, two years after the Supreme Court's *Buchanan* ruling banned racial assignments; with no reference to race, the ordinance pretended to be in compliance.[3]

Following Bartholomew's lead, city after city passed single-family zoning ordinances to perpetuate their race-based zoning. Kim notes that "since the restrictions had to appear race-neutral to be legal, they relied on economic means to keep out Black Americans, who had not accumulated wealth at the same rate as whites because of segregationist housing programs. . . . Many of these same ordinances continue to ensure that Black and white Americans remain separate and unequal."[4]

How unequal? In Boston, white households had a median net worth of $247,000 in 2015. For nonimmigrant Black households, that number was $8.[5] We can be confident that most Newton residents consider that circumstance socially unacceptable. But they like their neighborhoods the way they are, and they don't begin to see how their resistance to physical change is a powerful force standing in the way of social change.

To give you a sense of how hard this is: the most vocal opponents to the Riverside plan came not from any adjoining property, but from a neighborhood across I-95, an eight-lane highway. Instead of NIMBYs, you could call them NAMIs: Not Across My Interstate.

How did all this end? Well, I can send this book to press because the project was approved—but not until the number of apartments was cut by more than one hundred. Riverside was right-sized.

THINKING LIKE A STATE

Before you get all down on Newton, it bears pointing out that Newton is one of very few Boston suburbs that are making a concerted effort to diversify their housing stock and by extension their population. Most towns statewide, and nationwide, are unmotivated to add apartments, not even around their walkable Main Streets. As the meme goes, "We full."

It looks like that's about to change. A new Commonwealth of Massachusetts law will require every city or town with significant transit service to zone for apartments around that service, and in no small number. It's quite remarkable: within half a mile of rail, subway, bus, or ferry service, most communities will be required to provide a multifamily district at least fifty acres in size. This is state-mandated transit-oriented development; the more transit, the more development. As an example, Wellesley and Weston, two rich, rail-served suburbs, would be required to create zoning capacity for enough apartments to increase their housing stock by a full 25 percent.[6] That's more than three thousand homes.

This law will impact 175 cities and towns—most of eastern and central Massachusetts. Municipalities are of course free to pass on this mandate . . . if they never want to receive another penny of state funding. As one commentator joked on Twitter, "In ten years watch all the roads in Weston turn to dirt."

The political wrangling in these left-leaning communities will be fun to watch. Will their sense of equity allow them to share their privilege? Will they listen to David Roberts, who had this to say on the (absolutely essential) podcast *The War on Cars*?:

> You are just not allowed anymore to be a wealthy single-family homeowner fighting to keep people out of your neighborhood and calling yourself a liberal. I don't care if you have a hemp tote bag and drive a Prius, if you are keeping other people from creating dense urban areas, you are a conservative. You are a reactionary. That's what reactionaries do, is to preserve their privileges at the expense of newcomers.[7]

ATTACK OF THE FOURPLEXES

It will be fascinating to see how the Massachusetts law plays out. It could certainly be more carefully crafted—for example, eliminating parking minimums in the development zones—but its focus on placing density at transit makes it smart and sustainable. The same cannot be said of SB9, the new California law that is rocking the planning world. Signing SB9 was Gavin Newsom's first act as reaffirmed governor after surviving a recall challenge.[8] Similar to ordinances passed in Minnesota, Oregon, and Vermont—and being debated in Maryland, Nebraska, Virginia, and perhaps soon everywhere—the law effectively eliminates most single-family housing in California. All cities and "urbanized areas" must now allow property owners to build up to two duplexes on any single-family lot.

Sounds good so far, yes? Writing in *The Wall Street Journal*, two American Enterprise Institute scholars describe the law this way:

> In a best-case scenario, more than 500,000 units would be added over 10 years with benefits accruing to existing property owners and small-scale builders, not large, politically connected private developers. . . . SB9 applications are already being filed. The first was for a private home built in 1951 in Palo Alto, Calif., which sits on a 1-acre lot and is valued by Zillow at around $4.5 million. With four newly-built energy-efficient units, the lot's total value could double easily, now split over four units. The city's tax base would also double—all with minimal new infrastructure expenditures, no subsidies and no urban sprawl. What's not to like?[9]

On the surface, this law looks good indeed. First off, it's great to see Koch-funded conservatives attacking a conservative sacred cow—especially one with racist bona fides—promoted by Donald Trump as essential to the well-being of America's suburbs.[10]

Second, the law seems like a natural extension of the concept of the granny flat included in this book. My colleagues and I have been pushing for those since the 1980s and, honestly, I was not confident they would ever catch on. Backyard cottages hit their stride in 2016, when the State of California passed a statewide accessory dwelling unit ordinance,[11] and by 2020, California cities issued about thirteen thousand permits for ADUs. That's more than 10 percent of the state's new housing stock, and ten times what it was when *Walkable City* was published.[12]

Third, multiplexes on single-family lots sure feel like a great way to quickly lessen a housing shortage in a state whose NIMBY residents have had their heel on the throat of developers for decades. Things are so restrictive in the San Francisco region that the right to build a house on a piece of property has been valued at $409,000. University of Pennsylvania researchers call this the "zoning tax," and you can see why it's a real impediment to growing the housing supply.[13]

Finally, SB9 wisely limits parking requirements to one space per unit, or zero near a transit station or car share.[14] That's better than Massachusetts did.

So, what's not to like? I see two issues, a small one that points to a big one. The small issue is that minimum parking requirements allow minimal parking but don't guarantee it. Pasadena-based architects Liz Moule and Stef Polyzoides observe that the vast majority of subdivided lots end up completely paved, with any trees or gardens ripped out, so that all remains are houses floating in a sea of cars.[15]

And the cars point to the big issue, which is that, contrary to what the *The Wall Street Journal* says, most of these new units will indeed be sprawl, with all its concomitant environmental and economic impacts. New residents will be required to buy cars and use them all the time. This will not help with their house payments, let alone their diabetes risk.

People need not just affordable homes, but affordable lives. The Center for Housing Policy, in a study of twenty-eight U.S. metropolitan areas, found that working families spend just as much on transportation as they do on housing.[16] The average annual cost of owning a car in the United States is $9,666 and rising;[17] an annual systemwide pass on SFMTA Muni costs $1,176. Sticking half a million new homes into California's single-family sprawl will increase the housing supply and likely lower its cost. But the same homes, focused in higher densities on transit, would provide more people a viable lifestyle, while incidentally not cooking the planet.

In the end, we have to ask: Would we rather right past wrongs metaphorically, or actually? Nothing seems more satisfying a retribution for the legacy of race-based zoning than to start lobbing fourplexes into single-family sprawl. But, as Richard Rothstein notes, these units will remain mostly unaffordable to those populations that were disenfranchised by zoning in the first place; only subsidies will get us there.[18] Rothstein makes an airtight case that financial remedies are long overdue and should be pursued. Meanwhile, let's make more housing legal where it can do the most good: in downtowns and at transit stops.

WHAT ABOUT THE HOMELESS?[19]

Whether or not you believe that shelter is a basic human right that should be protected by society, you are probably aware that the costs of homelessness are profound, and not just for the homeless. Emergency-room visits—the way most homeless receive health care—are expensive. Policing services are expensive. Jail time is expensive. So are homeless shelters. And, from a pure walkability perspective, street people are cited by many as the reason they avoid walking around downtown. In some cities where few people walk, the majority of pedestrians appear to be homeless, reinforcing that condition.

Historically, a moralistic approach to homelessness has mandated a slow progression in which the homeless are expected to work their way through public shelters into transitional housing and eventually into independent housing, with each step up earned in part through clean living. These programs are not effective, because having a stable place to live can be a key component of overcoming substance abuse. How can your case worker visit you if you can't be found?

Beginning in the 1990s with the premise that shelter is a right, the Housing First movement reversed the process, and began providing long-term housing to the homeless with (almost) no strings attached. This housing was provided at a cost of 30 percent of the resident's income, whatever the income, and supplemented with wraparound social services, including mental health and substance treatment.[20]

As Housing First programs began to spread and be studied, few were surprised at their success at getting people off the streets. What surprised many, however, were the savings.

In terms of success: the State of Utah, an early adopter, managed to reduce homelessness by an astounding 72 percent in less than a decade.[21] Nationwide studies report that between 75 and 91 percent of Housing First participants remain housed after a year in the program, and most of these participants take advantage of the optional social services they are offered. This makes them considerably more likely to seek work or stay in school, stay off drugs and alcohol, and stay out of the hospital and jail.[22]

In terms of savings: the outcomes have been remarkable. One study found an average annual spending reduction of over fifteen thousand dollars per person in emergency services alone.[23] In Denver, emergency room costs were reduced by 34 percent, hospital inpatient costs by 66 percent, and incarceration costs by 76 percent.[24] In Seattle, each person who moved from the street into the Housing First program saved the city more than twenty-nine thousand dollars per year.[25] Results in Canada have been similar.

Still, despite all this evidence, most cities do not have Housing First programs.[26] To those cities, one can only ask: Are you really willing to spend twice as much on homelessness, and have twice as much of it, because you believe that people should be punished for addiction and mental illness? If not, what's keeping you?

I'VE SEEN THE FUTURE, AND IT'S CALLED CULDESAC

Wonderful things can come from the unlikeliest of places, in this case the suburbs of Phoenix, the "capital of sprawl." The story of

the next great thing in walkability begins on the intramural vol-
leyball courts at the University of Arizona, where roommates
Ryan Johnson and Jeff Berens faced off against Vanessa Valen-
zuela. Ryan went on to help found Opendoor, a digital real estate
disruptor that eventually sold for billions, as evidenced by his Jay
Leno–style stable of more than sixty vehicles—except Ryan's
rides are all e-bikes. Vanessa, the first in her family to attend
university, became Opendoor's top-rated manager. Jeff took a
different path, buying a one-way ticket to East Africa, where he
helped create a drinking-water treatment system that now serves
more than 4 million people.[27] Not your average millennial slack-
ers, they also shared a disdain for car ownership, reportedly inspired by a shelf of city planning books including this one.

Does a new community really need cars at all? That is the
question they asked themselves and others over many years of
late nights in dorm rooms and bars. Ryan selling his stake in
Opendoor allowed them to take the plunge and acquire a
seventeen-acre site at a light-rail stop in Tempe. The property
was already permitted for a hulking six-story apartment complex
surrounding 1,385 parking spaces, a building type I seem to design for my clients daily. They threw out all the residential
parking—about $20 million worth—cut the height in half, and
broke up the blocks. Their replacement plan puts more than a
thousand people in 761 units, most located in small buildings
lining pedestrian streets ("paseos"), with ample bike parking and
zero private cars.[28]

In many American cities, more than 50 percent of the land
area is pavement for moving and storing vehicles. In Culdesac,
that same amount of property will be dedicated to paseos, courtyards, plazas, and parks. While it has access to transit, it will also
include coffee shops, restaurants, markets, coworking spaces,
pools, and other amenities on site.

I have two problems with Culdesac. The first is that I had
nothing to do with it . . . they could have called. The second is

the name, which was chosen because it evokes a safe refuge for children to play in an otherwise car-dominated environment. That's strikingly accurate—look at Tempe—but ironically celebrates one of the worst features of sprawl. Thanks to the way they concentrate traffic on wide collector roads, places with frequent cul-de-sacs have 270 percent more fatalities than places with traditional street grids.[29]

Happily, there are no cul-de-sacs in Culdesac, but the name stuck, and is now becoming a movement. Backed by venture capital from Khosla Ventures, Y Combinator, and others, the company now has more than forty employees and a plan for world domination. Their goal is to replicate their car-free model nationwide at all scales, including—gasp—whole cities.

Standalone cities built from scratch bring with them an entirely separate set of sustainability challenges, too complex to receive ink here. But it is easy to see how every metropolitan area of significant size is ready for a car-free neighborhood. The fact is that, in any housing market, there are a certain number of renters, and even some buyers, who want to live car free and are ready to move. That number is pretty easy to estimate, and their housing choices easy to predict. A properly marketed Culdesac— and they're good at that—could be expected to absorb the majority of those households. In Tempe, the first phase of apartments, a full year before availability, leased up as fast as they could sign the paperwork.

If only it were legal! Tempe had to change its rules to allow a car-free community, and this remains the case almost everywhere, save for a few shining examples like Buffalo, Minneapolis, St. Paul, San Francisco, Berkeley . . . the list is growing.[30] Boston has even introduced some parking *maximums*.[31] Donald Shoup's influence is finally being felt nationwide, but 99.9 percent of American municipalities have yet to realize that what most NIMBYs fear is not more people but more cars. As long as neighbors can be guaranteed that Culdesac residents won't park on the street—an easy enough lease requirement—opposition should be limited to only the most unsavory curmudgeons.

While we're discussing car-free zones, a final word is needed on pedestrian malls. I'm sorry to say that I've seen my words in this book used to maintain heavy car traffic on some streets that don't need it. That was not my intention, nor what I said. In recognizing the history of ped mall failure, my advice was to test out any proposed car ban temporarily before making it permanent. But I am all for more of them, everywhere. What needs testing site-by-site is their viability for retail. Meanwhile, they are immediately viable for residential streets wherever the residents want them—presuming that snipping a bunch of connections in a capillary street network does not cause any of the surrounding streets to become wider. Barcelona's much heralded new superblock system—in which the hashtag of streets within each nine-square cluster of blocks has been closed to through traffic—demonstrates how neighborhoods can go from good to great by putting cars in their place.

There is no better environment in which to live than along a street with no motor traffic. Now, when we design new towns, we try to put a major portion of the homes on car-free streets, squares, greens, and paths. Visit Rosemary Beach in Florida, which I drew up in 1995, and you will see hundreds of houses strung along more than a mile of wooden boardwalks. A partial resort, it's a great place to visit with children you wish to wrangle only on occasion. Open the screen door, and they—and you—are free.

MORE ENGINEERING CONFESSIONS

Oversignaled; The streets we need; Culpable engineers;
Cars against free assembly; America the unfree;
How do you define freedom?; Transit in transition

The longest quote in *Walkable City*, longer even than Jane Jacobs's, is from Chuck Marohn, the former roadway engineer whose early *Grist* essay on the wrongheadedness of his profession rocked me to my core; reading it was my *When Harry Met Sally* delicatessen moment. Over the past decade, Chuck's message has become all the more necessary, and America may finally be ready for it. Happily, it has been published at length in a new book of the same title—*Confessions of a Recovering Engineer*—which you should read immediately after this one if you care about public safety.

Chuck is an expert at distilling a complex subject down to its essence. On the twin blights of the traffic-overrun Main Street and the traffic-clogged suburban strip, he reminds us that there should be only two types of throughfares: streets and roads. Streets are for local wealth generation and welcome traffic only at slow speed, because high speeds destroy the value of place. Roads are for moving vehicles quickly, and should be kept free of businesses, because every driveway impacts speed and also threatens safety. Our mistake over the years is that we have allowed streets to become half roads and roads to become half streets. On one, commerce has been sacrificed to speed. On the other, speed has been sacrificed to commerce. Chuck calls these places "stroads."

Chuck equates a stroad to a futon, "an uncomfortable couch that converts into an uncomfortable bed, something that performs two functions but does neither well."[1]

Once you have heard the word "stroad," you can't help but identify them everywhere you go. Wilshire Boulevard in Los Angeles is a stroad. So is just about every MLK Boulevard in America. These are the first type of stroad, local streets misunderstood as highways. U.S. Highway 1 on the outskirts of any eastern city is also a stroad, as is almost every postwar commercial strip coast to coast. These are the second type of stroad: roads designed around moving high volumes of traffic at speed, misunderstood as commercial centers. We have less interest in this second type, because these places will never be walkable. If your downtown is the strip, you should try to move.

But the first type of stroad can be found in the heart of almost every American city, from Miami's Biscayne Boulevard to Seattle's brand new and supposedly walkable Alaskan Way (more on that ill-fated effort ahead). They are mostly prewar Main Streets that were reamed out at the peak of the auto age and have been struggling to recover ever since. They are easy to fix, if the will is there. The key is convincing the local automotive hordes that one small part of their city deserves to be a street and not a road.

Probably the greatest stroad recovery I have witnessed is Lancaster Boulevard in Lancaster, California, a five-lane surface highway lined with struggling shops that Stef Polyzoides and Liz Moule transformed into a linear plaza in 2010. They reduced the five lanes to two and created a brick-paved median that welcomes either angled parking or merchants' tables, depending on the day. The rebuild cost $11.2 million of taxpayer money, and for what? Well how about cutting injury crashes by 49 percent while spurring the opening of fifty-seven new businesses, the construction of more than eight hundred homes—most of them affordable—and the creation of two thousand jobs, for an economic impact estimated at $282 million?

That's a deal most cities would take, if they could only get out of their own way. When presented with a similar challenge, the largely disinvested Main Street of Hammond, Indiana, I copied the Lancaster design almost exactly. Local leaders embraced the plan, even though it meant reducing the carrying capacity of the street. It's now under construction.

The Lancaster plan took a street that was carrying fifteen thousand cars each day and reduced that number to eleven thousand. We're doing the same thing in Hammond. We even designed a traffic sign that says IN A HURRY? → TURN RIGHT TO STATE LINE AVE. People who want only to blow through the downtown are welcome to shift from the street to the road, so that neither has to be a stroad.

This conversation is slightly trickier in small towns, where no parallel paths may exist. In this case, a community has to be convinced that slower speeds are a small price to pay to have a downtown worth visiting. But it's not always a trade-off: counterintuitively, many Main Streets can actually handle more traffic when speeds are lowered. The trick here is to replace signals with stop signs.

OVERSIGNALED

Briefly mentioned at the end of Step 5, Protect the Pedestrian, is the safety improvement that all-way stop signs offer over traffic signals. Not mentioned last time was the data: that when Philadelphia removed the signals from 472 intersections, replacing them with all-way stop signs, severe industry crashes dropped by 62.5 percent. In most streets, a city's investment in traffic signals, at six figures apiece, is an investment not in safety, but in high-speed driving—often from red light to red light.

And there's the rub. Because while green lights allow drivers to shoot through intersections at dangerous speeds, they are usually part of a system that actually delays trips across town. The high-speed driving is easily outweighed by time wasted idling at reds. As Marohn notes, "A city without traffic signals is a city where most of us arrive at our destinations sooner and all of us travel safer."[2]

That fact takes a while to sink in. Weren't traffic signals invented to make urban driving safer and more efficient? That may have been the intention, but at a certain point we have to acknowledge that they do the opposite.

I had a funny experience when, in my walkability study for downtown Albuquerque, I recommended the removal of seventeen signals. The city took me up on nine of them. But people complained—change is always hard—so the city put three of them back. Then people complained even louder, because they observed the signals made traffic worse. The headline on the TV news put it this way: "City Reinstalls Downtown Stop Signs to Reduce Traffic Pileup, Speeding."[3]

Sure, all-way stops can be a bit confusing to the inexperienced, requiring a level of neighborly cooperation that we are spared by signals. For many Americans, the experience of taking their turn at a four-way stop may be the only moment during their day when they are asked to interact with, and therefore build trust with, their fellow community members. That might be a good thing.

THE STREETS WE NEED

Of course, replacing signals with stop signs is just a way station on the path to the Safety Apotheosis also discussed in Step 5: naked streets. Even as almost no progress has been made stateside in the last decade, the naked streets revolution continues apace in Europe. In the Netherlands, all-way stops are now considered bad form; they are ripping them out and replacing them with . . . nothing. Drivers have grown accustomed to approaching every intersection as a negotiation, and it's become apparent that signs just get in the way. Streets have become understood properly as social space in which the most vulnerable participants dominate, and drivers proceed with care.

Sounds like a nightmare for drivers, right? Tell that to Waze: their analysis of the experiences of 65 million monthly users in 235 countries identified the Netherlands as "the most satisfying place in the world to drive."[4]

One aspect of naked streets has accidentally crept into American road design, however, and we should not neglect to use it: centerline removal. If you look around your town, you'll find that many streets don't have yellow lines down the center; they're common only on the bigger ones, where they ostensibly make driving safer by keeping everyone in their lane. Except they don't. Risk homeostasis alert! Centerlines give drivers confidence, enough confidence to drive seven miles per hour faster, according to one British study. For a pedestrian, that seven miles per hour roughly doubles the risk of death.[5] In my work, I remove centerlines wherever I can.

CULPABLE ENGINEERS

The understanding and nonstop trumpeting of risk homeostasis—more clearly described as "risk compensation"—is central to the fundamental rethinking that needs to occur if we are to reform the insanity that is American street design. We have three to six times the vehicular death rate of our European counterparts because we insist that the relationship between design and behavior flows in one direction and not the other. American engineers widen lanes, straighten out curves, and rip trees out of roadside "clear zones" to make high-speed driving safer, yet they won't admit that doing the opposite slows drivers down. They publish charts in which broader lane widths correlate with higher speeds, which they then reference exclusively to widen lanes but never to narrow them. As Marohn notes, "High speeds are a design issue but low speeds are an enforcement issue. This is incoherent, but it is consistent with an underlying set of values that prefers higher speeds."[6]

In northern Europe, engineers take the opposite approach, actively designing neighborhoods so that only low speeds feel comfortable. This is why, in Scandinavia, when they evoke "Vision Zero"—the global campaign to eliminate urban traffic deaths—they literally mean zero, and some of their cities are getting there. Neither Helsinki nor Oslo witnessed a single pedestrian fatality in 2019.[7] Here in the United States, Vision Zero can't help but feel like a sick joke. As of this writing, Atlanta's Vision Zero coordinator is in a coma, having been struck at high speed in a Chattanooga crosswalk.[8]

Speaking of crosswalks, the *Manual on Uniform Traffic Control Devices*—enforced in most cities—says that you can't stripe a crosswalk at a dangerous intersection unless more than ninety-three people are crossing per hour. These deadly conditions are self-perpetuating. As the former Vancouver chief planner Brent Toderian notes, "You can't judge the need for a bridge by counting the people swimming the river." Meanwhile, ninety-two pedestrians per hour are dodging SUVs. My question is: When can we sue?

Rather than making low-speed design the norm, American engineers' answer to speeding is to post a low speed limit. How's that working out? Well, in Portland they made the bold choice in 2018 to enact a citywide twenty-miles-per-hour speed limit in residential areas, down from twenty-five miles per hour previously. This change was promoted through a vast media campaign including seven thousand 20 IS PLENTY yard signs distributed to residents. A study of 214,320 observations at fifty-eight distinct locations found that speeds dropped . . . by a grand total of 1 percent.[9] That's a lot of effort to get people to drive one-quarter of a mile per hour slower.

In sum, American engineers habitually design streets to invite dangerous speeds and then claim that safety can be achieved through posting ineffective speed limits, arguing that designing for lower speeds would make the road less safe. Marohn likens this activity to professional malpractice and documents how it meets the standards of gross negligence. I repeat: When can we sue? Who is going to mount the massive public class action that properly lays bare the inner workings of this negligent industry? In America, for better or worse, progress seems to be made in the courts. It is hard to imagine any other venue through which we can begin to bring down the established standards that result in tens of thousands of excess deaths annually. Until we do, this institutionalized mass manslaughter will continue.

CARS AGAINST FREE ASSEMBLY

Speaking of manslaughter, it gets worse. As if cars were not enough of a problem, the last few years witnessed a newly proliferating category of traffic violence: the ramming of protestors. As Black Lives Matter supporters took to the streets in the wake of the George Floyd murder, both police and civilians used their cars and trucks to "reclaim public space," with many injured. In just six weeks in 2020, the researcher Ari Weil identified seventy-two incidents of vehicles ramming protestors in fifty-two cities.[10] These nasty encounters ran the gamut from overzealous riot control to panicked motorists to self-righteous vigilantism. Public reaction sorted itself cleanly along ideological lines, evidenced by Twitter posts like, "Run them over! I'm late for shopping," and, "Red Rover, Red Rover send the SUV over!"[11]

But it's not just web chat. Legislators in sixteen states introduced bills criminalizing in-street protests and/or protecting those who plow through them. Such measures have been enacted in Iowa, Oklahoma, and Florida.[12] The Oklahoma law protects protestor-rammers from criminal liability; Florida's protects them from civil liability as well. "It's the strongest anti-rioting, pro-law-enforcement piece of legislation in the country. There's nothing even close," boasted Governor Ron DeSantis at a press conference.[13] In Florida's statute, a gathering of three people can be labeled a "riot"—and, in a riot, it's no-holds-barred. One reporter's take: "If they're blocking the road and you feel frightened, it's generally OK to run them over with a car."[14]

As Alex Pareene concludes in *The New Republic*, "American conservatives are creating, really, a sort of Second Amendment for cars. . . . It's as if the right absorbed a left-wing critique of American automobile culture and decided the problem with the whole idea was that the violence wasn't literal enough."[15]

AMERICA THE UNFREE

I have a small number of libertarian friends, and only one of them is a city planner. Two libertarians, it turns out, live under my roof. They are Queso and Fundido, our house cats. They spend every day absolutely convinced of their own independence and self-determination, blissfully unaware of the intricate system of support that keeps them warm, healthy, and fed.

It might be better to avoid politics here, but it strikes me that city planning and libertarianism are largely incompatible by definition. The whole purpose of the former is to avoid the "tragedy of the commons," in which the optimization of many individuals' personal needs destroys the systems that they rely on to survive. That said, there are a good number of strong libertarian arguments to be made in favor of more walkable cities once you begin to recognize the degree to which our governments at every level subsidize automobile dependence.

But that conversation rarely happens. For most libertarians and other conservatives, the organization of our national landscape around cars rather than walking and transit is seen as a bedrock foundation for freedom. Nobody hammers this point home harder than Lauren Fix at the fracking-funded media outlet Prager University. Prager University is not a university, but it is enough of an institution to have received more than seven hundred thousand dollars in COVID relief funds (so much for small government). In its 2017 YouTube video "The War on Cars," Fix warns us of a top-down government attack on car culture, and lays out the libertarian auto-apologia in its purest form:

> They allow us to go wherever we want, whenever we want, with whomever we want. . . . Only cars allow us to be spontaneous. When you get behind the wheel, you are in control. You are free. The very reason people love cars—personal freedom—is also why regulators can't stand them.[16]

My favorite part of that quote is the "with whomever we want." Who, exactly, is it that Lauren does not want to travel with? Would it perhaps be acceptable if they kept to the back of the bus? In any case, the message is clear: America's car culture is integral to its freedom. But let's parse that one out a little bit. Three factors—road policing, car dependence, and street design—would together seem to conspire otherwise.

In the important book *Policing the Open Road*, Sarah Seo tells the story of how once-tiny, cash-strapped municipal police departments grew into their current behemoth state on the back of traffic ticketing, and how case law fairly quickly established the automobile as exempt from many of the same privacy protections as other personal property. While the police need a warrant to search your house or your handbag, by 1925 the car lost that status, due principally and understandably to the fact that it's an extremely dangerous device. We can hardly blame Chief Justice Taft for labeling cars "this great evil machine,"[17] but the automobile's potential use as a weapon caused the Supreme Court to grant vast discretion to police officers to sidestep Fourth Amendment prohibitions on unreasonable search and seizure. As a result, patrol cops now effectively operate as judge, jury, and possibly executioner on the road.

And the executions are frequent. A recent *New York Times* investigation found that police car stops have left more than four hundred unarmed Americans dead over the past five years, with officers routinely claiming that the car was a weapon. Rarely, when these shootings are reconstructed, is the officer found to have actually been in harm's way. According to the criminologist Geoffrey Alpert, "You see many where bullets are in the back of the car, in the side of the car. . . . In the high 90 percent of cases I've seen, the person is just trying to get away."[18]

In some of the cases studied by the *Times*, "the vehicle was stationary, even incapable of moving."

So, police are killing unarmed drivers at a rate of seven per month, but it's more than that. Pulling over "suspicious-looking" people has become the main thing that police departments do. In cities, the minor traffic violation is almost always just a pretext for enforcing other, more invasive laws that have nothing to do with the safety of the vehicle. And while the definition of "suspicious" may vary by state, it doesn't vary much. As the officer who detained and executed Philando Castile put it, "The driver looks like one of our suspects just because of the wide-set nose."[19]

Police power over motorists is the first step to making car culture less free than its advocates imagine. The second step is straightforward: auto dependence. We have created a landscape in which few of us are spared the requirement of inhabiting the public sphere principally as motorists, either as drivers or as passengers in these heavily policed private vehicles. This, too, incidentally, was discussed by the Supreme Court, which in 1997 acknowledged that driving was "a virtual necessity for most Americans."[20]

If those two factors were the whole story, that would be enough to impact our freedom. But the third factor, road design, truly seals the deal. As discussed, American engineers, unlike their counterparts in other countries, have standardized the practice of building roadways to invite speeds well in excess of their posted limit. The typical driver in downtown Albuquerque is doing thirty on a street that is posted at twenty-five and engineered for fifty.[21] The broad lanes, swooping corner radii, and rolled curbs, combined with our own instinct for risk compensation, create a circumstance in which many of us are speeding most of the time.

Tell me you're different. Even my own status as a pedestrian advocate is not enough to consistently lighten my foot. And on highways, with no pedestrians present, forget about it. To not speed on most American highways is to invite dirty looks, or worse.

The outcome of American engineering practice is that most Americans are breaking the law every time they drive. As Kalfani Ture, a former Georgia police officer, told *The New York Times*, "If I follow a car for five minutes, I can always find one or two moving violations."[22] Combine this situation with the fact that most of us must drive to survive, and that we relinquish our Fourth Amendment rights when we do so, and the picture that begins to emerge is a far cry from the freedom that libertarians imagine. To build streets that invite illegal speeds in a society where driving is unavoidable and cars are not protected by constitutional limits on search and seizure is to create a virtual police state.

Extracting ourselves from this woke-libertarian's nightmare will be a long slog, but it is achievable. The first step would be to eliminate the routine police stop, a reasonable strategy that

Chuck Marohn lays out convincingly in a surprising late chapter of *Confessions*. Only truly reckless driving should invoke contact with a police officer. All other violations—minor speeding, rolling stops, broken taillights—should be camera-documented from the police car and ticketed by mail.[23] Chuck and I disagree about speed cameras and red-light cameras—I believe they should be deployed wherever they reduce injuries, no matter how much of a windfall the city gets—but replacing pull-overs with point and click would go a long way toward what most thinking Americans want, which is to "defund the police" without defunding the police.

The second step, necessary for so many more reasons than personal liberty, would be to start restriping our streets to a design speed that happens to match how fast we want drivers to go. This is a huge job, but not if you break it down city by city, which is of course the only way it can be accomplished. It's already happening in a limited way in more than a few places, especially in downtowns, where it really counts: Newark, Cedar Rapids, Chicago . . . even Albuquerque, whose new parking-protected bike lanes are plainly (and anachronistically) visible in season five of *Better Call Saul*.

HOW DO YOU DEFINE FREEDOM?

A proper conversation about American freedom doesn't stop at its driving-induced police state, and must move on to the broader issues of housing, health, education, and the social safety net in general. How free are you if you face housing insecurity, as do between 10 and 15 percent of the population? How free are you if a single illness can drive you to bankruptcy, even if you are moderately well-off and insured? How free are you if you start your career with $39,400 in student debt, the American average? For a country that supposedly prizes innovation, entrepreneurship, and social mobility, it would be hard to find circumstances less conducive to those outcomes. Not many people start a company when they're $40K in the hole.

These issues are beyond the reach of this effort, but another definition of freedom is not, and it can be found in the book *Human Transit* by the transportation planner (and Stanford literature PhD) Jarrett Walker. That book came out at the same time as *Walkable City*, so its wisdom missed the cut, and can here provide a brief supplement to Step 4, Let Transit Work. That chapter seems to have been mostly right, but it did not go far enough to describe how cities should and can dramatically improve their transit service in short order.

The clearest thinking about transit available today can be found at the tip of Walker's pen. He talks about freedom this way:

> In transit, the real test of freedom is spontaneity. Can I change my plans suddenly? Can I get home if I need to, or to my child's school if something comes up? Can I simply move freely around my city, following whatever impulse I may feel at the moment? Some transit systems approach that level of convenience, at least in dense cities. In some of those same cities, you'll find that your car is an encumbrance. If you've ever been stuck in traffic on a busy downtown street while pedestrians and cyclists flow past you and subway trains zoom beneath you, you know that sometimes your car can become your prison.[24]

Visitors to truly urban downtowns like in Chicago and San Francisco know this feeling. In proper urbanism, the car limits your mobility, and transit can set you free. But even in less dense cities, where driving is not necessarily a burden, transit can present a competitive and even compelling choice if it is designed properly, and if service is frequent. In Jarrett Walker's world, frequency is freedom.

TRANSIT IN TRANSITION

Redesigning bus systems is Walker's bread and butter. What his team accomplished in Houston was typical of his work. Without adding a penny to the transit budget, they placed frequent bus service within a short walk of 110 percent more homes and 55 percent more jobs, quickly halting a long decline in ridership.[25]

I give buses a bit of a hard time in *Walkable City* and, let's face it, trains have their advantages. But most cities want to get people out of their cars quickly, and the new-build timeline is preposterously out of step with that objective. If buses are what we have, buses are what we shall use, and, as Houston demonstrates, we can use them so much better.

The key to Houston's turnaround was to reshape an archaic, meandering spiderweb of overlapping routes into a simple grid. The trade-off was between complexity and connections. Before, fewer connections were needed between destinations, but the resulting complexity of the routes made it impossible to provide frequent service on many of them. Simplifying the routes allowed more of them to become frequent, enough so that connections became convenient. Now most bus trips in Houston are L-shaped and require a single connection, but the connection is quick, and the initial wait is short. As a result, more people can get to more places, sooner.

Another recent transit star is Seattle, thanks to a similar rethinking of its bus system. In 2015, before the new plan, only 25 percent of Seattle households were located within a ten-minute walk of ten-minute-headway transit. Two years later, that number rose to 64 percent. No surprise, then, that solo driving dropped by 10 percent. In 2017, only 25 percent of city-center employees drove themselves to work. This is largely by choice: nine out of ten Seattle transit riders have access to a vehicle; they just find the bus more convenient.[26]

The heart of Seattle's upgraded bus system is dedicated lanes. Apparently, Seattle's leaders heeded Enrique Peñalosa's assertion that, if all people are equal under the law, "a bus with 100 people has a right to 100 times as much road as a car."[27] Eight downtown lanes are transit-only during rush hour, with signal priority over cross-streets. Four of these are on Third Avenue, which carries fifty-two thousand riders a day at a rate of four buses per minute on-peak.

Employers have helped in the effort, offering incentives like transit passes. The Gates Foundation dropped its 88 percent drive-alone rate to an impressive 34 percent. Weyerhaeuser went from 82 percent to 9 percent, but they cheated: they moved from the suburbs to downtown.[28]

Of course, COVID knocked all of this off course. Two years into the pandemic, with transmission rates coming off their highest peak yet, most transit lines are still down around 50 percent of their 2019 ridership, and rising only slowly. A pro-transit administration in Washington is doing its best to shore up the finances of local agencies, so that they are prepared to meet rider demand as the pandemic abates. Meanwhile, some cities are doing their part to goose ridership—and help poor people—by making transit free.

Foremost among these is probably Boston. Under the new leadership of Michelle Wu—a young, progressive, pro-planning mayor—the city is spending $8 million in federal pandemic relief funds to make three of its most important bus lines fully free for two years. These buses pass through the lower-income neighborhoods of Dorchester, Roxbury, and Mattapan, places that are underserved by rail. One of these free lines was piloted under the previous mayor, and quickly jumped back up near pre-pandemic ridership.[29]

This free-transit measure passed city council by a vote of twelve to one, mirroring public opinion. In a poll of registered voters statewide, fully 65 percent supported making public

transit—the entire MBTA—free to all.[30] This is a lovely sentiment, but Jarrett Walker would call it counterproductive. "The
strong worldwide consensus is that better service is more powerful than lower fares in boosting ridership," he insists.[31] But
subsidized fares for the poor, or free fares through poorer neighborhoods, are a great way to target COVID relief to those who
need it most.

INDUCED DEMAND REDUX

Carmageddon never comes—Alaskan Way update; More tunnels, this time for suckers; Uberis and nemesis; AVs: not on our watch

In Step 1, Put Cars in Their Place, I described traffic studies as bullshit. This implied that they are often wrong, which is true. One 2007 study across five continents found that half of traffic forecasts are off by more than 20 percent, and two additional studies found them to be off by an average of 35 and 42 percent, respectively. But the main problem with traffic forecasts is not that they are often wrong, but they are often right, because they are extremely effective at causing the very traffic that they predict.

This outcome is what results from a regulatory framework that promotes the steady flow of private vehicles as the sine qua non of human settlement. By assuming that everyone will get around by car, and expanding the roadway network to invite those cars, traffic forecasting is more often than not a self-fulfilling prophecy.

Meanwhile, the concept that you can fight traffic with road building is one myth that simply will not die, even as the data collection enters its seventieth year. The most recent analysis from Transportation for America goes as follows:

> We know that states alone spent more than $500 billion on highway capital investments in urbanized areas

between 1993 and 2017, with a sizeable portion going toward highway expansion. . . . In those 100 urbanized areas, congestion has grown by a staggering 144 percent, far outpacing [32 percent] population growth.[1]

So, half a trillion spent to make traffic more than twice as bad. In most states, this madness continues unchecked. As one example, the Central Virginia Transportation Authority's 2021 long-range budget dedicated 84 percent of all dollars to roadway expansion projects.[2] Only California has begun to show progress. In 2013, after decades of discussion, Senate Bill 743 reformed the state's environmental laws to eliminate "Level of Service" (aka traffic flow) as a key measure for determining the environmental impacts of new development.[3] Until this point, it was mistakenly presumed that traffic congestion, rather than traffic volume, destroyed the environment. Seven years after the law's passage, California's state DOT finally modified its environmental review process to include analysis of induced demand.[4] Will other states follow?

CARMAGEDDON NEVER COMES—ALASKAN WAY UPDATE

Remember the story of Seattle's Alaskan Way viaduct? As expected in 2012, the maximalist approach of a surface boulevard *and a tunnel* emerged victorious, thanks to ever-present congestion fears. Our contention that such a redundant system was unnecessary was tested during construction, when the entire six-lane highway, carrying almost one hundred thousand cars per day, was simply shut down. For three weeks in January 2019, as the new tunnel was about to come on line, all north-south traffic on Interstate 5—which reaches from Canada to Mexico—was diverted to local streets.

Day one of the shutdown was formally named the Period of

Maximum Constraint, and was anticipated with the usual dread. Even our normally sharp friends at *CityLab* predicted disaster.[5] People called it "the Seattle Squeeze," "Traffic Hell," and "Viadoom." Guess what? It never happened. If anything, downtown traffic on parallel routes improved during the shutdown as people adjusted their behavior.[6]

Of course, you say: fearing congestion, people chose not to drive. As Joe Cortright noted in his Seattle coverage, people "decide not to travel, change when they travel, change where they travel, or even change the mode of travel."[7] Why am I telling you this again? Because, ten years later, I have yet to see a single traffic forecasting effort properly consider "reduced demand," or its opposite. We continue to grow our highways and streets to elephantine proportions, laying waste to our cities, our lungs, and our planet, because an entire multibillion-dollar industry refuses to acknowledge that environment impacts behavior and treats travel demand as a fixed, irreducible quantity.

Since learning of the phenomenon of reduced demand from the removals of the Embarcadero Freeway, West Side Highway, and Cheonggyecheon Freeway—covered in these pages—the stories continue to pile up: bridge collapses on I-35 in Minneapolis and I-85 in Atlanta, and two separate shutdowns of the 405 Freeway in Los Angeles during its widening, have produced similar outcomes.[8]

This phenomenon is not limited to highways. Cortright notes, "The latest instance of this was . . . when New York closed 14th Street to most car traffic; speeds on parallel streets 13th and 15th were unaffected."[9] This is an important example, because Fourteenth Street was transformed into an express busway, vastly improving crosstown travel times and ridership. This is the sort of change that most cities reject as they run scared from traffic.

Despite the valuable told-you-so data, the Alaskan Way story is deeply disappointing, for many reasons. At the very least, the $4.5 billion underground roadway should have allowed the new surface boulevard to be something nice. Instead, traffic forecasting was allowed to rule the day, supplanting what could have been a spectacular green boulevard with four to eight lanes of high-speed tarmac. Perhaps advertising a guilty conscience, the right of way also includes a cycle track and dozens of substantial new trees; most of these, strangely, are planted on the wrong side of the sidewalk, where unlucky pedestrians can protect them from stray traffic. In sum, Seattle tore down one highway and got two in return.

MORE TUNNELS, THIS TIME FOR SUCKERS

Intrepid *Curbed* reporter Alissa Walker dropped in on Las Vegas during the annual Consumer Electronics Show, where a LIDAR manufacturer was demonstrating how their cars stop for child pedestrian dummies in crosswalks while autonomous Teslas routinely plow through them. She took a deep dive underground to check out the two tunnels that Elon Musk's Boring Company had dug beneath the convention center to spare visitors a twenty-minute walk. What she found was two crawling queues of drivers getting "stuck in seemingly ordinary traffic, except they're trapped inside what looks to be the world's longest MRI machine."[10]

The City of Las Vegas paid Musk $50 million for a contraption that was promised to move four thousand people per hour. What it got was a flashy casino sideshow that currently moves about thirteen hundred people per hour—roughly the capacity of any two-lane road in Nevada. The Boring Company made its promise to the city in 2019 with the expectation that the tunnels would be stocked not with ordinary Teslas but with "high-passenger urban density transport."[11] That's tech-bro speak for twelve-seat vans. In 2020, Musk said that the vans "should be ready for unveiling next year."[12] His follow-up, in 2021? "I think Tesla is definitely going to make an electric van at some point."[13]

Will the vans ever materialize? When they do, the transportation press will no doubt lavish universal praise on Musk for inventing what turns out to be an exceptionally low-capacity subway. In the meantime, San Bernardino County, Fort Lauderdale, and other municipalities are lining up for more Tesla tunnels. The Florida proposal, 2.7 miles of what is hoped will be a much larger network, is championed by Mayor Dean Trantalis as a potential solution to downtown gridlock.[14] And if you buy that, there is some slightly moist land in the Everglades I would like to show you.

For people who understand the dynamics of urban traffic, it is frustrating to see Musk—who is clearly smart about some things—get so close to the hoop and repeatedly flub the layup. He has helped develop a technology that purportedly reduces the cost of building a tunnel from $1 billion to $10 million a mile.[15] But instead of creating subways at a fraction of the cost, he is effectively just supplementing existing aboveground roads at five times the cost, and inducing more driving the whole time—not a surprising idea from a carmaker.

UBERIS AND NEMESIS

In October of 2017, I was invited to give a lecture at Uber's San Francisco headquarters. Staff there had read my books and were curious what I might have to say about the intersection of ride-hailing and the walkable city. I think they expected some good news. Certainly, their company's stated objective of ending private car ownership was well in keeping with my vision of less car-dependent communities. Personally, I was driving a lot less due to Uber—well, Lyft, actually (less toxic CEO)—and their advocacy for public transit was admirable. I did my best to put together an objective talk.

Unfortunately for them, my research included speaking to Alejandro Henao, a recent University of Colorado Denver graduate who had worked as an Uber and Lyft driver while earning his PhD in civil engineering—as well as a solid five-star rating. He had tracked his miles, polled his customers, and collected a ton of data that did not exactly comply with the dominant ride-hailing narrative.

First off, he found that, for every ten miles he drove a customer, his car had to move 16.9 miles thanks to "dead-heading" between rides. Well, if the goal is to reduce driving, that's a bad start. He also found that 45 percent of his customers, far from leaving the car at home, had opted into ride-hailing rather than taking transit, walking, biking, or simply not traveling. Strike two. Finally, he had observed that people seemed to be using ride-hailing as a path *toward* car ownership: driving for Uber and Lyft was enabling them to buy cars they otherwise couldn't afford.[16] Yikes.

The initial theory behind ride-hailing was that, by making most of the costs of driving variable rather than fixed, people would ditch their cars and drive less. The exact opposite seemed to be happening. Car ownership was not dropping[17] and, between dead-heading and customers stolen from other modes, each Uber and Lyft ride represented more than a tripling of automotive vehicle miles traveled.

Tripling? That's surprising, so let's do the math together. If one hundred people take Uber a mile, that causes 169 miles of driving. But forty-five of those people, without Uber, would not have driven at all. One hundred sixty-nine divided by the remaining fifty-five is more than three. (More recent data would adjust this number closer to four.)[18]

That's what I learned from Alejandro. I had also become painfully aware of how representatives of the car lobby were using the promise of Uber and Lyft to kill transit funding, with success. As Henry Grabar reported in *Slate*, "Cities across the country are cutting public transportation because they think ride-hailing services will fill the gap."[19] And the early data—later confirmed[20]—suggested that public transit ridership was dropping noticeably wherever ride-hailing entered a market.

I had also come across a billboard ad that cast some doubt on Uber and Lyft's much trumpeted "partnership" with transit. It showed a forlorn-looking waif staring in frustration down an empty subway tunnel, with the caption "You can't miss an Uber." By the way, Uber's real feelings on this matter were made clear during their 2019 IPO filing, when they described their TAM (Total Addressable Market) as including "all public transportation miles in all countries globally."[21]

Then there was the traffic data. Unsurprising for a service that was tripling vehicle miles traveled with every ride, traffic congestion in Uber-rich cities was through the roof. In Uber's hometown, a study found that trip times had risen 31 percent exclusively due to ride-hailing.[22] In early 2017, nearly two-thirds of congestion-related moving violations in downtown San Francisco were being committed by Uber and Lyft drivers.[23]

Finally, there was my own experience, watching every single Lyft I ever hailed waiting for me smack dab in the middle of the bike lane, even when ample curb parking was available five feet away. I asked the drivers if they had received a single word of instruction from HQ on bike safety. The answer was no.

All in all, ride-hailing was shaping up to be a terrible, horrible, no good, very bad idea. The first slide of my presentation showed Batman standing menacingly behind a seated Joker in an interrogation chamber. "Thanks for inviting me," it said. I suspect that we both thought of the other party as the Joker.

It was actually a cordial event, mostly because all of the Uber employees I met seemed pretty convinced they were saving the planet. I took their earnestness to heart, and asked them seriously: "What's the value proposition for cities?" I reminded them how cars (a dispersal tool) and cities (a concentration tool) work at cross purposes. I showed them Henao's data. I asked them about the billboard. I reviewed the defense they had published about ride-hailing's compatibility with transit. I presented my conclusions in two large-print all-text slides: I DON'T UNDERSTAND THE DEFENSE, and I DON'T SEE THE VALUE PROPOSITION FOR CITIES.

Like many VC-funded Silicon Valley startups, Uber's model was to "move fast and break things." As related by Sarah Goodyear on *The War on Cars*, Uber did both.[24] In half a decade, they broke yellow taxis, sending immigrant cab owners leaping into the East River. They broke transit, causing an average 9 percent drop in ridership.[25] They broke labor rights. They will eventually break their investors, having never turned a profit and having no visible path to profitability. Uber lost $6.8 billion in 2020. Lyft, being smaller, lost a mere $4.4 billion.

About a year after my visit, Uber got back in touch. Having ditched their pedestrian-killing autonomous vehicle division, they were now betting on flying taxis. Would I be willing to speak at the Uber Elevate Summit in Los Angeles? "Sure," I said, as long as they were comfortable with me telling the audience that Uber Air, as they had conceived it, was a terrible idea for cities, but not to worry because it would never happen. They declined my offer.

Uber sold off Elevate in 2020 for another huge loss. It's hard to see how there is any future for these companies beyond a return to their initial conception, which was to give a rich dude named Garrett Camp a premium ride to the nightclub.[26] Our cities will recover, but the Uber experience should not be forgotten, especially as we turn our attention to autonomous vehicles. "Oooh, shiny!" is no way to run a town.

AVS: NOT ON OUR WATCH

There is much discussion these days about how autonomous vehicles are going to revolutionize our cities. Most of this talk is optimistic, even Panglossian, and tends to fetishize new and disruptive technologies without considering the impacts of past analogous revolutions. Deeper consideration leads to a more cautious conclusion: if the city with autonomous vehicles is to be better than the city without them, there is a lot of work to be done.

While we are tracking my lecture circuit, I should quickly tell the story of my encounter with the U.S. Conference of Mayors. In the same year I visited Uber, I was given a chance to address a plenary at their winter meeting. "This is amazing," I thought. Imagine, hundreds of mayors and staffers all in one room, listening intently to the Ten Steps of Walkability! Truly a watershed moment for city planning nationwide!

About two weeks before the event, I got a call. Uh oh. "Don't worry, Jeff, you still get half an hour. The thing is, the only thing the mayors want to hear about is autonomous vehicles."

Fair enough. AVs were dominating the news, and cities wanted to know how to respond. To be accurate, most seemed to want to know how to pave the way. My session was to be sponsored in part by Uber and also by Ford, who were investing billions in self-driving technology. With the goal of giving an honest and helpful presentation, I started digging. Here's where I ended up, and haven't budged since:

The first obvious conclusion was that, if they can be perfected, self-driving cars will triumph. In *Technopoly: The Surrender of Culture to Technology* (1992), Neil Postman demonstrates how new technologies that increase convenience are unstoppable, even if their ultimate impacts on society are destructive (cars, anyone?).[27] We are already seeing on highways that drivers will hand over the wheel to their car as soon as the car is willing, as a solid twenty Tesla autopilot deaths will attest.[28] This speaks also to the unlikelihood that our lobbyist-run federal and state governments will be restricting their adoption in any way.

My second conclusion was that real AVs may never arrive in

our cities at all—good news, based on the next few conclusions. That assessment seems even more true today. We are now well past the 2020 deadline that boosters set for full autonomy. While driving on highways is relatively easy to program, the near infinite number of variables impacting city traffic, from all-way stop signs to gyrating disco Rollerbladers, seem more difficult to master . . . perhaps impossible. *The Wall Street Journal* reports that "self-driving cars could be decades away. . . . Experts aren't sure when, if ever, we will have truly autonomous vehicles that can drive anywhere without help."[29] Taking the long view, the historian Peter Norton notes that "automated driving has been 'only 20 years away' for over 60 years."[30]

Watching leaked video of automated Teslas and their human minders bumbling around cities, into occupied crosswalks and onto train tracks, does not inspire confidence. In one, Tech Bro A—perhaps a tad scripted—raves to Tech Bro B, "Now, with the software update, you can actually make thousands of people drive safer . . . overnight!" As he snaps his fingers, the car lurches right, with clear bloodlust, at a young cyclist in the bike lane. Tech Bro B yanks back the wheel. "Fuck! . . . Are we going to have to cut that?"[31]

Not to worry, there is a solution to mixing crackbrained Teslas, cyclists, and pedestrians in cities. It's called V2X technology, and it's commanded a noticeable chunk of the recent $1.2 trillion infrastructure bill.[32] V2X stands for "vehicle to everything," and refers to beaconization, equipping pedestrians and bike riders with transponders that can be spotted automatically by sensor-equipped cars. The Princeton researcher Zhuqi Li is bullish on this liberating device. "Both the pedestrians and the cars are working together toward the same goal, which is to make everyone safer."[33]

The beacon costs two thousand dollars to produce. If they can get the price down, it is expected to become a part of our cellphones—no equity issues there—which means that you should probably check your battery before you cross the street. Will false expectations of safety among the partially charged create a more hazardous situation than today's? Will V2X cause pedestrians and cyclists—pranksters or not—to jump in front of cars with impunity, negating any benefits to traffic flow generated by autonomy? Traffic experts like Sam Schwartz anticipate the second outcome, and properly worry that the industry response will be sidewalk corrals and cattle gates at crosswalks.[34]

After a point, this thought experiment wears us out. The conclusions worth remembering are that full autonomy in our lifetimes seems unlikely, and it is hard to model any partial-autonomy scenario that is not dystopian.

Easier to predict are the impacts that the path toward automation will have on our commutes and our environment. Due to technological limitations and the need for top-down restrictions, it is impossible to envision a future in which the dream of swarming AV fleets is achievable in America. We are a nation that has never shown the capacity to tell anyone where to not take their car, and we can be confident that any nascent swarm would quickly find itself infiltrated by uncoordinated civilians in jacked-up F-150s.

Instead of swarms, the likely outcome, in five years and fifty, is that ever more of us will own private vehicles that do ever more of the driving for us. We will be able to use our time behind the wheel more productively, and we will therefore be more willing to sit in traffic. Even AV-producer Elon Musk knows this, recently tweeting, "Self-driving car will amplify traffic to insane levels, as you won't feel the pain of driving yourself."[35] Like the tycoons happily conducting business from the back seats of their limos in gridlocked Jakarta, we will Zoom into work from our SUVs, creeping to and from homes located ever farther afield. Since the only real constraint to driving on congested highways is congestion, self-driving cars, by making congestion more bearable, will cause a lot more driving and sprawl. For this reason, a recent Harvard/MIT study concluded that "even limited uptake of the technology may produce a net increase in energy consumption and emissions."[36]

What do we do with this knowledge? Here's what I told the mayors: you can't stop sprawl, and you are not likely to be able to restrict AV use with laws. But you can legislate with lanes: you own the streets, or at least most of them. You can allow the growing traffic pressure of a second auto age to ream out your cities anew, or you can decide now how much additional space in each street to hand over as demand skyrockets. The proper answer, by the way, is zero.

As I say in Step 1, Put Cars in Their Place, we can have the kind of city we want. We can tell the car where to go and how fast. We can be a place not just for driving through, but for arriving at. Autonomy demands that we double down on that understanding.

CYCLING ASCENDANT

Sides matters; New gear; Gentrification lanes; Get greedy

There is no chapter in *Walkable City* more in need of an update than Step 6, Welcome Bikes. While progress has at times been frustrating, the revolution taking place in American cycling has outpaced most of our expectations. That revolution has produced data, and that data has proved some of my earlier conclusions wrong.

So much has changed in ten years. Our former nemesis, the vehicular cyclists, seem to have all died out, either by natural causes or dispatched by highway traffic. Janette Sadik-Khan's Prospect Park West cycle track emerged victorious after a protracted five-year legal battle; as described by *The Village Voice*, the "bike-hating NIMBY trolls grudgingly surrender[ed] to reality."[1] And bike share has become an even bigger deal than we thought. It's almost quaint to read my 2012 passage ostensibly introducing America to bike share. Since then, more than seven thousand docking stations have populated our shores.[2] New York's Citi Bike fleet has surpassed 100 million trips, often topping 125,000 per day.

I write these pages while I am visiting Miami, where I am making regular and remarkably efficient use of bike share and the eight-mile-long Miami Beach Boardwalk to get just about anywhere in twenty minutes. This combination—of shared bikes and cycle routes separated from car traffic—is making life noticeably better in more than sixty American cities.[3] While most smaller communities don't have bike share, almost every city with a serious planning department has thrown down at least one protected bike lane, and most seem ready for more.

SIDES MATTERS

These efforts, global trends, and mounting experiences in the United States make it clear that cycle tracks—bike lanes either removed from or protected from motor vehicles—are the future of cycling. Painting bike lanes into streets, especially where the driving lanes are too wide, is a good way to invite bikes; I still do it where nothing better is possible. But lanes alongside traffic, especially in the "door zone," are less than half as effective as protected lanes at convincing people to bike.[4] And, here's the kicker: they make biking no safer. A London 2020 study of 2,876 morning-commute cyclist injuries—including seven fatalities—found that cycle tracks reduced injuries by 65 percent, while unprotected (painted) bike lanes provided no safety improvements at all.[5]

And it gets worse: "advisory cycle lanes"—the British version of a sharrow—actually increased injuries by 34 percent.[6] Remember sharrows? They were the road marking of choice for a bit. Now they most decidedly are not. The British federal government, observing the data, announced that it would be funding only physically separated cycling facilities, and would no longer help communities provide paint-only bike lanes.

These outcomes were mirrored stateside in a thirteen-year study of seventeen thousand road fatalities and seventy-seven thousand severe injuries across twelve large U.S. cities. Unprotected bike lanes were found to have no meaningful impact on safety, while sharrows again made cycling more dangerous. In the words of the researcher Wes Marshall, "We found that they're worse than nothing. You're better off doing nothing."[7]

Interestingly, Marshall found that I (and many others) were wrong about "strength in numbers"; the study decidedly determined that biking population, while tracking with bike safety, was not its cause.[8]

What else did I get wrong? Well, I sincerely regret my admonition against bike lanes in lieu of parking on Main Streets. (I will be stepping back from public service to spend more time with my family.) While it's true that the best drivable shopping streets mix all users at very slow speeds, we have recently learned that cycle tracks—like the ones on Manhattan's Eighth and Ninth Avenues—are quite compatible with retail activity, and in fact can improve revenues.

Mayor Bloomberg was known for saying, "In God we trust; all others bring data." The data is in: after the implementation of a highly contested cycle track on Ninth Avenue, retailers who had insisted that the lanes would be the death of their business instead saw a sales increase of 49 percent.[9]

And it's not just New York. A Portland State University study of fourteen new cycling corridors across six U.S. cities found that eleven of the corridors "saw substantial increases in sales and/or employment."[10]

What concerned me in 2012 still concerns me now: most shopping streets still need some parking, and pedestrians and cyclists alike must be shielded from cars moving quickly. The ideal heavy-traffic shopping street today likely includes both parked cars and protected cycling.

NEW GEAR

On a recent visit to New York, I was surprised to see that about half the cyclists were on e-bikes. I was reminded of Beijing, where observed transportation choices run a remarkably smooth and multifarious spectrum from trike to motorcycle. If the rest of the country keeps following New York's lead, as New York seems to follow Beijing's, then we are in for a vast expansion of what it means to cycle. This is good and bad.

My initial knee-jerk reaction to e-bikes was dismissive; it looked like cheating. Why take the healthful exercise out of biking? Then I read that e-bikers get even more exercise than non-assisted bikers.[11] Really?

Well, the study—of ten thousand cyclists in seven European cities—is a bit misleading. It turns out that e-bikers are getting more exercise than bikers because the people who buy e-bikes are the ones who are already biking farther. Steady bikers who trade up to an e-bike actually experience a slight drop in physical activity.[12]

But it's not enough to matter. E-bikes, like bikes, are great for you.

It's worth noting that this study looked at pedal-powered e-bikes, not the throttle-controlled minimotorcycles that make up a large part of the Chinese and American fleets. European countries have limited the sale of e-bikes to the low-speed, pedal-powered models only, like the two-thousand-dollar Gazelle Medeo. This restriction has serious health benefits, and importantly protects their crowded bike lanes from hightailing hot rods.[13]

These e-cyclists who attain breakneck speed through unnatural means are the greatest risk that e-biking introduces to cities. Some states are wisely requiring licenses for e-bikes whose motors provide assistance over twenty miles per hour.[14] As e-bikes proliferate, cities too need to be vigilant—with both signage and enforcement—to keep bike lanes safe. If twenty is plenty for our streets, it is more than enough for our bike lanes, and mopeds disguised as e-bikes should be mixing with drivers, not cyclists.

Whether slow or fast, e-bikes are a potentially transformative technology for our cities. The experience, first in other countries and now at home, is that they get people out of their cars in great number.[15] For the efficiency of our communities, the health of the population, and the future of the planet, governments should be promoting e-bikes at every level. It was nice to see an up to 30 percent e-bike tax credit in Biden's Build Back Better bill. One hopes that bill's failure at the hands of one coal-state senator (plus one entire party) will not impede the passage of other e-bike legislation in the works. The federal government has spent more than $10 billion on tax breaks for electric cars;[16] the same money spent on e-bikes would have ten times the impact.

Other new gear to pop up in the 2010s were dock-less bike share and e-scooters. Just as buses aren't trains, shared bikes without docks did not convey or achieve the same permanence as their more infrastructural cousins. Many have since been replaced by e-scooters. What both technologies share is a tendency to litter our sidewalks and inconvenience people walking, especially e-scooters, whose riders have killed several pedestrians.

These deaths are unfortunate, but it is incredibly frustrating to watch them grab the headlines while thousands of car-on-pedestrian murders go underreported. In this way, they are like bike-on-pedestrian crashes, each of which dominates the news cycle for a week, creating the false impression that micromobility makes walking less safe. When asked, I am quick to remind folks that more people are crushed to death each year by vending machines than the number of pedestrians killed by cyclists.[17]

Because scooters, e-skateboards, and other mini travel accessories are all potentially "one less car," they deserve our affection and support. Cities should ease their adoption with reasonable rules about their storage and use. The best thing about them is that they make all too clear the need for bike lanes—now dubbed "micromobility facilities"—throughout our communities.

While we're talking safety: I advocated for wearing helmets in 2012. I still do. You should wear a bike helmet, because biking in America is dangerous, much more dangerous than in places like Europe where people don't wear helmets. But, if you are concerned for your safety, you should never require anyone else to wear a helmet, because doing so makes cycling more dangerous for everyone. Helmet laws suppress cycling. When New Zealand began enforcing helmet laws, cycling dropped by 51 percent and injury risk roughly doubled.[18]

GENTRIFICATION LANES

Anti-biking backlash has been known to create strange bedfellows. Where else do wealthy white commuters and historic Black churches find common ground? In *Bike Lanes Are White Lanes*, Melody Hoffmann documents recent skirmishes on the transportation equity battlefield, in which fears of gentrification join fears of traffic as motivation for cancelling new bike lanes that would disproportionately benefit people of color.[19]

One such lane, a beautifully protected cycle track that stretches one and a quarter miles along Washington, D.C.'s M Street—from Thomas Circle clear to Georgetown—dumps unceremoniously into traffic for just one block along its run, thanks to fervid opposition from the Metropolitan AME Church. "When slaves built our church, they were not thinking about bike lanes."[20] Ouch.

In these conflicts, it's important to distinguish symbolism from reality while also acknowledging the power that symbolism holds. The reality is clear: fully 38.5 percent of bike commuters come from the poorest 25 percent of income earners, and people of color rely disproportionately on cycling to get around their neighborhoods.[21] Black cyclists are much more likely to be hit and killed than white ones. Yet urban cycling is still regarded as an elite activity. The image of the entitled, recreational MAMIL— the middle-aged man in Lycra—simply will not die.

It doesn't help that books like this one, and people who look like me, consistently trumpet cycling infrastructure as key to attracting young, educated talent to cities. Where will this talent find housing, and won't that push costs up?

Except, apparently, it doesn't. A ten-year study of 11,010 miles of new bike lanes across twenty-nine U.S. cities found that, while cycling facilities often follow gentrification, gentrification does not follow cycling facilities. To wit: "The causality relationships between bicycling facilities and socio-economic-demographic changes were weak and largely non-significant . . . bicycling facilities were not linked to displacement."[22]

The confusion of symptom for cause that characterizes so much contemporary urban thinking must be attacked head-on. But the fact remains that bike lanes are one very visible part of a larger set of economic processes through which improving neighborhoods, as they gain value, tend to spit out many of their more vulnerable residents. We can say that bike lanes don't cause displacement, but if we don't act to stem displacement as we install bike lanes, we can't honestly claim to care.

This is a conundrum that we city planners face every day. It's our job to make places better. But making them better often makes them more valuable, and therefore more expensive. When this happens, renters can get priced out, and owners can end up with property taxes too high to pay. Happily, there are a number of time-tested measures that city governments can use to counter these trends, including renter-to-owner programs, community land trusts, and property tax freezes. Sadly not many city governments, even as they bemoan displacement, feel a moral obligation to pursue them.

This is why, although bike lanes don't cause displacement, cities building bike lanes need to be asked to fight displacement. In his essay "We Can't Walk If We Can't Breathe," Morgan State University's Lawrence T. Brown puts it this way:

Racial equity means . . . protected bike lanes or transit lanes that are designed and installed with Black neighborhoods at the center. It also means putting strong measures in place to prevent gentrification as such bike lanes are often viewed with skepticism rooted in the repeated uprooting of Black neighborhoods.[23]

In 2009 I was embedded in the Town Hall of Babylon, New York, working on the vision plan for Wyandanch Rising, a $500 million "downtown from scratch" at Long Island's most economically disadvantaged rail stop. As I sat there drawing, I got to listen to a phone bank operating in the adjacent cubicles. Day after day, they were calling every renter they could locate in the area, turning them into homeowners with a down-payment assistance program to be funded by the future developer. They were also working to identify local unemployed workers they could train to work on the construction site. Neither of these programs cost the town much money, but they led to massive improvement with minimal displacement. As Wyandanch rose, so did its residents.

GET GREEDY

If there is one passage of this book that I would like to retract, it is Step 6's "Don't Get Greedy." Sure, bike advocates are specialists, and we need our cities to be designed by generalists. As I noted, there isn't enough room in the streets for every specialist to get what they want. But here's what I got wrong: I have yet to see a city do anything requested by a bike advocate that has not made that city better for everyone. I've finally been to Copenhagen, and biked miles of downtown without the slightest fear for my eight- and ten-year-old boys in front of me. If you haven't had that life-changing experience, don't begin to think you know what you are doing when you deny a cyclist anything. The cycling city is the city we all need, and remembering Copenhagen fills me alternately with joy and rage. Just today, Milan announced $271 million in funding for a 466-mile citywide bike network.[24] Paris recently upped its biking investment to half a billion dollars, in order to achieve a "100 percent cycling city."[25] Meanwhile, the Boston Cyclists Union clamors enthusiastically for an increase in the city's bike budget . . . to $2.6 million.[26] And Boston's one of the good ones.

So get greedy. Don't settle for scraps. Demand more, one hundred times more, and don't stop until the very last bike-hating motorist throws up their hands and decamps permanently for the suburbs.

MORE COMFORT

More trees; Return of the natives; Streets of character;
Don't let terrorists design your city

In Step 7 of this book, I briefly railed against the indiscriminate use of shadow studies and how they can impede the creation of spaces with good edges. Now, as our cities get hotter, good edges become even more essential. A recent study of urban heat islands found a sixteen-degree difference between the hottest and coolest parts of Washington, D.C., on a blistering summer day. No surprise that the coolest areas were in forested places like Rock Creek Park; the surprise was that, street by street, it was the presence of tall buildings that had the greatest impact on local temperatures.[1]

This outcome mirrored earlier studies in Richmond, Virginia. Computer modeling in Australia—where the sun is upside down but no less intense—has determined that the classic 1:1 height-to-width ratio is an important threshold. It is precisely the "street canyon" effect that most cities fear that creates the shadows necessary to cool our urban spaces. A similar 2016 study in Portland found that no factor was more powerful than building heights in determining local temperature variations.[2]

This conversation reminds me of a favorite photo of mine, tweeted by Jake Schmidt, who witnessed a throng of activists along a street on New York's Upper East Side, protesting a proposed medical tower, with signs proclaiming SAVE OUR SUN-LIGHT and FIGHT FOR LIGHT. It's a sunny day, and about fifty participants wander in the bright foreground, squinting. A bit harder to see are the remaining protestors—perhaps one hundred—who huddle with their signs across the street in the welcome shade of a medical building.[3]

MORE TREES

Also noticeable in the photo is the complete lack of trees on the sunny side of the street, the precise thing that would have made it comfortable. I am pleased that I dedicated a full chapter of *Walkable City* to urban trees but, in retrospect, it could have been a lot more. We are only beginning to understand all the ways that trees are essential to cities.

In fact, were it not for trees, the vast majority of the continental United States would be mostly lifeless desert. Evaporation from oceans only directly moistens land within a few hundred miles of the coasts. Over the millennia, trees have absorbed coastal rainfall and passed it inland, creating the ecosystems that make most of America habitable.[4]

I can tell you this because I have spent a good part of the past eighteen months focused on trees. On August 10, 2020, Cedar Rapids, Iowa, was hit by a record-breaking derecho (straight-wind) storm, with gusts hitting 140 miles per hour. In just one hour, the city lost fully two-thirds of its canopy. In a place historically called the "Emerald City" for its lush tree coverage, whose very city seal is a picture of a tree, more than 660,000 trees came down. It is doubtful that any other storm in modern history has killed so many urban trees.

Within a week of the storm, the city manager was on the phone. I had previously redesigned their street network—turning a downtown of half four-lane one-ways into mostly two-lane two-ways—with the expected results. Would I help them get their trees back? The resulting plan, ReLeaf Cedar Rapids, was my first urban forestry plan, and I did it with a ton of help.[5] Working on it taught me more about trees, and reinforced some of the suspicions already voiced in Step 8 about where the practice of urban forestry has lost its way.

I also found a bunch more information on all the good that trees do. Not only do they improve our health, raise our property values, provide UV protection, eliminate urban heat islands, reduce car crashes, and absorb greenhouse gases and stormwater. They also provide vital wildlife habitat—if chosen properly—as they improve student performance and fight crime.

The educational and crime data is astounding. One University of Illinois study of more than fifty thousand Washington State middle schoolers found that "the more tree cover around a school, the better its standardized test scores in both math and reading."[6] This study controlled for seventeen other factors including neighborhood demographics. Remarkably, what mattered was tree cover close to the school. Neither neighborhood greenery nor schoolyard grass had a similar impact. "Even if the larger neighborhood was leafy, students were no better off if the schoolyard wasn't."[7] As your child's school district struggles to improve its test scores, how much is it investing in trees?

Meanwhile, the removal of 646 trees devastated by the emerald ash borer in Cincinnati provided a rare opportunity for a longitudinal study in which other factors were held constant. In this case, the loss of trees was associated with "an uptick in property crimes, assaults, and violent crimes."[8] Happily, the reverse also proved true. A thirty-eight-month randomized trial of five hundred properties in Philadelphia found that, compared to others left unchanged, those planted with trees experienced a significant reduction in crime, including a 29 percent drop in gun violence in neighborhoods below the poverty line.[9]

The fact that trees reduce crime is better understood than the reasons behind that fact. But we need not understand why trees make places safer to act upon our confidence that they do.

RETURN OF THE NATIVES

My biggest recent education around trees surrounds their contribution to the food web, something I did not think much about until I met the entomologist Doug Tallamy. Before I read his recent book, I was as likely to recommend a nonnative tree as a native one for the streets I designed. I know better now.

In *Nature's Best Hope*, Tallamy describes how climate change and unchecked development have launched the Earth's sixth mass extinction event. Currently, 52 percent of insects, 13 percent of birds, and 25 percent of mammals face extinction risk due to habitat loss. Key to human survival are the pollinators, which include butterflies, bats, hummingbirds, and especially bees. We rely on pollinators for 30 percent of our food crops and 87 percent of all plant life. In many places, bees are experiencing colony collapse disorder. In the last fifty years, half of the Midwest's native bee species have disappeared.[10]

Just as crops, plants, and trees need bees and other pollinators, pollinators need trees, both as habitat and for food. And only native trees are food, because native insects can't eat nonnative plants.

For many years, urban foresters have debated the importance of planting native trees in streets and yards rather than the wide variety of attractive imported species that have been planted across the continent. What the foresters have questioned, the biologists have now confirmed: nonnative trees can provide many useful ecosystem services, but one thing they do not do is support the food web. In fact, they actively undermine it.

The reason for this is simple: plants and animals have evolved in tandem across the millennia. They change very slowly. It literally takes hundreds of thousands of generations for insects to alter their diets. Moreover, most creatures are diet specialists; 90 percent of insect herbivores are restricted to eating just a few plants. Monarch butterflies, for example, have evolved to eat milkweed, and milkweed is the only thing they can eat.[11]

In this way, native plants support native wildlife, while importing foreign plants does not cause foreign wildlife to populate our shores. Case in point, Tallamy notes that "after nearly 500 years in residence in North America, *Phragmites australis*, the common reed, supports only 3 percent of the insects it supports in its European homeland [5 species versus 170]."[12]

But it gets worse. Imported trees and plants arrive without their collection of natural enemies, "the insects, mammals, and diseases that keep them in check in their homeland."[13] This gives them an unfair advantage over native species, which they can quickly overrun. Planting an imported tree is not merely a missed opportunity to plant a native tree; rather, it usually leads to a net loss in native trees overall. And fewer native trees means less food for native creatures.

The tree list we created for Cedar Rapids does not rule out all imported tree species. Rather, they are "contingent": the city is instructed to never plant a nonnative tree in a location where a native tree will thrive. Meanwhile, local nurseries are ramping up production of native seedlings as the city plans to spend close to $40 million in public and private funds rebuilding its canopy over the next decade.

STREETS OF CHARACTER

Google the phrase "beautiful tree-lined street" and tell me what you see: it is image after image of streets flanked on both sides by rows of nearly identical trees, something that many cities no longer allow. When I argued ten years ago against the typical urban forester's tutti-frutti approach to diversity, I thought that I was offering readers a reasonable trade-off: place-making versus resilience. Both have their value, and it seemed worth it to trade a little of the latter for a lot of the former.

It turns out I was wrong, but not in the way you may suspect. Like many people who are paid to know better, I was suffering from a superficial understanding of diversity. For decades, urban foresters have regarded these street-by-street "tree monocultures" as unnatural and unhealthy. That was wrong. As Peter Wohlleben teaches in *The Hidden Life of Trees*, the most resilient groups of trees are family members that help one another. Same-species trees are most likely to intertwine their roots underground, where they share nutrients and information and support each other against dangerous winds.[14]

It is essential that cities maintain an overall diversity of tree stock to protect against future blights. In 1999, Frank Santamour of the National Arboretum suggested what has become known as the 10-20-30 Rule: cities should plant no more than 10 percent of any one species (like white oak), no more than 20 percent of any one genus (like oak), and no more than 30 percent of any one family (like beech, to which oak belongs).[15] Since then, this advice has become a standard practice. But the mandate for overall diversity should not be confused with demanding diversity on every block, where an individual species can be used to establish a continuous canopy and make resilient places of unique character.

Santamour put it this way:

> Strips or blocks of uniformity should be scattered through the city to achieve spatial as well as biological diversity. Twenty to fifty trees of a single species, or even a single clone, do not constitute a "dangerous" monoculture. . . . Genetic diversity is achieved by mixtures of uniformity.[16]

Many streets in our cities currently enjoy a pleasant potpourri of tree species, and that should not change. But when the beauty of local uniformity is possible, that is a goal that should drive our plans.

DON'T LET TERRORISTS DESIGN YOUR CITY[17]

The scene is devastating: a terrorist plows a pickup truck down a Manhattan bike path, killing eight people and injuring almost a dozen more. The public demands a government response, and Mayor Bill de Blasio rises to the occasion, immediately budgeting $50 million for new vehicle barriers around the city, including funding for fifteen hundred steel bollards costing thirty thousand dollars apiece.[18]

While people are still on edge, this commitment is largely met with approval, and a feeling that "our leaders are working to keep us safe." But there remains in the air a general sense that something is amiss. While it is hard to think rationally about terrorism, a cool-headed analysis of the terror threat in our cities leads to four difficult conclusions that could dramatically impact our policies and practices.

First, we need to acknowledge that a bloody death is a bloody death, whatever its cause. Somehow, when a death is intentional, and an "accident" is instead a murder, preventing its recurrence becomes inordinately worthy of public funding—especially if the perpetrators are brown. But those who have personally witnessed a fatal car crash will confirm that the anguish, trauma, and tragic repercussions are no less than what accompanies any other violent death. A rational public safety policy would treat all lives as equal. Remarkably, taxpayers invested less than twenty-two thousand dollars per victim to put an end to the car-crash deaths on New York City's Queens Boulevard, while so far allocating approximately $1.7 billion per victim to ostensibly prevent another 9/11.[19] This discrepancy deserves our attention.

Second, it must be stated that terrorism is statistically insignificant. There are different ways to do the math, but an objective accounting of several decades of data suggests that you are 568 times less likely to die in a terror attack than a car crash. Fewer people were killed in the New York truck attack than have died in traffic practically every two weeks before and since. A proper epidemiological approach to public health and safety would allocate resources proportionally to the dangers they address.

Third, there is always a soft target. It is impossible to harden an entire city. This fact is perhaps the greatest source of cognitive dissonance surrounding New York's bollard campaign. For every bike path and sidewalk newly protected, there will remain hundreds exposed. If all public spaces receive bollards—an impossibility—a terrorist need only take an AR-15 to a hotel room window. In this way, we are doomed to be always protecting against the last attack instead of the next, and misspending millions on what is effectively "security theater."[20]

Finally, the anti-terror landscape can itself be terrifying. The purpose of terrorism is not principally to hurt people, but to cause panic and to unravel the social fabric. In that regard, a built environment that loudly proclaims the expectation of attack is in itself a form of terrorism, inciting fear, uncertainty, and suspicion of one's fellow man. Just like subway stop-and-frisks and a constant barrage of "See something, say something" messages, explicitly hardened public spaces are best understood as artifacts of a complicit terror-industrial complex that profits by keeping us scared. The fact that most actors in this drama are well-meaning should not distract us from resisting its grip.

The above arguments are unlikely to win many converts, and I will not be running for public office any time soon. But we can keep them quietly in the back of our minds as we make decisions about the design of our cities. It is also worth remembering that, as discussed in Step 9, bollards can be nice. They are traditional street furniture and, if designed well, need not participate in a terrorist threat that they may be naively responding to. If they are attractive, well-crafted, and well-located, they can become a positive feature of the spaces that they inhabit, rather than a permanent emblem of our panic, concrete evidence that the terrorists are winning.

It turns out there is more to the story of the Manhattan bike path. As related in Jessie Singer's powerful new book *There Are No Accidents*, that path was frequently breached by errant drivers. People had been complaining about it for years. Jessie's dear friend Eric Ng was killed there by a drunk driver in 2006, and others were mowed down before and after. Activists had been clamoring for a redesign of the many locations where drivers seemed to be welcomed onto the path.[21] But nothing was done, because the deaths were "accidental," even though they were eminently preventable. Only when the deaths became intentional did they merit the city's attention.

Public safety dollars can be spent in a way that has a real impact. With a limited investment, child traffic deaths in the Netherlands went from more than four hundred in 1971 to just fourteen in 2010.[22] A small fraction of our current anti-terror budgets, transferred to road design, would save thousands of lives.

THE ROLE OF CITY PLANNING

This book begins with the statement that "Jane Jacobs, who wrote in 1960, won over the planners by 1980." This is largely true as it relates to strategies for the inner city but, on reflection, is less accurate when it comes to how our cities and rural areas have been allowed to grow. By 1980, urban renewal was discredited and nobody smart was advocating for more inner-city highways, but the juggernaut of sprawl was only gaining momentum. Anyone who has traveled America over the past forty years can bear witness to how our cities continue to decant outward into the countryside, as even the most rural crossroads manage to attract a soulless detritus of Speedways and Dollar Generals. Sadly, this growth—destructive as it is to local economy, culture, and nature—was often guided by professional planners, who administer the zoning codes and development standards that give it shape.

Fighting urban, suburban, and rural sprawl, which many of us have identified as the biggest physical mistake that America has ever made, is where I began my design career, turning only later to the problems and promise of our older towns and cities. We designed new towns like Seaside, Florida, and Kentlands, Maryland, hoping that these traditionally organized neighborhoods, based on walking rather than driving, would become beloved and therefore replace the single-use sprawl paradigm that everyone seemed to hate.

Only the former occurred. Every new neighborhood we built, unless expressly directed at low-income populations, quickly escalated into the luxury market as buyers voted with their feet. Developers took notice. There are now hundreds of New Urban communities around the United States, but each one is an anomaly, and the car-dependent development pattern continues unabated.

It seems like we've tried everything. But that "we" is still narrowly defined, and the fight for more walkable communities actually, unbelievably, lacks the full-throated support of the planning profession. The American Planning Association (APA), the organization that has dictated the conduct of professional planners since the midcentury, has never taken a bold stance on sprawl. It has a sustainability division—not to mention a New Urbanism division—just as it has a Latino division and an LGBTQ division, as if socially responsible planning is some sort of demographic rather than the very reason for planners to organize in the first place. It oversees planner certification and ethical standards with a heavy hand, but it has little to say about the shape of our communities.

I can't suggest with any confidence that transforming the planning profession from rubber-stamping enablers into anti-sprawl warriors will be enough to reverse seventy-five years of poor decisions, but it seems worth a shot. As a fellow of the organization—at least until they read this—I would like here to launch a campaign to make this change. Jumping well ahead to its conclusion, I have proposed a first draft of the open letter that a properly reformed APA would issue to its membership and the media. It contains, in addition to a long-overdue mea culpa, something I am calling the Planner's Pledge, a commitment each planner would make to plan well and not badly. It's a first draft, but I welcome the APA to run with it.

AN OPEN LETTER TO ALL PROFESSIONAL PLANNERS
AND THE GENERAL PUBLIC FROM THE AMERICAN
PLANNING ASSOCIATION.[1]

As an establishment organization that has pushed for
what it believed to be best practices while inevitably ad-
vancing the dominant ideology of its society, the American Planning Association wishes to formally apologize
for the significant role that it has played in creating the
unsustainable suburban sprawl development pattern
that now constitutes most of the American built environment, reinforcing race and class segregation while bur-
dening the vast majority of citizens with the mandate of
car ownership.

To put it bluntly, we have participated and continue
to participate in the creation of a landscape that sepa-
rates us ruthlessly both from different activities and
from different people, such that we are inordinately dependent on our automobiles and less connected to one
another. While citizens of other nations enjoy daily life
in walkable, mixed-use, diverse neighborhoods, the typical American lives in a cluster of economically identical
single-family houses where it is impossible to safely walk
to work, school, shopping, recreation, or worship. The
outcomes of this pattern of growth could not be more
profound. We have gained weight, lost economic resiliency, exacerbated inequity, and undermined the social
fabric as our daily driving cooks the planet.

This changes today. Professional planners, who sit in
city and town halls across the nation and create the rules
that shape our growth, in being directly responsible for
the current circumstances, must take responsibility for
changing them. Apologies are not enough. We must step
forward with a new model of professional conduct designed to undo nearly a century of misdirection.

It will take many years to reverse the zoning laws and transportation standards that created and reinforce our car-dependent landscape. Politics will continue to favor business as usual. The homebuilding and road-building industries will keep pushing for more of the same, and will keep funding politicians who do their bidding. But municipal planners, as a profession, can take a stand. In some places we will be effective in changing the rules—it is already happening in Minneapolis, Seattle, and elsewhere—and every place makes a difference.

This effort is enforceable. Planners are professionally certified within the American Planning Association by the American Institute of Certified Planners. Not every planner is certified, especially younger ones, but AICP certification is considered the hallmark of full professional status. Maintaining this status, which requires continuing education and adherence to a strictly enforced code of ethics, is something planners take seriously. The AICP certification is the tool that the planning profession can use to hold its members to a higher standard, one that acknowledges that it is neither professional nor ethical to build a landscape that actively damages our health, our social fabric, and our environment.

As of today, the American Planning Association will make AICP certification dependent on signing the Planner's Pledge below. Those who object are welcome to create their own, alternative certifying body, perhaps the AICSP, the American Institute of Certified Sprawl Planners. Towns and cities, for their part, are welcome to continue to plan badly, defying everything we know about what makes for sustainable places. But they will do so without the blessing of a profession that is finally acting on decades of evidence that planning around the automobile makes America worse.

Some may say that the American Planning Association is a lumbering institution more concerned with its own preservation than with its impact on society. Most young planners question the value of AICP certification. With this act, we hope to reinvigorate the AICP imprimatur by giving it meaning. Planners who wish to earn or maintain AICP certification beyond 2023 will be planners who can be trusted to implement current best practices, which means throwing off many years of destructive convention. Just as doctors who prescribe leeches are no longer likely to maintain their licenses, planners who create or abet car-dependent sprawl will henceforth be relegated to ply their trade in the proverbial back alley, beyond the bounds of respected practice.

THE PLANNER'S PLEDGE IS AS FOLLOWS:

WHEREAS:

- Car-dependent development is destructive to our health, our economy, our environment, and our social fabric;
- Planning around the car is a self-fulfilling prophesy: traffic studies and parking minimums perpetuate and worsen the very car dependence that they hope to mitigate;
- Land-use zoning, beyond its original purpose of separating housing from noxious uses, creates car dependence;
- Most negative impacts of car-based planning will not be alleviated by electrification, especially the wasteful consumption patterns caused by decentralization;

- Single-family zoning, invented to perpetuate racial segregation in the face of civil rights laws, is morally bankrupt and destructive to overcoming past injustices;
- Income diversity within neighborhoods is a social good that developers will typically not allow for unless required to do so by local ordinance;
- Affordable housing is not truly affordable if its residents cannot lead productive lives car-free;
- Walkable, bikeable communities provide their inhabitants with a superior quality of life and must be acknowledged as an unmitigated good;
- Achieving walkability depends on the creation of a physical framework in which walking is truly useful, safe, comfortable, and interesting;
- The majority of the American built environment is car dependent; these places should be allowed to grow, but only in ways that lessen that dependency;
- Homelessness is a condition that cities can address most affordably by first providing housing and only subsequently placing any demands upon the person housed;
- Primary schooling is best provided in neighborhoods in which it can be reached on foot; the same is true of daycare, playgrounds, parks, pools, and other municipal amenities.

I PLEDGE THAT I WILL:

- Encourage more housing in walkable areas;
- Encourage the construction of schools that most students can reach on foot or bike;
- Encourage the construction of small local parks and other amenities;

- Mandate inclusionary zoning;
- Allow accessory dwelling units everywhere;
- Support Housing First policymaking to fight homelessness;
- Work to eliminate all on-site parking requirements;
- Require all apartment properties to decouple parking fees from rents;
- Require all large employers to offer transit passes, bike subsidies, or simple cash payouts to employees who do not drive, of equal value to a parking space;
- Work to locate dense development along frequent transit routes and vice versa;
- Encourage the implementation of docked bike-share programs;
- Insist that all new streets and roads offer low-stress micromobility routes, either through protected lanes or mixing with truly low-speed traffic;
- Encourage congestion pricing for crowded roadways;
- Encourage the adoption of Vision Zero policies;
- Engineer new roads with a design speed no higher than the desired driver speed;
- Advocate for firefighting equipment that fits streets and not vice versa;
- Replace traffic signals with all-way stop signs wherever feasible;
- Work toward a goal of continuous tree canopy above all thoroughfares and parking lots;
- Advocate against bike helmet laws as they suppress ridership and worsen safety.

I PLEDGE THAT I WILL NOT:

- Encourage or assist in the consolidation of schools or parks into larger facilities;

- Encourage or assist in the proliferation of ride-hailing services like Uber and Lyft in places with significant transit ridership;
- Encourage or assist in the development of any autonomous driving technology (or any technology) that limits the freedom of pedestrians and cyclists;
- Build or abet the building of any new highways or highway lanes;
- Allow traffic studies to limit new development or mandate wider streets;
- Build or abet the building of any new throughfare that does not safely welcome pedestrians and cyclists;
- Locate any parking lots between a right-of-way edge and a front door;
- Locate any parking structures facing a sidewalk without another use at ground level;
- Encourage the destruction of any substantial sidewalk-facing building facade more than one hundred years old.

In signing this pledge, I understand that it is equally binding as the AICP code of ethics, and that any violation thereof is grounds for revocation of my professional certification.

Thank you for your consideration as you embark upon this profound change to our way of serving the public. To professional planners, we ask for your understanding and compliance. To everyone else, we ask for your forgiveness.

The American Planning Association and American Institute of Certified Planners had nothing to do with this text. It is fiction, a mere proposal. But wouldn't it be nice?

ACKNOWLEDGMENTS*

This is the first book on design that I have written without
Andres Duany or Elizabeth Plater-Zyberk, but don't be fooled:
it would not have been possible, or at least any good, without
them. Not only are a significant percent of this book's ideas
theirs; so too is the strategy of organizing those ideas into a ruthlessly instrumental framework, one that I can only hope is up to
their standard.

When this book was almost finished, I sent it along to Andres so he could call my attention to any of their ideas that I had
not properly credited. He declined to take on this task, a choice
that embodies two of his dominant personality traits: a violent
allergy to wasting time, and an intellectual generosity of truly
historic proportion. For that reason, if you read something you
like, there is a good chance that I got it from Andres—not that
he would want the credit.

I first heard Andres lecture in 1988, and I had a very specific
reaction: Oh My God, this has to be a book. The result was
Suburban Nation. More than twenty years later, I was fortunate
enough to have that scenario play out in reverse when, after my
lecture to her former organization, CEOs for Cities, Carol Coletta thanked me with the same words. Unlike my suggestion to

*From the original 2012 edition.

Andres, Carol was not offering to write the book for me; that would still be my job. But without Carol this book would not have been written.

In addition to their encouragement, Carol and CEOs for Cities can be thanked for securing a grant that allowed me to take the time off to write. That grant came from the Fund for the Environment and Urban Life, whose founder, Richard Oram, had made the mistake of asking me: "Is there anything interesting out there we should be supporting?" I hope that I can be forgiven for responding so selfishly.

With the promise of a grant, I created a proposal for my brilliantly skeptical agent, Neeti Madan. She demanded three rewrites, and just as I was about to give up, she sold it to Farrar, Straus and Giroux, the publishers of *Suburban Nation*. Given our wholly positive experience creating that book, I was unsurprised to learn that I had been assigned no less an editor than Sean McDonald, who, in addition to being famously smart about books, is probably the one person on earth who cares more about city planning than I do. He also has zero tolerance for TMI, so, if you find any of this book boring, it is because I overruled some of his cuts. Then again, if you wish the book were longer, please call him repeatedly on his home phone.

Four additional editors, unpaid, contributed heavily to this effort, all of them Specks. Father Mort provided executive-level direction. Mother Gayle and brother Scott, essayists of the first rank, pored over every sentence and improved many. And wife Alice served as a daily sounding board, not to mention source of inspiration. She also carved out a space for me to write by miraculously corralling two young children in an unchildproofed country.

That country was Italy, where I was generously hosted by two tremendously supportive organizations: the American Academy in Rome, and the Bogliasco Foundation's Liguria Study Center. I am personally grateful to Adele Chatfield-Taylor and the

Harrison family for their enthusiastic encouragement, and also for overlooking the baby damage.

I have dozens of people to thank for the information and stories that make up this book. As the text and notes suggest, certain chapters depend heavily on the thought leaders in their subjects, roughly as follows: economics: Chris Leinberger and Joe Cortright; health: Richard Jackson, Howie Frumkin, and Lawrence Frank; parking: Donald Shoup; transit: Yonah Freemark; safety: Dan Burden; biking: Jeff Mapes and Robert Hurst; and urban triage: Andres Duany.

While this list is by no means complete, I also received important help from Adam Baacke, Kaid Benfield, Scott Bernstein, Ron Bogle, Tom Brennan, Amanda Burden, Norman Garrick, Robert Gibbs, Alex Gorlin, Vince Graham, Charlie Hales, Blake Kreuger, Bill Lennertz, Matt Lerner, Todd Litman, Mike Lydon, Michael Mehaffy, Charles Marohn, Paul Moore, Wes Marshall, Eileen McNeil, Darrin Nordahl, Brian O'Looney, Eva Otto, David Owen, Jay Primus, Shannon Ramsay, Ginny Seyferth, Christian Sottile, Boo Thomas, Brent Toderian, John Torti, Harriet Tregoning, and Sam Zimbabwe.

Finally, it was mayors who helped me understand the need for this book, the issues that it had to address, and the requirement that its recommendations be both reality-based and actionable now. These include Steve Bellone (Babylon, NY), Jim Brainard (Carmel, IN), John Callahan (Bethlehem, PA), Mick Cornett (Oklahoma City), Frank Cownie (Des Moines, IA), Manny Diaz (Miami), A C Wharton (Memphis), and the incomparable Joe Riley (Charleston, SC), who has demonstrated over ten consecutive terms that city design matters more than most of us can imagine.

NOTES

A GENERAL THEORY OF WALKABILITY
1. Andres Duany, Elizabeth Plater-Zyberk, and Jeff Speck, *Suburban Nation*, 164.
2. Andres Duany and Jeff Speck, *The Smart Growth Manual*, Point 10.7.

I: WHY WALKABILITY?
1. Andres Duany, Elizabeth Plater-Zyberk, and Jeff Speck, *Suburban Nation*, 217.

WALKING, THE URBAN ADVANTAGE
1. Jack Neff, "Is Digital Revolution Driving Decline in U.S. Car Culture?"
2. J. D. Power press release, October 8, 2009.
3. Richard Florida, "The Great Car Reset."
4. The Segmentation Company, "Attracting College-Educated, Young Adults to Cities," 7.
5. Patrick C. Doherty and Christopher B. Leinberger, "The Next Real Estate Boom."
6. Ibid.
7. Christopher B. Leinberger, *The Option of Urbanism*, 89.
8. Ibid.
9. Ibid., 90.
10. David Byrne, *Bicycle Diaries*, 283.
11. Carol Morello, Dan Keating, and Steve Hendrix, "Census: Young Adults Are Responsible for Most of D.C.'s Growth in Past Decade."
12. Christopher B. Leinberger, "Federal Restructuring of Fannie and Freddie Ignores Underlying Cause of Crisis."

13. Christopher B. Leinberger, "The Next Slum."
14. Leinberger, *Option*, 96–98.
15. Ibid., 101, and Anton Troianovski, "Downtowns Get a Fresh Lease."
16. Leinberger, *Option*, 91, 8–9.
17. Joe Cortright, "Walking the Walk: How Walkability Raises Home Values in U.S. Cities," 20.
18. Belden Russonello & Stewart, "What Americans Are Looking for When Deciding Where to Live," 3, 2.
19. Joe Cortright, "Portland's Green Dividend," 1.
20. Ibid., 1–2, and Joe Cortright, "Driven Apart."
21. Ibid., 3.
22. Poster, Intelligent Cities Initiative, National Building Museum.
23. Leinberger, *Option*, 20.
24. Barbara J. Lipman, "A Heavy Load: The Combined Housing and Transportation Costs of Working Families," iv.
25. Ibid., 5.
26. Doherty and Leinberger, "The Next Real Estate Boom."
27. Ibid.
28. Leinberger, "Federal Restructuring."
29. Catherine Lutz and Anne Lutz Fernandez, *Carjacked*, 207.
30. Leinberger, *Option*, 77–78, and "Here Comes the Neighborhood"; Jeff Mapes, *Pedaling Revolution*, 143.
31. Jon Swartz, "San Francisco's Charm Lures High-Tech Workers."
32. David Brooks, Lecture, Aspen Institute; and David Brooks, "The Splendor of Cities."
33. Mapes, 268.
34. Jonah Lehrer, "A Physicist Solves the City," 3.
35. Ibid., 4.
36. Hope Yen, "Suburbs Lose Young Whites to Cities"; Leinberger, *Option*, 170.
37. Ibid.

WHY JOHNNY CAN'T WALK

1. Jim Colleran, "The Worst Streets in America."
2. Jeff Speck, "Our Ailing Communities: Q&A: Richard Jackson."
3. Ibid.
4. Lawrence Frank, Lecture to the 18th Congress for the New Urbanism.
5. Molly Farmer, "South Jordan Mom Cited for Neglect for Allowing Child to Walk to School."
6. Howard Frumkin, Lawrence Frank, and Richard Jackson, *Urban Sprawl and Public Health*, xii.
7. Thomas Gotschi and Kevin Mills, "Active Transportation for America," 27.

8. Jan Gehl, *Cities for People*, 111.
9. Neal Peirce, "Biking and Walking: Our Secret Weapon?"
10. Gotschi and Mills, 44.
11. Jeff Mapes, *Pedaling Revolution*, 230.
12. Elizabeth Kolbert, "XXXL: Why Are We So Fat?"
13. Christopher B. Leinberger, *The Option of Urbanism*, 76.
14. Catherine Lutz and Anne Lutz Fernandez, *Carjacked*, 165.
15. Frumkin, Frank, and Jackson, 100.
16. Ibid.
17. Erica Noonan, "A Matter of Size."
18. American Dream Coalition website.
19. Richard Jackson, "We Are No Longer Creating Wellbeing."
20. Kevin Sack, "Governor Proposes Remedy for Atlanta Sprawl," A14.
21. Lutz and Lutz Fernandez, 172–73; American Lung Association, "State of the Air 2011 City Rankings"; Lutz and Lutz Fernandez, 173.
22. Asthma and Allergy Foundation of America, "Cost of Asthma"; John F. Wasik, *The Cul-de-Sac Syndrome*, 68.
23. WebMD slideshow, "10 Worst Cities for Asthma."
24. Charles Siegel, *Unplanning*, 30.
25. Lutz and Lutz Fernandez, 182.
26. Frumkin, Frank, and Jackson, 110.
27. All traffic fatality data collected by Drive and Stay Alive, Inc.
28. Frumkin, Frank, and Jackson, 112.
29. Speck, "Our Ailing Communities."
30. Jane Ford, "Danger in Exurbia: University of Virginia Study Reveals the Danger of Travel in Virginia," *University of Virginia News*, April 30, 2002.
31. Doug Monroe, "The Stress Factor," 89.
32. Mapes, 239.
33. Deborah Klotz, "Air Pollution and Its Effects on Heart Attack Risk," *The Boston Globe*, February 28, 2011.
34. Frumkin, Frank, and Jackson, 142; Lutz and Lutz Fernandez, 156; Alois Stutzer and Bruno S. Frey, "Stress That Doesn't Pay," as described in Joe Cortright, "Portland's Green Dividend," 2.
35. Mainstreet.com, quoted in "Survey Says" by Cora Frazier, *The New Yorker*, March 19, 2012.
36. Dan Buettner, *Thrive*, 189.
37. Frumkin, Frank, and Jackson, 172.
38. Dom Nozzi, http://domz60.wordpress.com/quotes/.

THE WRONG COLOR GREEN

1. Terry Tamminen, *Lives per Gallon*, 207.
2. Michael T. Klare, quoted in Catherine Lutz and Anne Lutz Fernandez, *Carjacked*, 90.
3. Josh Dorner, "NBC Confirms That 'Clean Coal' Is an Oxymoron."
4. Bill Marsh, "Kilowatts vs. Gallons."
5. Firmin DeBrabander, "What If Green Products Make Us Pollute More?"
6. Ibid.
7. Michael Mehaffy, "The Urban Dimensions of Climate Change."
8. David Owen, *Green Metropolis*, 48, 104.
9. *A Convenient Remedy*, Congress for the New Urbanism video.
10. Witold Rybczynski, *Makeshift Metropolis*, 189.
11. The study was prepared by Jonathan Rose Associates, March 2011.
12. New Urban Network, "Study: Transit Outperforms Green Buildings."
13. Kaid Benfield, "EPA Region 7: We Were Just Kidding About That Sustainability Stuff."
14. Ibid.
15. Dom Nozzi, http://domz60.wordpress.com/quotes/.
16. Owen, 19, 23.
17. Andres Duany, Elizabeth Plater-Zyberk, and Jeff Speck, *Suburban Nation*, 7–12.
18. Edward Glaeser, "If You Love Nature, Move to the City."
19. Owen, 2–3, 17.
20. Peter Newman, Timothy Beatley, and Heather Boyer, *Resilient Cities*, 7, 88.
21. Ibid., 92.
22. John Holtzclaw, "Using Residential Patterns and Transit to Decrease Auto Dependence and Costs."
23. "2010 Quality of Living Worldwide City Rankings," Mercer.com.
24. Newman, Beatley, and Boyer, 99.

STEP 1: PUT CARS IN THEIR PLACE

1. Dom Nozzi, http://domz60.wordpress.com/quotes/.
2. Ralph Waldo Emerson, "Experience" (1844), quoted in Cotton Seiler, *Republic of Drivers*, 16; Walt Whitman, "Song of the Open Road" (1856).
3. Seiler, 94.
4. David Byrne, *Bicycle Diaries*, 8.
5. Patrick Condon, "Canadian Cities American Cities: Our Differences Are the Same," 16.
6. Ibid., 8.
7. Witold Rybczynski, *City Life*, 160–61.

8. Donald Shoup, *The High Cost of Free Parking*, 65.
9. Bob Levey and Jane Freundel-Levey, "End of the Roads," 1.
10. Ibid., 2–3.
11. Ibid., 2–4.
12. Terry Tamminen, *Lives per Gallon*, 60–61.
13. Christopher B. Leinberger, *The Option of Urbanism*, 164.
14. Randy Salzman, "Build More Highways, Get More Traffic."
15. Charles Siegel, *Unplanning*, 29, 95.
16. Federal Highway Administrator Mary Peters, Senate testimony, quoted in Nozzi, http://domz60.wordpress.com/quotes/.
17. Peter Newman, Timothy Beatley, and Heather Boyer, *Resilient Cities*, 102.
18. Texas Transportation Institute, Texas A&M University, "2010 Urban Mobility Report."
19. Nozzi, op. cit.
20. Andres Duany, Elizabeth Plater-Zyberk, and Jeff Speck, *Suburban Nation*, 16.
21. Information from an e-mail exchange with Dan Burden.
22. Jane Jacobs, *Dark Age Ahead*, 73.
23. Ibid., 74–79.
24. Yonah Freemark and Jebediah Reed, "Huh?! Four Cases of How Tearing Down a Highway Can Relieve Traffic Jams (and Save Your City)."
25. Kamala Rao, "Seoul Tears Down an Urban Highway, and the City Can Breathe Again," *Grist*, November 4, 2011.
26. Ibid.
27. Ibid.
28. Siegel, 102; William Yardley, "Seattle Mayor Is Trailing in the Early Primary Count."
29. "Removing Freeways—Restoring Cities," preservenet.com.
30. Jan Gehl, *Cities for People*, 9.
31. Ibid., 13.
32. Newman, Beatley, and Boyer, 117.
33. Jeff Mapes, *Pedaling Revolution*, 81.
34. Witold Rybczynski, *Makeshift Metropolis*, 83.
35. Jeff Speck, "Six Things Even New York Can Do Better."
36. Ken Livingstone, winner commentary by Mayor of London, World Technology Winners and Finalists.
37. Data taken alternately from two sources: Ibid., and Wikipedia, "London Congestion Charge."
38. Ibid.
39. Stewart Brand, *Whole Earth Discipline*, 71.
40. Wikipedia, "New York Congestion Pricing."
41. Ibid.

42. Ibid.
43. Nozzi, op. cit.
44. Bernard-Henri Lévy, *American Vertigo.*
45. Ivan Illich, *Toward a History of Needs.*
46. Ibid., 119.
47. Duany, Plater-Zyberk, and Speck, 91n.
48. Catherine Lutz and Anne Lutz Fernandez, *Carjacked*, 145.

STEP 2: MIX THE USES

1. Andres Duany, Elizabeth Plater-Zyberk, and Jeff Speck, *Suburban Nation*, 10.
2. Conversation with Adam Baacke, June 14, 2011.
3. Nicholas Brunick, "The Impact of Inclusionary Zoning on Development," 4.
4. Judy Keen, "Seattle's Backyard Cottages Make a Dent in Housing Need."
5. Data from the City of Seattle Department of Planning and Development.
6. Tim Newcomb, "Need Extra Income? Put a Cottage in Your Backyard," time.com, May 28, 2011.

STEP 3: GET THE PARKING RIGHT

1. Martha Groves, "He Put Parking in Its Place."
2. Ibid.
3. Eric Betz, "The First Nationwide Count of Parking Spaces Demonstrates Their Environmental Cost."
4. Donald Shoup, *The High Cost of Free Parking*, 189.
5. Catherine Lutz and Anne Lutz Fernandez, *Carjacked*, 8.
6. Ibid.
7. Shoup, 83.
8. Ibid., 591.
9. Ibid., 2.
10. Ibid., 208–14.
11. Ibid., 24.
12. Ibid., 559.
13. Philip Langdon, "Parking: A Poison Posing as a Cure."
14. Ibid.
15. Langdon.
16. Betz.
17. Shoup, 81.
18. Sarah Karush, "Cities Rethink Wisdom of 50s-Era Parking Standards."

19. Washington, D.C., Economic Partnership (2008), "2008 Neighborhood Profiles—Columbia Heights."
20. Interview with architect Brian O'Looney of Torti Gallas and Partners.
21. Paul Schwartzman, "At Columbia Heights Mall, So Much Parking, So Little Need."
22. Ibid.
23. Shoup, 43.
24. Ibid., 8.
25. Andres Duany, Elizabeth Plater-Zyberk, and Jeff Speck, *Suburban Nation*, 163n.
26. Shoup, 131.
27. Ibid., 157.
28. Langdon; Shoup, 146.
29. Langdon.
30. Shoup, 150.
31. Ibid.
32. Noah Kazis, "NYCHA Chairman: Parking Minimums 'Working Against Us.'"
33. Wikipedia, "Carmel-by-the-Sea, California."
34. Shoup, 102–103, 230, 239.
35. Ibid., 239.
36. Ibid., 262.
37. Ibid., 498.
38. Ibid., 122.
39. Ibid., 327, 310, 14, 359.
40. Ibid., 328.
41. Ibid., 400.
42. Ibid., 380–81.
43. Douglas Kolozsvari and Donald Shoup, "Turning Small Change into Big Changes."
44. Shoup, 299.
45. Ibid., 383.
46. Ibid., 391–92.
47. Groves.
48. Bill Fulton, mayor of Ventura, blog posting, September 14, 2010.
49. Ibid.
50. Groves.
51. Shoup, 309.
52. Rachel Gordon, "Parking: S.F. Releases Details on Flexible Pricing."
53. Ibid.
54. Kolozsvari and Shoup; Shoup, 417.
55. Kolozsvari and Shoup.

56. Shoup, 417, 434, 415.
57. Ibid., 348–53.
58. Kolozsvari and Shoup; Shoup, 417.
59. Kolozsvari and Shoup.
60. Langdon.
61. Kolozsvari and Shoup.
62. Shoup, 397.
63. Ibid., 275.
64. Ibid., 299.
65. Alex Salta, "Chicago Sells Rights to City Parking Meters for $1.2 Billion."
66. Ibid.

STEP 4: LET TRANSIT WORK

1. Yonah Freemark, "Transit Mode Share Trends Looking Steady." Data from U.S. Census Bureau's American Community Survey, October 13, 2010.
2. Donald Shoup, *The High Cost of Free Parking*, 2.
3. Peter Newman, Timothy Beatley, and Heather Boyer, *Resilient Cities*, 86–87.
4. Freemark, "Transit Mode Share Trends Looking Steady."
5. Daniel Parolec, presentation to the Congress for the New Urbanism, June 2, 2011.
6. Terry Tamminen, *Lives per Gallon*, 112.
7. David Owen, *Green Metropolis*, 127.
8. Ibid., 121.
9. Andres Duany and Jeff Speck, *The Smart Growth Manual*, Point 3.2.
10. Newman, Beatley, and Boyer, 109.
11. Christopher B. Leinberger, *The Option of Urbanism*, 166.
12. John Van Gleson, "Light Rail Adds Transportation Choices on Common Ground," 10.
13. Todd Litman, "Raise My Taxes, Please!"
14. Yonah Freemark, "The Interdependence of Land Use and Transportation."
15. dart.org, 2008.
16. Wendell Cox, "DART's Billion Dollar Boondoggle."
17. Yonah Freemark, "An Extensive New Addition to Dallas' Light Rail Makes It America's Longest."
18. Van Gleson, 10.
19. Freemark, "An Extensive New Addition."
20. San Miguel County Local Transit and Human Service Transportation Coordination Plan, LSC Transportation Consultants in association with the URS Corporation, Colorado Springs, 2008, pages III-6 through III-7.

21. Charles Hales, presentation at Rail-Volution, October 18, 2011.
22. American Public Transportation Association Transit Ridership Report, 1st quarter 2011. Washington, D.C.
23. D.C. Surface Transit, "Value Capture and Tax-Increment Financing Options for Streetcar Construction."
24. Ibid.
25. Ibid.
26. American Public Transportation Association Transit Ridership Report, 1st quarter 2011.
27. D.C. Surface Transit.
28. Equilibrium Capital, "Streetcars' Economic Impact in the United States," PowerPoint presentation.
29. D.C. Surface Transit.
30. Ibid.
31. Andres Duany, Elizabeth Plater-Zyberk, and Jeff Speck, *Suburban Nation*, 202–203.
32. Darrin Nordahl, *My Kind of Transit*, ix.
33. Ibid., 126–43.
34. Mark Jahne, "Local Officials Find Fault with Proposed Hartford–New Britain Busway."
35. U.S. Government Accounting Office, "Bus Rapid Transit Shows Promise."
36. Morgan Clendaniel, "Zipcar's Impact on How People Use Cars Is Enormous."

STEP 5: PROTECT THE PEDESTRIAN

1. Wesley Marshall and Norman Garrick, "Street Network Types and Road Safety," table 1.
2. Andres Duany, Elizabeth Plater-Zyberk, and Jeff Speck, *Suburban Nation*, 160n.
3. Dan Burden and Peter Lagerwey, "Road Diets: Fixing the Big Roads."
4. Reid Ewing and Eric Dumbaugh, "The Built Environment and Traffic Safety," 363.
5. Robert Noland, "Traffic Fatalities and Injuries," cited in Catherine Lutz and Anne Lutz Fernandez, *Carjacked*, chapter 9, note 19.
6. "Designing Walkable Urban Thoroughfares."
7. NCHRP Report 500, "Volume 10: A Guide for Reducing Collisions Involving Pedestrians," 2004.
8. 20splentyforus.org.uk.
9. Duany, Plater-Zyberk, and Speck, 36–37.
10. Malcolm Gladwell, "Blowup," 36; also in Duany, Plater-Zyberk, and Speck, 37n.
11. Tom McNichol, "Roads Gone Wild."

12. Tom Vanderbilt, *Traffic*, 199.
13. McNichol.
14. Jeff Mapes, *Pedaling Revolution*, 62.
15. McNichol.
16. David Owen, *Green Metropolis*, 186.
17. McNichol.
18. Ibid.
19. Duany, Plater-Zyberk, and Speck, 64.
20. Christian Sottile, "One-Way Streets: Urban Impact Analysis," commissioned by the city of Savannah (unpublished).
21. Ibid.
22. Melanie Eversley, "Many Cities Changing One-Way Streets Back."
23. Alan Ehrenhalt, "The Return of the Two-Way Street."
24. Ibid.
25. Ibid.
26. Duany, Plater-Zyberk, and Speck, 71.
27. Jan Gehl, *Cities for People*, 186.
28. Mapes, 85.
29. Michael Grynbaum, "Deadliest for Walkers: Male Drivers, Left Turns."
30. Damien Newton, "Only in LA: DOT Wants to Remove Crosswalks to Protect Pedestrians."
31. Owen, 185.

STEP 6: WELCOME BIKES

1. Ron Gabriel, "3-Way Street by ronconcocacola," Vimeo.
2. Hayes A. Lord, "Cycle Tracks."
3. Jan Gehl, *Cities for People*, 105.
4. Allison Aubrey, "Switching Gears: More Commuters Bike to Work."
5. Jeff Mapes, *Pedaling Revolution*, 24.
6. Robert Hurst, *The Cyclist's Manifesto*, 176.
7. Gehl, 104–105.
8. Mapes, 14.
9. John Pucher and Ralph Buehler, "Why Canadians Cycle More Than Americans," 265.
10. Jay Walljasper, "The Surprising Rise of Minneapolis as a Top Bike Town."
11. Pucher and Buehler, "Why Canadians," 273.
12. Ibid., 265.
13. Mapes, 65, 70.
14. Jay Walljasper, "Cycling to Success: Lessons from the Dutch."
15. Mapes, 71; John Pucher and Lewis Dijkstra, "Making Walking and Cycling Safer: Lessons from Europe," 9.
16. Mapes, 62.

17. Russell Shorto, "The Dutch Way: Bicycles and Fresh Bread."
18. Ibid.
19. Gehl, 185–87.
20. Mapes, 81.
21. Wikipedia, "Modal Share," data from urbanaudit.org.
22. Mia Burke, "Joyride."
23. Mapes, 155.
24. Burke.
25. bikerealtor.com.
26. Mapes, 158, 143.
27. Ibid., 139.
28. Noah Kazis, "New PPW Results: More New Yorkers Use It, Without Clogging the Street"; Gary Buiso, "Safety First! Prospect Park West Bike Lane Working."
29. Gary Buiso, "Marty's Lane Pain Is Fodder for His Christmas Card."
30. Ibid.
31. Andrea Bernstein, "NYC Biking Is Up 14% from 2010; Overall Support Rises."
32. Lord.
33. Hurst, 81.
34. Ibid., 175.
35. Bernstein.
36. Thomas Gotschi and Kevin Mills, "Active Transportation for America," 28.
37. Ibid., 24.
38. Ibid., 225.
39. Children's Safety Network, "Promoting Bicycle Safety for Children."
40. John Forester, *Bicycle Transportation*, 2nd ed., 3.
41. Hurst, 90.
42. John Pucher and Ralph Buehler, "Cycling for Few or for Everyone," 62–63.
43. Mapes, 40.
44. Tom Vanderbilt, *Traffic*, 199.
45. Hurst, 94.
46. Steven Erlanger and Maïa de la Baume, "French Ideal of Bicycle-Sharing Meets Reality."
47. Wikipedia, "Bicycle Sharing System."
48. Clarence Eckerson, Jr., "The Phenomenal Success of Capital Bikeshare."
49. Christy Goodman, "Expanded Bike-Sharing Program to Link D.C., Arlington."
50. "Capital Bikeshare Expansion Planned in the New Year," D.C. DOT, December 23, 2010.
51. Wendy Koch, "Cities Roll Out Bike-Sharing Programs."

52. David Byrne, *Bicycle Diaries*, 278.
53. Lord.

STEP 7: SHAPE THE SPACES
1. Thomas J. Campanella, *Republic of Shade*, 135.
2. Jan Gehl, *Cities for People*, 4.
3. Ibid., 120, 139, 34.
4. Ibid., 50.
5. Christopher Alexander, *A Pattern Language*, 115.
6. Gehl, 42.
7. Ibid., 171–73.
8. Jane Jacobs, *The Death and Life of Great American Cities*, 203.
9. Andres Duany and Jeff Speck, *The Smart Growth Manual*, Point 10.5.
10. Gehl, 146.

STEP 8: PLANT TREES
1. R. S. Ulrich et al., "View Through a Window May Influence Recovery from Surgery."
2. "The Value of Trees to a Community," arborday.org/trees/benefits.cfm.
3. Dan Burden, "22 Benefits of Urban Street Trees."
4. Howard Frumkin, Lawrence Frank, and Richard Jackson, *Urban Sprawl and Public Health*, 119.
5. Eric Dumbaugh, "Safe Streets, Livable Streets," 285–90.
6. Burden.
7. U.S. Department of Agriculture, Forest Service Pamphlet #FS-363.
8. Burden.
9. Henry F. Arnold, *Trees in Urban Design*, 149.
10. Zoe G. Davies, Jill L. Edmondson, Andreas Heinemeyer, Jonathan R. Leake, and Kevin J. Gaston, "Mapping an Urban Ecosystem Service: Quantifying Above-Ground Carbon Storage at a City-Wide Scale."
11. David Whitman, "The Sickening Sewer Crisis in America."
12. Greg Peterson, "Pharmaceuticals in Our Water Supply Are Causing Bizarre Mutations to Wildlife."
13. "Rainfall Interception of Trees, in Benefits of Trees in Urban Areas," coloradotrees.org.
14. Burden.
15. Kim Coder, "Identified Benefits of Community Trees and Forests."
16. Charles Duhigg, "Saving US Water and Sewer Systems Would Be Costly."
17. Whitman.
18. Thomas J. Campanella, *Republic of Shade*, 89.

19. Ibid., 75–77.
20. Anthony S. Twyman, "Greening Up Fertilizes Home Prices, Study Says."
21. Geoffrey Donovan and David Butry, "Trees in the City."
22. Ibid.
23. Jan Gehl, *Cities for People*, 180.
24. See milliontreesnyc.org.

STEP 9: MAKE FRIENDLY AND UNIQUE FACES

1. Jan Gehl, *Cities for People*, 88.
2. Ibid., 137.
3. Ibid., 77.
4. Ibid., 151.
5. Andres Duany, Elizabeth Plater-Zyberk, and Jeff Speck, *Suburban Nation*, 175–78.
6. Chris Turner, "What Makes a Building Ugly?"
7. James Fallows, "Fifty-Nine and a Half Minutes of Brilliance, Thirty Seconds of Hauteur."
8. Ethan Kent, "Guggenheim Museum Bilbao," Project for Public Spaces Hall of Shame.
9. Léon Krier, *The Architecture of Community*, 70.
10. Jane Jacobs, *The Death and Life of Great American Cities*, 291.
11. David Owen, *Green Metropolis*, 178.
12. Ibid., 181.
13. Jacobs, 91.
14. Ibid., 91n.

STEP 10: PICK YOUR WINNERS

1. Andres Duany, Elizabeth Plater-Zyberk, and Jeff Speck, *Suburban Nation*, 166.
2. Blair Kamin, "Ohio Cap at Forefront of Urban Design Trend."
3. Andres Duany and Jeff Speck, *The Smart Growth Manual*, Point 7.8.
4. Rick Reilly, "Life of Reilly: Mile-High Madness."

DO I NEED TO REMIND YOU WHY?

1. Gregory Hodkinson, "Cities Alive: Towards a Walking World."
2. Alicia Adamczyk, "Millennials Are Fleeing Big Cities for the Suburbs."
3. Jordyn Holman and Lauren Coleman-Lochner, "Stores That Defined American Malls Eye a Freestanding Future."
4. Lauren Thomas, "25% of U.S. Malls Are Expected to Shut Within 5 Years. Giving Them a New Life Won't Be Easy."

5. Marie Patino, Aaron Kessler, and Sarah Holder, "More Americans Are Leaving Cities, But Don't Call It an Urban Exodus."

6. Lane Lambert, "Commuting Hurts Productivity and Your Best Talent Suffers Most."

7. Ibid.

8. James Fanelli, "Lousy Management, Knucklehead Hires Plague Operations of Real-Life Sopranos."

9. John Elflein, "Obesity Prevalence Among U.S. Adults Aged 20 and Over 1997–2018."

10. Alex Hutchinson, "Does Owning a Car Hurt Your Health?"

11. National Highway Traffic Safety Administration, "Newly Released Estimates Show Traffic Fatalities Reached a 16-Year High in 2021."

12. Angie Schmitt, *Right of Way*, 2.

13. Smart Growth America, "Dangerous by Design."

14. Angie Schmitt, *Right of Way*, 9.

15. Jim Gorzelany, "Study Says SUVs Are More Deadly Than Cars When Striking Pedestrians."

16. Manoli Katakis, "2020 GMC Sierra HD Design: The Origin Story."

17. Bob Segall, "Millions of Vehicles Have Unexpected, Dangerous Front Blind Zone."

18. Susan Koeppen, "Increasing Number of Children Killed in 'Frontover' Accidents"; Scottie Hunter, "Blind Zones on Cars Pose Hidden Danger for Kids."

19. Ellen Goldbaum, "Passenger Car Drivers Are More Likely to Die in Crashes with SUVs, Regardless of Crash Safety Ratings."

20. Jennifer Chu, "Study: Air Pollution Causes 200,000 Early Deaths Each Year in the U.S."

21. Julianne Cuba, "Harvard Study: Car Pollution in NYC Claims 1,400 Lives, Billions in Costs."

22. Gregory H. Shill, "Americans Shouldn't Have to Drive, But the Law Insists on It."

23. Cypress Hansen, "Sounding the Alarm: How Noise Hurts the Heart."

24. Ibid.

25. Andrew Gregory, "Transport Noise Linked to Increased Risk of Dementia, Study Finds."

26. Adele Peters, "50 Reasons Why Everyone Should Want More Walkable Streets."

27. Søren Kierkegaard, letter to his niece Henriette Lund, 1847.

28. Arianna Huffington, "Solution to Many a Problem: Take a Walk."

29. Amy Fleming, "'It's a Superpower': How Walking Makes Us Healthier, Happier and Brainier."

30. Maria Popova, "Nietzsche on Walking and Creativity."

31. Fleming, "'It's a Superpower.'"

32. Ibid.
33. Jessica Stroope, "Active Transportation and Social Capital: The Association Between Walking or Biking for Transportation and Community Participation."
34. "Revisiting Donald Appleyard's Livable Streets," StreetfilmsVlog.
35. Brittany Roffel, "B.C.'s Heat Wave Likely Contributed to 719 Sudden Deaths in a Week, Coroner Says—Triple the Usual Number."
36. *Derecho 8/10/20*, 7.
37. "Marshall Fire," Wikipedia.
38. Kevin DeGood, "Why an All-of-the-Above Transportation Strategy Doesn't Work."
39. Brad Plumer, Nadja Popovich, and Blacki Migliozzi, "Electric Cars Are Coming. How Long Until They Rule the Road?"
40. Jose Martinez, "MTA to Get Slim Slice of Federal Infrastructure Bill as Cars Outpace Mass Transit."
41. David Schaper, "Critics Say Infrastructure Projects Won't Make a Big Enough Impact on Climate Change."
42. John Kerry, remarks, Chantilly, France.
43. Farhad Manjoo, "There's One Big Problem with Electric Cars."
44. Shill, "Americans Shouldn't Have to Drive."
45. Jack Ewing, "The City Where Cars Are Not Welcome."
46. Farhad Manjoo, "Help. I've Fallen for That Cadillac Escalade."
47. Make I-45 Better Coalition.
48. Ibid.
49. Leah Binkovitz, "Houston's Air Quality Is Improving, but Asthma Disparities Persist."
50. "Living Near Highways and Air Pollution," American Lung Association.
51. Liam Dillon and Ben Poston, "Freeways Force out Residents in Communities of Color—Again."
52. Destiny Thomas, "Opinion: Urbanism Is Complicit in Infra-Structural Racism—And Reparations Have a Place in the Built Environment."
53. Nicholas N. Ferenchak and Wesley E. Marshall, "Bicycling Facility Inequalities and the Causality Dilemma with Socioeconomic/Sociodemographic Change."
54. Smart Growth America, "Dangerous by Design."
55. Topher Sanders, Kate Rabinowitz, and Benjamin Conarck, "Walking While Black."
56. Alan Ehrenhalt, "Jaywalking and the Dilemma of 'Victimless' Crimes."
57. Megan Wright, "Commonwealth Communities Kicks Off with Engaging, Expert-Led Session on Walkability."
58. Schmitt, *Right of Way*, 35.
59. U.S. Census Bureau, American Community Survey, 2008–2012.

LONG COVID

1. Andrew Cuomo (@NYGovCuomo), Twitter, March 22, 2020.
2. "Mortality Analyses," Coronavirus Resource Center at Johns Hopkins University; "Latest Data," City of Chicago COVID-19 site.
3. John Anderer, "Surprising Study: Urban Density Doesn't Cause More COVID-19 Infections, Even Promotes Lower Death Rates."
4. Matthew Keegan, "Why Cities Are Not as Bad for You as You Think."
5. Anderer, "Surprising Study."
6. Ibid.
7. Jimmy Carr, *Jimmy Carr: His Dark Material*.
8. Chris Morris, "Home Sales in the Suburbs Are Red Hot Right Now."
9. Tom Vanderbilt, "The Pandemic Shows What Cars Have Done to Cities."
10. Carlton Reid, "The Car Is Like a Virus, Says Urban Planner but This Is One Pandemic that Politicians Can Prevent."
11. Janette Sadik-Khan and Seth Solomonow, "Surrendering Our Cities to Cars Would Be a Historic Blunder."
12. Emily Baumgaertner and Russ Mitchell, "Car Crash Deaths Have Surged During COVID-19 Pandemic. Here's Why."
13. Ally Schweitzer, "D.C. Is Taking a Closer Look at Converting Downtown Office Space into Housing."
14. Richard Florida, "Parking Has Eaten American Cities."
15. Walter Isaacson, *The Code Breaker*, 464–65.
16. Hannah Devlin, "Palm Scent: The Science of Smelling After a Handshake."
17. Sadik-Khan and Solomonow, "Surrendering Our Cities."
18. Jeff Speck, presentation to Boston City Council, May 12, 2020.
19. Cities People Love (@citiespllove), Twitter, June 1, 2021.
20. Vivienne Walt, "'We Heard Birds': Paris Mayor Anne Hidalgo on How Lockdown Offered a Glimpse at a Greener City."
21. Ibid.
22. Sadik-Khan and Solomonow, "Surrendering Our Cities."
23. "Boston-Area Voters Support Changes to Local Streets Even If It Means Less Space for Cars."

AMERICAN HOUSING: PICK YOUR CRISIS

1. Up for Growth Action.
2. Noah Y. Kim, "A Test of White Support for Black Lives."
3. Richard Rothstein, *The Color of Law*, 49.
4. Kim, "A Test of White Support."
5. Ibid.
6. Christian MilNeil, "New State Rule Would Force Suburbs to Legalize Thousands of New Apartments Near T Stops."

7. Doug Gordon, Sarah Goodyear, and Aaron Naparstek, "Barcelona's Superblocks with David Roberts of Vox."

8. Marisa Kendall, "Gov. Newsom Abolishes Most Single-Family Zoning in California."

9. Edward Pinto and Tobias Peter, "California's Free-Market Housing Fix."

10. Donald J. Trump and Ben Carson, "We'll Protect America's Suburbs."

11. Jeff Speck, *Walkable City Rules*, 29.

12. Conor Dougherty, "Where the Suburbs End."

13. Susie Neilson, "This Is How Much Single-Family Zoning Is Costing San Franciscans."

14. Robert Steuteville, "California Zoning Reform: Are Form-Based Codes the Answer?"

15. Email to CNU Fellows listserv, February 4, 2022.

16. Barbara J. Lipman, "A Heavy Load: The Combined Housing and Transportation Burdens of Working Families," 4.

17. Keira Wingate, "Owning a New Vehicle Costs Nearly $10,000 a Year, AAA Says."

18. Charles Russo, "Un-forgetting the Segregationist History of Palo Alto (and Daly City, and San Francisco, and . . .)"

19. This passage is reprinted, with modifications, from Speck, *Walkable City Rules*.

20. "Housing First," Wikipedia.

21. Utah Housing and Community Development Division, "Comprehensive Report on Homelessness," 6.

22. Thomas Byrne et al., "Predictors of Homelessness Among Families and Single Adults After Exit from Homelessness Prevention and Rapid Re-Housing Programs."

23. Ibid.

24. Jennifer Perlman and John Parvensky, "Cost Benefit Analysis and Program Outcomes Report."

25. Mary E. Larimer et al., "Health Care and Public Service Use and Costs Before and After Provision of Housing for Chronically Homeless Persons with Severe Alcohol Problems."

26. "Housing First," National Alliance to End Homelessness.

27. "Building the Neighborhood of the Future."

28. The plan can be found at the website of the urban planners. "Culdesac Tempe: A Car-Free Neighborhood," Opticos.

29. Jonathan Becher, "The Curse of the Cul-de-Sac."

30. Frederick Melo, "St. Paul Eliminates Parking Minimums."

31. Christian MilNeil, "Boston Establishes New Limits on Parking in Large Developments."

MORE ENGINEERING CONFESSIONS

1. Charles L. Marohn Jr., *Confessions of a Recovering Engineer*, 21.
2. Marohn, *Confessions*, 103.
3. "City Reinstalls Downtown Stop Signs to Reduce Traffic Pileup, Speeding," KRQE 13 News.
4. Chris Bruntlett and Melissa Bruntlett, "Surprise: Bike-Friendly Netherlands Named Best Place in the World to Be a Driver."
5. Jeff Speck, *Walkable City Rules*, 168–69.
6. Marohn, *Confessions*, 6.
7. Ryan Cooper, "The Case Against American Truck Bloat."
8. John Ruch, "Manager of City Program to Eliminate Traffic Injuries Is Hurt by Alleged DUI Driver."
9. Jason C. Anderson, Christopher Monsere, and Sirisha Kothuri, "Effect of Residential Street Speed Limit Reduction on Driving Speeds in Portland, Oregon."
10. Tess Owen, "Florida 'Anti-Rioting' Law Will Make It Much Easier to Run Over Protesters with Cars."
11. Liam Hogan (@Limerick1914), Twitter, July 18, 2016.
12. Jim Puzzanghera, "Putting the Law on the Driver's Side."
13. Florida's new law protects drivers from civil liability. (Owen, "Florida 'Anti-Rioting' Law.")
14. Owen, "Florida 'Anti-Rioting' Law."
15. Alex Pareene, "The Right to Crash Cars into People."
16. Lauren Fix, "The War on Cars."
17. Doug Gordon, Sarah Goodyear, and Aaron Naparstek, "Policing the Open Road with Sarah Seo."
18. Kim Barker, Steve Eder, David D. Kirkpatrick, and Arya Sundaram, "How Police Justify Killing Drivers: The Vehicle Was a Weapon."
19. Marohn, *Confessions*, 191.
20. Neal R. Wooley, etc., et al., Appellants, v. George Maynard et ux.
21. Speck, *Walkable City Rules*, 105.
22. David D. Kirkpatrick, Steve Eder, Kim Barker, and Julie Tate, "Why Many Police Traffic Stops Turn Deadly,"
23. Marohn, *Confessions*, 196.
24. Jarrett Walker, *Human Transit*, 31.
25. Data provided by Jarrett Walker and Associates.
26. Laura Bliss, "Why Seattle Is America's Bus-Lovingest Town"; Laura Bliss, "How Seattle Is Winning the War on the Car Commute."
27. Speck, *Walkable City Rules*, note 83.
28. Bliss, "Why Seattle Is America's Bus-Lovingest Town"; Bliss, "How Seattle Is Winning the War on the Car Commute."
29. Taylor Dolven, "Boston's 28 Bus Will Remain Free for an Extra Month

After Coming in Under Budget"; Christopher Gavin, "City Council Passes Mayor Wu's $8 Million Vision for 3, Fare-Free MBTA Bus Lines."

30. "Boston-Area Voters Support Changes to Local Streets Even If It Means Less Space for Cars," Mass Inc. Polling Group.

31. Private email correspondence from Jarrett Walker, February 5, 2022.

INDUCED DEMAND REDUX

1. "The Congestion Con," Transportation for America.

2. Wyatt Gordon (@yitgordon), Twitter, June 30, 2021.

3. "Rethinking How We Build So Californians Can Drive Less," Caltrans.

4. Ibid.

5. Gregory Scruggs, "As an Elevated Highway Closes, Seattle Braces for Traffic Hell."

6. Joe Cortright, "Why Carmaggedon Never Comes (Seattle Edition)."

7. Ibid.

8. That last road-building effort, which promised to reduce congestion, actually increased driving times by one minute. As reported by NBC 4 Los Angeles, "After more than four years of construction, $1 billion, two 'Carmageddons' and a Jamzilla, a notoriously traffic-choked stretch of the San Diego (405) Freeway has a new carpool lane but not a whole lot of relief to show for it" (Ted Chen and Katherine Hafner, "Commute Times Increase One Minute After Freeway Widening Project").

9. Joe Cortright, "Carmaggedon Does a No-Show in Seattle, Again."

10. Alissa Walker, "Two of Elon Musk's Terrible Ideas Both Flopped in Las Vegas This Week."

11. Fred Lambert, "Tesla Is Making 12 Passenger Electric Van for Boring Company, Says Official."

12. Ibid.

13. Fred Lambert, "A Tesla Electric Van Is Coming as Soon as There Are Batteries for It."

14. Susannah Bryan, "So Elon Musk Wants to Build a Tunnel to the Beach. And That May Just Be the Beginning."

15. Ibid.

16. Private conversations with Alejandro Henao. Much of the information can be found in this article: Alejandro Henao, "The Good, the Bad and the Unknown of Uber and Lyft." The car-ownership stories have since been confirmed, as Uber and Lyft have been shown to increase private car ownership an average of 0.7 percent in urban areas, putting more than one hundred thousand additional vehicles on U.S. roads (Matthew Beedham, "Oh, Great—Uber and Lyft Are Actually Increasing Car Ownership in U.S. Cities").

17. Beedham, "Oh, Great—Uber and Lyft."
18. Regina R. Clewlow and Gouri Shankar Mishra, "Disruptive Transportation: The Adoption, Utilization, and Impacts of Ride-Hailing in the United States." A UC Davis study raised the 45 percent number to between 49 and 61 percent.
19. Henry Grabar, "'They Can Just Take an Uber.'"
20. Mi Diao, Hui Kong, and Jinhua Zhao, "Impacts of Transportation Network Companies on Urban Mobility."
21. Uber Technologies, Inc., SEC S-1 Registration Statement.
22. Yoann Le Petit, "Uber and Lyft Increase Pollution and Undermine Public Transport, Study Shows."
23. Joe Fitzgerald Rodriguez, "SFPD: Uber, Lyft Account for Two-Thirds of Congestion-Related Traffic Violations Downtown."
24. Doug Gordon, Sarah Goodyear, and Aaron Naparstek, "What Uber Hath Wrought."
25. Diao, Kong, and Zhao, "Impacts of Transportation."
26. Gordon, Goodyear, and Naparstek, "What Uber Hath Wrought."
27. Neil Postman, *Technopoly*.
28. Rick Newman, "It's Time to Notice Tesla's Autopilot Death Toll."
29. Christopher Mims, "Self-Driving Cars Could Be Decades Away, No Matter What Elon Musk Said."
30. Peter Norton, *Autonorama*.
31. Warren J. Wells (@WarrenJWells), Twitter, February 9, 2022. See also Faiz Siddiqui and Reed Albergotti, "'Full Self-Driving' Clips Show Owners of Teslas Fighting for Control, and Experts See Deep Flaws."
32. Carlton Reid, "Biden's $1.2 Trillion Infrastructure Bill Hastens Beacons for Bicyclists and Pedestrians Enabling Detection by Connected Cars."
33. Jon Christian, "Scientists: Pedestrians Could Wear Devices to Protect Themselves from Self-Driving Cars."
34. Jessie Singer, "All Hail the Robot Car?"
35. Elon Musk (@elonmusk), Twitter, March 6, 2022.
36. Ashley Nunes, Laurena Huh, Nicole Kagan, and Richard B. Freeman, "Estimating the Energy Impact of Electric, Autonomous Taxis: Evidence from a Select Market."

CYCLING ASCENDANT

1. Max Rivlin-Nadler, "Bike-Hating NIMBY Trolls Grudgingly Surrender to Reality."
2. "Bikeshare and E-Scooter Systems in the U.S.," U.S. Department of Transportation.
3. Ibid.

4. Jon Woodward, "'If You Build It, They Will Come': Study Says New Bike Lane Doubles Chances People Will Cycle."

5. Thomas Adams and Rachel Aldred, "Cycling Injury Risk in London: Impacts of Road Characteristics and Infrastructure."

6. Ibid.

7. Aaron Short, "Separated Bike Lanes Means Safer Streets, Study Says."

8. Wesley E. Marshall and Nicholas N. Ferenchak, "Why Cities with High Bicycling Rates Are Safer for All Road Users."

9. Melissa Bruntlett and Chris Bruntlett, *Building the Cycling City: The Dutch Blueprint for Urban Vitality*, 49.

10. Jessica Coulon, "Bike Lanes Can Benefit Local Businesses (!), According to This Study."

11. Lloyd Alter, "E-Bikers Ride Much Farther and More Frequently Than Regular Bikers."

12. Alberto Castro et al., "Physical Activity of Electric Bicycle Users Compared to Conventional Bicycle Users and Non-Cyclists: Insights Based on Health and Transport Data from an Online Survey in Seven European Cities."

13. Ibid.

14. "Do You Need a License to Drive an Electric Bike?," Aventon.

15. Selene Yeager, "E-Bikes Are Getting More People Out of Their Cars."

16. Karen K. Ho, "Only One of Harley-Davidson's Electric Bikes Would Qualify for a Proposed Tax Credit. Here Are 3 Ways the 118-Year-Old Company Has Committed to Sustainability—and Customer Satisfaction."

17. Jason Rodrigues, "Five Things More Likely to Kill You Than a Shark."

18. "How to Escape Bicycle Helmet Fines in Australia," Cyclists' Rights Action Group.

19. Nedra Deadwyler, "Whose Bike Lanes? A Review of *Bike Lanes Are White Lanes*."

20. Mike DeBonis, "How a Downtown Bike Lane Has Become a Political Headache."

21. American Association of State Highway and Transportation Officials, 2006–2010 U.S. Census Transportation Planning Products.

22. Nicholas N. Ferenchak and Wesley E. Marshall, "Bicycling Facility Inequalities and the Causality Dilemma with Socioeconomic/Sociodemographic Change."

23. Lawrence T. Brown, "We Can't Walk If We Can't Breathe: The Imperative for Racial Equity."

24. Ryan Mallon, "Milan Confirms Ambitious New Cycling Network Linking 80% of the City to Bike Paths."

25. Will Bolton, "Paris to Become '100 Per Cent Cycling City' Within Next Four Years."

26. Bike Union Staff, "Tell City Council: I Support the Boston Bike Budget."

MORE COMFORT

1. Jeremy S. Hoffman, "How Housing Density Can Help Keep Cities Cooler."
2. Ibid.
3. Jake Schmidt (@TheJakeSchmidt), Twitter, May 23, 2021.
4. Peter Wohlleben, *The Hidden Life of Trees: What They Feel, How They Communicate—Discoveries from a Secret World*, 105–106.
5. ReLeaf Cedar Rapids was completed in partnership with Confluence, Inc., in service to the City of Cedar Rapids and Trees Forever, a remarkable environmental nonprofit based in Iowa. The plan can be found by searching for ReLeaf Cedar Rapids or at the Town of Cedar Rapids' website.
6. "Trees Set Sixth-Graders Up for Success," Science Daily.
7. Ibid. And here's a second study: Sivajanani Sivarajah, Sandy M. Smith, and Sean C. Thomas, "Tree Cover and Species Composition Effects on Academic Performance of Primary School Students."
8. Jackie Flynn Mogensen, "The Surprising Science of Fighting Crime with . . . Trees."
9. Ibid.
10. Douglas W. Tallamy, *Nature's Best Hope: A New Approach to Conservation That Starts in Your Yard*, 82, 157, 158.
11. Ibid., 93, 100, 104.
12. Ibid., 82, 121–22.
13. Ibid., 93.
14. Wohlleben, *Hidden Life of Trees*, 3–4.
15. Frank Santamour Jr., "Trees for Urban Planting: Diversity, Uniformity, and Common Sense," 57.
16. Ibid., 57, 60.
17. This passage is adapted from Jeff Speck, *Walkable City Rules*.
18. Jake Offenhartz, "City to Spend $30,000 Apiece on Anti-Terror Bollards."
19. Linda Bilmes, "The Financial Legacy of Iraq and Afghanistan: How Wartime Spending Decisions Will Constrain Future National Security Budgets."
20. Offenhartz, "City to Spend $30,000."
21. Jessie Singer, *There Are No Accidents*, 194–96.
22. "How the Dutch Got Their Cycle Paths," BicycleDutch.

THE ROLE OF CITY PLANNING

1. Again, this is my writing and did not involve the APA or AICP in any way.

WORKS CITED

BOOKS

Alexander, Christopher. *A Pattern Language*. New York: Oxford University Press, 1977.

Arnold, Henry F. *Trees in Urban Design*, 2nd ed. New York: John Wiley, 1992.

Brand, Stewart. *Whole Earth Discipline: Why Denser Cities, Nuclear Power, Transgenic Crops, Restored Wetlands and Geoengineering Are Necessary*. New York: Penguin, 2009.

Bruntlett, Melissa, and Chris Bruntlett. *Building the Cycling City: The Dutch Blueprint for Urban Vitality*. Washington, D.C.: Island Press, 2018.

Buettner, Dan. *The Blue Zones: Lessons for Living Longer from the People Who've Lived the Longest*. Washington, D.C.: National Geographic, 2008.

———. *Thrive: Finding Happiness the Blue Zones Way*. Washington, D.C.: National Geographic, 2010.

Byrne, David. *Bicycle Diaries*. New York: Viking, 2009.

Campanella, Thomas J. *Republic of Shade: New England and the American Elm*. New Haven: Yale University Press, 2003.

Derecho 8/10/20. Cedar Rapids, IA: *The Gazette*, 2020.

Designing Walkable Urban Thoroughfares: A Context-Sensitive Approach: An ITE Recommended Practice. Institute of Transportation Engineers and Congress for the New Urbanism, Washington, D.C., 2010.

Duany, Andres, Elizabeth Plater-Zyberk, and Jeff Speck. *Suburban Nation: The Rise of Sprawl and the Decline of the American Dream*. New York: North Point Press, 2000.

Duany, Andres, and Jeff Speck. *The Smart Growth Manual*. New York: McGraw-Hill, 2010.

Forester, John. *Bicycle Transportation*, 2nd ed. Cambridge, Mass.: MIT Press, 1994.

Frumkin, Howard, Lawrence Frank, and Richard Jackson. *Urban Sprawl and Public Health: Designing, Planning, and Building for Healthy Communities*. Washington, D.C.: Island Press, 2004.

Gehl, Jan. *Cities for People*. Washington, D.C.: Island Press, 2010.

Hart, Stanley I., and Alvin L. Spivak. *The Elephant in the Bedroom: Automobile Dependence and Denial: Impacts on the Economy and Environment*. Pasadena, Calif.: New Paradigm Books, 1993.

Higham, Charles. *Trading with the Enemy: An Exposé of the Nazi-American Money Plot, 1933–1949*. New York: Delacorte Press, 1983.

Hurst, Robert. *The Cyclist's Manifesto: The Case for Riding on Two Wheels Instead of Four*. Helena, Mont.: Globe Pequot Press, 2009.

Illich, Ivan. *Toward a History of Needs*. New York: Pantheon, 1977. First published in 1973.

Isaacson, Walter. *The Code Breaker: Jennifer Doudna, Gene Editing, and the Future of the Human Race*. New York: Simon & Schuster, 2021.

Jacobs, Alan. *The Boulevard Book*. Cambridge, Mass.: MIT Press, 2002.

———. *Great Streets*. Cambridge, Mass.: MIT Press, 1993.

Jacobs, Jane. *Dark Age Ahead*. New York: Random House, 2004.

———. *The Death and Life of Great American Cities*. New York: Vintage, 1961.

Koolhaas, Rem, Hans Werlemann, and Bruce Mau. *S,M,L,XL*. New York: Monacelli Press, 1994.

Krier, Léon. *The Architecture of Community*. Washington, D.C.: Island Press, 2009.

Leinberger, Christopher B. *The Option of Urbanism: Investing in a New American Dream*. Washington, D.C.: Island Press, 2009.

Lévy, Bernard-Henri. *American Vertigo: On the Road from Newport to Guantanamo*. London: Gibson Square, 2006.

Lutz, Catherine, and Anne Lutz Fernandez. *Carjacked: The Culture of the Automobile and Its Effect on Our Lives*. New York: Palgrave Macmillan, 2010.

Mapes, Jeff. *Pedaling Revolution: How Cyclists Are Changing American Cities*. Corvallis: Oregon State University Press, 2009.

Marohn, Charles L., Jr. *Confessions of a Recovering Engineer: Transportation for a Strong Town*. Hoboken, NJ: Wiley, 2021.

Newman, Peter, Timothy Beatley, and Heather Boyer. *Resilient Cities: Responding to Peak Oil and Climate Change*. Washington, D.C.: Island Press, 2009.

Nordahl, Darrin. *My Kind of Transit: Rethinking Public Transportation in America*. Chicago: The Center for American Places, 2008.

Norton, Peter. *Autonorama: The Illusory Promise of High-Tech Driving*. Washington, D.C.: Island Press, 2021.

Owen, David. *Green Metropolis: Why Living Smaller, Living Closer, and Driving Less Are the Keys to Sustainability*. New York: Penguin, 2009.

Postman, Neil. *Technopoly: The Surrender of Culture to Technology*. New York: Knopf, 1992.

Rothstein, Richard. *The Color of Law: A Forgotten History of How Our Government Segregated America*. New York: Liveright, 2018.

Rybczynski, Witold. *City Life: Urban Expectations in a New World*. New York: Scribner, 1995.

———. *Makeshift Metropolis: Ideas About Cities*. New York: Scribner, 2010.

Schmitt, Angie. *Right of Way: Race, Class, and the Silent Epidemic of Pedestrian Deaths in America*. Washington, D.C.: Island Press, 2020.

Seiler, Cotton. *Republic of Drivers: A Cultural History of Automobility in America*. Chicago: University of Chicago Press, 2008.

Shoup, Donald. *The High Cost of Free Parking*. Chicago: Planners Press, 2004.

Siegel, Charles. *Unplanning: Livable Cities and Political Choices*. Berkeley, Calif.: The Preservation Institute, 2010.

Singer, Jessie. *There Are No Accidents*. New York: Simon & Schuster, 2022.

Speck, Jeff. *Walkable City Rules: 101 Steps to Making Better Places*. Washington, D.C.: Island Press, 2018.

Tallamy, Douglas W. *Nature's Best Hope: A New Approach to Conservation That Starts in Your Yard*. Portland, OR: Timber Press, 2019.

Tamminen, Terry. *Lives per Gallon: The True Cost of Our Oil Addiction*. Washington, D.C.: Island Press, 2006.

Vanderbilt, Tom. *Traffic: Why We Drive the Way We Do (and What It Says About Us)*. New York: Knopf, 2008.

Walker, Jarrett. *Human Transit: How Clearer Thinking About Public Transit Can Enrich Our Communities and Our Lives*. Washington, D.C.: Island Press, 2012.

Wasik, John F. *The Cul-de-Sac Syndrome: Turning Around the Unsustainable American Dream*. New York: Bloomberg Press, 2009.

Whyte, William. *City: Rediscovering the Center*. New York: Doubleday, 1988.

Wohlleben, Peter. *The Hidden Life of Trees: What They Feel, How They Communicate—Discoveries from a Secret World*. Vancouver, BC: Greystone Books, 2016.

ARTICLES AND REPORTS

AAA. "Your Driving Costs," 2010. aaa.com.

Adamczyk, Alicia. "Millennials Are Fleeing Big Cities for the Suburbs." CNBC, September 29, 2019. cnbc.com/2019/09/29/millennials-are-fleeing-big-cities-for-the-suburbs.html.

Adams, Thomas, and Rachel Aldred. "Cycling Injury Risk in London: Impacts of Road Characteristics and Infrastructure." *Findings* (December 15, 2020). https://findingspress.org/article/18226-cycling-injury-risk-in-london-impacts-of-road-characteristics-and-infrastructure.

Alter, Lloyd. "E-Bikers Ride Much Farther and More Frequently Than Regular Bikers." *Treehugger*, August 31, 2020. treehugger.com/e-bikers-ride-much-farther-and-more-frequently-than-regula-bikers-5076231.

American Association of State Highway and Transportation Officials. 2006–2010 U.S. Census Transportation Planning Products.

American Lung Association. "State of the Air 2011 City Rankings." stateoftheair.org/2011/city-rankings.

American Public Transportation Association. "Transit Ridership Report, 1st Quarter 2011."

"America's Top-50 Bike Friendly Cities." bicycling.com, undated.

Anderer, John. "Surprising Study: Urban Density Doesn't Cause More COVID-19 Infections, Even Promotes Lower Death Rates." Study Finds, June 26, 2020. studyfinds.org/surprising-study-urban-density-doesnt-cause-more-covid-19-infections-even-promotes-lower-death-rates/.

Anderson, Jason C., Christopher Monsere, and Sirisha Kothuri. "Effect of Residential Street Speed Limit Reduction on Driving Speeds in Portland, Oregon." *Findings* (January 2022). https://findingspress.org/article/31956-effect-of-residential-street-speed-limit-reduction-on-driving-speeds-in-portland-oregon.

Asthma and Allergy Foundation of America. "Cost of Asthma." aafa.org, undated.

Barker, Kim, Steve Eder, David D. Kirkpatrick, and Arya Sundaram. "How Police Justify Killing Drivers: The Vehicle Was a Weapon." *The New York Times*, November 6, 2021. nytimes.com/2021/11/06/us/police-traffic-stops-shooting.html.

Baumgaertner, Emily, and Russ Mitchell. "Car Crash Deaths Have Surged During COVID-19 Pandemic. Here's Why." *Los Angeles Times*, December 8, 2021. latimes.com/world-nation/story/2021-12-08/traffic-deaths-surged-during-covid-19-pandemic-heres-why.

Becher, Jonathan. "The Curse of the Cul-de-Sac." *Forbes*, April 9, 2012. forbes.com/sites/sap/2012/04/09/the-curse-of-the-cul-de-sac/.

Beedham, Matthew. "Oh, Great—Uber and Lyft Are Actually Increasing Car Ownership in U.S. Cities." *The Next Web*, January 13, 2021. https://thenextweb.com/news/oh-great-uber-and-lyft-are-actually-increasing-car-ownership-in-us-cities.

Belden Russonello & Stewart Research and Communications. 2004 National Community Preference Survey, November 2004.

———. "What Americans Are Looking for When Deciding Where to Live." 2011 Community Preference Survey, March 2011.

Benfield, Kaid. "EPA Region 7: We Were Just Kidding About That Sustainability Stuff." sustainablecitiescollective.com, April 18, 2011.

Bernstein, Andrea. "NYC Biking Is Up 14% from 2010; Overall Support Rises." transportationnation.org, July 28, 2011.

Berreby, David. "Engineering Terror." *The New York Times*, September 10, 2010.

Betz, Eric. "The First Nationwide Count of Parking Spaces Demonstrates Their Environmental Cost." *The Knoxville News Sentinel*, December 1, 2010.

"Bikeshare and E-Scooter Systems in the U.S." U.S. Department of Transportation, Bureau of Transportation Statistics, February 15, 2022. https://data.bts.gov/stories/s/Bikeshare-and-e-scooters-in-the-U-S-/fwcs-jprj/.

Bike Union Staff. "Tell City Council: I Support the Boston Bike Budget." Boston Cyclists Union, April 30, 2020. https://bostoncyclistsunion.org/tell-city-council-i-support-the-boston-bike-budget.

Bilmes, Linda. "The Financial Legacy of Iraq and Afghanistan: How Wartime Spending Decisions Will Constrain Future National Security Budgets." Harvard Kennedy School Faculty Research Working Paper Series, RWP13-006, March 2013. https://research.hks.harvard.edu/publications/workingpapers/citation.aspx?PubId=8956&type=WPN.

Binkovitz, Leah. "Houston's Air Quality Is Improving, but Asthma Disparities Persist." Kinder Institute for Urban Research, Rice University, January 24, 2017. https://kinder.rice.edu/2017/01/24/houstons-air-quality-is-improving-but-asthma-disparities-persist.

Bliss, Laura. "How Seattle Is Winning the War on the Car Commute." *Bloomberg*, February 16, 2018. bloomberg.com/news/articles/2018-02-16/seattle-s-slashes-its-downtown-driving-rate.

———. "Why Seattle Is America's Bus-Lovingest Town." *Bloomberg*, May 11, 2018. bloomberg.com/news/articles/2018-05-11/seattle-has-a-4-step-plan-to-building-bus-ridership.

Bolton, Will. "Paris to Become '100 Per Cent Cycling City' Within Next Four Years." Road.cc, October 24, 2021. https://road.cc/content/news/paris-become-100-cent-cycling-city-next-four-years-287285.

"Boston-Area Voters Support Changes to Local Streets Even If It Means Less Space for Cars." Mass Inc. Polling Group, June 10, 2021. massincpolling.com/the-topline/boston-area-voters-support-changes-to-local-streets-even-if-it-means-less-space-for-cars.

Branyan, George. "What Is an LPI? A Head Start for Pedestrians." ddotdish.com, December 1, 2010.

Brooks, David. "The Splendor of Cities." Review of *Triumph of the City* by Edward L. Glaeser (New York: Penguin, 2011). *The New York Times*, February 7, 2011.

Brown, Lawrence T. "We Can't Walk If We Can't Breathe: The Imperative for

Racial Equity." America Walks, October 13, 2020. https://americawalks
.org/we-cant-walk-if-we-cant-breathe-the-imperative-for-racial-equity/.

Brunick, Nicholas. "The Impact of Inclusionary Zoning on Development."
Report of Business and Professional People for the Public Interest,
bpichicago.org, 2004, 4.

Bruntlett, Chris, and Melissa Bruntlett. "Surprise: Bike-Friendly Netherlands
Named Best Place in the World to Be a Driver." *Daily Hive*, September 19, 2016. https://dailyhive.com/vancouver/best-place-in-the-world-to
-be-a-driver-netherlands.

Bryan, Susannah. "So Elon Musk Wants to Build a Tunnel to the Beach. And
That May Just Be the Beginning." *Sun Sentinel*, October 31, 2021. sun
-sentinel.com/local/broward/fort-lauderdale/fl-ne-tunnel-beach-fort-lau
derdale-details-20211031-5gcg7miffbgttkp3wcdnnyek5u-story.html.

"Building the Neighborhood of the Future." *Eller*, Spring 2021. https://eller
.arizona.edu/sites/default/files/Eller%20Magazine%20Spring%20
2021%20WEB_0.pdf, 23.

Buiso, Gary. "Marty's Lane Pain Is Fodder for His Christmas Card." *The
Brooklyn Paper*, December 12, 2010.

———. "Safety First! Prospect Park West Bike Lane Working." *The Brooklyn
Paper*, January 20, 2011.

Burden, Dan. "22 Benefits of Urban Street Trees." ufei.org/files/pubs
/22benefitsofurbanstreettrees.pdf, May 2006.

Burden, Dan, and Peter Lagerwey. "Road Diets: Fixing the Big Roads." Walkable Communities Inc., 1999. walkable.org/assets/downloads/roaddiets
.pdf.

Burke, Mia. "Joyride: Pedaling Toward a Healthier Planet." planetizen.com,
February 28, 2011.

Byrne, Thomas, Dan Treglia, Dennis P. Culhane, John Kuhn, and Vincent
Kane. "Predictors of Homelessness Among Families and Single Adults
After Exit from Homelessness Prevention and Rapid Re-Housing Pro-
grams: Evidence from the Department of Veterans Affairs Supportive
Services for Veterans Program." *Housing Policy Debate*, 2015.

"Call for Narrower Streets Rejected by Fire Code Officials." New Urban
News. bettercities.net, December 1, 2009.

Castro, Alberto, et al. "Physical Activity of Electric Bicycle Users Compared
to Conventional Bicycle Users and Non-Cyclists: Insights Based on
Health and Transport Data from an Online Survey in Seven European
Cities." *Transportation Research Interdisciplinary Perspectives* 1 (June
2019). sciencedirect.com/science/article/pii/S259019821930017X.

Chen, Donald. "If You Build It, They Will Come . . . Why We Can't Build Ourselves Out of Congestion." *Surface Transportation Policy Project Progress* VII: 2 (March 1998): 1, 4.

Chen, Ted, and Katherine Hafner. "Commute Times Increase One Minute

After Freeway Widening Project." NBCLA, October 8, 2014. nbclos
angeles.com/news/added-405-carpool-lane-was-it-worth-the-delays
/63017/.

Children's Safety Network. "Promoting Bicycle Safety for Children," 2.
childrenssafetynetwork.org, 2011.

Christian, Jon. "Scientists: Pedestrians Could Wear Devices to Protect Themselves from Self-Driving Cars." The Byte, March 8, 2021. https://futurism
.com/the-byte/devices-protect-self-driving-cars.

Chu, Jennifer. "Study: Air Pollution Causes 200,000 Early Deaths Each Year in
the U.S." MIT News, August 29, 2013. https://news.mit.edu/2013/study-air
-pollution-causes-200000-early-deaths-each-year-in-the-us-0829.

"City Reinstalls Downtown Stop Signs to Reduce Traffic Pileup, Speeding."
KRQE 13 News, August 14, 2018. krqe.com/news/city-reinstalls-down
town-stop-signs-to-reduce-congestion-speeding/.

Clendaniel, Morgan. "Zipcar's Impact on How People Use Cars Is Enormous." fastcompany.com, July 19, 2011.

Clewlow, Regina R., and Gouri Shankar Mishra. "Disruptive Transportation:
The Adoption, Utilization, and Impacts of Ride-Hailing in the United
States." Institute of Transportation Studies, University of California,
Davis (October 2017). https://usa.streetsblog.org/wp-content/uploads
/sites/5/2017/10/2017_UCD-ITS-RR-17-07.pdf.

Coder, Rim D. "Identified Benefits of Community Trees and Forests." University of Georgia study, October 1996. warnell.forestry.uga.edu/service
/library/for96=039/for96=039.pdf.

Colleran, Jim. "The Worst Streets in America." planetizen.com, March 21, 2001.

Condon, Patrick. "Canadian Cities American Cities: Our Differences Are
the Same." Smart Growth on the Ground Initiative, University of British Columbia, February 2004. jtc.sala.ubc.ca/newsroom/patrick_condon
_primer.pdf.

"The Congestion Con." Transportation for America, March 2020. https://
t4america.org/wp-content/uploads/2020/03/Congestion-Report-2020
-FINAL.pdf.

Cooper, Ryan. "The Case Against American Truck Bloat." The Week, August 14, 2020. https://theweek.com/articles/929196/case-against-american
-truck-bloat.

Cortright, Joe. "Carmaggedon Does a No-Show in Seattle, Again." City Observatory, December 11, 2019. https://cityobservatory.org/seattle_carmag
gedon-noshow/.

———. "Driven Apart: Why Sprawl, Not Insufficient Roads, Is the Real
Cause of Traffic Congestion." CEOs for Cities White Paper, September 29,
2010.

———. "Portland's Green Dividend." CEOs for Cities White Paper, July
2007.

————. "Walking the Walk: How Walkability Raises Home Values in U.S. Cities." CEOs for Cities White Paper, August 2009.

————. "Why Carmaggedon Never Comes (Seattle Edition)." City Observatory, January 16, 2019. https://cityobservatory.org/seattle_carmaggedon/.

Cortright, Joe, and Carol Coletta. "The Young and the Restless: How Portland Competes for Talent." Portland, Ore: Impresa, Inc., 2004.

Coulon, Jessica. "Bike Lanes Can Benefit Local Businesses (!), According to This Study." *Bicycling*, April 28, 2020. bicycling.com/news/a32306169 /bike-lanes-benefit-local-businesses-study/.

Cox, Wendell. "DART's Billion Dollar Boondoggle." *Dallas Business Journal*, June 16, 2002.

Cuba, Julianne. "Harvard Study: Car Pollution in NYC Claims 1,400 Lives, Billions in Costs." Streetsblog, June 8, 2021. https://nyc.streetsblog.org /2021/06/08/harvard-study-car-pollution-in-nyc-claims-1400-lives-billions -in-costs/.

"Culdesac Tempe: A Car-Free Neighborhood." Opticos. https://opticosdesign .com/work/culdesac-tempe/.

Davies, Zoe G., et al. "Mapping an Urban Ecosystem Service: Quantifying Above-Ground Carbon Storage at a City-Wide Scale." *Journal of Applied Ecology* 48 (2011): 1125–34.

D.C. Surface Transit. "Value Capture and Tax-Increment Financing Options for Streetcar Construction." Report commissioned by D.C. Surface Transit from the Brookings Institution, HDR, Re-Connecting America, and RCLCO, June 2009.

Deadwyler, Nedra. "Whose Bike Lanes? A Review of *Bike Lanes Are White Lanes*." *Atlanta Studies*, September 3, 2019. atlantastudies.org/2019/09 /03/nedra-deadwyler-whose-bike-lanes-a-review-of-bike-lanes-are-white -lanes/.

DeBonis, Mike. "How a Downtown Bike Lane Has Become a Political Headache." *The Washington Post*, August 15, 2013. washingtonpost.com/blogs /mike-debonis/wp/2013/08/15/how-a-downtown-bike-lane-has-become -a-political-headache/.

DeBrabander, Firmin. "What If Green Products Make Us Pollute More?" *The Baltimore Sun*, June 2, 2011.

DeGood, Kevin. "Why an All-of-the-Above Transportation Strategy Doesn't Work." Center for American Progress, November 13, 2019. american progress.org/issues/economy/reports/2019/11/13/477004/transportation -strategy-doesnt-work/.

Devlin, Hannah. "Palm Scent: The Science of Smelling After a Handshake." *The Guardian*, March 3, 2015. theguardian.com/science/2015/mar/03 /palm-scent-the-science-of-smelling-after-a-handshake.

Diao, Mi, Hui Kong, and Jinhua Zhao. "Impacts of Transportation Network Companies on Urban Mobility." *Nature Sustainability* 4 (June 2021). nature.com/articles/s41893-020-00678-z.pdf.

Dillon, Liam, and Ben Poston. "Freeways Force out Residents in Communities of Color—Again." *Los Angeles Times*, November 11, 2021. latimes.com/projects/us-freeway-highway-expansion-black-latino-communities/.

District Department of Transportation, Washington, D.C. "Capital Bikeshare Expansion Planned in the New Year," December 23, 2010.

Doherty, Patrick C., and Christopher B. Leinberger. "The Next Real Estate Boom." *The Washington Monthly*, November/December 2010.

Doig, Will. "Are Freeways Doomed?" salon.com, December 1, 2011.

Dolven, Taylor. "Boston's 28 Bus Will Remain Free for an Extra Month After Coming in Under Budget." *The Boston Globe*, November 8, 2021. bostonglobe.com/2021/11/08/metro/bostons-28-bus-will-remain-free-an-extra-month-after-coming-under-budget/.

Donovan, Geoffrey, and David Butry. "Trees in the City: Valuing Trees in Portland, Oregon." *Landscape and Urban Planning* 94 (2010): 77–83.

Dorner, Josh. "NBC Confirms That 'Clean Coal' Is an Oxymoron." Huffington Post, November 18, 2008.

Dougherty, Conor. "Where the Suburbs End." *The New York Times*, October 8, 2021. nytimes.com/2021/10/08/business/economy/california-housing.html.

"Do You Need a License to Drive an Electric Bike?" Aventon, October 15, 2021. aventon.com/blogs/aventon_bikes/do-you-need-a-license-to-drive-an-electric-bike.

Duhigg, Charles. "Saving US Water and Sewer Systems Would Be Costly." *The New York Times*, March 14, 2010.

Dumbaugh, Eric. "Safe Streets, Livable Streets." *Journal of the American Planning Association* 71, no. 3 (2005): 283–300.

Duranton, Gilles, and Matthew Turner. "The Fundamental Law of Road Congestion: Evidence from U.S. Cities." *American Economic Review* 101 (2011): 2616–52.

Durning, Alan. "The Year of Living Car-lessly." daily.sightline.org, April 28, 2006.

Eckerson, Clarence, Jr. "The Phenomenal Success of Capital Bikeshare." streetfilms.org, August 2, 2011.

Ehrenhalt, Alan. "Jaywalking and the Dilemma of 'Victimless' Crimes." *Governing*, January 8, 2021. governing.com/assessments/jaywalking-and-the-dilemma-of-victimless-crimes.html.

———. "The Return of the Two-Way Street." governing.org, December 2009.

Elflein, John. "Obesity Prevalence Among U.S. Adults Aged 20 and Over 1997–2018." *Statista*, October 15, 2020. statista.com/statistics/244620/us-obesity-prevalence-among-adults-aged-20-and-over/.

El Nasser, Haya. "In Many Neighborhoods, Kids Are Only a Memory." *USA Today*, June 3, 2011.

Erlanger, Steven, and Maïa de la Baume. "French Ideal of Bicycle-Sharing Meets Reality." *The New York Times*, October 30, 2009.

Eversley, Melanie. "Many Cities Changing One-Way Streets Back." *USA Today*, December 20, 2006.

Ewing, Jack. "The City Where Cars Are Not Welcome," *The New York Times*, February 28, 2021, nytimes.com/2021/02/28/business/heidelberg-cars-environment.html.

Ewing, Reid, and Robert Cervero. "Travel and the Built Environment: A Meta-Analysis." *Journal of the American Planning Association* 76, no. 3 (2010): 11.

Ewing, Reid, and Eric Dumbaugh. "The Built Environment and Traffic Safety: A Review of Empirical Evidence." *Journal of Planning Literature* 23, no. 4 (2009): 347–67.

Fallows, James. "Fifty-Nine and a Half Minutes of Brilliance, Thirty Seconds of Hauteur." theatlantic.com, July 3, 2009.

Fanelli, James. "Lousy Management, Knucklehead Hires Plague Operations of Real-Life Sopranos." *The Wall Street Journal*, October 4, 2021. wsj.com/articles/lousy-management-knucklehead-hires-plague-operations-of-real-life-sopranos-11633360973.

Farmer, Molly. "South Jordan Mom Cited for Neglect for Allowing Child to Walk to School." *The Deseret News*, December 15, 2010.

Ferenchak, Nicholas N., and Wesley E. Marshall. "Bicycling Facility Inequalities and the Causality Dilemma with Socioeconomic/Sociodemographic Change." *Transportation Research Part D: Transport and Environment* 97 (August 2021). sciencedirect.com/science/article/abs/pii/S1361920921002194.

Fleming, Amy. "'It's a Superpower': How Walking Makes Us Healthier, Happier and Brainier." *The Guardian*, July 28, 2019. theguardian.com/lifeandstyle/2019/jul/28/its-a-superpower-how-walking-makes-us-healthier-happier-and-brainier.

Florida, Richard. "The Great Car Reset." theatlantic.com, June 3, 2010.

———. "Parking Has Eaten American Cities." *Bloomberg*, July 24, 2018. bloomberg.com/news/articles/2018-07-24/the-overparked-states-of-america.

Flynn Mogensen, Jackie. "The Surprising Science of Fighting Crime With . . . Trees." *Mother Jones*, May/June 2019. motherjones.com/environment/2019/04/trees-crime-cincinnati-philadelphia-ida-b-wells-chicago/.

Ford, Jane. "Danger in Exurbia: University of Virginia Study Reveals the Danger of Travel in Virginia." *University of Virginia News*, April 30, 2002.

Freemark, Yonah. "An Extensive New Addition to Dallas' Light Rail Makes It America's Longest." thetransportpolitic.com, December 5, 2010.

———. "The Interdependence of Land Use and Transportation." thetrans portpolitic.com, February 5, 2011.

———. "Transit Mode Share Trends Looking Steady." thetransportpolitic .com, October 13, 2010.

Freemark, Yonah, and Jebediah Reed. "Huh?! Four Cases of How Tearing Down a Highway Can Relieve Traffic Jams (and Save Your City)." infrastructurist.com, July 6, 2010.

Fremont, Calif., City of. "City Council Agenda and Report," May 3, 2011.

Fried, Ben. "What Backlash? Q Poll Finds 54 Percent of NYC Voters Support Bike Lanes." streetsblog.org, March 18, 2011.

Garrett-Peltier, Heidi. "Estimating the Employment Impacts of Pedestrian, Bicycle, and Road Infrastructure. Case Study: Baltimore." Political Economy Research Institute, University of Massachusetts, Amherst, December 2010.

Gavin, Christopher. "City Council Passes Mayor Wu's $8 Million Vision for 3, Fare-Free MBTA Bus Lines." Boston.com, December 2, 2021. boston .com/news/politics/2021/12/02/city-council-passes-mayor-wus-8-million -vision-for-3-fare-free-mbta-bus-lines/.

Gerstenang, James. "Cars Make Suburbs Riskier Than Cities, Study Says." *The Los Angeles Times*, April 15, 1996.

Gladwell, Malcolm. "Blowup." *The New Yorker*, January 22, 1996.

Glaeser, Edward. "If You Love Nature, Move to the City." *The Boston Globe*, February 10, 2011.

Goldbaum, Ellen. "Passenger Car Drivers Are More Likely to Die in Crashes with SUVs, Regardless of Crash Safety Ratings." University at Buffalo News Center, May 14, 2013. buffalo.edu/news/releases/2013/05/026.html.

Goodman, Christy. "Expanded Bike-Sharing Program to Link D.C., Arlington." *The Washington Post*, May 23, 2010.

Gordon, Rachel. "Parking: S.F. Releases Details on Flexible Pricing." sfgate .com, April 2, 2011.

Gorzelany, Jim. "Study Says SUVs Are More Deadly Than Cars When Striking Pedestrians." *Forbes*, June 17, 2020. forbes.com/sites/jimgorzelany /2020/06/17/study-says-suvs-are-more-deadly-striking-pedestrians-than -cars/?sh=2984e7331ebd.

Gotschi, Thomas, and Kevin Mills. "Active Transportation for America: The Case for Increased Federal Investment in Bicycling and Walking." railstotrails.org, October 20, 2008.

Grabar, Henry. "'They Can Just Take an Uber.'" *Slate*, December 14, 2016. slate.com/business/2016/12/cities-are-cutting-transportation-service -because-they-think-uber-will-fill-the-gap.html.

Gregory, Andrew. "Transport Noise Linked to Increased Risk of Dementia, Study Finds." *The Guardian*, September 9, 2021. theguardian.com/society

/2021/sep/09/transport-noise-linked-to-increased-risk-of-dementia-study -finds.

Gros, Daniel. "Coal vs. Oil: Pure Carbon vs. Hydrocarbon." achangeinthewind .com, December 28, 2007.

Groves, Martha. "He Put Parking in Its Place." *The Los Angeles Times*, October 16, 2010.

Grynbaum, Michael. "Deadliest for Walkers: Male Drivers, Left Turns." *The New York Times*, August 16, 2010.

Haddock, Mark. "Salt Lake Streets Have Seen Many Changes over Past 150 Years." *Deseret News*, July 13, 2009.

Hansen, Cypress. "Sounding the Alarm: How Noise Hurts the Heart." *Knowable Magazine*, February 12, 2021. https://knowablemagazine.org/article /health-disease/2021/how-noise-pollution-affects-heart-health.

Hansen, Mark, and Yuanlin Huang. "Road Supply and Traffic in California Urban Areas." *Transportation Research*, part A: *Policy and Practice* 31, No. 3 (1997): 205–18.

Heller, Nathan. "The Disconnect." *The New Yorker*, April 16, 2012.

Henao, Alejandro. "The Good, the Bad and the Unknown of Uber and Lyft." LinkedIn, May 9, 2019. linkedin.com/pulse/good-bad-unknown-uber -lyft-alejandro-henao-phd.

Ho, Karen K. "Only One of Harley-Davidson's Electric Bikes Would Qualify for a Proposed Tax Credit. Here Are 3 Ways the 118-Year-Old Company Has Committed to Sustainability—and Customer Satisfaction." *Business Insider*, December 8, 2021. businessinsider.com/premium-electric-bike -brand-serial-1-signals-an-industry-evolution-2021-12.

Hodkinson, Gregory. "Cities Alive: Towards a Walking World." Arup, June 2016. arup.com/perspectives/cities-alive-towards-a-walking-world.

Hoffman, Jeremy S. "How Housing Density Can Help Keep Cities Cooler." Greater Greater Washington, July 1, 2019. https://ggwash.org/view/72767 /housing-density-can-help-mitigate-the-impacts-of-climate-change.

Holman, Jordyn, and Lauren Coleman-Lochner. "Stores That Defined American Malls Eye a Freestanding Future." *Bloomberg*, March 21, 2021. bloomberg.com/news/articles/2021-03-21/stores-that-defined-american -malls-bet-on-a-freestanding-future.

Holtzclaw, John. "Using Residential Patterns and Transit to Decrease Auto Dependence and Costs." Natural Resources Defense Council, 1994. docs.nrdc.org/SmartGrowth/files/sma_09121401a.pdf.

"Housing First." National Alliance to End Homelessness. http://endhomeless ness.org/resource/housing-first/.

"Housing First." Wikipedia. https://en.wikipedia.org/wiki/Housing_First.

"How to Escape Bicycle Helmet Fines in Australia." Cyclists' Rights Action Group, January 6, 2017. https://crag.asn.au.

Huffington, Arianna. "Solution to Many a Problem: Take a Walk." *The Balti-*

more Sun, September 3, 2013. baltimoresun.com/opinion/bs-xpm-2013 -09-03-bal-solution-to-many-a-problem-take-a-walk-20130830-story .html.

Hunter, Scottie. "Blind Zones on Cars Pose Hidden Danger for Kids." KSLA News 12, January 4, 2021. ksla.com/2021/01/04/investigators-blind-zones -cars-pose-hidden-danger-kids/.

Hutchinson, Alex. "Does Owning a Car Hurt Your Health?" *The Globe and Mail*, February 17, 2020. theglobeandmail.com/life/health-and-fitness /article-does-owning-a-car-hurt-your-health/.

Jackson, Richard. "We Are No Longer Creating Wellbeing." dirt.asla.org, September 12, 2010.

Jahne, Mark. "Local Officials Find Fault with Proposed Hartford–New Britain Busway." mywesthartfordlife.com, January 18, 2010.

J. D. Power and Associates. Press release, October 8, 2009.

Johnson, Kevin, Judy Keen, and William M. Welch. "Homicides Fall in Large American Cities." *USA Today*, December 29, 2010.

Kamin, Blair. "Ohio Cap at Forefront of Urban Design Trend." *The Chicago Tribune*, October 27, 2011.

Karush, Sarah. "Cities Rethink Wisdom of 50s-Era Parking Standards." *USA Today*, September 20, 2008.

Katakis, Manoli. "2020 GMC Sierra HD Design: The Origin Story." Muscle Cars & Trucks, September 4, 2019. musclecarsandtrucks.com/2020-gmc -sierra-hd-design-the-origin-story/.

Kazis, Noah. "East River Plaza Parking Still Really, Really Empty, New Research Shows." streetsblog.org, April 20, 2012.

———. "New PPW Results: More New Yorkers Use It, Without Clogging the Street." streetsblog.org, December 8, 2010.

———. "NYCHA Chairman: Parking Minimums 'Working Against Us.'" streetsblog.org, October 17, 2011.

Keates, Nancy. "A Walker's Guide to Home Buying." *The Wall Street Journal*, July 2, 2010.

Keegan, Matthew. "Why Cities Are Not as Bad for You as You Think." BBC Future, December 1, 2020. bbc.com/future/article/20201201-the-surpris ing-upsides-to-living-in-cities.

Keen, Judy. "Seattle's Backyard Cottages Make a Dent in Housing Need." usatoday.com, May 26, 2010.

Kendall, Marisa. "Gov. Newsom Abolishes Most Single-Family Zoning in California." *The Mercury News*, September 16, 2021. mercurynews .com/2021/09/16/gov-newsom-abolishes-single-family-zoning-in-cali fornia/.

Kent, Ethan. "Guggenheim Museum Bilbao." Project for Public Spaces Hall of Shame, pps.org.

Kim, Noah Y. "A Test of White Support for Black Lives." *The Boston Globe*,

August 21, 2020. https://edition.pagesuite.com/popovers/dynamic_article_popover.aspx?artguid=0eb3f70e-df77-4d63-8089-116a09340b12.

Kirkpatrick, David D., Steve Eder, Kim Barker, and Julie Tate. "Why Many Police Traffic Stops Turn Deadly." *The New York Times*, October 31, 2021. nytimes.com/2021/10/31/us/police-traffic-stops-killings.html.

Klotz, Deborah. "Air Pollution and Its Effects on Heart Attack Risk." *The Boston Globe*, February 28, 2011.

Koch, Wendy. "Cities Roll Out Bike-Sharing Programs." *USA Today*, May 9, 2011.

Koeppen, Susan. "Increasing Number of Children Killed in 'Frontover' Accidents." KidsAndCars.org, May 8, 2017. kidsandcars.org/2017/06/05/increasing-number-of-children-killed-in-frontover-accidents/.

Kolbert, Elizabeth. "XXXL: Why Are We So Fat?" *The New Yorker*, July 20, 2009.

Kolozsvari, Douglas, and Donald Shoup. "Turning Small Change into Big Changes." *Access*, no. 23 (2003). shoup.bol.ucla.edu/SmallChange.pdf.

Kooshian, Chuck, and Steve Winkelman. "Growing Wealthier: Smart Growth, Climate Change and Prosperity." Washington, D.C.: Center for Clean Air Policy, January 2011.

Kruse, Jill. "Remove It and They Will Disappear: Why Building New Roads Isn't Always the Answer." *Surface Transportation Policy Project Progress* VII: 2 (March 1998): 5, 7.

Kuang, Cliff. "Infographic of the Day: How Bikes Can Solve Our Biggest Problems." Co.Design, 2011. fastcodesign.com/1665634/infographic-of-the-day-how-bikes-can-solve-our-biggest-problems.

Kurzius, Rachel. "Poll: 46 Percent of Trump Voters Believe 'Pizzagate' Theory." DCist, December 28, 2016. https://dcist.com/story/16/12/28/poll/.

Lambert, Fred. "Tesla Is Making 12 Passenger Electric Van for Boring Company, Says Official." Electrek, June 5, 2020. https://electrek.co/2020/06/05/tesla-electric-van-boring-company-12-passengers-official/.

————."A Tesla Electric Van Is Coming as Soon as There Are Batteries for It." Electrek, January 29, 2021. https://electrek.co/2021/01/29/tesla-electric-van-coming-batteries/.

Lambert, Lane. "Commuting Hurts Productivity and Your Best Talent Suffers Most," Harvard Business School Working Knowledge, March 30, 2021. https://hbswk.hbs.edu/item/commuting-kills-productivity-and-your-best-talent-suffers-most.

Langdon, Philip. "Parking: A Poison Posing as a Cure." *New Urban News*, April/May 2005.

————. "Young People Learning They Don't Need to Own a Car." *New Urban News*, December 2009.

Larimer, Mary E., et al. "Health Care and Public Service Use and Costs Before and After Provision of Housing for Chronically Homeless Persons with Severe Alcohol Problems." *JAMA* 301, no. 13 (April 1, 2009): 1349–57.

"Latest Data." City of Chicago COVID-19 site. chicago.gov/city/en/sites/covid -19/home/latest-data.html.

Lehrer, Jonah. "A Physicist Solves the City." *The New York Times Magazine*, December 17, 2010.

Leinberger, Christopher B. "Federal Restructuring of Fannie and Freddie Ignores Underlying Cause of Crisis." *Urban Land*, February 1, 2011.

———. "Here Comes the Neighborhood." *The Atlantic Monthly*, June 2010.

———. "The Next Slum." *Atlantic Monthly*, March 2008.

———. "Now Coveted: A Walkable, Convenient Place." *The New York Times*, May 25, 2012.

Le Petit, Yoann. "Uber and Lyft Increase Pollution and Undermine Public Transport, Study Shows." Transport & Environment, September 2, 2019. transportenvironment.org/discover/uber-and-lyft-increase-pollution-and -undermine-public-transport-study-shows/.

Levey, Bob, and Jane Freundel-Levey. "End of the Roads." *The Washington Post*, November 26, 2000.

Lipman, Barbara J. "A Heavy Load: The Combined Housing and Transportation Costs of Working Families." Center for Housing Policy, October 2006. https://community-wealth.org/sites/clone.community-wealth.org/files /downloads/article-lipman.pdf.

Litman, Todd. "Economic Value of Walkability." Victoria Transport Policy Institute, May 21, 2010.

———. "Rail in America: A Comprehensive Evaluation of Benefits." Victoria Transport Policy Institute, December 7, 2010.

———. "Raise My Taxes, Please! Evaluating Household Savings from High-Quality Public Transit Service." Victoria Transport Policy Institute, February 26, 2010.

———. "Smart Congestion Reductions: Reevaluating the Role of Highway Expansion for Improving Urban Transportation." Victoria Transport Policy Institute, February 2, 2010.

———. "Terrorism, Transit, and Public Safety: Evaluating the Risks." Victoria Transport Policy Institute, December 2, 2005.

———. "Whose Roads? Defining Bicyclists' and Pedestrians' Right to Use Public Roadways." Victoria Transport Policy Institute, November 30, 2004.

"Living Near Highways and Air Pollution." American Lung Association, last updated January 5, 2021. lung.org/our-initiatives/healthy-air/outdoor/air -pollution/highways.html.

Lord, Hayes A. "Cycle Tracks: Concept and Design Practices." The New York City Experience. New York City Department of Transportation, February 17, 2010.

LSC Transportation Consultants. "San Miguel County Local Transit and Human Service Transportation Plan. Colorado Springs, 2008."

Lyall, Sarah. "A Path to Road Safety with No Signposts." *The New York Times*, January 22, 2005.

Mallon, Ryan. "Milan Confirms Ambitious New Cycling Network Linking 80% of the City to Bike Paths." Road.cc, January 8, 2022. https://road.cc/content/news/milan-confirms-new-bike-network-289375.

Manjoo, Farhad. "Help. I've Fallen for That Cadillac Escalade." *The New York Times*, February 4, 2022. nytimes.com/2022/02/04/opinion/self-driving-car-escalade.html.

———. "There's One Big Problem with Electric Cars." *The New York Times*, February 18, 2021. nytimes.com/2021/02/18/opinion/electric-cars-SUV.html.

Marohn, Charles. "Confessions of a Recovering Engineer." Strong Towns, November 22, 2010. strongtowns.org/journal/2010/11/22/confessions-of-a-recovering-engineer.html.

Marsh, Bill. "Kilowatts vs. Gallons." *The New York Times,* May 28, 2011.

Marshall, Wesley, and Norman Garrick. "Street Network Types and Road Safety: A Study of 24 California Cities." *Urban Design International*, August 2009.

Marshall, Wesley E., and Nicholas N. Ferenchak. "Why Cities with High Bicycling Rates Are Safer for All Road Users." *Journal of Transport & Health* 13 (June 2019). sciencedirect.com/science/article/abs/pii/S2214140518301488?via%3Dihub.

"Marshall Fire." Wikipedia. https://en.wikipedia.org/wiki/Marshall_Fire.

Martinez, Jose. "MTA to Get Slim Slice of Federal Infrastructure Bill as Cars Outpace Mass Transit." *The City*, August 15, 2021. thecity.nyc/transportation/2021/8/15/22625350/mta-gets-slim-slice-of-federal-infrastructure-bill-finds.

Mayer, Jane. "The Secret Sharer." *The New Yorker*, May 23, 2011.

McNichol, Tom. "Roads Gone Wild." *Wired*, December 12, 2004.

Mehaffy, Michael. "The Urban Dimensions of Climate Change." planetizen.com, November 30, 2009.

Melo, Frederick. "St. Paul Eliminates Parking Minimums." *Pioneer Press*, August 18, 2021. twincities.com/2021/08/18/st-paul-eliminates-parking-minimums/.

Meyer, Jeremy P. "Denver to Eliminate Diagonal Crossings at Intersections." denverpost.com, April 6, 2011.

Miller, Jon R., M. Henry Robison, and Michael L. Lahr. "Estimating Important Transportation-Related Regional Economic Relationships in Bexar County, Texas." VIA Metropolitan Transit, 1999. vtpi.org/modeshift.pdf.

MilNeil, Christian. "Boston Establishes New Limits on Parking in Large Developments." Streetsblog, October 13, 2021. https://mass.streetsblog.org/2021/10/13/boston-establishes-maximum-parking-rules-for-large-developments/.

———. "New State Rule Would Force Suburbs to Legalize Thousands of New Apartments Near T Stops." Streetsblog, January 13, 2022. https://mass.streetsblog.org/2022/01/13/new-state-rule-would-force-suburbs-to-legalize-thousands-of-new-apartments-near-t-stops/.

Mims, Christopher. "Self-Driving Cars Could Be Decades Away, No Matter What Elon Musk Said." *The Wall Street Journal*, June 5, 2021. wsj.com/articles/self-driving-cars-could-be-decades-away-no-matter-what-elon-musk-said-11622865615.

Monroe, Doug. "Taking Back the Streets." *Atlanta* magazine, February 2003, 85–95.

———. "The Stress Factor." *Atlanta* magazine, February 2003.

Morello, Carol, Dan Keating, and Steve Hendrix. "Census: Young Adults Are Responsible for Most of D.C.'s Growth in Past Decade." *The Washington Post*, May 5, 2011.

Morris, Chris. "Home Sales in the Suburbs Are Red Hot Right Now!" *Fortune*, November 23, 2021. https://fortune.com/2021/11/23/home-sales-suburbs-are-red-hot/.

"Mortality Analyses." Coronavirus Resource Center at Johns Hopkins University. https://coronavirus.jhu.edu/data/mortality.

Nairn, Daniel. "New Census Numbers Confirm the Resurgence of Cities." discoveringurbanism.blogspot.com, December 15, 2010.

National Highway Traffic Safety Administration. "Newly Released Estimates Show Traffic Fatalities Reached a 16-Year High in 2021," May 17, 2022. nhtsa.gov/press-releases/early-estimate-2021-traffic-fatalities.

NCHRP Report 500, "Volume 10: A Guide for Reducing Collisions Involving Pedestrians." NCHRP, 2004.

Neff, Jack. "Is Digital Revolution Driving Decline in U.S. Car Culture?" *Advertising Age*, May 31, 2010.

Neilson, Susie. "This Is How Much Single-Family Zoning Is Costing San Franciscans." *San Francisco Chronicle*, July 18, 2021. sfchronicle.com/sf/article/This-is-how-much-single-family-zoning-is-costing-16305216.php.

Newcomb, Tim. "Need Extra Income? Put a Cottage in Your Backyard." time.com, May 28, 2011.

Newman, Rick. "It's Time to Notice Tesla's Autopilot Death Toll." Yahoo! News, April 19, 2021. https://news.yahoo.com/its-time-to-notice-teslas-autopilot-death-toll-195849408.html.

Newton, Damien. "Only in LA: DOT Wants to Remove Crosswalks to Protect Pedestrians." la.streetsblog.org, January 23, 2009.

New Urban Network. "Study: Transit Outperforms Green Buildings." bettercities.net/article/study-transit-outperforms-green-buildings-14203, undated.

Noland, Robert. "Traffic Fatalities and Injuries: The Effect of Changes in Infrastructure and Other Trends." Center for Transport Studies, London, 2002.

Noonan, Erica. "A Matter of Size." *The Boston Globe*, March 7, 2010.

Nunes, Ashley, Laurena Huh, Nicole Kagan, and Richard B. Freeman. "Estimating the Energy Impact of Electric, Autonomous Taxis: Evidence from a Select Market." *Environmental Research Letters* 16, no. 9 (2021). https://iopscience.iop.org/article/10.1088/1748-9326/ac1bd9.

Offenhartz, Jake. "City to Spend $30,000 Apiece on Anti-Terror Bollards." *The Village Voice*, January 3, 2018. villagevoice.com/2018/01/03/city-to-spend-30000-apiece-on-anti-terror-bollards/.

"Off with Their Heads: Rid Downtown of Parking Meters." *Quad City Times* editorial, August 8, 2010.

Owen, Tess. "Florida 'Anti-Rioting' Law Will Make It Much Easier to Run Over Protesters with Cars." *Vice*, April 19, 2021. vice.com/en/article/88n95a/florida-anti-rioting-law-will-make-it-much-easier-to-run-over-protesters-with-cars.

Pareene, Alex. "The Right to Crash Cars into People." *The New Republic*, April 24, 2021. https://newrepublic.com/article/162163/republicans-anti-riot-laws-cars.

Patino, Marie, Aaron Kessler, and Sarah Holder. "More Americans Are Leaving Cities, But Don't Call It an Urban Exodus." *Bloomberg*, April 26, 2021. bloomberg.com/graphics/2021-citylab-how-americans-moved/.

Peirce, Neal. "Biking and Walking: Our Secret Weapon?" citiwire.net, July 16, 2009.

———. "Cities as Global Stars." Review of *Triumph of the City* by Edward Glaeser. citiwire.net, February 18, 2011.

Perlman, Jennifer, and John Parvensky. "Cost Benefit Analysis and Program Outcomes Report." Colorado Coalition for the Homeless, December 11, 2006.

Peters, Adele. "50 Reasons Why Everyone Should Want More Walkable Streets." *Fast Company*, August 24, 2016. fastcompany.com/3062989/50-reasons-why-everyone-should-want-more-walkable-streets.

Peterson, Greg. "Pharmaceuticals in Our Water Supply Are Causing Bizarre Mutations to Wildlife." alternet.com, August 9, 2007.

Pinto, Edward, and Tobias Peter. "California's Free-Market Housing Fix." *The Wall Street Journal*, February 3, 2022. wsj.com/articles/california-free-market-housing-fix-sb9-lots-units-four-value-crisis-zoning-requirements-property-rights-11643922512.

Plumer, Brad, Nadja Popovich, and Blacki Migliozzi. "Electric Cars Are Coming. How Long Until They Rule the Road?" *The New York Times*,

March 10, 2021. nytimes.com/interactive/2021/03/10/climate/electric-vehicle-fleet-turnover.html.

Popova, Maria. "Nietzsche on Walking and Creativity." *The Marginalian*, December 12, 2021. themarginalian.org/2021/12/12/nietzsche-walking/.

Pucher, John, and Ralph Buehler. "Cycling for Few or for Everyone: The Importance of Social Justice in Cycling Policy." *World Transport Policy and Practice* 15, no. 1 (2009): 57–64.

———. "Why Canadians Cycle More Than Americans: A Comparative Analysis of Bicycling Trends and Policies." Institute of Transport and Logistics Studies, University of Sydney, Newtown, NSW, Australia. *Transport Policy* 13 (2006): 265–79.

Pucher, John, and Lewis Dijkstra. "Making Walking and Cycling Safer: Lessons from Europe." *Transportation Quarterly* 54, no. 3 (2000): 25–50.

Puzzanghera, Jim. "Putting the Law on the Driver's Side." *The Boston Globe*, November 2, 2021. https://apps.bostonglobe.com/news/nation/2021/10/vehicle-rammings-against-protesters/legislation/.

"Rainfall Interception of Trees, in Benefits of Trees in Urban Areas." coloradotrees.org, undated.

Rao, Kamala. "Seoul Tears Down an Urban Highway, and the City Can Breathe Again." *Grist*, November 4, 2011.

"Recent Lessons from the Stimulus: Transportation Funding and Job Creation." Smart Growth America report, February 2011.

Redmond, Tim. "Uber's Plans Include Attacking Public Transit." 48hills, May 6, 2019. https://48hills.org/2019/05/ubers-plans-include-attacking-public-transit/.

Reid, Carlton. "Biden's $1.2 Trillion Infrastructure Bill Hastens Beacons for Bicyclists and Pedestrians Enabling Detection by Connected Cars." *Forbes*, November 6, 2021. forbes.com/sites/carltonreid/2021/11/06/bidens-12-trillion-infrastructure-bill-hastens-beacon-wearing-for-bicyclists-and-pedestrians-to-enable-detection-by-connected-cars/.

———. "The Car Is Like a Virus, Says Urban Planner but This Is One Pandemic that Politicians Can Prevent." *Forbes*, May 26, 2020. forbes.com/sites/carltonreid/2020/05/26/the-car-is-like-a-virus-says-urban-planner-but-this-is-one-pandemic-that-politicians-can-prevent/.

Reilly, Rick. "Life of Reilly: Mile-High Madness." si.com, October 23, 2007.

"ReLeaf Cedar Rapids." Town of Cedar Rapids. cedar-rapids.org/residents/parks_and_recreation/releaf_cedar_rapids_.php.

"Removing Freeways—Restoring Cities." preservenet.com, undated.

"Research: Trees Make Streets Safer, Not Deadlier." *New Urban News*, bettercities.net, September 1, 2006.

"Rethinking How We Build So Californians Can Drive Less." Caltrans. https://dot.ca.gov/programs/sustainability/sb-743.

Reynolds, Gretchen. "What's the Single Best Exercise?" *The New York Times Magazine*, April 17, 2011.

Rivlin-Nadler, Max. "Bike-Hating NIMBY Trolls Grudgingly Surrender to Reality." *The Village Voice*, September 21, 2016. villagevoice.com/2016/09/21/bike-hating-nimby-trolls-grudgingly-surrender-to-reality/.

Rodrigues, Jason. "Five Things More Likely to Kill You Than a Shark." *The Guardian*, December 7, 2010. theguardian.com/theguardian/2010/dec/07/things-likely-kill-than-shark.

Rodriguez, Joe Fitzgerald. "SFPD: Uber, Lyft Account for Two-Thirds of Congestion-Related Traffic Violations Downtown." *San Francisco Examiner*, September 26, 2017. sfexaminer.com/news/sfpd-uber-lyft-account-for-two-thirds-of-congestion-related-traffic-violations-downtown/.

Roffel, Brittany. "B.C.'s Heat Wave Likely Contributed to 719 Sudden Deaths in a Week, Coroner Says—Triple the Usual Number." CBC News, July 2, 2021. cbc.ca/news/canada/british-columbia/heat-wave-719-deaths-1.6088793.

Rogers, Shannon H., John M. Halstead, Kevin H. Gardner, and Cynthia H. Carlson. "Examining Walkability and Social Capital as Indicators of Quality of Life at the Municipal and Neighborhood Scales." *Applied Research in the Quality of Life* 6, no. 2 (2010): 201–53.

Ruch, John. "Manager of City Program to Eliminate Traffic Injuries Is Hurt by Alleged DUI Driver." *Saporta Report*, October 21, 2021. https://saportareport.com/drmanager-of-city-program-to-eliminate-traffic-injuries-is-hurt-by-alleged-dui-driver-driver/sections/reports/johnruch/.

Russo, Charles. "Un-forgetting the Segregationist History of Palo Alto (and Daly City, and San Francisco, and . . .)." *Palo Alto Online*, June 28, 2020. https://paloaltoonline.com/news/2020/06/28/un-forgetting-the-segregationist-history-of-palo-alto-and-daly-city-and-san-francisco-and.

Sack, Kevin. "Governor Proposes Remedy for Atlanta Sprawl." *The New York Times*, January 26, 1999: 14.

Sadik-Khan, Janette, and Seth Solomonow. "Surrendering Our Cities to Cars Would Be a Historic Blunder." *The Atlantic*, April 16, 2021. theatlantic.com/ideas/archive/2021/04/cars-will-take-streets-back-unless-cities-act-quickly/618615/.

Salta, Alex. "Chicago Sells Rights to City Parking Meters for $1.2 Billion." ohmygov.com, December 24, 2008.

Salzman, Randy. "Build More Highways, Get More Traffic." *The Daily Progress*, December 19, 2010.

Sanders, Topher, Kate Rabinowitz, and Benjamin Conarck. "Walking While Black." ProPublica, November 16, 2017. https://features.propublica.org/walking-while-black/jacksonville-pedestrian-violations-racial-profiling/.

Santamour, Frank, Jr. "Trees for Urban Planting: Diversity, Uniformity, and Common Sense." *Proceedings of the 7th Conference Metropolitan Tree Improvement Alliance* (1990).

Schwartzman, Paul. "At Columbia Heights Mall, So Much Parking, So Little Need." *The Washington Post*, October 8, 2009.

Schweitzer, Ally. "D.C. Is Taking a Closer Look at Converting Downtown Office Space into Housing." DCist, December 14, 2021. https://dcist.com/story/21/12/14/dc-downtown-office-housing-conversion/.

Scruggs, Gregory. "As an Elevated Highway Closes, Seattle Braces for Traffic Hell." *Bloomberg*, January 14, 2019. bloomberg.com/news/articles/2019-01-14/-viadoom-time-for-the-seattle-squeeze-traffic-hell.

Segall, Bob. "Millions of Vehicles Have Unexpected, Dangerous Front Blind Zone." 13 WTHR, April 25, 2019. wthr.com/article/news/investigations/13-investigates/13-investigates-millions-vehicles-have-unexpected-dangerous-front-blind-zone/531-9521c471-3bc1-4b55-b860-3363f0954b3b.

The Segmentation Company, "Attracting College-Educated, Young Adults to Cities." Prepared for CEOs for Cities, May 8, 2006.

Shill, Gregory H. "Americans Shouldn't Have to Drive, But the Law Insists on It." *The Atlantic*, July 9, 2019. theatlantic.com/ideas/archive/2019/07/car-crashes-arent-always-unavoidable/592447/.

Short, Aaron. "Separated Bike Lanes Means Safer Streets, Study Says." Streetsblog, May 29, 2019. https://usa.streetsblog.org/2019/05/29/protect-yourself-separated-bike-lanes-means-safer-streets-study-says/.

Shorto, Russell. "The Dutch Way: Bicycles and Fresh Bread." *The New York Times*, July 30, 2011.

Siddiqui, Faiz, and Reed Albergotti. "'Full Self-Driving' Clips Show Owners of Teslas Fighting for Control, and Experts See Deep Flaws." *The Washington Post*, February 10, 2022. washingtonpost.com/technology/2022/02/10/video-tesla-full-self-driving-beta.

Singer, Jessie. "All Hail the Robot Car?" *Reclaim Magazine*, October 11, 2018. https://medium.com/reclaim-magazine/all-hail-the-robot-car-8d672221b18e.

Sivarajah, Sivajanani, Sandy M. Smith, and Sean C. Thomas. "Tree Cover and Species Composition Effects on Academic Performance of Primary School Students." *PLoS One* 13, no. 2 (2018). ncbi.nlm.nih.gov/pmc/articles/PMC5825089/.

Smart Growth America. "Dangerous by Design." 2021. https://smartgrowthamerica.org/dangerous-by-design/.

Smiley, Brett. "Number of New Yorkers Commuting on Bikes Continues to Rise." *New York*, December 8, 2011. With link to New York City Department of Transportation press release.

Smith, Rick. "Cedar Rapids Phasing Out Back-In Angle Parking." *The Gazette*, June 9, 2011.

Snyder, Tanya. "Actually, Highway Builders, Roads Don't Pay for Themselves." dc.streetsblog.org, January 4, 2011.

Sottile, Christian. "One-Way Streets: Urban Impact Analysis." Commissioned by the City of Savannah, as yet unpublished.

Speck, Jeff. "Our Ailing Communities: Q&A: Richard Jackson." metropolismag.com, October 11, 2006.

"Status of North American Light Rail Projects." lightrailnow.org, 2002.

Steuteville, Robert. "California Zoning Reform: Are Form-Based Codes the Answer?" *Public Square: A CNU Journal*, September 22, 2021. cnu.org /publicsquare/2021/09/22/california-zoning-reform-are-form-based -codes-answer.

Stroope, Jessica. "Active Transportation and Social Capital: The Association Between Walking or Biking for Transportation and Community Participation." *Preventive Medicine* 150 (September 2021). https://pubmed.ncbi .nlm.nih.gov/34087322/.

Stutzer, Alois, and Bruno S. Frey. "Stress That Doesn't Pay: The Commuting Paradox." Institute for Empirical Work in Economics, University of Zurich, Switzerland, ideas.repec.org/p/zur/iewwpx/151.html.

Summers, Nick. "Where the Neon Lights Are Bright—and Drivers Are No Longer Welcome." *Newsweek*, February 27, 2009.

Swartz, Jon. "San Francisco's Charm Lures High-Tech Workers." *USA Today*, December 6, 2010.

Thomas, Destiny. "Opinion: Urbanism Is Complicit in Infra-Structural Racism—And Reparations Have a Place in the Built Environment." Streetsblog, July 27, 2020. https://usa.streetsblog.org/2020/07/27/opinion -urbanism-is-complicit-in-infra-structural-racism-and-reparations-have -a-place-in-the-built-environment/.

Thomas, Lauren. "25% of U.S. Malls Are Expected to Shut Within 5 Years. Giving Them a New Life Won't Be Easy." CNBC, August 27, 2020. cnbc .com/2020/08/27/25percent-of-us-malls-are-set-to-shut-within-5-years -what-comes-next.html.

Transportation for America. *Dangerous by Design 2011*. Undated.

"Trees Set Sixth-Graders Up for Success." Science Daily, November 9, 2020. sciencedaily.com/releases/2020/11/201109124724.htm.

Troianovski, Anton. "Downtowns Get a Fresh Lease." *The Wall Street Journal*, December 13, 2010.

Trump, Donald J., and Ben Carson. "We'll Protect America's Suburbs." *The Wall Street Journal*, August 16, 2020. wsj.com/articles/well-protect-amer icas-suburbs-11597608133.

Turner, Chris. "The Best Tool for Fixing City Traffic Problems? A Wrecking Ball." Mother Nature Network, mnn.com, April 15, 2011.

———. "What Makes a Building Ugly?" Mother Nature Network, mnn.com, August 5, 2011.

"2010 Quality of Living Worldwide City Rankings." Mercer.com.

"2010 Urban Mobility Report." Texas Transportation Institute, Texas A&M University, 2010.

Twyman, Anthony S. "Greening Up Fertilizes Home Prices, Study Says." *The Philadelphia Inquirer*, January 10, 2005.

Uber Technologies, Inc. SEC S-1Registration Statement, U.S. Securities and

Exchange Commission. sec.gov/Archives/edgar/data/1543151/00011931
2519103850/d647752ds1.htm.

Ulrich, R. S., et al. "View Through a Window May Influence Recovery from
Surgery." *Science* 224, 420 (1984): 420–21.

U.S. Census Bureau. American Community Survey, 2008–2012.

U.S. Department of Agriculture. "Benefits of Trees in Urban Areas." Forest
Service Pamphlet #FS-363.

U.S. Environmental Protection Agency. "Location Efficiency and Housing
Type—Boiling It Down to BTUs." USEPA Report prepared by Jonathan
Rose Associates, March 2011.

U.S. Government Accounting Office. "Bus Rapid Transit Shows Promise."
September 2001.

Utah Housing and Community Development Division. "Comprehensive Report on Homelessness." State Community Services Office, 2014. https://
jobs.utah.gov/housing/scso/documents/homelessness2014.pdf.

"The Value of Trees to a Community." Arbor Day Foundation, arborday.org
/trees/benefits.cfm.

Vanderbilt, Tom. "The Pandemic Shows What Cars Have Done to Cities." *The
Atlantic*, April 24, 2020. theatlantic.com/ideas/archive/2020/04/pandemic
-shows-what-cities-have-surrendered-cars/610423/.

Van Gleson, John. "Light Rail Adds Transportation Choices on Common
Ground." National Association of Realtors (2009): 4–13.

Vlahos, James. "Is Sitting a Lethal Activity?" *The New York Times Magazine*,
April 14, 2011.

Walljasper, Jay. "Cycling to Success: Lessons from the Dutch." citiwire.net,
September 23, 2010.

———. "The Surprising Rise of Minneapolis as a Top Bike Town." citiwire
.net, October 22, 2011.

Walker, Alissa. "Two of Elon Musk's Terrible Ideas Both Flopped in Las Vegas
This Week." *Curbed*, January 7, 2022. curbed.com/2022/01/elon-musk
-las-vegas-tunnel-ces.html.

Walt, Vivienne. "'We Heard Birds': Paris Mayor Anne Hidalgo on How Lockdown Offered a Glimpse at a Greener City." *Time*, July 9, 2020. https://
time.com/5864707/paris-green-city-2/.

Washington, D.C., Economic Partnership. "2008 Neighborhood Profiles—
Columbia Heights."

Whitman, David. "The Sickening Sewer Crisis in America." aquarain.com,
undated.

Wieckowski, Ania. "The Unintended Consequences of Cul-de-Sacs." *Harvard
Business Review*, May 2010.

Wingate, Keira. "Owning a New Vehicle Costs Nearly $10,000 a Year, AAA
Says." *USA Today*, August 19, 2021. usatoday.com/story/money/cars/2021
/08/19/new-vehicle-suv-truck-car-ownership-costs-aaa/8181082002/.

Woodward, Jon. "'If You Build It, They Will Come': Study Says New Bike Lane Doubles Chances People Will Cycle." CTV News Toronto, June 2, 2021. https://toronto.ctvnews.ca/if-you-build-it-they-will-come-study-says -new-bike-lane-doubles-chances-people-will-cycle-1.5453674.

Wooley, Neal R., etc., et al., Appellants, v. George Maynard et ux. No. 75-1453., U.S. Supreme Court. law.cornell.edu/supremecourt/text/430/705.

Wright, Megan. "Commonwealth Communities Kicks Off with Engaging, Expert-Led Session on Walkability." Smart Growth America, October 14, 2021. https://smartgrowthamerica.org/commonwealth-communities-kicks -off-with-engaging-expert-led-session-on-walkability/.

Yardley, William. "Seattle Mayor Is Trailing in the Early Primary Count." *The New York Times*, August 19, 2009.

Yeager, Selene. "E-Bikes Are Getting More People Out of Their Cars." *Bicycling*, March 21, 2018. bicycling.com/news/a20049844/ebike-study-car -trips/.

Yen, Hope. "Suburbs Lose Young Whites to Cities: Younger, Educated Whites Moving to Urban Areas for Homes, Jobs." Associated Press, May 9, 2010.

RADIO, TELEVISION, FILM, AND SLIDESHOWS

Aubrey, Allison. "Switching Gears: More Commuters Bike to Work." NPR *Morning Edition*, November 29, 2010.

Barnett, David C. "A Comeback for Downtown Cleveland." NPR *Morning Edition*, June 11, 2011.

Carr, Jimmy. *Jimmy Carr: His Dark Material*. Netflix, 2021.

A Convenient Remedy. Congress for the New Urbanism video.

Equilibrium Capital. "Streetcars' Economic Impact in the United States." PowerPoint presentation, May 26, 2010.

Fix, Lauren. "The War on Cars." PragerU, July 31, 2017. YouTube video. you tube.com/watch?v=k8Lo0ieyQtQ.

Gabriel, Ron. "3-Way Street by ronconcocacola." Vimeo.

Gordon, Doug, Sarah Goodyear, and Aaron Naparstek. "Barcelona's Super-blocks with David Roberts of Vox." *The War on Cars*, April 19, 2019. Podcast. https://thewaroncars.org/2019/08/19/twoc-bonus-barcelonas -superblocks-with-david-roberts-of-vox/.

———. "Policing the Open Road with Sarah Seo." *The War on Cars*. Podcast. https://thewaroncars.org/episode-30-policing-the-open-road-with-sarah -seo/.

———. "What Uber Hath Wrought." *The War on Cars*. Podcast. https://the waroncars.org/episode-29-what-uber-hath-wrought-final-web-tran script/.

"How the Dutch Got Their Cycle Paths." BicycleDutch, October 9, 2011. YouTube video. youtube.com/watch?v=XuBdf9jYj7o&feature=youtu.be&t =2m3s.

"Revisiting Donald Appleyard's Livable Streets." StreetfilmsVlog, December 15, 2020. YouTube video. youtube.com/watch?v=ESgkcFbGiL8.

Schaper, David. "Critics Say Infrastructure Projects Won't Make a Big Enough Impact on Climate Change." NPR *All Things Considered*, January 25, 2022. npr.org/2022/01/25/1075624848/critics-say-infrastructure-projects-won-t-make-a-big-enough-impact-on-climate-ch.

WebMD. "10 Worst Cities for Asthma." Slideshow. webmd.com/asthma/slideshow-10-worst-cities-for-asthma.

LECTURES AND CONFERENCES

Brooks, David. Lecture. Aspen Institute, March 18, 2011.

Frank, Lawrence. Lecture to the 18th Congress for the New Urbanism, Atlanta, Georgia, May 20, 2010.

Gladwell, Malcolm. Remarks. Downtown Partnership of Baltimore Annual Meeting, November 17, 2010.

Hales, Charles. Presentation at Rail-Volution, October 18, 2011.

Kerry, John. Remarks at the first summit of the Université de la Ville de Demain. Chantilly, France, July 8, 2021.

Livingstone, Ken. Winner commentary by Mayor of London. World Technology Winners and Finalists, World Technology Network, 2004.

Parolec, Daniel. Presentation to the Congress for the New Urbanism, June 2, 2011.

Ronkin, Michael. "Road Diets." PowerPoint presentation, New Partners for Smart Growth, February 10, 2007.

Speck, Jeff. Presentation to Boston City Council, May 12, 2020.

———. "Six Things Even New York Can Do Better." Presentation to New York City Planning Commission, January 4, 2010.

WEBSITES

20's Plenty for Us: 20splentyforus.org.uk.

American Dream Coalition: americandreamcoalition.org.

Better! Cities & Towns: Walkable Streets (source of many quotes): bettercities.net/walkable-streets.

Brookings VMT Cities Ranking: scribd.com/doc/9199883/Brookings-VMT-Cities-Ranking.

Dallas Area Rapid Transit: dart.org.

Dom's Plan B Blog: http://domz60.wordpress.com/quotes/.

Jane's Walk: janeswalk.net.

Kaufman, Kirsten: bikerealtor.com.

Lonely Planet readers poll: Top 10 Walking Cities. lonelyplanet.com/blog/2011/03/07/top-cities-to-walk-around/.

Make I-45 Better Coalition. https://i-45coalition.org.

Mercer.com: Quality of Living Worldwide City Rankings 2010.
Million Trees NYC: milliontreesnyc.org.
Up for Growth Action. https://upforgrowthaction.org.
Urban Audit: urbanaudit.org.
Walk Score: walkscore.com.

TWEETS

Cities People Love (@citiesppllove). Twitter, June 1, 2021. https://twitter.com
/citiesppllove/status/1399611159066468352?s=20.
Cuomo, Andrew (@NYGovCuomo). Twitter, March 22, 2020. https://twitter
.com/nygovcuomo/status/1241750717939007490.
Gordon, Wyatt (@yitgordon). Twitter, June 30, 2021. https://twitter.com/yit
gordon/status/1410337996331786240?s=11.
Hogan, Liam (@Limerick1914). Twitter, July 18, 2016. https://twitter.com
/Limerick1914/status/755132030493556736.
Musk, Elon (@elonmusk). Twitter, March 6, 2022. https://twitter.com/elonmusk
/status/1500475796623749120.
Schmidt, Jake (@TheJakeSchmidt). Twitter, May 23, 2021. https://twitter.com
/thejakeschmidt/status/1396533546819497990.
Wells, Warren J. (@WarrenJWells). Twitter, February 9, 2022. https://twitter
.com/WarrenJWells/status/1491487543455465472.

IMAGES

Poster, Intelligent Cities Initiative, National Building Museum, Washington,
D.C.

GEOGRAPHIC INDEX

GENERAL INDEX